Lecture Notes in Computer Science 15711

Founding Editors

Gerhard Goos
Juris Hartmanis

AF166661

The series Lecture Notes in Computer Science (LNCS), including its subseries Lecture Notes in Artificial Intelligence (LNAI) and Lecture Notes in Bioinformatics (LNBI), has established itself as a medium for the publication of new developments in computer science and information technology research, teaching, and education.

LNCS enjoys close cooperation with the computer science R & D community, the series counts many renowned academics among its volume editors and paper authors, and collaborates with prestigious societies. Its mission is to serve this international community by providing an invaluable service, mainly focused on the publication of conference and workshop proceedings and postproceedings. LNCS commenced publication in 1973.

Khin Than Win · Raian Ali ·
Evangelos Karapanos · George A. Papadopoulos ·
Kiemute Oyibo · Elena Vlahu-Gjorgievska
Editors

Persuasive Technology

20th International Conference, PERSUASIVE 2025
Limassol, Cyprus, May 5–7, 2025
Proceedings

 Springer

Editors

Khin Than Win (ID)
University of Wollongong
Wollongong, NSW, Australia

Raian Ali (ID)
Hamad Bin Khalifa University
Doha, Qatar

Evangelos Karapanos (ID)
Cyprus University of Technology
Limassol, Cyprus

George A. Papadopoulos (ID)
University of Cyprus
Nicosia, Cyprus

Kiemute Oyibo (ID)
York University
Toronto, ON, Canada

Elena Vlahu-Gjorgievska (ID)
University of Wollongong
Wollongong, NSW, Australia

ISSN 0302-9743   ISSN 1611-3349 (electronic)
Lecture Notes in Computer Science
ISBN 978-3-031-94958-6   ISBN 978-3-031-94959-3 (eBook)
https://doi.org/10.1007/978-3-031-94959-3

This Springer imprint is published by the registered company Springer Nature Switzerland AG
The registered company address is: Gewerbestrasse 11, 6330 Cham, Switzerland

If disposing of this product, please recycle the paper.

Preface

In a world in which technology is increasingly present in people's lives, and changing human behavior and attitudes is often the key to solving many societal and personal problems, studying how technology might be used to influence humans (in their behavior, attitudes and information processing) is paramount.

Persuasive Technology is a vibrant interdisciplinary research field, focusing on the design, development and evaluation of interactive technologies aimed at influencing people's attitudes and behavior through persuasion, but not through coercion or deception. The research community aims at enriching people's lives in various domains such as health and sustainability by supporting people in setting and achieving their own goals, thus helping them change their behavior.

The PERSUASIVE conference series is the leading venue to meet and discuss cutting-edge theoretical, methodological and technical perspectives and to present recent insights from research and development. The conference provides a venue for networking between researchers and practitioners from all corners of the world and has been held in previous years in different places such as Chicago, USA; Padua, Italy; Linköping, Sweden; Oulu, Finland; Sydney, Australia; Amsterdam, The Netherlands; Salzburg, Austria; Waterloo, Canada; Limassol, Cyprus; Aalborg, Denmark; Bournemouth, UK; Doha, Qatar; Eindhoven, The Netherlands and Wollongong, Australia.

The 20th International Conference on Persuasive Technology (PERSUASIVE 2025) was hosted in Limassol, Cyprus, from May 5–7, 2025. The first day was dedicated to the Doctoral Consortium, the 13th International Workshop on Behavior Change Support Systems (BCSS 2025), the 1st International Workshop on Upholding Ethical Designs (I-WOULD 2025) and a tutorial on EngageAI: AI-Driven Persuasive Technology to Enhance Student Engagement in Digital Learning Environments. On May 6–7, the main conference featured seven single-track sessions, including oral presentations of accepted papers. Full papers were allocated 15+5 minutes (Q&A), while Short Papers and papers in the Late-Breaking Results and Extended Abstract tracks were given 10+5 minutes (Q&A). The program also included a keynote by Philip Cash (Northumbria University) on "Exploring the Processes and Practices of Persuasive Intervention Development: Perspectives, Challenges, and Opportunities." A poster-and-demo session was also held, with opportunities for oral presentations.

This volume contains the accepted Full and Short papers in the main track of the conference, i.e., the Full and Short Papers. Eighty-four (84) submissions were made by 178 authors from 30 countries around the globe, out of which 49 were submitted to the main track. The papers were reviewed by the program committee in a double-blind review process conducted in EasyChair. Overall, 67 reviewers were assigned to review the papers. Each paper received at least 3 detailed and constructive reviews, which not only provided the program chairs with significant insight concerning the individual submissions but also ensured that the authors were provided with high-quality feedback and recommendations for the final versions of their paper. The final list of papers to be presented at the conference was decided after a careful assessment of the reviews. Out of the 49 submissions, 17 were accepted as full papers (acceptance rate of 34.6% for full papers) and 6 were accepted as short papers. In these proceedings, the accepted full and short papers are grouped into the following sections based on their content: Personalized Persuasion, Theory and Exploration, Design and Solutions, Emotions and Behavior, Behavior Change Games, and Personality and Individual Differences.

We would like to thank all reviewers and organizers that contributed to the success of PERSUASIVE 2025. In particular, we would like to thank the authors who submitted their papers to the conference. We would also like to thank the program committee for the critical role they played in the review process and for helping to promote the conference.

Khin Than Win
Raian Ali
Evangelos Karapanos
George Λ. Papadopoulos
Kiemute Oyibo
Elena Vlahu-Gjorgievska

Organization

General Chairs

Evangelos Karapanos   Cyprus University of Technology, Cyprus
George A. Papadopoulos   University of Cyprus, Cyprus

Program Chairs

Raian Ali   Hamad Bin Khalifa University, Qatar
Khin Than Win   University of Wollongong, Australia

Workshops and Tutorial Chairs

Rhodora Abadia   University of South Australia, Australia
Kaoru Sumi   Future University of Hakodate, Japan
Wenzhen Xu   Hitotsubashi University, Japan

Doctoral Consortium Chairs

Jaap Ham   Eindhoven University of Technology, Netherlands
Sriram Iyengar   University of Arizona, USA
Roberto Legaspi   KDDI Research, Inc., Japan
Shahla Meedya   Australian Catholic University, Australia

Demo, Poster and Artefacts Track Chairs

Ruben Hgouveia   Universidade de Lisboa, Portugal
Hanne Spelt   Philips, Netherlands

Late Breaking Results Chairs

Areej B. Babiker   Hamad Bin Khalifa University, Qatar
Jaap Ham   Eindhoven University of Technology, Netherlands
Isaac Wiafe   University of Ghana, Ghana

Proceedings Chairs

Kiemute Oyibo   York University, Canada
Elena Vlahu-Gjorgievska   University of Wollongong, Australia

Publicity Chair

Ifeoma Adaji   University of British Columbia, Canada

Program Committee Members

Rhodora Abadia   University of South Australia, Australia
Ifeoma Adaji   University of British Columbia, Canada
Syed Ishtiaque Ahmed   University of Toronto, Canada
Dena Al-Thani   Hamad Bin Khalifa University, Qatar
Aftab Alam   Hamad Bin Khalifa University, Qatar
Mona Alhasani   Dalhousie University, Canada
Raian Ali   Hamad Bin Khalifa University, Qatar
Alaa Ali S. Almohanna   University of Wollongong, Australia
Nawaf Almutairi   University of Hail, Saudi Arabia
Sameha Alshakhsi   Hamad Bin Khalifa University, Qatar
Alaa Alslaity   Dalhousie University, Canada
Saleh Altuwayrib   University of Hail, Saudi Arabia
Yutaka Arakawa   Kyushu University, Japan
Emily Arden-Close   Bournemouth University, UK
Areej Babiker   Hamad bin Khalifa University, Qatar
Shlomo Berkovsky   Macquarie University, Australia
Barbara Caci   University of Palermo, Italy
Luca Chittaro   University of Udine, Italy
Nelly Condori Fernández   Universidad Santiago de Compostela, Spain
Peter De Vries   University of Twente, Netherlands
Huseyin Dogan   Bournemouth University, UK
Dimitra Dritsa   Eindhoven University of Technology, Netherlands
Alia El Bolock   American University of Cairo, Egypt
Alexander Felfernig   TU Graz, Austria
Mark Freeman   University of Sydney, Australia
Nanami Furue   Hitotsubashi University, Japan
Yann Glémarec   INRIA Rennes, Université de Rennes 1, France
Luke Haliburton   LMU Munich, Germany
Jaap Ham   Eindhoven University of Technology, Netherlands
Sanaul Haque   LUT University, Finland

Sponsoring Organizations

Contents

Personalized Persuasion

Design of a Personalised AI Coaching Assistant for Occupational Health
and Safety 3
  Jonathan Vitale, Shlomo Berkovsky, Shun Takeuchi, Amin Beheshti,
  Kexuan Xin, Junya Saito, and Sosuke Yamao

Analysing User Feedback on Commercial Diet Tracking App 18
  Joohyun Lee, Vivienne Guan, and Khin Than Win

Personalized Social Proof for Persuasive Human-Robot Interaction 32
  Rosalyn Langedijk, Lars C. Jensen, and Kerstin Fischer

Personalized Digital Interventions for Behavior Change: Insights
from the MoM App Study 46
  Fawad Taj, Michel Klein, and Aart van Halteren

Theory and Exploration

Exploring the Potential and Limitations of Large Language Models
to Control the Behavior of Embodied Persuasive Agents 61
  Christian Corrò and Luca Chittaro

Insights into the Design of Ethical and Trustworthy Persuasive Technologies ... 74
  Parinda Rahman and Ifeoma Adaji

Effect of Competitive and Cooperative Learning Contexts in Controversial
Information Search: Preliminary Results 89
  Cheyenne Dosso, Mohamed Benlamine, Tiffany Morisseau,
  Christophe Heintz, and Jean-Sébastien Vayre

The Heuristic Evaluation of Manipulative Interfaces 105
  Frank Lewis and Julita Vassileva

Digital Persuasion: Understanding the Impact of Online Influencers
on Public Opinion 117
  Omran Berjawi, Rida Khatoun, and Giuseppe Fenza

Design and Solutions

LifeLink: The Design and Evaluation of an mHealth App for Caregivers
Supporting Individuals with Suicidality 131
  Smriti Jha, Gerry Chan, and Rita Orji

Bridging Research and Practice in Persuasive Mobile Stress Management
Apps: A 21-Year Comparative Analysis and Novel Design Framework 147
  Mona Alhasani, Oladapo Oyebode, and Rita Orji

Designing Behavior Change Support Systems for Recovery
from Addictions: Mapping Software Features with Counseling Strategies 165
  Hasan Selkan Taskan and Harri Oinas-Kukkonen

Investigation of the Eye Donor Aust App's Persuasiveness 176
  Waraporn Chumkasian, Constantinos Petsoglou,
  Elena Vlahu-Gjorgievska, and Khin Than Win

MyHealthCore: Towards a Community-Engaged HIV Prevention
Persuasive mHealth App for Black Communities in Canada 188
  Kaminda Natasha Musumbulwa, Gerry Chan, Oladapo Oyebode,
  and Rita Orji

Emotions and Behaviour

Health Risk Management Using Persuasive Technology: A Scoping Review ... 203
  Stanley Ebhohimhen Abhadiomhen,
  Emmanuel Onyekachukwu Nzeakor, and Kiemute Oyibo

Evaluation of an Emotion-Aware Persuasive Framework Based
on Peripheral Interaction for Reducing Physical Strain in Office
Environments 217
  Franci Suni-Lopez and Nelly Condori-Fernandez

On People's Susceptibility to Persuasive Techniques in Social Engineering:
Is It About the Technique or Their Readiness to Be Persuaded? 232
  Aya Muhanad, Ala Yankouskaya, Khaled M. Khan,
  Mahmoud Barhamgi, and Raian Ali

Behavior Change Games

AMRageddon V1: The Design and Usability Evaluation of a Digital
Escape Room Game for Antimicrobial Resistance Education Through
Persuasive Technology 249
    Avis Anya Nowbuth, Vikram Singh Parmar, Andrea Porras Elizo,
    Aslak Irgens Steinsbekk, and Ashis Jalote Parmar

PetBuddy: An Examination of Augmented Reality Mobile Health Game
for Promoting Physical Activity 264
    Priyal Srivastava, Gerry Chan, Oladapo Oyebode, and Rita Orji

The Motivational Appeal of Persuasive Strategies in a Healthy Eating
Behaviour Change Game 281
    Chinenye Ndulue, Oladapo Oyebode, and Rita Orji

Personality and Individual Differences

(Un)sustainable Personalities: The Role of Personality When Persuading
to Adopt Sustainable Behaviours 299
    Elena Minucci, Martin Lages, and Simone Stumpf

Non-binary People are Harder to Persuade: Evidence and Insights 315
    Victor Sonego, Annye Braca, and Pierpaolo Dondio

Gamified vs. Non-Gamified Language Learning: The Role of Working
Memory and Gaming Disorder 330
    Areej Babiker, Sameha Alshakhsi, Rabab Ali Abumalloh,
    Ala Yankouskaya, Dena Al-Thani, Magnus Liebherr, and Raian Ali

Author Index 341

Personalized Persuasion

Design of a Personalised AI Coaching Assistant for Occupational Health and Safety

Jonathan Vitale[1](✉)(iD), Shlomo Berkovsky[1](iD), Shun Takeuchi[1,3](iD), Amin Beheshti[2](iD), Kexuan Xin[1](iD), Junya Saito[3], and Sosuke Yamao[3]

[1] Australian Institute of Health Innovation, Macquarie University, Macquarie Park, Australia
{jonathan.vitale,shlomo.berkovsky,kexuan.xin}@mq.edu.au
[2] Centre for Applied Artificial Intelligence, Macquarie University, Sydney, Australia
amin.beheshti@mq.edu.au
[3] Artificial Intelligence Laboratory, Fujitsu Research, Kanagawa, Japan
{s.takeuchi,saito.junya,yamao.sosuke}@fujitsu.com

Abstract. This work presents a personalised AI coaching system to enhance occupational health and safety using a bottom-up design approach inspired by Lean UX and Agile principles. Leveraging Large Language Models and Computer Vision, the pilot integrated automated reporting and role-playing simulations to address safety challenges. Prototyping with existing and adapted AI tools demonstrated feasibility, with positive feedback from managers highlighting its potential to improve compliance and the need for staff involvement. The study underscores AI's role as a collaborative coaching mediator and the effectiveness of bottom-up design in aligning solutions with user needs, while naturally integrating persuasive technology principles.

Keywords: Human-Centred Design · Personalised Coaching · Persuasive Technologies · Collaborative AI · Occupational Health and Safety Agile Methodologies · Role-Playing · LLMs

1 Introduction

Occupational Health and Safety (OHS) safeguards workers' physical and psychological well-being [39]. Warehouses pose heightened risks due to hazardous materials and regular use of heavy machinery, e.g. forklifts [23], that could potentially lead to severe injuries or fatalities [37]. Other common incidents include slips, trips, and improper manual handling [32], which may cause musculoskeletal disorders, chronic conditions, and operational disruptions [5,34]. A proactive safety culture with continuous training and strict adherence to protocols reduces risks [23,37]. While all employees must follow OHS guidelines, OHS managers

K. T. Win et al. (Eds.): PERSUASIVE 2025, LNCS 15711, pp. 3–17, 2025.
https://doi.org/10.1007/978-3-031-94959-3_1

carry the primary duty of identifying, mitigating, and eliminating safety hazards [30]. Despite this, hazards can still be overlooked, rules ignored for convenience, and human errors made [39].

AI can be used to mitigate workplace risks by processing multimodal data to detect hazards and unsafe behaviour [1, 24, 31, 39, 47]. Automating tasks like document review and surveillance reduces managerial workload, while Large Language Models (LLMs) enhance reporting [33], cause-effect analysis [4], and natural interactions. As Socially Intelligent Agents (SIAs) [12,13], LLMs can understand and respond to social behaviour [27, 48]. Designed as socio-technical tools [46], they integrate with ubiquitous technologies for situational awareness, recognising specific users, preferences, mental states, actions, and needs [49]. This capability not only fosters seamless human-machine collaboration but also supports the delivery of personalised assistance, defined here as tailoring experiences to the unique preferences, behaviours, and needs of individual users [8].

These capabilities extend to the identification of workplace issues impacting OHS, reporting them efficiently, and assisting with the implementation of personalised solutions to mitigate risks before incidents occur [35]. Additionally, these technologies can be used to *persuade* users toward safer and more compliant behaviours. For instance, AI can deliver timely and context-sensitive recommendations to encourage adherence to OHS protocols via the *principle of suggestion* [16], gradually fostering a culture of compliance. However, poorly designed AI tools can introduce unintended risks or exacerbate existing issues, potentially increasing the volume of OHS incident reports [6]. This underscores the critical importance of adhering to proper design processes that ensure AI systems are effective and align with desired outcomes, a goal that is central to the aim of this work.

This work lies at the intersection of OHS and persuasive technologies (PT) design, leveraging recent advancements in LLMs. To the best of our knowledge, this is the first study to integrate LLMs and PT in addressing OHS challenges. PT design methodologies typically adopt a top-down approach [2,11,15], relying on predefined behavioural change interventions, problems or selected persuasive principles, even when stakeholders are included in participatory activities [22,41] or bottom-up elements are integrated in the design process [26]. In contrast, we take a different perspective. We employ a *full* bottom-up design methodology inspired by Lean UX and Agile methodologies, which starts with uncovering user needs to enhance their experience in the considered context, allowing insights to emerge organically and inform the design process without being constrained by a predefined behavioural intervention or problem. This ensures that solutions remain grounded in the complexities of real-world contexts, addressing practical challenges faced by users.

We present the design process followed and its initial outcomes, demonstrating how a bottom-up approach, previously applied in social robotics [42], can guide the development of user-centred solutions aligned with PT design principles. We specifically focus on design of PT incorporating coaching by human experts, such as OHS managers, and position AI as coaching mediator to augment human expertise, fostering collaboration and enhancing OHS compliance. Hence, the work contributes PT research in several ways. *First*, we explore the adaptation of a bottom-up design to PT, detailing its phases and activities used to generate outcomes, while demonstrating its effectiveness in uncovering user needs and naturally integrating persuasive principles. *Second*, we present an early-stage pilot of a personalised AI coaching assistant for the OHS domain, showcasing how the capabilities of LLMs can enable persuasive design principles, such as simulation and rehearsal, to enhance coaching effectiveness. *Third*, we propose a new interpretation of PT for coaching applications, positioning AI as a mediator that supports and augments human expertise, enabling collaborative and context-aware behavioural change interventions.

2   Design Process

This work originates from a collaborative project with Fujitsu Japan, aimed at developing AI-based personalised coaching solutions in an industrial setting. Such solutions leverage AI technologies, including Computer Vision, for activity recognition and aim to integrate LLMs for natural, socially intelligent, and tailored coaching. To design them, we adapted Tonkin et al.'s methodology [42] originally conceived for designing innovative commercial social robotics applications with positive user experience. This methodology was chosen for its adaptability and flexibility in refining design problems iteratively.

The methodology's *adaptability* lies in its integration of technology, user context, and situated interaction, allowing it to adjust flexibly to different use cases and technologies by reconfiguring these key components as needed. Originally conceived for social robots, its principles extends to SIAs embedded in physical settings through cameras and smart devices. This integration has proven beneficial for PT design [28], yet few studies detail how to achieve it through specific design activities [26], highlighting the need for more works like the one reported here. In addition, the methodology's *flexibility* allows it to evolve within the same project as stakeholder insights emerge, fostering exploration to identify relevant use cases based on observed user needs. Combining Lean UX [20] for creating minimum viable products (MVPs) with Agile Science [21] for testing and refinement ensures that the technology is both practical and evidence-based.

The following paragraphs outline the design process and its outcomes[1], limited to the first five phases of the methodology [42] and culminating in a preliminary pilot assessed for technical feasibility and user feedback.

Phase 1: Define the Challenge. The first phase focussed on identifying a suitable context for implementing the desired personalised AI coaching. Warehouse management emerged as the promising context for developing the AI coaching solution. To guide the subsequent design, this phase ended with a situated

---

[1] Design deliverables, pilot, and prompts used for fast prototyping LLM's features can be found in the online addendum, https://osf.io/kd2pq/?view_only=782b7dde4aef41228eec3f6b1dec0121.

How-Might-We (HMW) statement, a concise question that frames challenges in a solution-oriented manner [3,40]. The resulting HMW statement was:

> *"How might we use AI to enhance the work experience of managers and staff at Fujitsu's warehouse by delivering personalised coaching that supports their individual needs?"*

This HMW statement points the design to the targeted AI technology, specifying the context and users, while keeping the desired outcome, i.e., enhancing the work experience, broad enough to encourage exploration of the problem space. At this stage, specific user needs and behavioural interventions deliberately remain unknown, following a bottom-up approach to allow flexibility in exploring how AI can address emerging needs within the chosen context.

Phase 2: Observe. In this phase, sample warehouse surveillance footage was obtained and processed with Computer Vision. The footage was automatically annotated with bounding boxes and labels for people and objects, depicting staff activities, ranging from basic actions like walking and bending to more complex scenarios, e.g., "close to a moving forklift". The footage familiarised the team with the warehouse environment in preparation for meetings with managers.

Subsequently, the team met with the warehouse managers to deepen the understanding of critical operations, focussing on internal logistics, item dispatch, and risk management. While limited needs were identified in logistics and dispatch, significant opportunities emerged in risk management, also aligning well with the motivating use-case for AI coaching. The team then conducted an on-site visit, to obtain detailed insight on warehouse risks and past incidents. By the end of this phase, the team gained an awareness and understanding of the warehouse environment. Key insights around staff training and risk management were documented and reinforced in discussions with OHS managers, forming solid foundations for the subsequent design phases.

Phase 3: Form Insights. The insights and notes gathered during the observation phase were organised in an Empathy Map [36,43], with each detail placed in the appropriate quadrant: what users see, think, feel, and do. This structure helped the team empathise with users' needs, emotions, experiences and actions. Each insight was then classified as a 'gain' (positive aspect to preserve) or 'pain point' (area to improve/mitigate), or was kept neutral. The notes in each quadrant of the Empathy Map were re-organised using affinity mapping [36], which organised similar insights into themes, highlighting key strengths and challenges in warehouse operations.

An analysis of the identified themes followed. On the positive side, warehouse staff benefitted from continuous training and licensing, supported by a new national program certifying machinery competency. Regular use of machinery was found to reduce risks, whereas incident investigations effectively prevented repeated issues. Encouraging staff to acknowledge mistakes promoted accountability and reduced escalation risks. However, several challenges were identified. Personal differences among staff, over-confidence, and complacency with OHS rules contributed to breaches. Annual training sessions and reading materials were found inadequate, with staff often prioritising convenience over safety. On-site monitoring was time-consuming for OHS managers and investigating incidents added burden. The analysis also uncovered several tension points, specific areas of conflict creating opportunities for solutions. While clear OHS guidelines had been available to staff, these were often disregarded due to low perception of risks. Likewise, the confidence gained from mandatory training sometimes led to complacency, undermining safety practices. Finally, the new training program was praised by managers but deemed insufficient due to its low frequency, highlighting the need for ongoing reinforcement.

This phase concluded with the creation of an end-to-end journey map [40], focussing on the activities, emotions, and challenges of the OHS managers and highlighting risk management operation points with a low user experience.

Phase 4: Frame Opportunities. Each identified low user experience point is an opportunity for improvement. Thus, we crafted a corresponding HMW statement to highlight these opportunities for targeted solutions. This led to the following HMW statements: (i) How might we reinforce OHS compliance knowledge among staff to lead to fewer OHS breaches and ensure that OHS managers feel valued and heard?; (ii) How might we coach staff to prioritise OHS-compliant and safe behaviour, discouraging them from choosing convenient but unsafe actions?; (iii) How might we ensure staff remains focussed on OHS-compliant behaviour and avoids overconfidence while performing tasks in the warehouse?

The three HMW statements were consolidated into one *contextualised statement*, incorporating the use of AI as a guiding constraint. This ensured alignment with the project objectives, while informing the subsequent ideation phase:

"How might we use AI to assist warehouse managers in coaching staff to prioritise OHS-compliant and safe behaviour over convenience, while reinforcing their OHS knowledge, maintaining focus on safe practices, and fostering attentiveness to their activities, thereby reducing OHS breaches?"

Phase 5: Brainstorm. The contextualised HMW statement inspired ideas for brainstorming, where the team was encouraged to propose even unconventional ideas to foster creativity. The session emphasised collaboration, with the team members building on each other's ideas to explore diverse perspectives and refine concepts into innovative solutions. Over 70 ideas were generated and analysed, yielding eight overarching themes.

The *"Data Integration and Processing"* theme focussed on ideas leveraging multimodal data to prevent and identify OHS breaches. The theme of *"Data Explainability"* encompassed ideas aimed at providing managers with insights on the causes of the detected issues, enhancing their awareness and ability to resolve underlying problems. Ideas under the *"Automatic Generation of OHS Materials"* theme proposed automating the creation of tailored OHS content and reports, reducing manual effort and aligning outputs with user profiles.

The *"AI as Coaching Mediator"* theme positioned AI as a facilitator between managers and staff, enabling personalised coaching simulations and improving communication. The theme of *"Managers in Control of AI"* highlighted ideas empowering OHS managers to provide ongoing feedback and ensure alignment with their needs. Meanwhile, the *"Real-time Activity Monitoring"* theme covered ideas around using live surveillance video to detect risky behaviour and signs of employee fatigue, enabling timely notifications. Finally, the *"Gamification and OHS Compliance Rewards"* theme explored ideas incorporating rewards to promote adherence to OHS protocols, while the theme of *"Centralised Collaborative Platform"* envisioned a shared network of warehouses to share best practices, coaching recommendations, and risk management resources.

Following the analysis, these themes were ranked based on technical feasibility and their potentials in mitigating OHS incidents. The highest-ranked concepts and ideas were used to guide the design of a pilot addressing the identified needs. This marked the final step of the design process reported in this work, aligned with the incremental approach that emphasises iterative design cycles incorporating evaluation and preliminary feedback. The remaining steps outlined by Tonkin et al. [42] were beyond the scope of this paper and will be reported in future works.

3   HIRO, the AI Coaching Assistant

Building on the previously generated ideas, we identified and refined concept solutions addressing the challenges and needs uncovered by the design process. These were materialised into a high-fidelity pilot AI coach called HIRO (Hazards, Incidents, and Risks Operations), designed to assist OHS managers (see Fig. 1). While the pilot resembled the intended coach's functionality and interactions, its features were emulated to demonstrate how the coach would work in practice.

Fig. 1. HIRO.

3.1   Pilot Features

The designed pilot incorporated three key features tailored to address critical aspects of warehouse OHS risk management:

Data Integration and Reporting: A preliminary analysis of the current situation is crucial for identifying safety management needs, enabling OHS managers to assess warehouse issues and propose effective solutions [44]. As such, this feature integrates warehouse data selected by managers to identify issues and uncover root causes. Managers can query HIRO about specific problems or needs, and receive insights based on contextual data analysis. Additionally, HIRO includes an automatic report-generation tool that presents visual findings, such as plots or surveillance shots. These tools streamline reporting, enhance *situational awareness*, and provide actionable insights to support decision-making.

(a) Human-Sensing technology.

(b) Role-Play Simulation with LLM.

Fig. 2. Examples of prototyped features leveraging available AI technologies.

Role-Playing Coaching Simulations for Staff: Frequent employee training is essential for raising the safety standards and ensuring employees are educated on reducing risks [44]. Staff needing OHS training can be identified through the data integration feature and assigned to coaching interventions. HIRO generates personalised scenarios following OHS managers' requests for customised coaching simulations addressing specific training needs. Staff interacts with these simulations through natural dialogue and receives tailored improvement recommendations. The manager receives a report too, which includes additional recommendations and suggestions for future staff training.

Role-Playing Simulations Vignettes for Managers: OHS managers can use HIRO to simulate and rehearse meetings with staff. HIRO can simulate worker personas with realistic attitudes and reactions. These scenarios test managers' professional and interpersonal skills, helping them refine strategies for addressing non-compliance. Upon completing the simulation, HIRO evaluates the manager's performance and offers recommendations for improvement.

These features provide *personalised assistance* [8] by tailoring role-playing simulations to the coaching needs of OHS managers, customising scenarios, adapting worker personas, and generating tailored reports to support both managerial and staff development.

Building on the key features outlined in the proposed pilot, we explored existing AI technologies to fast prototype the core functionalities needed for their implementation, following the Agile principle of rapid iterations. Figure 2 exemplifies two technologies used to demonstrate the pilot's functionalities. Figure 2a showcases Fujitsu's human sensing AI, Fujitsu Kozuchi for Vision [17,18], applied to pre-processed warehouse video footage. The system uses bounding boxes to identify people and warehouse machinery, labelling them with corresponding actions. Simple actions, such as standing, bending, or walking, represent basic movements or poses of staff. In contrast, complex actions, such as detecting unsafe proximity between a staff member and a moving forklift, involve interactions between multiple entities and rely on editable inference rules. These rules are managed through a user interface allowing users to define, compose, and modify rules, including adding support for recognising new entities. Once recognised, these actions were further represented as Action-Scene Graphs [25], providing a structured and detailed representation of warehouse activities, which were then utilised by a Retrieval-Augmented Generation (RAG) system to efficiently retrieve and inject relevant information to an LLM for the generation of contextual insights [19]. This representation enhances the system's ability to analyse and interpret multimodal data, enabling the identification of unsafe behaviours and supporting timely reporting to warehouse staff and managers.

Figure 2b shows an excerpt from a GPT-4-generated dialogue where the manager can practice interpersonal skills by interacting with a simulated worker, handling resistance to encourage OHS compliance. The model was used as-is, with task-specific prompt engineering to align with the application domain. Although the initial prompts did not include domain-specific knowledge or worker profiling details, the LLM was shown to be adaptable to craft scenarios testing a manager's communication and interpersonal skills. The prompt included an initial interaction, where the LLM asked questions to personalise the coaching scenario based on the manager's needs. The model then generated a unique tailored vignette and concluded with actionable recommendations for improvement. This proof-of-concept highlighted the potential of LLMs to facilitate coaching across domains, with future implementations aiming at enabling dynamic prompt personalisation and reducing the need for extensive prompt engineering.

3.2 OHS Managers' Feedback

The feedback of OHS managers on the pilot was generally positive, transitioning from a neutral starting mood to enthusiasm, as they realised the potential of Computer Vision and LLMs to their field. One manager remarked that multimodal data integration for incident analysis would simplify the way incidents are investigated at the warehouse. The pilot's role-playing dialogues also resonated with OHS managers, who highlighted its realism and even noted how accurately the simulated responses mirrored workers' reactions to OHS enforcement.

A senior OHS manager provided constructive suggestions, emphasising the importance of involving staff in the design process to ensure acceptance and engagement. He cautioned that introducing the technology without their participation might lead to resistance, as staff could perceive it as a surveillance tool rather than a beneficial resource. Aligned with this perspective, privacy by design principles have been embedded from the outset, ensuring that transparency and user control mitigate privacy concerns while enhancing trust and user experience [45]. To further foster a sense of ownership, he recommended involving team leaders in future design iterations, highlighting that demonstrating the technology's impact on reducing incidents would help staff recognise its value. He noted: "*If we can show staff how this technology reduces incidents and makes the workplace safer, they'll see the value themselves*". Additionally, he suggested using concrete metrics, such as monthly incident reduction, to effectively communicate the benefits of the pilot. Such metrics not only illustrate its impact but also serve as an efficacy measure for the PT, reinforcing its role in reducing non-compliant behaviour. Another key concern was false positives in incident detection, potentially increasing OHS managers' workload. The senior manager noted: "*Incorrect data would mean more work, as we'd have to manually review and dismiss false incidents*". The team clarified that the pilot would generate aggregate statistics to minimise individual errors and include a feedback mechanism for managers to flag inaccuracies, refining AI performance through human-in-the-loop input.

Overall, OHS managers endorsed the proposed pilot and supported staff involvement in future design phases and testing, reflecting a shared vision for the AI coach and its potential to enhance OHS attitudes and behaviours.

4   Retrospective Analysis and Key Learnings

Building on managers' feedback, this design work ensured alignment with practical needs, with an Agile approach enabling iterative improvements. The methodology advances through the *Experiment* and *Measure* phases [42], using user experiments to assess impact via qualitative and quantitative measures. While these phases extend beyond this paper, the strong foundations laid so far ensure future development follows a robust design framework. This section reflects on the reported design activities, using retrospective analysis [38] to extract key learnings that contribute more broadly to the field of PT.

4.1   Bottom-Up Emergence of PT Principles

The work demonstrates the effectiveness of a bottom-up design, contrasting the top-down methods traditionally employed in PT. Top-down approaches use expert-defined interventions and tailored persuasive design principles to drive behavioural change, but may overlook user needs or the causes of the behaviour targeted for change. In contrast, our process did not initiate with a fixed intervention, goal, or principles, focussing instead on exploring the potential of the AI coaching technology for the chosen context. This open-ended approach allows the design to evolve through iterative stakeholder engagement and insights, gradually uncovering pain points and tailoring innovative solutions.

The bottom-up methodology offers notable advantages. Its adaptability enables exploration and selection of use cases aligned with emergent needs, such as improving OHS compliance. The process naturally uncovered the root causes of the targeted behaviour, ensuring it addresses not only the behavioural goal but also systemic issues, such as inefficiencies in monitoring, shortcomings in training methods, or the need for managers to instil OHS compliance more effectively.

The outcomes of the design process notably aligned with established PT principles [9, 10, 16], which were not imposed top-down but emerged organically. For example, the *reduction* principle can be observed in features enabling OHS managers to streamline data integration and processing to identify safety risks efficiently, and deliver personalised OHS coaching with the AI acting as a mediator. Similarly, *tailoring* is reflected in customised coaching simulations and reports, dynamically adapted to the user's role and needs. The design incorporates the *simulated cause-and-effect* and *simulated environments* principles, offering realistic role-playing vignettes for managers and staff. These allow users to rehearse behaviours, observe decision outcomes in real-time, address knowledge gaps, and improve professional and interpersonal skills. Moreover, the *suggestion* principle enhances decision-making by delivering timely and actionable recommendations grounded in integrated data or following the role-playing interactions. To encourage compliance, the *surveillance* principle uses ubiquitous AI to enable managers to monitor staff OHS behaviour, promoting compliance through awareness of being observed. Finally, the *authority* principle strengthens adherence by framing simulations as directives from managers and referencing OHS rules, reinforcing the importance of training and compliance.

What does this mean for the PT community? In some cases, traditional top-down design may be an effective way to address the target behaviour, specifically when the underlying causes are well-understood and clear strategies for intervention can be identified. As an analogy, take a 'supervised' machine learning approach, where the ground truth is known and the training process is guided by existing labels. Similarly, when use case-specific knowledge is not required and general pre-existing knowledge is sufficient, selecting PT principles and ideating solutions around them can be appropriate. However, when the target behaviour is unclear, the underlying causes are not fully understood, or it is uncertain if a behaviour change is beneficial for the considered context, a bottom-up approach offers a solid complementary solution. Analogous to 'unsupervised' machine learning, where patterns and insights emerge without labels, bottom-up approach facilitates an in-depth exploration of users' needs and pain points without relying on predefined assumptions. For example, in our work, the holistic investigation of the warehouse environment revealed that coaching interventions were needed not only for warehouse staff but also for OHS managers. Managers required solutions to improve their situational awareness and develop interpersonal skills, enabling them to address staff non-compliance more effectively.

By focussing on user-centred design activities, the process shifts from applying pre-selected PT design principles to understanding the users' context and problems. Only after a target behaviour is identified, can PT principles be layered onto the design process to refine solutions effectively. This adaptive approach allows the PT community to explore a broader solution space, grounding interventions in user insights, fostering innovation, and developing technologies that are more attuned to real-world needs and user expectations.

4.2   Collaborative Human-and-AI Coaching

This work brings to the fore a new perspective on the role of coaching PT. Traditionally, PT are designed to function independently of human coaches or experts, directly engaging with users to drive behavioural change [16]. In such cases, the expertise and strategies of human coaches or experts are distilled and embedded into PT to increase scalability and eliminating the need for continuous human input [16]. While this is advantageous in contexts where experts

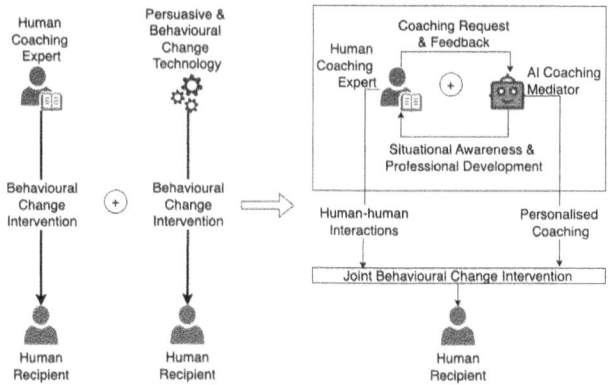

Fig. 3. Combining human-and-AI coaching fosters collaboration and enhances behavioural change, while maintaining workplace interactions.

are unavailable or can be safely removed, it may be a notable limitation, e.g., in the OHS setting explored by this work. OHS managers play a pivotal role in delivering guidance, as well as fostering trust and accountability. By replacing OHS managers, PT may alienate staff and diminish the impact of behavioural interventions, as interpersonal dynamics are critical for ensuring OHS compliance [29]. In general, fully delegating behavioural interventions to PT in high-risk and mission-critical domains may be unacceptable and have legal consequences.

As shown in Fig. 3, our design yielded an alternative solution, positioning AI coaching not as a replacement to humans, but as a collaborative mediator augmenting the humans. This positions AI, beyond the means to generate and deliver personalised coaching, also as a resource that enhances the human coach's knowledge, awareness, and skills, thus, more effectively guiding and influencing the recipient of the coaching interventions through direct interpersonal interactions [29]. In the context of OHS, this dual effort can enhance compliance and ultimately reduce OHS incidents, a key evaluation metric for the PT.

The versatility of this framework may extend to other coaching domains, e.g., education, where AI can deliver personalised learning to students while providing teachers with insights on classroom dynamics and student needs. This can help educators adjust strategies to improve learning outcomes. Our work shows how PT embedding expert coaching can elevate recipient-focused tools into holistic collaborative support technologies. By integrating human expert and AI, we can enhance interventions through a dynamic, feedback-driven partnership.

4.3   Limitations and Future Directions

This work highlighted the value of a bottom-up design methodology in uncovering PT principles organically and positioning AI as a collaborative mediator for AI coaching. Despite establishing a robust foundation, several limitations, which are at the same time opportunities for future research, should be discussed.

First, our participatory design process was limited to the research and development team and OHS managers, without direct involvement from broader warehouse staff. This decision was driven by the need to initially establish a clear understanding of managerial workflows and priorities before expanding the stakeholder engagement. Concerns around potential resistance to new technologies at early development stages also influenced this decision. Future iterations will actively involve broader staff through participatory sessions, to incorporate their unique perspectives and ensure the system addresses their needs. Such a phased approach enables robust foundational development, while creating opportunities to refine the system based on staff feedback and fostering engagement and ownership [26].

Another limitation is the absence of a comprehensive user study evaluating HIRO's effectiveness in tackling OHS non-compliance. This aligns with the current focus on the design process rather than empirical validation. The chosen design methodology [42] includes subsequent experimental phases that build on the design outcomes presented here. These will involve structured user studies with quantitative metrics, such as comparing the accuracy of OHS managers in identifying non-compliance in video footage with or without the AI technology, task performance times, and more. Ultimately, short- and long-term trends in OHS incidents before and after deploying the complete solution will be analysed. Qualitative assessments, including user experience evaluation to understand satisfaction and usability, as well as think-aloud protocols [7,14] to capture real-time thoughts during interactions, will complement the quantitative metrics.

Finally, an important limitation of this paper refers to the lack of detailed technical descriptions. These include the implementation of the computer vision and LLM features, as well as their integration underpinning the proposed solution. This omission was a deliberate choice to ensure the paper focusses on the design methodology and its broader implications for the PT community. The LLM prompts used to generate the sample coaching simulations presented in the pilot are available in the online addendum referred to in Sect. 2, while the technical details of the full implementation will be presented in future publications. The limited presentation of the design outcomes was primarily dictated by page constraints, with these outputs also accessible in the online addendum.

5   Conclusions

This work highlights the effectiveness of a bottom-up design approach in identifying user needs and addressing OHS challenges in warehouses. The AI coach, HIRO, supports OHS managers in fostering compliance and safety culture, with positive feedback validating the participatory approach's role in user trust and adoption.

A retrospective analysis underscored the value of AI coaching as a collaborative mediator that enhances rather than replaces human coaches. AI provides tailored insights, reinforcing interpersonal interactions and strengthening OHS managers' capabilities. Additionally, the bottom-up design naturally integrated

PT principles, enabling adaptive, realistic coaching interventions without predefined behaviours or goals.

Acknowledgments. This work is based on results obtained by Fujitsu Macquarie AI Research Lab.

References

1. Akinsemoyin, A., Awolusi, I., Chakraborty, D., Al-Bayati, A.J., Akanmu, A.: Unmanned aerial systems and deep learning for safety and health activity monitoring on construction sites. Sensors **23**(15), 6690 (2023)
2. Almohanna, A.A.S., Meedya, S., Vlahu-Gjorgievska, E., Win, K.T.: Exploring user experiences with a persuasive mhealth app for breastfeeding: an empirical investigation. International J. Hum.–Comput. Interact. 1–18 (2024)
3. Asano, Y.: Defining the problems solution to lead to the ideation phase: a case study on the use of how might we.... In: International Conference on Human-Computer Interaction, pp. 27–37. Springer, Cham (2023)
4. Ashwani, S., et al.: Cause and effect: can large language models truly understand causality? In: Proceedings of the AAAI Symposium Series, vol. 4, pp. 2–9 (2024)
5. Basahel, A.M.: Investigation of work-related musculoskeletal disorders (MSDs) in warehouse workers in Saudi Arabia. Procedia Manuf. **3**, 4643–4649 (2015)
6. Cebulla, A., Szpak, Z., Knight, G.: Preparing to work with artificial intelligence: assessing WHS when using AI in the workplace. Int. J. Workplace Health Manag. **16**(4), 294–312 (2023)
7. Charters, E.: The use of think-aloud methods in qualitative research an introduction to think-aloud methods. Brock Educ. J. **12**(2) (2003)
8. Chen, J., et al.: When large language models meet personalization: perspectives of challenges and opportunities. World Wide Web **27**(4), 42 (2024)
9. Cialdini, R.B.: The science of persuasion. Sci. Am. **284**(2), 76–81 (2001)
10. Cialdini, R.B.: Influence: Science and Practice, vol. 4. Pearson Education, Boston (2009)
11. Colusso, L., Do, T., Hsieh, G.: Behavior change design sprints. In: Proceedings of the 2018 Designing Interactive Systems Conference, pp. 791–803 (2018)
12. Dautenhahn, K.: The art of designing socially intelligent agents: science, fiction, and the human in the loop. Appl. Artif. Intell. **12**(7–8), 573–617 (1998)
13. Dautenhahn, K., Bond, A., Cañamero, L., Edmonds, B.: Socially Intelligent Agents: Creating Relationships with Computers and Robots. Springer, Cham (2002)
14. Eccles, D.W., Arsal, G.: The think aloud method: what is it and how do I use it? Qual. Res. Sport Exercise Health **9**(4), 514–531 (2017)
15. Fogg, B.J.: Creating persuasive technologies: an eight-step design process. In: Proceedings of the 4th International Conference on Persuasive Technology, pp. 1–6 (2009)
16. Fogg, B.J.: Persuasive technology: using computers to change what we think and do. Ubiquity **2002**(December), 2 (2002)
17. Fujitsu Limited: Technology for behavioral analysis Actlyzer: AI that understands, predicts, and judges like a human being. https://www.fujitsu.com/global/about/research/technology/actlyzer/. Accessed 18 Dec 2024

18. Fujitsu Limited: Fujitsu launches AI platform "Fujitsu Kozuchi", streamlining access to AI and ML solutions to contribute to a sustainable society (2023) https://www.fujitsu.com/global/about/resources/news/press-releases/2023/0420-02.html. Accessed 18 Dec 2024
19. Gao, Y., et al.: Retrieval-augmented generation for large language models: a survey. arXiv preprint arXiv:2312.10997 (2023)
20. Gothelf, J.: Lean UX: Applying Lean Principles to Improve User Experience. O'Reilly Media Inc. (2013)
21. Hekler, E.B., et al.: Agile science: creating useful products for behavior change in the real world. Transl. Behav. Med. **6**(2), 317–328 (2016). https://doi.org/10.1007/s13142-016-0395-7
22. Hietbrink, E.A.G., et al.: A digital lifestyle coach (E-Supporter 1.0) to support people with type 2 diabetes: participatory development study. JMIR Hum Factors **10**, e40017 (2023). https://doi.org/10.2196/40017. https://humanfactors.jmir.org/2023/1/e40017
23. Hofstra, N., Petkova, B., Dullaert, W., Reniers, G., De Leeuw, S.: Assessing and facilitating warehouse safety. Saf. Sci. **105**, 134–148 (2018)
24. Isailovic, V., et al.: Compliance of head-mounted personal protective equipment by using YOLOv5 object detector. In: 2021 International Conference on Electrical, Computer and Energy Technologies (ICECET), pp. 1–5. IEEE (2021)
25. Ji, J., Krishna, R., Fei-Fei, L., Niebles, J.C.: Action genome: actions as compositions of spatio-temporal scene graphs. In: Proceedings of the IEEE/CVF Conference on Computer Vision and Pattern Recognition, pp. 10236–10247 (2020)
26. Keizer, J., Jong, N.B., Naiemi, N.A., van Gemert-Pijnen, J.: Persuading from the start: participatory development of sustainable persuasive data-driven technologies in healthcare. In: Gram-Hansen, S.B., Jonasen, T.S., Midden, C. (eds.) PERSUASIVE 2020. LNCS, vol. 12064, pp. 113–125. Springer, Cham (2020). https://doi.org/10.1007/978-3-030-45712-9_9
27. Kihlstrom, J.F., Cantor, N.: Social intelligence. Handb. Intell. **2**, 359–379 (2000)
28. Kip, H., de Jong, N.B., Kelders, S.M., van Gemert-Pijnen, L.J.: The CeHRes Roadmap, chap. 7, pp. 103–102, 2 edn. Routledge (2024). https://doi.org/10.4324/9781003302049-9
29. Klein, C., DeRouin, R.E., Salas, E.: Uncovering workplace interpersonal skills: a review, framework, and research agenda. Int. Rev. Ind. Organ. Psychol. **2006**(21), 79–126 (2006)
30. Nelson, L.: Managing managers in occupational health and safety. Asia Pac. J. Hum. Resour. **32**(1), 13–28 (1994)
31. Niu, Y., Fan, Y., Ju, X.: Critical review on data-driven approaches for learning from accidents: comparative analysis and future research. Saf. Sci. **171**, 106381 (2024)
32. Prameswara, D., Djunaidi, Z.: Occupational health and safety in warehouse area. In: International Conference of Occupational Health and Safety (ICOHS 2017) (2018)
33. Pu, H., Yang, X., Li, J., Guo, R.: AutoRepo: a general framework for multimodal LLM-based automated construction reporting. Expert Syst. Appl. **255**, 124601 (2024)
34. Rahman, M.N.A., Zuhaidi, M.F.A.: Musculoskeletal symptoms and ergonomic hazards among material handlers in grocery retail industries. In: IOP Conference Series: Materials Science and Engineering, vol. 226. IOP Publishing (2017)
35. Reiman, T., Pietikäinen, E.: Leading indicators of system safety-monitoring and driving the organizational safety potential. Saf. Sci. **50**(10), 1993–2000 (2012)

36. Rodrí§guez, M.C.: Íñigo Cuiñas: Definition, chap. 4 (in "Design thinking for engineering: a practical guide"), pp. 57–72. IET manufacturing series, Institution of Engineering and Technology (2023). https://doi.org/10.1049/PBME024E_ch4. https://digital-library.theiet.org/doi/abs/10.1049/PBME024E_ch4

37. Saric, S., Bab-Hadiashar, A., Hoseinnezhad, R., Hocking, I.: Analysis of forklift accident trends within Victorian industry (Australia). Saf. Sci. **60**, 176–184 (2013)

38. Schön, D.A.: The Reflective Practitioner: How Professionals Think in Action. Routledge (2017)

39. Shah, I.A., Mishra, S.: Artificial intelligence in advancing occupational health and safety: an encapsulation of developments. J. Occup. Health **66**(1), uiad017 (2024)

40. Stanford School: Design Thinking Bootleg. https://dschool.stanford.edu/resources/design-thinking-bootleg. Accessed 10 Dec 2024

41. Taype, G., Calani, M.: Extending persuasive system design frameworks: an exploratory study. In: Rocha, Á., Ferrás, C., Montenegro Marin, C.E., Medina García, V.H. (eds.) ICITS 2020. AISC, vol. 1137, pp. 35–45. Springer, Cham (2020). https://doi.org/10.1007/978-3-030-40690-5_4

42. Tonkin, M., Vitale, J., Herse, S., Williams, M.A., Judge, W., Wang, X.: Design methodology for the UX of HRI: a field study of a commercial social robot at an airport. In: Proceedings of the 2018 ACM/IEEE International Conference on Human-Robot Interaction, pp. 407–415 (2018)

43. Tschimmel, K.: Design thinking as an effective toolkit for innovation. In: ISPIM Conference Proceedings, p. 1. The International Society for Professional Innovation Management (ISPIM) (2012)

44. Đurđević, D., Andrejić, M., Pavlov, N.: Framework for improving warehouse safety. In: Proceedings of the 5th LOGIC Conference, pp. 304–314 (2022)

45. Vitale, J., Tonkin, M., Ojha, S., Williams, M.A., Wang, X., Judge, W.: Privacy by design in machine learning data collection: a user experience experimentation. In: 2017 AAAI Spring Symposium Series (2017)

46. Voria, G., Catolino, G., Palomba, F.: Is attention all you need? Toward a conceptual model for social awareness in large language models. In: Proceedings of the 2024 IEEE/ACM First International Conference on AI Foundation Models and Software Engineering, pp. 69–73 (2024)

47. Vukicevic, A.M., Petrovic, M.N., Knezevic, N.M., Jovanovic, K.M.: Deep learning-based recognition of unsafe acts in manufacturing industry. IEEE Access (2023)

48. Walker, R.E., Foley, J.M.: Social intelligence: its history and measurement. Psychol. Rep. **33**(3), 839–864 (1973)

49. Wang, L., Zhong, H.: LLM-SAP: large language models situational awareness-based planning. In: 2024 IEEE International Conference on Multimedia and Expo Workshops (ICMEW), pp. 1–6. IEEE (2024)

Analysing User Feedback on Commercial Diet Tracking App

Joohyun Lee[✉] ⓘ, Vivienne Guanⓘ, and Khin Than Winⓘ

University of Wollongong, Wollongong, NSW, Australia
jrl970@uowmail.edu.au

Abstract. This study consists of advanced text mining and Natural Language Processing (NLP) technique to analyse user reviews on commercial diet tracking apps, focusing on enhancing user engagement and satisfaction through persuasive System Design (PSD) model. By systematically categorising user feedback into areas such as primary task, dialogue, social and credibility, the research identifies key patterns and factors impacting user interactions, as well as provide deeper insight into how app features influence sustained user engagement and adherence to health goals. The categorised user feedback provides a distinct user reviews into four categorises which allow developers to pin point specific areas of where users are satisfied or requires specific refinements according to the four PSD models. The findings illustrate the diverse influences of PSD elements on user satisfaction and engagement. This methodological approach not only addresses a significant gap in understanding user feedback but also serves as pioneer attempt of using NLP incorporated with PSD model to refine health app features, thereby improving user outcomes and retention in specific areas of persuasive design models.

Keywords: User Reviews · Persuasive Systems Design · Sentiment Analysis · Topic Modelling · NLP

1 Introduction

In today's digital landscape, mobile health applications are integral to personal health management, particularly due to their accessibility and user-friendly design, amplified by the ubiquity of smartphones [1]. Among these, diet tracking apps stand out by providing essential services such as food logging and nutrient tracking, playing a crucial role in guiding users towards healthier lifestyle choices. The success of these applications largely hinges on user engagement and satisfaction, which are influenced by how well these apps meet users' needs [2]. A pivotal aspect of continual app enhancement involves the rigorous analysis of user feedback available through app reviews.

To address these challenges, this study employs advanced text mining and Natural Language Processing (NLP) techniques to perform topic modeling and sentiment analysis on user reviews of commercial diet tracking applications. By systematically categorizing feedback into dimensions such as persuasive systems design, primary task support, social interactions, dialogue facilitation, and credibility, this research aims to

© The Author(s), under exclusive license to Springer Nature Switzerland AG 2025
K. T. Win et al. (Eds.): PERSUASIVE 2025, LNCS 15711, pp. 18–31, 2025.
https://doi.org/10.1007/978-3-031-94959-3_2

unearth underlying patterns and crucial factors that affect user engagement and satisfaction. The concept of persuasive systems design is particularly central to our analysis, providing a framework to understand how different app features persuade and motivate users towards sustained app usage and adherence to health-related goals [3]. By integrating these analytical dimensions, the study offers developers nuanced insights into user sentiment and practical directives for user-centric enhancements.

2 Literature

The prevalence of mobile health apps, particularly for diet tracking, underscores the necessity of enhancing user experience to sustain engagement and satisfaction. Key to this is understanding app usability which significantly influences user retention [4]. Current literature suggests that user feedback via app reviews offers invaluable insights into app functionality and user satisfaction, essential for iterative development [1, 2]. Moreover, incorporating persuasive systems design into app features can significantly enhance user motivation and adherence to health-related goals by making the apps more engaging and interactive [3, 5].

Advanced text mining and sentiment analysis techniques provide a robust framework for extracting meaningful patterns from user feedback, helping developers prioritize improvements and align updates more closely with user expectations [6, 7].

Existing studies have shown the effectiveness of topic modeling for analyzing user comments to evolve software requirements but have often overlooked health-specific functionalities [1, 2, 8]. This oversight highlights an opportunity to adapt such methodologies for health applications, especially to tackle unique challenges in diet-tracking apps like health outcomes, usability, and data privacy [2, 4]. Moreover, while comprehensive analyses of user feedback in diet-tracking apps have been conducted throughout numerous studies [1, 2], implications of adapting persuasive design model in analysing these user feedback has not been explored. Thus, paper serves to improve the field of persuasive technology and consolidate prior research in user feedback analysis.

This research aims to bridge that gap by integrating the persuasive design model, providing a deeper and more nuanced analysis of user requirements and engagement in commercial diet tracking apps. It explores how persuasive elements can be effectively designed to increase user interaction, potentially leading to better health outcomes and higher retention rates [6, 9]. This approach seeks to empower developers with strategies that transform passive users into active participants, enhancing their overall health engagement with the app. This focused methodology fills a critical research void and offers practical tools for developers to improve user satisfaction and app success. This gap highlights the need for research focused on the application of user feedback analysed through NLP techniques to enhance app features effectively, leading to the research question: How are user satisfaction and perceptions towards the persuasive design elements of diet-tracking apps are expressed and what specific user satisfaction or improvement areas can be identified through NLP?

3 Methodology

Initially, MyFitnessPal and Calorie Counter by LoseIt! were selected, considering numerous factors such as popularity, ratings, number of downloads and the available reviews. User reviews from 2011 to 2024 were extracted from Google play store using *SerpAPI* through pagination. The initial dataset consists of; MyFitnessPal being 50,149, Calorie Counter by LoseIt! of 46,691. Upon collection and initial exploratory descriptive statistical analysis, a comprehensive data cleaning process, shown in Fig. 1, was undertaken using Python, to ensure the quality and compatibility for analysis to address inconsistencies, errors and noises commonly found in raw data [10].

Fig. 1. Data Cleaning Process in Detail

After implementing the data cleaning methods on the initial dataset, reviews were meticulously processed, resulting in a final dataset 96,840 reviews. Furthermore, in compliance with the General Data Protection Regulation (GDPR), any data related to usernames and labels that could identify users was anonymized. Sentiment Analysis was initially performed on the cleaned dataset across all of the reviews throughout all the applications in order to identify individual quantitative emotion score for each review as well as for the combination for topic modelling later on.

Roberta was chosen for the sentiment analysis as it's a pre-trained model, provided by hugging face, trained on large-scale corpora enables it to generalize well across different datasets, making it highly adaptable for analysing diverse user reviews. Unlike simpler models that might struggle with sarcasm or ambiguous wording, Roberta's enables it to capture context deeply, ensuring more accurate predictions of sentiment [11].

3.1 Topic Modelling with Categorisation of Persuasive Technology of User Reviews

Categorisation. The categorization process begins with the automated grouping of reviews into predefined categories of persuasive systems design, namely 'primary task support', 'dialogue support.', 'social support' and 'credibility support' This process involves several steps:

(Step1: Initialization of Category Scores) A numerical score is initiated at zero for each category.

(Step 2: Keyword Matching) The entire review text is scanned for predefined keywords that have been set based on the nature of the application that is associated with each category. When a match is found, the corresponding category's score is incremented.
(Step 3: Category Assignment) The review is assigned to the category with the highest score. If no keywords match, the review is classified as 'uncategorized'.

This automated categorization facilitates unbiased and consistent classification, leveraging a keyword-matching scoring system that minimizes human error and subjective bias. Once the categorisation is complete, then reviews are assigned with each of category name as well as uncategorised.

Selection of category-specific keywords for initial categorization in persuasive technologies, we utilize established frameworks within persuasive systems design, notably those by Oinas-Kukkonen and Harjumaa [3]. These frameworks outline the essential elements that influence user behaviour through technology. The keywords are meticulously chosen based on the primary functionalities and user interactions specific to health and fitness applications.

These keywords are validated against user reviews and app descriptions, ensuring they accurately reflect the most engaged-with features. This approach is not only grounded in theoretical research but is also continuously refined through empirical data, ensuring relevance and efficacy in categorizing persuasive technology elements [2, 9].

Topic Modelling. Following categorization, topic extraction is performed within each category using topic modelling via KMeans clustering:

In the process of topic modelling shown in Fig. 2, the first step involves pre-processing where textual reviews are cleansed of URLs, special characters, and common stopwords to refine the data for analysis. Following this, text embedding techniques using Universal Sentence Encoder employed to transform the cleaned text into numerical vectors that capture semantic meanings of words based on their contextual usage. After transforming text data into numerical vectors via embedding, clustering is performed using the K-Means algorithm, guided by an "elbow plot" to determine the optimal number of clusters [12]. This plot, which displays the number of clusters against inertia, helps identify the point where increases in cluster count yield diminishing improvements, ensuring the clustering's relevance and accuracy [12].

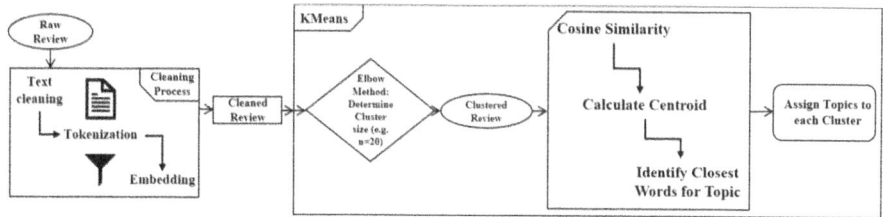

Fig. 2. Flow of the Topic Modelling process using Embedding and KMeans Clustering

This structured approach ensures that the topics extracted are not only relevant but are also distinctly representative of the specific categories, enhancing both the interpretability and applicability of the findings in understanding user sentiments and preferences in the reviews.

4 Results

4.1 Descriptive Statistical Analysis

The descriptive statistics reveal that LoseIt is generally more positively received, with higher average ratings (4.2) and more consistent feedback. MyFitnessPal, on the other hand, shows greater variability (Mean 3.3, SD 1.65), suggesting that while some users find it excellent, others have significant complaints. This difference is further emphasized by the tighter clustering of ratings around the mean for LoseIt compared to the broader spread of ratings for MyFitnessPal (Table 1).

Table 1. Descriptive statistics on ratings.

Ratings	Count	Mean	SD
Calorie counter by LoseIt!	46691	4.2	1.32
MyFitnessPal	50148	3.3	1.65

The lower average rating and higher standard deviation suggest that user opinions about MyFitnessPal are more polarized.

4.2 Sentiment Analysis

The sentiment analysis applied to user reviews for MyFitnessPal and LoseIt! provided a breakdown of the emotional tone expressed in user feedback (Table 2).

Table 2. Sentiment Percentage for LoseIt! and MyFitnessPal

Percentage	Calorie Counter by LoseIt!	MyFitnessPal
Positive	65.96%	43.50%
Negative	10.54%	28.16%
Neutral	23.50%	28.34%

The statistics reveal a clear difference in user sentiment between Calorie Counter by LoseIt! and MyFitnessPal. LoseIt! has a significantly higher percentage of positive reviews at 65.96%, compared to 43.50% for MyFitnessPal, indicating that a larger proportion of users are highly satisfied with LoseIt! In contrast, MyFitnessPal has a considerably higher percentage of negative reviews at 28.16%, while LoseIt! only has 10.54% negative reviews, suggesting greater dissatisfaction among MyFitnessPal users. Both applications share the same percentage of neutral reviews at 23.50%, reflecting a similar proportion of users with mixed or moderate opinions.

Each review was assigned a sentiment score ranging from -1 to 1, where −1 indicates negative sentiment, 0 indicates neutral sentiment, and 1 indicates positive sentiment.

Scores reflect the general emotional tone of the reviews for each app, with higher average scores indicating more positive feedback and lower scores indicating more negative feedback. The average sentiment score reflects each of the app's components such as LoseIt! indicating neutral and leaning more towards slightly positive sentiment on average, MyFitnessPal being moderately positive sentiment.

Table 3 shows the average sentiment scores for the reviews, highlighting that LoseIt! has a higher sentiment score compared to MyFitnessPal. This might contrast with the ratings, as people who give a five-star rating often just leave a rating, whereas those who give lower ratings tend to also comment on the issues that led them to such ratings.

Table 3. Average Sentiment Score per each application

Average Sentiment (−1 to 1)	Calorie Counter by LoseIt!	MyFitnessPal
Sentiment Score	0.53	0.13

Figure 3 below Fig. 3 illustrates a distinct correlation between sentiment scores and numerical ratings for both LoseIt! and MyFitnessPal. Each bar represents the average sentiment score corresponding to ratings from 1 to 5. The small black lines on each bar indicate the variability of sentiment scores, reflecting the consistency of sentiments associated with each rating level. LoseIt! demonstrates a clear positive correlation between ratings and average sentiment, indicating that higher ratings consistently correspond with more positive reviews. In contrast, MyFitnessPal shows generally negative average sentiments for ratings from 1 to 3, suggesting that users tend to leave more critical reviews that align closely with lower ratings. This pattern may indicate that LoseIt! users

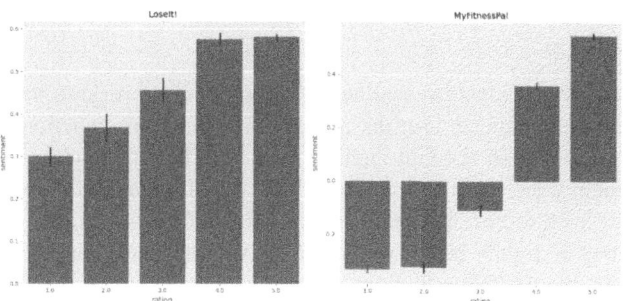

Fig. 3. Sentiment Score and Ratings Correlations

typically provide positive feedback, while MyFitnessPal users often express significant criticisms directly related to their ratings.

4.3 Topic Modelling with Categorisation of Persuasive Technology of User Reviews

Once reviews were categorised and grouped into primary task, dialogue, credibility, social support and additionally uncategorised, then topic modelling was performed within each group. As illustrated in Tables 4 and 5, key topic keywords along with their calculated average sentiment scores are displayed, categorized under different aspects of persuasive technology. This arrangement allows us to pinpoint the crucial persuasive features that these apps employ to influence user behaviour.

Credibility Support. In MyFitnessPal, the mixed sentiment scores observed for keywords related to reliability and security suggest a nuanced user experience with the application's performance. On one hand, terms such as "hacked, privacy, compromised and security" and "glitchy, unreliable and buggy" are associated with notably low sentiment scores of -0.776663 for security-related issues and -0.601097 for reliability issues. These negative scores highlight user concerns regarding the app's security and reliability, suggesting that there are noticeable issues affecting trust and satisfaction.

Conversely, high sentiment scores of 0.892361 for accurate and reliable functionalities indicate that other aspects of the app are highly regarded by users, particularly in terms of accuracy in tracking and the utility of sync features. This positive reception suggests that when the app functions as intended, users find it effective and reliable, enhancing their overall experience (Table 4).

This indicates that while MyFitnessPal generally supports its users well in certain functionalities like accurate tracking, there remains a critical need to address inconsistencies in application security and performance to ensure reliability.

LoseIt! faces challenges with features related to uninstalling and privacy, as evidenced by the low sentiment score of -0.499501 for keywords like "uninstalled, privacy, installed, inaccurate, uninstalling." However, the app also receives high sentiment scores for terms associated with accuracy and reliability, such as "accurate," "reliable," "trustworthy," and "precise." This contrast suggests that while there are concerns about certain functional and privacy aspects, the app excels in delivering precise and reliable service where it counts, particularly in calorie tracking and diet management [7].

Addressing these issues could help stabilize user trust and enhance the overall credibility of the app.

Social Support. The analysis of sentiment scores from user reviews for MyFitnessPal and LoseIt! reveals significant user dissatisfaction with certain functionalities, notably those related to email and account management. Specifically, MyFitnessPal has very negative sentiment scores for topics shown in Table 4 with "email and error" and "sign-in, login and error" with scores of -0.822030 and -0.790667 respectively.

LoseIt! shows a slightly better, yet still negative sentiment score of -0.690347 for similar issues (Table 5). These findings suggest challenges in these areas, though it is important to note that the topics covered in user reviews may not fully capture all aspects of the apps' social support features [9].

Table 4. Average Sentiment Score per Categorised Topics for MyFitnessPal Reviews

Credibility		Social		Primary task		Dialogue		Uncategorised	
Hacked, privacy, compromised, security, secure	-0.78	email, emails, gmail, protonmail, error	-0.82	login,loggin,logins, relogging,relog	-0.72	error,signin, unable, invalid, troubleshooting	-0.76	error,unable,signin, invalid, redownloaded	-0.78
Uninstall, uninstalled, privacy, uninstall, setting	-0.77	signin, login, error, loggin, accout	-0.79	playstore,laggy,syn cs, crashes,glitchy	-0.59	unsubscribed,unsub scribing, notifications, alerts,cancelation	-0.72	canceling, cancelling, cancel, subscription, cancelation	-0.76
glitchy, unreliable, buggy, reliable, glitches	-0.60	passwords, signin, password, logins, phishing	-0.78	syncs, smartwatch, resync, playstore, sync	-0.46	premium,subscripti on,uninstalled,subs cribed,subscription s	-0.52	laggy,crashes,oxyg enos, crashing,lags	-0.62
barcodes, premium, scanner, scanning, barcode	-0.47	gmail, authenticator, error, email, acount	-0.78	adfree,freemium,ba rcodes,barcode,trac ker	-0.41	notifications, alerts, notification, annoying, popup	-0.52	adfree,adverts,ads, advertisements,adv ert	-0.53
updating, updates, fixes, laggy, glitchy	-0.25	cancelling, canceling, cancelation, cancel, subscription	-0.73	menus,meals,recipi es, recipes,menu	0.00	barcodes, barcode, scanner, scanned,scanning	-0.48	barcode,barcodes,a dfree,scanner,scann ers	-0.44
inaccurate, accurately, menus, omly, accuracy	-0.14	error, disconnects, connectivity, troubleshooting, reconnecting	-0.68	playstore,calorie,sy ncs, tracker,caloric	0.23	notifications, notification,alerts, reminders, annoying	-0.47	premium,paywall,s ubscription,premiu ms,overpriced	-0.38
syncs, sync, synced, syncing, android	-0.11	playstore, oxygenos, syncs, connectivity, error	-0.64	calorie,caloric,calor ies, cals,kcals	0.35	adfree,premium,adv erts,popups, uninstalled	-0.43	barcode,barcodes,s canners, scanner,scanned	-0.22
Barcodes, barcode, scanner, scanners, scanning	-0.02	syncs, sync, disconnects, synced, syncing	-0.55	tracker,smartwatch, calorie,syncs,kcal	0.56	syncs,laggy,sync, crashes,lagging	-0.40	adfree,premium,sub scription, monetization,lite	-0.21
calorie, caloric, calories, dieting, cals	0.42	barcodes, barcode, scanner, scanners, scanning	-0.51	barcodes,barcode, scanner,scanners, scanning	0.56	notifications, notification,notified , notifying, reminders	-0.40	syncs,smartwatch,s ync,syncing,synced	-0.01
accurately, accurate, syncs, useful, reliable	0.89	samsung, huawei, android, syncs, sync	-0.42	calorie,caloric,kcals ,kcal,dieting	0.70	reminders, notifications,syncs, reminder,alerts	0.22	playstore,syncs,swi ping, android,ios	0.20
		syncs, instagram, adfree, uninstalled, android	0.08	caloric,kcals,calorie s, calorie,dieters	0.70	syncs,reminders,ux, notifications,ui	0.28	recipies,cookbooks, menus, cookbook,recipes	0.24
		syncs,tracker,huaw ei,sync,playstore	0.19	dieters,dieted,dietin g, recomp,weightloss	0.79	dieting,recipes,keto , calorie,dietary	0.62	handy,usefull,clunk y, cumbersome,easier	0.25
		smartwatch, syncs, android, whatsapp, huawei	0.22	weightloss,dieting, dieted,calorie,bariat ric	0.82	calorie,keto,excerci ses,useful,diets	0.89	dieting,caloric,calor ie,diets, carbs	0.64
		dieters, keto, menus, recipies, dieting	0.32	macros,calorie,kcal s, tracker,dieting	0.83			calorie,dieted,calori c,syncs, iifym	0.77
		calorie, syncs, tracker, kcal, caloric	0.58	calorie,caloric,sync s, kcal,dieting	0.94			weightloss,dieting,c alorie,diet,caloric	0.83

Table 5. Average Sentiment Score per Categorised Topics for LoseIt! Reviews

Credibility		Social		Primary Task		Dialogue		Uncategorised	
uninstalled,privacy, installed,inaccurate, uninstalling	-0.50	email,account, password,gmail, emails	-0.69	relogging, crashes, signout, laggy, error	-0.50	freemium,premium, subscription,notific ations, uninstalled	-0.47	laggy,crashes,apk, android,uninstalled	-0.42
updates,updated, update,improved, refresh	-0.11	refunded,refunds, emailed,cancelled, cancel	-0.65	adfree, syncs, calorie, tracker, smartwatch	0.09	notifications, alerts, notification,notify, reminders	-0.27	scumbag,sucks,hate s,useless,dislike	-0.22
accurate,inaccurate, dependable,extreme lygreat	0.15	account,logins, password,error, accounts	-0.60	calorie, dieters, exercising, exercise, excersize	0.31	android,widget, reminders,tablet, amoled	0.30	premium,playstore, subscription,fdroid, uninstalled	-0.14
calorie,calories, accurate,counting,c al	0.19	emails,email,gmail, emailed,spam	-0.46	calories, calorie, caloric, cals, dieting	0.40	diets,keto, diet, calorie, caloric	0.60	premium,fdroid, playstore, subscription, uninstalled	0.34
syncs,tracker, calorie, android,ui	0.29	error,glitch,proble m, problems,glitching	-0.41	calorie, dieters, caloric, dieting, calories	0.52	calorie,syncs, reminders,dieting, tracker	0.67	great,good,helps, awesome,really	0.34
barcodes,barcode, scanned,scanning, scanner	0.36	subscription,premiu m,free,api, uninstalled	-0.41	meals,overeat,dieti ng,overeating,meal	0.69	reminders,sync, reminder, simplicity,intuitive	0.78	dieters,dieting, overeat,calorie,calo ric	0.48
dieting,caloric, calorie,diets,calorie s	0.59	laggy,playstore, connectivity, crashes,error	-0.38	calorie,caloric,kcals , kcal,cals	0.72	recipies,useful,tips, intuitive, easy	0.81	weightloss,25lbs, dieted,30lbs,dieting	0.62
accurate,brilliant, inaccurate,reliable, intuitive	0.80	connectivity,connec ting,connection, connected,connect	-0.29	barcodes,barcode, scanner,scanning, scanners	0.73	reminders, reminder,tracker, notifications, motivational	0.82	weightloss,dieting, weight,overweight, diet	0.70
accurate,reliable, easy,effective,trust worthy	0.83	smartwatch, wearables, gps, jawbone, sync	0.04	tracker,tracking, trackers,tracked, monitoring	0.74	motivate,motivated, encouragement, motivation, accomplishment	0.85	playstore,syncs, android, applications, ios	0.80
accurately, easy,accurate, reliable,precise	0.88	samsung, android, lg, huawei, iphone	0.15	weightloss,dieted, dieting,nutrisystem, diets	0.77			great,nice, awesome, fantastic, good	0.81
		menus,ui,calorie, recipes,syncs	0.46	weightloss,dieting, weight,diets,diet	0.78			weightloss,maigrir, dieted, dieters, c25k	0.83
		syncs,android,calor ie,wearables, tracker	0.50	calorie,calories, caloric,cals,tracker	0.80			brilliant,good,nice, fantastic,dope	0.83
		friends,friendships, friend,sharing, facebook	0.54	motivating,helps, motivate, motivation, motivational	0.83			easy,handy,easiest, convenient,ease	0.84
		android,ios, supportive, recommending, facebook	0.85	weightloss,dieted, nutrisystem,dieting, calorie	0.88			brilliant,great, awesome,excellent, fantastic	0.92
		weightloss,dieted, dieting,25lbs,30lbs	0.86	syncs,tracker, instagram,calorie, reminders	0.94			brilliant,dope, fantastic,love, amazing	0.96

Primary Task Support. Both apps excel in primary task support, focusing on core functionalities such as calorie tracking and diet management. MyFitnessPal particularly stands out, receiving high sentiment scores for keywords like weight loss, calorie counting, tracking, dieting, and macros (as shown in Table 4).

This indicates that the app effectively supports its primary tasks, enhancing user engagement and satisfaction by aligning well with the app's goals of facilitating weight loss and efficient calorie management.

Similarly, LoseIt! also demonstrates effectiveness in its primary task support, receiving positive feedback for keywords such as weight loss, tracking, calories, and nutrisystems. These high scores suggest that the app is successful in persuading users and aiding them in their dietary management goals. However, there are areas needing improvement, as indicated by negative sentiments associated with functionalities like "sign in, troubleshooting, barcodes, and scanning."

Overall, the strong performance of both apps in primary task support underscores their usefulness, particularly in features like barcode scanning and activity tracking, which are integral to their functionality and user satisfaction. This alignment with their primary goals not only aids users in managing their diet and weight but also enhances the overall persuasiveness of the apps [3].

Dialogue Support. MyFitnessPal's dialogue support features, including "notifications, alerts, popup, reminders," often receive negative to neutral sentiment ratings, as highlighted in Table 4. The frequent mention of terms like "annoying" in user reviews points to deficiencies in these aspects of the app's dialogue support, suggesting areas where improvements are needed to enhance user satisfaction.

In contrast, LoseIt! demonstrates more successful implementation of similar dialogue features. Positive sentiments associated with terms such as "motivate, encouragement, accomplishment, and reminders," as recorded in Table 5, indicate that these features effectively persuade and motivate users. This suggests that LoseIt! has managed to refine its dialogue support to better meet user expectations and enhance engagement.

5 Discussion

Sentiment score and Topics of user reviews from two different commercial diet tracking application has been completed, as well as frequently mentioned topics, average sentiment per topics. Sentiment analysis helps to gauge the general opinion or emotional tone users have towards each identified topic [13].

5.1 MyFitnessPal

The analysis of MyFitnessPal user reviews reveals that various persuasive technology features have been implemented in the application with varying levels of success. In the credibility category, topics such as "hacked, privacy, compromised, security" and "subscription, unsubscribed, cancellation" received highly negative sentiment scores of -0.776663 and -0.722201, highlighting significant concerns regarding privacy and subscription issues. These findings indicate that while credibility features are present, improvements are needed to rebuild user trust [3].

The application's strongest performance was in the primary task support category, where core functionalities such as calorie tracking and barcode scanning received the most positive sentiment scores. Topics like "calorie, dietary, recipes" and "calorie, keto, diets" demonstrate strong user satisfaction with these features as indicated by sentiment score of 0.624167 and 0.888407 [9, 13].

In the social support category, features related to syncing and social connectivity showed moderate positive sentiments (0.192390), such as "sync, tracker, Instagram", reflecting appreciation but also revealing room for improvement in technical execution. Certain uncategorized themes, like "play store, crashing, laggy" with a sentiment of −0.632356, indicate technical issues that detract from the overall user experience and fall outside defined persuasive technology categories.

Moreover, MyFitnessPal face somewhat challenges with their dialogue support features, particularly in how notifications and reminders are implemented. Reasoning for these issues may related to that dialogue support may be inherently difficult to optimize, as users have varied preferences regarding the frequency and tone of notifications and reminders with topic such as laggy, sync, notification and alerts associated with negative sentiments (Tables 4 and 5).

Additionally, the effectiveness of dialogue support depends on reward, reminder, suggestion and appeal to the user. If notifications are generic, poorly timed, or irrelevant, they may have the opposite of the intended persuasive effect, reducing engagement rather than enhancing it [4].

5.2   Calorie Counter by LoseIt!

The analysis of LoseIt! user reviews reveals that the application integrates various persuasive technology features, with user sentiment varying across the categories. In terms of credibility, topics such as "uninstalled, privacy, inaccurate" and "email, account, password, cancelled" reflect significant concerns, as evidenced by negative sentiment scores of −0.499501 and −0.690347. These findings suggest a pressing need to enhance trust-building features, particularly in areas related to privacy, security, and user account management [2, 9].

Dialogue support features, including notifications, reminders, and motivational messages, generally received positive sentiment, with topics like "reminders, motivational, tracker" and "motivate, encouragement, accomplishment" scoring 0.820468 and 0.854573, respectively, demonstrating user appreciation for well-designed motivational elements [5]. However, certain dialogue elements, particularly those related to premium features and intrusive notifications, such as "freemium, subscription, notifications" (−0.473209), were met with negative sentiment, indicating the need for refinement to improve user perception [9].

Primary task support stands out as a key strength of LoseIt! with highly positive sentiment for features like calorie tracking, weight loss, and dieting. Topics such as "calorie, tracker, diets, calories" with sentiment 0.798904 and "weightloss, dieting, nutritious, diet" with sentiment of 0.883214 highlight strong user satisfaction and reinforce the application's effectiveness in meeting its core functional goals [1, 9].

Social support features, including syncing capabilities and fostering connections, were generally well-received, as indicated by topics like "syncs, tracker, Instagram" and "friends, friendships, sharing" with corresponding sentiment of 0.933223 and 0.538881. These findings underscore the utility of social connectivity features, though there is room for further enhancement. Additionally, uncategorized themes highlighted technical challenges, such as "laggy, crashes, apk" with sentiment −0.420832, and negative user experiences like "useless, dislike" with −0.219328 sentiment, which disrupt the user experience and need to be addressed to ensure smoother functionality [1].

5.3 Key Strengths and Weaknesses of Each Application

Both applications illustrated their outstanding capabilities in primary functionalities, particularly in areas like calorie tracking and diet management, earning significant praise for their effectiveness and user-friendliness. This proficiency in core tasks is well-supported by motivational features, such as reminders and encouragements, which are crucial for sustaining user engagement and motivation, key principles of persuasive technology, which aims to influence behavior through persuasion and social influence rather than through coercion [3].

Despite these strengths, the applications face distinct challenges that can impact their persuasive effectiveness. Addressing these issues aligns with the principles of credibility and trust, fundamental tenets of the persuasive model. For instance, one application is criticized for issues related to account management and data accuracy, with specific user feedback pointing to 'uninstalled, privacy, inaccurate' and 'email, account, password, cancelled.' This feedback underscores the need to bolster the security and reliability of user data management, enhancing the system's credibility and thereby increasing its potential [2, 9].

Applying the principle of tailoring from persuasive technology, where information is customized to meet the needs and interests of individual users, could significantly improve the acceptance and effectiveness of these features [2, 7, 9].

Technical issues like 'laggy, crashes, apk' further complicate the user experience, directly undermining the functionality and reliability of the apps. In the context of persuasive technology, a reliable and smoothly functioning app is more likely to influence behavior effectively. Addressing these technical problems is crucial for maintaining user engagement and trust, thereby supporting the persuasive intent of the technology [3, 5].

By enhancing system credibility, improving data privacy, refining dialogue interactions, and ensuring technical stability, these applications can better adhere to the principles of persuasive technology. Implementing these improvements will not only enhance user satisfaction and trust but also increase the effectiveness of the apps in changing user behaviors related to diet and health management.

5.4 Limitation

This study, while exploring the application of persuasive system design categories to analyze user reviews of diet-tracking apps, encounters several limitations that warrant discussion.

Firstly, the study is limited by the small sample size, as only two diet-tracking apps were analyzed. This restricts the generalizability of the findings, as different apps may implement persuasive elements in diverse ways. Expanding the dataset to include more apps would provide a broader and more representative perspective on the application of persuasive system design in mobile health contexts.

Another significant challenge in the study is the categorization of user feedback, particularly the process of applying the persuasive design framework. Although the categories, primary task support, dialogue support, credibility support, and social support are designed to segment user feedback into distinct groups, they do not function as entirely independent categories [3]. Usability issues often span multiple persuasive design elements, demonstrating the interconnected nature of user experiences and app functionalities [4]. For instance, features such as barcode scanning, while primarily aligning with primary task support, often overlap with credibility and social support as they influence perceptions of usability, trust, and user interaction [3, 4]. This overlap suggests that persuasive features contribute to a cohesive user experience rather than operating as isolated elements [4].

Additionally, analysis of user feedback in apps faces significant challenges due to the absence of explicitly labelled persuasive design elements, necessitating inferential categorization that may not accurately reflect the developers' intended interaction paradigms, potentially leading to topic misclassification. Additionally, the reliance on a keyword-based classification approach introduces bias, as it fails to capture the varied expressions of user feedback, missing some persuasive elements and overrepresenting others due to ambiguous terminology. To overcome these limitations, more structured topic modelling techniques such as LDA or Topical N-gram could provide a more nuanced and data-driven categorization, uncovering emergent themes beyond predefined keyword categories and offering a more accurate reflection of user perceptions and interactions [1, 2, 13].

6 Conclusion

This paper provided a framework for analyzing user reviews, focusing on the categorization of topics and sentiments within the context of persuasive systems design. By categorizing persuasive features specifically, it enhances the understanding of how different elements influence user satisfaction, requirements, and engagement [10]. This approach provides not only in-depth insights into user behavior but also guides other researchers on the nuances of identifying and implementing effective persuasive strategies in app development. These insights are critical for refining app functionalities to improve user interaction and retention [2]. This holistic approach to improving both the persuasive elements and technical aspects of the applications can significantly contribute to the broader field of persuasive technologies by providing robust examples of how technology can effectively support health and wellness goals [14].

References

1. Zečević, M., Mijatović, D., Kos Koklič, M., Žabkar, V., Gidaković, P.: User perspectives of diet-tracking apps: reviews content analysis and topic modeling. J. Med. Internet Res. **23**(4), e25160 (2021)

2. Carreño, L.V.G., Winbladh, K.: Analysis of user comments: an approach for software requirements evolution. In: 2013 35th International Conference on Software Engineering (ICSE), pp. 582–591. IEEE, San Francisco, CA, USA (2013)
3. Oinas-Kukkonen, H., Harjumaa, M.: Persuasive systems design: key issues, process model, and system features. Commun. Assoc. Inform. Syst **24**, 28 (2009)
4. Win, K.T., Roberts, M.R.H., Oinas-Kukkonen, H.: Persuasive system features in comput-er-mediated lifestyle modification interventions for physical activity. Inform. Health Soc. Care **44**(4), 376–404 (2019)
5. Oliveira, A.D.A., Dos Santos, P.S.H., Marcílio Júnior, W.E., Aljedaani, W.M., Eler, D.M., Eler, M.M.: Analyzing accessibility reviews associated with visual disabilities or eye conditions. In: Proceedings of the 2023 CHI Conference on Human Factors in Computing Systems (CHI'23), p. 37, Association for Computing Machinery, New York, NY, USA (2023)
6. Serrano-Guerrero, J., Olivas, J.A., Romero, F.P., Herrera-Viedma, E.: Sentiment analysis: a review and comparative analysis of web services. Inform. Sci. **311**, 18–38 (2015)
7. Syakur, M.A., Khotimah, B.K., Rochman, E.M.S., Satoto, B.K.: Integration k-means clustering method and elbow method for identification of the best customer profile cluster. In: IOP Conference Series: Materials Science and Engineering, vol. 336, no. 1, IOP Publishing (2018)
8. Kotsiantis, S., Kanellopoulos, D., Pintelas, P.: Data preprocessing for supervised learning. Int. J. Comput. Sci. **1**, 111–117 (2006)
9. Chang, T.R., Kaasinen, E., Kaipainen, K.: Persuasive design in mobile applications for mental well-being: multidisciplinary expert review. In: Godara, B., Nikita, K.S. (eds.) MobiHealth 2012. LNICSSITE, vol. 61, pp. 154–162. Springer, Heidelberg (2013). https://doi.org/10.1007/978-3-642-37893-5_18
10. Meedya, S., Sheikh, M.K., Win, K.T., Halcomb, E.: Evaluation of breastfeeding mobile health applications based on the persuasive system design model. In: Oinas-Kukkonen, H., Win, K.T., Karapanos, E., Karppinen, P., Kyza, E. (eds.) PERSUASIVE 2019. LNCS, vol. 11433, pp. 189–201. Springer, Cham (2019). https://doi.org/10.1007/978-3-030-17287-9_16
11. Liu, Y., et al.: 'RoBERTa: A robustly optimized BERT pretraining approach'. arXiv preprint arXiv:1907.11692 (2019)
12. Medhat, W., Hassan, A., Korashy, H.: Sentiment analysis algorithms and applications: a survey. Ain Shams Eng. J. **5**(4), 1093–1113 (2014)
13. Simmerer, M.: Mobile Health Applications – A Natural Language Processing Review Analysis. Dissertation, MSc in Strategy & Entrepreneurship, Universidade Católica Portuguesa, 7th April 2021
14. Wang, C., Qi, H.: Influencing factors of acceptance and use behavior of mobile health application users: systematic review. Healthcare **9**, 357 (2021)

Personalized Social Proof for Persuasive Human-Robot Interaction

Rosalyn Langedijk[1], Lars C. Jensen[2], and Kerstin Fischer[1]([✉])

[1] University of Southern Denmark, Sønderborg, Denmark
kerstin@sdu.dk
[2] EWII, Kolding, Denmark

Abstract. Dehydration is an important challenge, especially in elderly care. This study investigates the effects of a verbal statement of personalized social proof, i.e., an utterance that evokes participants' gender identity, on the persuasiveness of a robot when encouraging people to drink more. In the scenario used, the robot suggests participants to drink more water once over the course of a 10–15 min interaction. At the end of the experiment, while filling out a questionnaire, participants who heard the utterance containing personalized social proof drink significantly more water than those who did not hear a persuasive utterance. Also the evaluation of the robot is influenced by the persuasive message. Thus, appealing to participants' social identity when evoking social proof is effective in verbal human-robot interaction.

Keywords: Persuasion · Human-Robot Interaction · Personalization

1 Introduction

This study aims to shed light on the extent to which persuasive messages are effective when used by a robot, and whether the personalization of these messages can contribute to their effectiveness. The persuasive message in focus is the strategy of social proof [7]; it addresses the fact that in situations of uncertainty, people may look at other people's decisions to inform their own. Utterances that appeal to other people's choices have been found to be highly effective (e.g. [18]). A prior field study with written messages of social proof also suggests that personalization may lead to behavioral changes [14]; whether this also applies to human-robot interactions is however unknown, as is what effects such messages have on the way the speaker, here a service robot, is perceived.

The behavior change investigated in this study concerns water consumption; especially older people tend to drink too little water, which can lead to dehydration and serious consequences for their health and wellbeing. In elder care facilities, to address dehydration, considerable effort from the staff is needed. Thus, delegating the task to remind residents to drink more water to a robot was identified as a promising use case for robots in elder care [13].

© The Author(s), under exclusive license to Springer Nature Switzerland AG 2025
K. T. Win et al. (Eds.): PERSUASIVE 2025, LNCS 15711, pp. 32–45, 2025.
https://doi.org/10.1007/978-3-031-94959-3_3

2   Previous Work

Previous work concerns studies that address persuasion in human-robot interactions and the role of personalization by evoking social identity in persuasive communication.

2.1   Persuasion in Human-Robot Interaction

In general, there is little work in human-robot interaction that investigates how robots can influence people's behavior. Some studies have shown that embodied agents like robots can be convincing and persuasive, for instance, by making people choose an energy-saving program on a washing machine [29] or reducing people's snacking behavior [23].

Some studies suggest that the extent to which a robot functions as a situated, multimodal interaction partner influences its persuasiveness; for example, indicating that the robot perceives the environment by means of verbal statements (e.g. about the weather) and gestures towards a jug of water, as well as concurrent comments about the participant's performance during a physical exercise (e.g. "lift you left arm higher, yes, good") influence to what extent people follow the robot's advice to drink more water [10]. Similarly, robots that use bodily cues such as proximity, gaze and gestures are complied with more [6], and especially mutual gaze seems to increase the robot's persuasiveness [11, 16].

Furthermore, speaking style has been shown to have significant effects in some studies of human-robot interaction; for instance, speech melody [12], rhetorical strategies [1] and cues to expertise [2] significantly affect the extent to which people follow a robot's advice. Relatedly, also the personalization of the perceived age of speaker to participants' age group has proven effective, showing preferences for, and higher credibility ratings of, artificial voices that exhibit characteristics corresponding to the respective participants' age [8].

But also the use of the strategies of influence outlined by Cialdini [7] by robots can be very effective; for instance, Winkle et al. [30] investigated the effect of displays of expertise and goodwill and of emphasizing similarity with the user, where displays of goodwill and emphasizing similarity with the user were based on Cialdini's principle of *liking*. In the study, the users were asked by a robot to carry out therapeutic exercises. The authors found significant effects of the display of goodwill and of emphasizing similarity on participants' compliance. Also Bernier and Scassellati [4] find that similarity has a great effect on how people rate the robot. Specifically, robots that appear to have the same preference in working style as their operators were rated more trustworthy, which is relevant since trust has a positive impact on people's willingness to collaborate with a robot.

Lee and Liang [20] employed the principle of *commitment and consistency* described by Cialdini [7]; they find that the robot was more persuasive if it used the 'foot-in-the-door' principle; i.e. the robot makes initially a small request (complete 30 tasks for 15min) and later a larger request (complete 50 tasks for 25min), which is granted more readily when presented in two steps.

Similarly, the principle of *reciprocity* [7] was found to be equally effective with robots as with human interaction partners [25]. Moreover, robots have been shown to evoke *social proof*, such that people were found to change their answers to the unanimous opinion of a group of robots, even if that answer was wrong [24]. However, the effects of appealing to and personalizing the human interactants' social identity by a robot has not yet been investigated in human-robot interaction research.

To sum up, robots have been found to be able to persuade users, both by employing strategies of influence and by gaining credibility through multimodal demonstrations of situatedness and displays of expertise.

2.2   Personalization of Persuasive Strategies

Several studies have shown that personalization can increase the effectiveness of persuasive communication; for instance, Kaptein [18] applied personal profiling to persuasion on the internet and showed that personalization is a strong influencing factor, especially in e-commerce.

Personalization has also been found to be relevant in human-robot interaction. In his overview of the role of personalization in human-robot interaction, Ham [15] suggests that personalizing human-robot interactions increases the respective robot's persuasiveness. He argues that research on personalization needs to consider to which user characteristics persuasive robots should be personalized; what role the particular situation of a user plays; and which robot characteristics are to be personalized. Robot characteristics that may be adapted include the robot's appearance, communication behavior, robot personality and displays of its affect, while user characteristics to be adapted to include people's appearance (gender or culture (e.g. common language or speaking style [2])), their behavior [1,2,6,12], as well as their cognitive and affective capabilities and preferences. In addition, Ham [15] suggests the social and physical situation to influence how the robot can be personalized to influence the human user.

One type of personalization to the respective addressee concerns appeals to their social identity when using the strategy of influence of social proof [14], where social proof is taken to account for the fact that in situations of uncertainty, people tend to look at what other people do in order to plan their own behavior [7]. Cialdini [7] argues that the degree to which social proof is relevant is influenced by the similarity between the model and the person to be influenced, but also that the relevance of a particular social identity also depends on the situational context. Correspondingly, Goldstein et al. [14] show that "the more important a social category is to an individual's social identity, the more likely he or she will be to follow the norms of that category". The authors put five different towel hangers into hotel rooms that encouraged hotel guests to re-use their towels. The first hanger featured the standard environmental message; the second hanger referred to the guests of the hotel, stating that most of the hotel guests would re-use their towels, thus appealing to social proof and participants' identity as hotel guests. The other hangers made use of the same principle of social proof but narrowed down the model group in different ways: One hanger appealed to guests' gender identity, one to their identity as citizens, and the last one to the guests' social identity as users of that particular hotel room. While all messages that made use of social proof were more effective than the standard environmental message, the message that was tailored most specifically to the situation the respective guest was in turned out to be the most effective message in terms of towel re-use. Thus, the authors argue that social proof can be very effective, especially if personalized based on people's social or situational identity (cf. also [15]).

It is likely that personalizing the strategy of social proof will also be effective in human-robot interaction since people have been shown to respond more favorably to artificial agents that show some similarity with the respective user [3,28]; furthermore, personalization always suggests that the speaker is adjusting his or her behavior to the specific addressee (cf. [9]), leading to additional pragmatic effects; for instance, participants may feel more seen because the robot seems to take them more into account, or they may ascribe higher credibility to it because it displays higher capabilities (cf. [10]).

2.3   Hypotheses

In this study, we therefore explore the effects of social proof in human-robot interaction, hypothesizing that personalization of social proof will render persuasive communication by robots even more effective. In particular, we study whether references to experiment participants in general serve to encourage participants to drink more water and whether a more personalized reference to experiment participants' gender makes the robot even more persuasive. Furthermore, we expect that also the perception of the robot in terms of competence, warmth and discomfort (cf. [5]) will be influenced by the use of (personalized) social proof. The hypotheses that guide this research are thus the following:

H1a: Robot dialog that uses social proof by alluding to the recipient's identity as a participant in the current experiment will lead to higher water consumption than the same robot dialog without a persuasive utterance.

H1b: Robot dialog that uses social proof by alluding to the recipient's gender identity and identity as a participant in the current experiment will lead to higher water consumption than the same robot dialog without a persuasive utterance.

H2a: Robot dialog that uses personalized social proof will lead to higher attributions of competence than the same robot dialog without a persuasive utterance.

H2b: Robot dialog that uses personalized social proof will lead to higher attributions of warmth than the same robot dialog without a persuasive utterance.

H2c: Robot dialog that uses personalized social proof will lead to lower perceptions of discomfort than the same robot dialog without a persuasive utterance.

3   Method

In the study carried out, a robot guides the participants through a room, indicates to them what objects to collect, and offers to carry the objects for them. The objects people are instructed to collect are objects needed to set a table. The robot communicates with the participants in polite, task-oriented verbal utterances, and when it instructs them to pick up a glass, in the experimental conditions, the manipulation takes place.

3.1   Experimental Conditions

The experiment is carried out in a between-subject experimental design with three conditions. In the first condition, the participants are referred to as 'participants', where the robot says "It is important to drink enough water during the day. Most participants drink half a liter after this game". This condition is referred to as the PEOPLE condition. The second condition specifies the gender of the participants. Depending on participants' respective gender, the robot says either, "It is important to drink enough water during the day. Most male participants drink half a liter after this game" or "It is important to drink enough water during the day. Most female participants drink half a liter after this game". For instance, if a male participant interacts with the robot, the robot says "Most male participants...". This condition is referred to as the GENDER condition. These two conditions are based on the strategy of social proof by Cialdini [7] and are inspired by the study by Goldstein et al. [14] on hotel hangers. In the third condition, the robot simply asks participants to pick up a glass. This condition constitutes the baseline, control condition.

The personalization of the persuasive message was carried out based on participants' self-identification in the pre-experimental questionnaire (male, female or other).

3.2   Participants

52 students and staff from a university (anonymized for peer review) agreed to participate in the study. The participants include students (76%), members of the faculty, students' parents, as well as in-house personnel. Students range from second semester bachelor level to Ph.D. students and were studying Mechatronics (37.4%), European Studies (11.7%), and Business Administration (11.7%), as well as Economics, Communication Studies, Power Electronics or Phonetics.

One data set was removed because the participant tried to sit on the robot so that the experimenter had to interrupt the session. Mean age of the remaining participants is 28.2 (SD = 11). Men are overrepresented in the study, so that only 31% self-identified as women, while the rest self-identified as men. However, these are balanced between the experimental conditions. Participants with previous experience with robots are likewise equally distributed between the experimental conditions, yet none of the participants had previously interacted with this robot before; more than half of the participants (55%) had seen robots only on television or had encountered a robot only once before in real-life, and only two participants work with robots regularly. Participants were recruited randomly in the university building and were rewarded with a bar of chocolate.

3.3 Subjective Measures

Participants were presented with a questionnaire before and after the experiment. In the pre-experimental questionnaire, demographic information and previous experiences with robots were elicited, while participants' subjective evaluations of the robot were elicited in the post-experimental questionnaire. The post-experimental questionnaire consisted of the Robotic Social Attributes Scale [5]. The scale consists of the three indices WARMTH, COMPETENCE, and DISCOMFORT. Each index comprises a collection of adjectives on the basis of which the participants are asked to rate the robot. All items are rated on a 5-point Likert scale where 1 corresponds to 'not at all' and 5 to 'very much'. The COMPETENCE scale comprises the adjectives *capable, responsive, interactive, reliable, competent,* and *knowledgeable.* The WARMTH scale comprises the adjectives *happy, feeling, sociable, compassionate, organic,* and *emotional.* The DISCOMFORT scale comprises the adjectives *scary, strange, awful, awkward, dangerous,* and *aggressive.* Some additional questions addressed participants' perceived engagement and the robot's persuasiveness, namely *likeable, engaging, credible, persuasive, enthusiastic, boring,* and *convincing.*

Fig. 1. Robot with Items to Set the Table

3.4 Objective Measures

As an objective measure of the robot's persuasiveness, participants' water consumption was measured in milliliters; in particular, we measured how much water was missing from the 1 liter jug and from participants' glasses after they were done filling out the post-experimental questionnaire.

3.5   Robot and Software

The robot used for this experiment is a Turtlebot 2 on a Yujin Kobuki mobile base. The robot is equipped with an Orbbec Astra 3D camera and is controlled by an Intel NUC running Canonical Ubuntu 16.04 LTS and ROS Kinetic. The robot was semi-autonomous, which means that the robot moved autonomously from point to point. However, target locations were set by a remote wizard using RViz. The autonomous navigation is enabled by SLAM map building [21]. Cameras were placed around the room on walls and on ceilings and were live-streamed to a PC in an adjacent room. The robot was a low-fidelity prototype (see Fig. 1).

The robot's speech was presynthesized using IVONA TTS (voice *George*). The robot's verbal actions were controlled via a series of shell scripts, thereby limiting the options available to the wizard at any given time during the experiment. This was done to decrease the cognitive load of the wizard and to increase the comparability of the interactions such that, with very little variations in timing, the participants were exposed to the same robot behaviors.

3.6   Interaction Protocol

Participants were greeted, led into an adjacent room and asked to fill out a consent form and the pre-experimental questionnaire. They were informed that their participation was voluntary, that they could withdraw from the experiment at any time, that the interaction was videotaped and were then asked for their explicit agreement to different uses of the video footage.

After that, they were taken to the lab and introduced to the robot, where the experimenter turned on the cameras and left the room. The participant remained alone in the lab with the robot. Then, the robot introduced itself and led the participant through the experiment based on the predefined script.[1]

Figure 2 describes the setup of the experiment in the lab. Robot and participant start in position (1), where the participant is greeted by the robot. Next, the robot moves to position (2), where the robot instructs the participant to pick up a plate and a napkin. Then, the robot moves to position (3), where it instructs the participant to pick up a glass. Here, the robot either moves to the next (BASELINE condition) or says "It's important to drink enough water during the day. Most participants drink half a liter after this game" (PEOPLE condition) or "It's important to drink enough water during the day. Most male/female participants drink half a liter after this game" (GENDER condition). This utterance is played based on the respective participant's gender, which the wizard specifies at the beginning of the experiment based on the participant's answer in the

---

[1] To see some example interactions, please see the video here: https://www.youtube.com/watch?v=hjKhQAkkvtk&t.

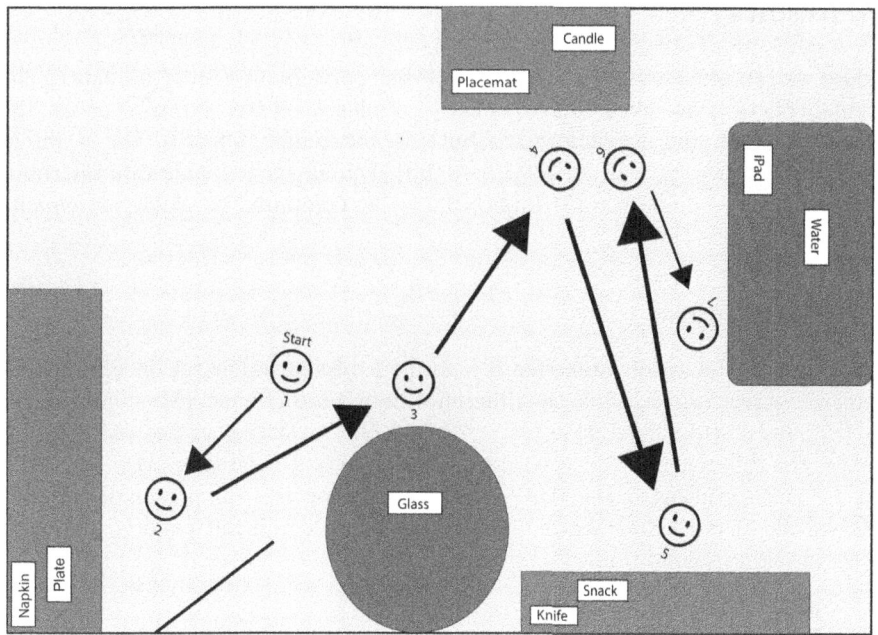

Fig. 2. Experiment Map

pre-questionnaire. At position (4), the participant is asked to pick up a placemat. Here the robot explicitly displays its situation awareness by commenting on the placemat the participant picks up (from a set of two) by claiming that the one chosen is its favorite, too. If no items have been placed on the robot by then, the robot offers to carry them for the participant. Next, the robot moves to position (5) and instructs the participants to pick up a snack. Here, participants can choose between a cookie and a fruit. At position (6), participants are asked to find a candle in a drawer. Finally, the robot moves to position (7) and instructs participants to set the table, to have a seat, to enjoy their snack and to fill out the post-experimental questionnaire, which is prepared for them on a tablet (see Fig. 1), next to a jug of water. All participants complied with the robot's instructions and had collected all items to set their table by the end of the experiment.

3.7 Analysis

To assess the effectiveness of the intervention, we measured how much water participants drank from the jug of water while filling out the final questionnaire (in milliliters).

A univariate analysis of variance was carried out to assess effects of the three conditions (BASELINE, PEOPLE, and GENDER), as well as post hoc analyses to analyze the differences between the three groups further.

4   Results

Before we ran our analysis, we tested whether participant gender influences the results. There is no effect of participant gender on water intake, nor on the ROSAS warmth and discomfort attributions, but a main effect on the rating of robot competence, $F(1, 49) = 4.931$, p = .031. Female participants rate the robot overall as more competent (M = 4.0, SD = .8) compared to male participants (M = 3.5, SD = .7).

4.1   Water Intake

We measured the water intake for N = 50 (+2 missing values). Concerning participants' water intake, while the difference between BASELINE (M = 55.3 ml, SD = 70.7) and PEOPLE-condition (M = 72.7 ml, SD = 95.1) does not reach significance, the difference between BASELINE and GENDER-condition (M = 111.7 ml, SD = 81) is significant (p = .048) Thus, if the robot uses the personalized GENDER-specific persuasive message, participants drink significantly more, compared to the BASELINE condition.

4.2   Questionnaire

The analysis of the RoSAS questionnaire reveals significant differences between the persuasion conditions and the BASELINE (see Table 1).

The analysis of the competence ratings shows a significant main effect between conditions, $F(2, 48) = 6.228$, p = .004; the post hoc test shows significant differences between the PEOPLE-condition and the BASELINE (p = .002) as well as between the GENDER-condition and the BASELINE (p = .007).

The analysis of the warmth ratings reveals only a statistical tendency: $F(2, 48) = 2.782$, p = .072. Post hoc testing reveals a significant difference between the PEOPLE-condition and the BASELINE (p = .025), but not for GENDER-condition (p = .135).

Furthermore, the analysis of the discomfort ratings shows a statistical tendency, $F(2, 48) = 1.029$, p = .065. Post hoc tests show a significant difference between the GENDER-condition and the BASELINE (p = .021) but not for the PEOPLE-condition (p = .149). Thus, people feel significantly more comfortable around the robot in the GENDER-condition in comparison to the BASELINE.

Table 1. Overview of mean ratings (standard deviation) of the three RoSAS indices

	competence	warmth	discomfort
BASELINE	3.2 (0.7)	2.4 (0.8)	2.1 (0.6)
PEOPLE	4 (0.7)	3.1 (0.6)	1.8 (0.5)
GENDER	3.9 (0.7)	2.8 (1.1)	1.6 (0.6)

Concerning the additional questionnaire items (see Table 2), our analysis shows a significant main effect between conditions for participants' rating of engagement, $F(2, 48) = 4.944$, $p = .011$. Thus, participants find the robot to be significantly more engaging in the PEOPLE-condition ($p = .005$) and in the GENDER-condition ($p = .021$), compared to the BASELINE condition. Furthermore, we see a tendency that people find the robot less boring in the GENDER-condition ($p = .089$) and more convincing in the PEOPLE-condition ($p = .052$).

Table 2. Overview of mean ratings (standard deviation) of additional items

	engaging	boring	convincing
BASELINE	3.3 (0.7)	2.3 (1.0)	3.3 (0.8)
PEOPLE	4.1 (0.9)	2.0 (1.0)	3.9 (1.0)
GENDER	3.9 (0.8)	1.7 (1.0)	3.7 (1.0)

5 Discussion

The results show that participants drink significantly more water when the robot employs a message using social proof that appeals to the communication partner's social identity. In other words, the persuasive utterance that is tailored to the identity of the respective participant, here concerning his or her gender, proves to be persuasive. Thus, Hypothesis 1b, which suggests that persuasive messages based on personalized social proof lead to more water consumption is supported, while social proof that referred to participants' identity as experiment participants alone (H1a) was not supported.

Furthermore, the persuasion conditions have a sufficient impact on people's evaluation of the robot. Our results show that the robot that uses both personalized and nonpersonalized social proof is rated as more competent. Thus, hypothesis 2a is accepted; participants find the robot that makes use of social proof to be more competent in comparison to the BASELINE.

Interestingly, we see differences in the ratings of warmth and discomfort between the two persuasion conditions; people rate the robot to be warmer when it employs a message using general social proof and less strange and awkward when it employs a message using personalized social proof. This means that hypotheses 2b and 2c are partly accepted since only one of the intervention conditions shows an effect in participants' ratings of the robot. In other words, participants find the robot warmer when it makes use of the general social proof, and they perceive less discomfort when it uses personalized social proof.

Both the behavioral results and the results on the perception of the robot are quite remarkable given that the difference between the conditions is one single utterance in an interaction that took about 10 to 15 min on the whole. Consequently, our results show that a single utterance about (personalized) social proof has a consistent significant impact on people's experience with the robot, even in the context of a 10–15 minute long interaction. This suggests that dialog design should be carried out with extreme care, and that the effects of persuasive messages last across a time span of at least several minutes.

Our results replicate Goldstein et al.'s [14] findings in a very different scenario, and for human-robot interaction; if the robot identifies the interaction partner more precisely, the persuasive message is more effective. What is not known is whether the effect may wear off if repeated; however, the same applies to social proof in other situations, like the one addressed by Goldstein et al. [14]. Regarding human-robot interactions, our results are also in line with the study by Salomons et al. [24], which shows that social proof works when coming from a group of robots, so that people change their answers and thus conform to robots even if the robots are wrong. Our results add nicely to this by showing that also messages of social proof are effective in human-robot interaction. Similarly, our work adds to other work on the persuasiveness of robots, for instance, Ramachandran et al. [22], Winkle et al. [30], and Vossen et al. [29], which show that robots can be persuasive in general.

A possible limitation of the experiment is that the proportion of female participants was rather low. We also saw an effect of participant gender on competence ratings of the robot, such that female participants rated the robots on average as more competent, which is consistent with previous findings on the differences between men and women and how they perceive robots, e.g. [26,27]. Nevertheless, our statistical analysis suggests that participant gender had no effect on participants' compliance with the robot's suggestion to drink more water, and hence it should not influence the effectiveness of social proof as a persuasive strategy or the personalization of social proof.

Given that only two participants were very familiar with robots, our participant pool does not allow us to study the effect of prior experience with robots on the effect of persuasive messages; however, manual inspection of the data shows that the two robot experts drank on average 120ml, and thus rather more than less than the other participants. This suggests that experience with robots does not necessarily prevent persuasive messages provided by robots to be effective. Nevertheless, future research is necessary to confirm this initial observation.

Another possible limitation could be that all participants were recruited in an academic environment. Other populations may respond differently.

Furthermore, in addition to its utterance that evoked social proof, the robot also pointed to the importance of drinking enough water in the two experimental conditions. This may have introduced a possible confounding factor in the comparison between the baseline and experimental conditions, such that the difference may not only be due to the message of (personalized) social proof. However, both experimental conditions used this utterance, whereas only the condition that made use of personalized social proof led to significantly higher water intake, so that the possible confound does not seem to play a role for the difference between BASELINE and GENDER condition.

The interactions may also have been influenced by the embodiment and the low-fidelity design of the robot. We did not compare different embodiments to see if they have an effect on the robot's persuasiveness. Hegel [17], for instance, has demonstrated that the 'degree of designedness' of a robot influences its evaluations, which may also affect the respective robot's persuasiveness. Our participants understood the robot's affordances from its design with the exception of one participant who tried to sit on it. Still, it is likely that a more well-designed robot may be even more credible and hence persuasive than our prototype. Nevertheless, since the robot's appearance is the same across conditions, it would have influenced people equally in all conditions so that appearance cannot account for the differences between the conditions.

Another possible limitation may be that personalization in human-robot interaction may lead to negative unwanted effects such as feelings of eeriness; for instance, during an experiment in the field in which we tested the same utterances [19], a participant commented that it was creepy that the robot knew that she was female. This may be different if the robot is employed in an elderly care facility where participants are familiar with the robot. Nevertheless, participants' discomfort ratings were lower for the personalized robot than for the robot in the BASELINE condition, and hence whether there are general limits to personalized persuasive utterances by robots is not yet known.

6   Conclusion

The results of the study demonstrate that the personalization of social proof can make the suggestion to drink more water more effective in a human-robot interaction context, leading to greater compliance with the robot's suggestion. Specifically, the persuasiveness of the robot's advice is apparent from a generally higher water intake, which reaches significance when the robot addresses the participant more precisely by mentioning the respective person's gender in the dialog.

The personalization of social proof in human-robot interaction was also shown to affect how the robot is perceived: participants rate the persuasive robot as more competent and more warm. Furthermore, people experience the interactions as more comfortable when the robot uses social proof.

Future work will have to determine potential limits of personalization of social proof and effects of long-term exposure to persuasive utterances in human-robot interactions.

References

1. Andrist, S., Spannan, E., Mutlu, B.: Rhetorical robots: making robots more effective speakers using linguistic cues of expertise. In: 2013 8th ACM/IEEE International Conference on Human-Robot Interaction (HRI), pp. 341–348. IEEE (2013). https://doi.org/10.1109/HRI.2013.6483608
2. Andrist, S., Ziadee, M., Boukaram, H., Mutlu, B., Sakr, M.: Effects of culture on the credibility of robot speech: a comparison between English and Arabic. In: Proceedings of the Tenth Annual ACM/IEEE International Conference on Human-Robot Interaction, pp. 157–164 (2015). https://doi.org/10.1145/2696454.2696464

3. Bailenson, J.N., Iyengar, S., Yee, N., Collins, N.A.: Facial similarity between voters and candidates causes influence. Public Opin. Q. **72**(5), 935–961 (2008). https://doi.org/10.1093/poq/nfn064
4. Bernier, E.P., Scassellati, B.: The similarity-attraction effect in human-robot interaction. In: 2010 IEEE 9th International Conference on Development and Learning, pp. 286–290. IEEE (2010). https://doi.org/10.1109/DEVLRN.2010.5578828
5. Carpinella, C.M., Wyman, A.B., Perez, M.A., Stroessner, S.J.: The robotic social attributes scale (RoSAS) development and validation. In: Proceedings of the 2017 ACM/IEEE International Conference on Human-Robot Interaction, pp. 254–262 (2017). https://doi.org/10.1145/2909824.3020208
6. Chidambaram, V., Chiang, Y.H., Mutlu, B.: Designing persuasive robots: how robots might persuade people using vocal and nonverbal cues. In: Proceedings of the Seventh Annual ACM/IEEE International Conference on Human-Robot Interaction, pp. 293–300 (2012). https://doi.org/10.1145/2157689.2157798
7. Cialdini, R.B., Cialdini, R.B.: Influence: The Psychology of Persuasion, vol. 55. Collins, New York (2007)
8. Edwards, C., Edwards, A., Stoll, B., Lin, X., Massey, N.: Evaluations of an artificial intelligence instructor's voice: social identity theory in human-robot interactions. Comput. Hum. Behav. **90**, 357–362 (2019)
9. Fischer, K.: Designing Speech for a Recipient: The Roles of Partner Modeling, Alignment and Feedback in So-Called 'Simplified Registers', vol. 270. John Benjamins Publishing Company (2016)
10. Fischer, K., Jensen, L.C., Zitzmann, N.: In the same boat: the influence of sharing the situational context on a speaker's (a robot's) persuasiveness. Interact. Stud. **22**(3), 489–516 (2022)
11. Fischer, K., Langedijk, R.M., Nissen, L.D., Ramirez, E.R., Palinko, O.: Gaze-speech coordination influences the persuasiveness of human-robot dialog in the wild. In: International Conference on Social Robotics, pp. 157–169. Springer, Cham (2020)
12. Fischer, K., Niebuhr, O., Jensen, L.C., Bodenhagen, L.: Speech melody matters-how robots profit from using charismatic speech. ACM Trans. Hum.-Robot Interact. (THRI) **9**(1), 1–21 (2019)
13. Fischer, K., et al.: Integrative social robotics hands-on. Interact. Stud. **21**(1), 145–185 (2020)
14. Goldstein, N.J., Cialdini, R.B., Griskevicius, V.: A room with a viewpoint: using social norms to motivate environmental conservation in hotels. J. Consum. Res. **35**(3), 472–482 (2008). https://doi.org/10.1086/586910
15. Ham, J.: Influencing robot influence: personalization of persuasive robots. Interact. Stud. **22**(3), 464–487 (2021)
16. Ham, J., Cuijpers, R.H., Cabibihan, J.-J.: Combining robotic persuasive strategies: the persuasive power of a storytelling robot that uses gazing and gestures. Int. J. Soc. Robot. **7**(4), 479–487 (2015). https://doi.org/10.1007/s12369-015-0280-4
17. Hegel, F.: Effects of a robot's aesthetic design on the attribution of social capabilities. In: 2012 IEEE RO-MAN: The 21st IEEE International Symposium on Robot and Human Interactive Communication, pp. 469–475. IEEE (2012). https://doi.org/10.1109/ROMAN.2012.6343796
18. Kaptein, M.: Persuasion profiling: how the internet knows what makes you tick. Business Contact (2015)
19. Langedijk, R.M., Fischer, K.: Persuasive robots in the field. In: International Conference on Persuasive Technology, pp. 251–264. Springer, Cham (2023)

20. Lee, S.A., Liang, Y.J.: Robotic foot-in-the-door: using sequential-request persuasive strategies in human-robot interaction. Comput. Hum. Behav. **90**, 351–356 (2019). https://doi.org/10.1016/j.chb.2018.08.026
21. Pajaziti, A., Avdullahu, P.: Slam-map building and navigation via ROS. Int. J. Intell. Syst. Appl. Eng. **2**(4), 71–75 (2014). https://doi.org/10.18201/ijisae.08103
22. Ramachandran, A., Litoiu, A., Scassellati, B.: Shaping productive help-seeking behavior during robot-child tutoring interactions. In: 2016 11th ACM/IEEE International Conference on Human-Robot Interaction (HRI), pp. 247–254. IEEE (2016). https://doi.org/10.1109/HRI.2016.7451759
23. Robinson, N.L., Connolly, J., Hides, L., Kavanagh, D.J.: Social robots as treatment agents: pilot randomized controlled trial to deliver a behavior change intervention. Internet Interv. **21**, 100320 (2020). https://doi.org/10.1016/j.invent.2020.100320
24. Salomons, N., van der Linden, M., Strohkorb Sebo, S., Scassellati, B.: Humans conform to robots: disambiguating trust, truth, and conformity. In: Proceedings of the 2018 ACM/IEEE International Conference on Human-Robot Interaction, pp. 187–195 (2018). https://doi.org/10.1145/3171221.3171282
25. Sandoval, E.B., Brandstetter, J., Obaid, M., Bartneck, C.: Reciprocity in human-robot interaction: a quantitative approach through the prisoner's dilemma and the ultimatum game. Int. J. Soc. Robot. **8**(2), 303–317 (2015). https://doi.org/10.1007/s12369-015-0323-x
26. Siegel, M., Breazeal, C., Norton, M.I.: Persuasive robotics: the influence of robot gender on human behavior. In: 2009 IEEE/RSJ International Conference on Intelligent Robots and Systems, pp. 2563–2568. IEEE (2009). https://doi.org/10.1109/IROS.2009.5354116
27. Thellman, S., et al.: He is not more persuasive than her: no gender biases toward robots giving speeches. In: Proceedings of the 18th International Conference on Intelligent Virtual Agents, pp. 327–328 (2018). https://doi.org/10.1145/3267851.3267862
28. Verberne, F.M., Ham, J., Midden, C.J.: Trusting a virtual driver that looks, acts, and thinks like you. Hum. Factors **57**(5), 895–909 (2015)
29. Vossen, S., Ham, J., Midden, C.: Social influence of a persuasive agent: the role of agent embodiment and evaluative feedback. In: Proceedings of the 4th International Conference on Persuasive Technology, pp. 1–7 (2009). https://doi.org/10.1145/1541948.1542007
30. Winkle, K., Lemaignan, S., Caleb-Solly, P., Leonards, U., Turton, A., Bremner, P.: Effective persuasion strategies for socially assistive robots. In: 2019 14th ACM/IEEE International Conference on Human-Robot Interaction (HRI), pp. 277–285. IEEE (2019). https://doi.org/10.1109/HRI.2019.8673313

Personalized Digital Interventions for Behavior Change: Insights from the MoM App Study

Fawad Taj[1]([⊠]) [iD], Michel Klein[1] [iD], and Aart van Halteren[1,2] [iD]

[1] Vrije Universiteit Amsterdam, Amsterdam, The Netherlands
fawadtaj1@gmail.com
[2] Philips Research, Eindhoven, The Netherlands

Abstract. This study evaluates the effectiveness of the digital intervention delivered using the MoM mobile app. The app uses different behavior as change techniques to bring about change via an explicit model of motivation as a mechanism of action for physical activity behavior. For a two-arm, single-blind experimental trial, 41 participants were randomly assigned to intervention (n = 20) and control (n = 21) groups. The Intervention group participants used a model-based personalized and adaptive app (MoM) for 40 days. Control participants used the same app without the motivation model, which was neither fully personalized nor adaptive. 9 days of baseline data and 40 days of treatment period data were collected for both intervention and control groups. Based on the linear mixed effect model, participants in the intervention group demonstrated more significant increases in steps per day (95% CI = 873.97–3497.19 p = 0.001) compared to their baseline. Still, changes in daily steps between-groups are not so significantly different. At the same time, enjoyment is the most related motive (95%, CI = 71.87–1339.14 p = 0.029) for calculating reward prediction error and increasing daily physical activity. Using an explicit model for the targeted determinant increases the effectiveness and gives more control to design personalized and adaptive interventions.

Keywords: mhealth · cognitive modeling · persuasive technologies · digital health behavior · behavior change systems · motivation model · dopamine reward system

1 Introduction

Digital interventions (devices and programs that employ digital technology to stimulate or support behavior change) are becoming more common, with patient diagnosis and treatment, chronic illness self-management, and primary prevention. They've been hailed as having the ability to revolutionize how people monitor and improve their health behaviors and care by increasing results, lowering costs, and enhancing the patient experience. However, with the advancement of digital technologies, understanding and changing behavior poses new challenges, requiring new or updated research methodologies for developing and evaluating intervention techniques using these technologies [1].

Digital health interventions usually apply Behaviour Change Techniques (BCTs). These individual BCTs have effects on behavior through different processes. Some BCTs

K. T. Win et al. (Eds.): PERSUASIVE 2025, LNCS 15711, pp. 46–58, 2025.
https://doi.org/10.1007/978-3-031-94959-3_4

might change behavior through a change in belief; others might impact memory, attention, intention or motivation, etc. These processes or constructs are called Mechanisms of Action (MoA) [2]. The recent and influential work in the Human Behavior Change project is to establish a link between behavior change techniques and the mechanism of action [2]. These two components, i.e., BCT and MoA, are essential for personalized, adaptive, and effective digital intervention when adequately modeled and integrated into a digital behavior change intervention.

2   Background

In our previous work we observed that many digital interventions lack a solid theoretical foundation, often failing to adequately report Behavior Change Techniques (BCTs) or explain their mechanisms of action (MoAs) [3]. This raises critical questions about what drives behavior change, for whom, and under what conditions. To address these gaps, a computational model of motivation was developed to serve as a mechanism of action in behavior change interventions [4].

Motivation is represented as the function directly proportional ($\propto$) to the overall difference between the cost and outcome of net reward (see Eq. 1). This idea of motivation is based on the prospect of the dopaminergic reward pathway, which states that each action we perform depends on the outcome value of it. The higher the reward value of the action, the more often we do it, and the higher the costs (negative consequences, money, physical effort, etc.) no action is taken [5]. Another important factor in the equation is temporal discounting (γ), which represents the inclination for a person to see a desired outcome in the future as less important than one in the present. Temporal discounting is also subjective; some costs or rewards may be close by but highly discounted, whereas in another case, costs and rewards may be further away. Still, it is a very less discounted [6].

$$\text{Motivation(t)} \propto \text{Reward\_outcome(t)} - \gamma_1 \times \text{costs}_1(t) - \gamma_2 \times \text{costs}_2(t) - \gamma_3 \times \text{costs}_3(t) \tag{1}$$

The motivation model is used to simulate two processes i.e. motivation generation and motivation maintenance. Motivation generation is based on value-based reward anticipation, because motivation depends on the subjective value of a reward at a given time [5]. Higher reward value leads to stronger motivation. For example, increasing the perceived benefits, such as improved health or monetary rewards, can effectively motivate behavior change. Motivation maintenance is modeled using Reward Prediction Error (RPE), which calculates the difference between expected and received rewards (Eq. 2) [5]. This process helps sustain motivation over time by continuously updating the perceived value of actions.

$$\text{RPE(t)} = \text{Received Reward(t)} - \text{Net expected reward(t)} \tag{2}$$

Here, Received Reward(t) denotes the actual reward received at time t, while Net Expected Reward(t) represents the predicted reward at the same time. This error value, rooted in neuroscience, triggers dopamine release and facilitates learning of the action-outcome connection [5].

In this study, the motivation model is integrated into the Motivation to Move (MoM) mobile app to deliver personalized and adaptive physical activity interventions. The main aim is to evaluate the short-term effectiveness of the MoM intervention (app with model) over 40 days compared to a simplified version of the app without the model. Additionally, the study explores how the integration of the motivation model can make behavior change strategies more adaptive and personalized and identifies the critical parameters in this process. The specific hypotheses tested in the study are:

Primary Outcome: How do daily steps change over time for the MoM app with a motivation model compared to the app without the model?

Secondary Outcome: What factors within the motivation model influence the number of daily steps in the MoM app?

3   Methods

3.1   Study Design, Setting, and Participants

A two-arm, parallel-group, single-blinded trial tested the model-based MoM app against the non-model version. Eligible participants were healthy adults aged 18 or with Android phones. Participants were randomly assigned to either the intervention or control group, without knowledge of their group assignment.

3.2   Recruitment

Participants were recruited via email, social media, and university channels from June to August 2022.

3.3   Intervention vs Control Group

The intervention was designed based on the Behavior Change Intervention Ontology (BCIO) [7], with three core behavior change strategies: goal-setting, feedback on behavior, and incentives (see Table 1).

Table 1. Components of MoM intervention according to behavior change ontology.

Context & setting	Intervention content	MoA	Behavior
Any healthy adult above 18	Three strategies:	Motivation	Physical activity (step count)
Use the MoM android app for 40 days	• 1.3 Goal setting (outcome)		
Daily steps count against the given goal	• 2.2 Feedback on behavior (outcome)		
	• 10.8 Incentive (outcome)		

The above mentioned BCTs are personalized and made adaptive for intervention group in the app using Reward Prediction Error (RPE) and their performance. In contrast, the control group used a version of the app with fixed goals and feedback, with no personalized adjustments. Both groups followed a 40-day intervention after a 9-day baseline period. Figure 1 outlines the intervention flow. In the treatment phase, weekly RPE scores, calculated from motives assessed via the MPAM-R scale [8], were used to adjust BCTs, e.g. the intervention group's goals were updated based on weekly performance percentiles (20th–90th) [9], while the control group's goals remained at the 60th percentile.

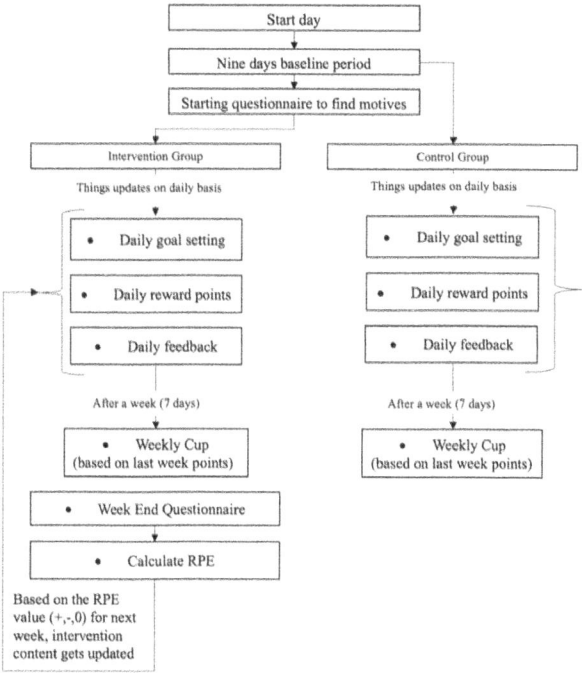

Fig. 1. Flow chart of the whole intervention

4 MoM App Overview

The Motivation to Move (MoM) app was developed using Google's Flutter framework, leveraging the Dart programming language [10]. The app's interface was designed in Adobe XD, and Android Studio was used for development. Data storage, authentication, and analytics were managed through Google Firebase. The app employs the "pedometer 3.0.0" package for step counting, developed by Copenhagen Center for Health Technology (CACHET), Denmark. Development took eight months[1].

---

[1] https://pub.dev/packages/pedometer.

4.1 App Features

The MoM intervention app includes four key features to support behavior change:

1. Account Creation: Users must create an account (Fig. 2a), complete a consent process (Fig. 2b), and verify their account via Google Firebase for secure data collection and spam prevention.
2. Baseline Period: During the nine-day baseline, the app records daily step counts for both groups to aid analysis and goal-setting. Progress is displayed (Fig. 2c), and data is uploaded nightly or when the device is online.
3. Questionnaire: Fifteen questions are asked at the start and end of each intervention week for RPE calculation (Fig. 2d). Responses update BCTs and are stored in Firebase.
4. Home Screen: Displays progress, points, and feedback (Fig. 2e), with sections for each BCT. Additional screens include targets and steps (Fig. 2f), rewards (Fig. 2g), and daily feedback messages (Fig. 2h).

Moreover some other screen are as follow: Fig. 2(f) where all the previous targets and steps can be seen. Figure 2(g) depicts the reward screen where daily earned reward points and weekly trophies can be seen. Figure 2(h) shows the feedback screen, where the participants can see the daily feedback message they received from the app. Table 2 details the integration of three BCTs with its relation with the App features.

Table 2. BCTs (code) used within the app are taken from Michie et al.'s taxonomy.

BCT	Related app feature
Goal setting (behavior) (1.1)	Daily adaptive goals
Feedback on behavior (2.2)	Daily motivational messages and specific messages for different motives
Incentive (outcome) (10.10)	Daily rewards and weekly trophy

4.2 Measurements

Physical activity changes were measured using daily step counts. If steps weren't recorded due to technical issues, a zero value was logged. Weekly responses to motive-related questions tracked motivation, while user engagement was analyzed via Google Analytics.

4.3 Data Management, Monitoring, and Safety

All data was collected electronically through the app. Google Firebase authenticated users and anonymized data by assigning unique IDs to participants.

(a) Account crea-   (b) Consent and   (c) 9 days base-   (d) Questionnaire
    tion screen   instruction form   line screen   screen

(e) Home screen   (f) Previous goals   (g) Reward   (h) Feedback
                        and steps   screen   screen

Fig. 2. MoM Mobile App features

5   Statistical Analysis

Recent studies show that inaccurate level specification in modeling longitudinal data can lead to skewed results [11]. To address this, we used a mixed-effects model with random intercepts to account for the nested structure of the data [12, 13]. We tested data normality using the Shapiro-Wilk test, histograms, and Q-Q plots. Data analysis was performed in R (version 2022.02.3) using the lmer package [14].

Linear mixed models (LMMs) extend linear regression to handle correlated errors and random effects. The simplest LMM includes a random intercept to capture variation across individuals. While repeated measures ANOVA is common for longitudinal data, it struggles with missing data and within-person relationships over time. Mixed-effects regression overcomes these limitations by combining fixed and random effects.

Dependent/outcome variable: Steps

Independent variable – Time – (Baseline vs. treatment) – For within-group analysis
Independent variable – Groups –(Intervention vs. control) – between-subject analysis

5.1 Sample Size and Participant Distribution

The app is available on the google play store for the general public. The app was downloaded by many people (100+) in different regions of the world. The number of people who signed the consent form and showed a willingness to participate was 41, among which randomly 20 was assigned to intervention group and 21 to control group. Completed the whole intervention.

5.2 Intervention Effects

Longitudinal data were assessed using linear mixed models to account for intraindividual differences. Differences in step count changes in the function of the condition (group allocation) will be evaluated using models that include the following fixed effects: group, period, and group × period interaction. We considered random intercepts and linear slopes for repeated measures at the participant level. The normality of residuals is checked. The results will be expressed using effect sizes and 95% CIs. Linear mixed effect modeling is the best option to fit the model, where the data is complex with repeated and group observation [15] and to account for the baseline and treatment periods (pre and post) and the random effects in the data.

Secondary outcome variables were scores of motivational determinants. The motives (i.e., appearance, enjoyment, fitness) were observed weekly, and the change in these motives was analyzed as their correlation with intervention. Descriptive analyses were conducted for all variables—means and SDs (continuous variables) or frequencies and proportions (categorical variables). Chi-square tests (categorical variables) and two-way mixed ANOVAs (continuous variables) were conducted to test for differences between groups at baseline.

6 Results

All participants completed the 9-day baseline period. However, four participants from the intervention group and three from the control group dropped out before finishing the baseline. Additionally, five participants from the intervention group and seven from the control group did not complete the 40-day treatment period (see Fig. 3). Four participants dropped out due to technical issues with the pedometer package on some Samsung phones (e.g., Samsung A32, Samsung Galaxy A10).

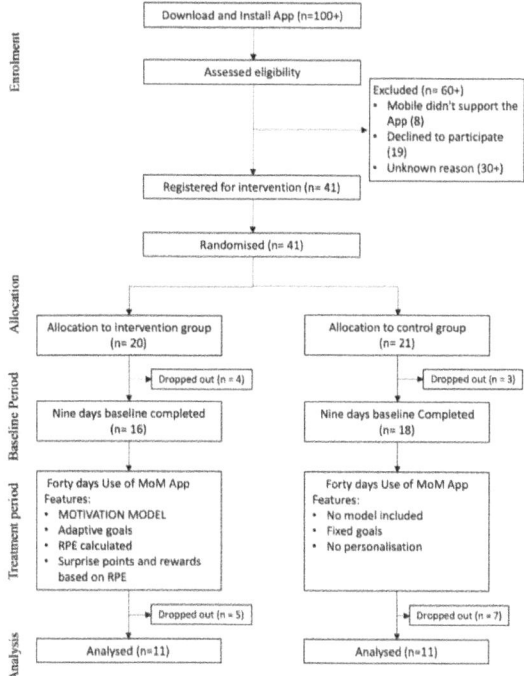

Fig. 3. Study design flow chart.

6.1 Quantitative Analysis

Table 3 presents descriptive statistics (frequencies, mean, SD) for the data. Data from 11 out of 21 participants (52%) in the control group and 11 out of 20 participants (55%) in the intervention group were analyzed. In the 9-day baseline period, 96/99 observations (97%) were collected for the control group, and 94/99 observations (95%) for the intervention group. The mean steps increased for both groups: control group (5,389 steps) and intervention group (4,736 steps). However, this descriptive data doesn't account for the repeated measures nature of the data.

Table 3. Descriptive statistics of physical activity data (daily steps) of baseline and treatment period

User type	Period	Observations (n)	Mean (SD)
Control	Baseline	96	5389 (4374)
Control	Treatment	413	5622 (4666)
Intervention	Baseline	94	4736 (4135)
Intervention	Treatment	404	7264 (5356)

6.2 Assumptions Testing for Linear Regression

Before applying linear mixed-effects regression, we checked several assumptions. The regression diagnostics (Fig. 4) suggest some issues:

- Residuals vs. Fitted: The plot indicates increasing variance with increasing fitted values, violating the homogeneity assumption.
- Normal Q-Q: The Shapiro-Wilk test revealed that the data is not normally distributed ($p < 2.2e-16$). This is expected, as the data is longitudinal.
- Scale-Location: The plot suggests heteroscedasticity (uneven spread of points).
- Residuals vs. Leverage: No extreme values influenced the regression results.

Since normality could not be achieved, we used a random intercept in the mixed linear model. This approach does not require normal distribution assumptions. Additionally, because observations within groups are nested (i.e., repeated measurements from the same participants), we included a random effect term for participants in the model to account for this non-independence.

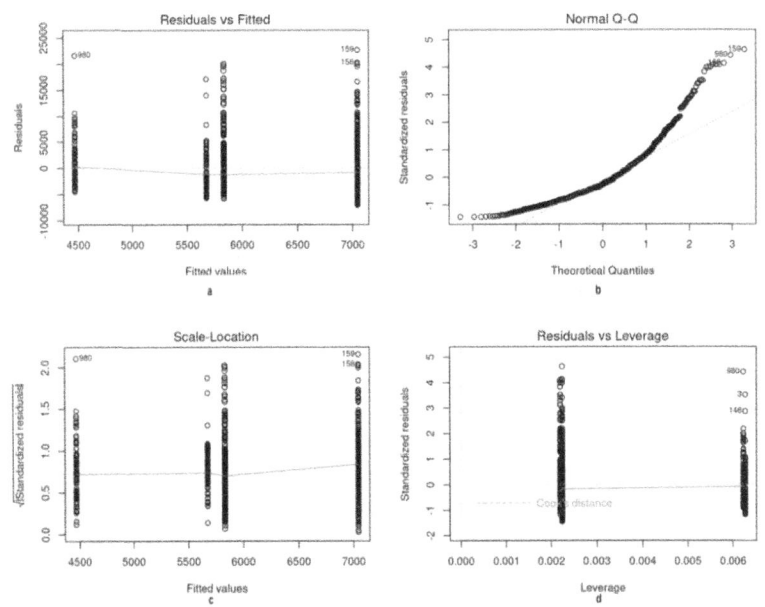

Fig. 4. Linear model assumptions

6.3 Effects on Primary Outcomes

The box plots in Fig. 5 show steps for two time periods, colored by time points and faceted by user type showing an increase in the number of steps. The green line shows the change in mean value from one time period to another for both groups.

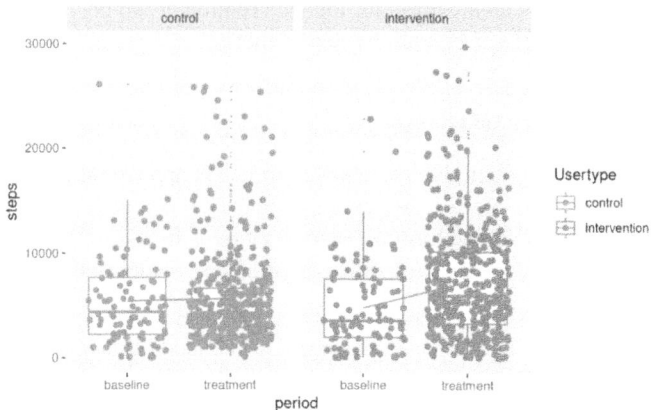

Fig. 5. Boxplot shows the steps count of each group with the green line from the mean of baseline to treatment period in each group (Color figure online).

The linear mixed effect model (steps ~ period*Usertype + (1|Userid)) fit by REML is defined to accommodate the random intercept for each participant within the group.

Table 4. The result of the mixed effect model with adding Userid as a random effect

Predictors	steps		
	Estimates	CI	p
(Intercept)	5406.28	3566.00–7246.57	**< 0.001**
period [treatment]	411.32	−511.45–1334.09	0.382
Usertype [intervention]	−689.50	−3295.07–1916.07	0.604
period [treatment] * Usertype [intervention]	2185.58	873.97–3497.19	**0.001**
Random Effects			
σ2	17153804.56		
τ00 Userid	7707745.74		
ICC	0.31		
N Userid	22		
Observations	1007		
Marginal R2/Conditional R2	0.032/0.332		

Significant p values are marked in bold.
Model1: $\gamma_{ij} = \beta 1 period + \beta 2 usertype + \beta 3\ Period * Usertype + (1|Userid)\ \varepsilon_{ij} + \mu_{ij}$.

Table 4 shows that overall there is no significant difference between the control and intervention groups. However, the interaction between the baseline and treatment period of intervention group participants shows a significant increase in the number of steps (p = 0.001). It can be seen that there is a statistically significant two-way interaction between baseline and treatment period for the intervention group $F(1, 983.30) = 20.26$, $p = 0.001$, $\eta 2 = 0.0034$ (User type), $\eta 2 = 0.652$ (period).

6.4 Effect on Secondary Outcomes

Similarly to the primary effect, the linear mixed model is applied to find the dependent variable of 'daily steps' with the components of the motivation model, i.e., fitness, enjoyment, and appearance. The formula (steps ~ enjoy + fitness + appearance + User type + (1 | Userid)) is used to accommodate the nested structure of our data.

Table 5. The result of the mixed effect model for different motives, with adding Userid as a random effect.

	steps		
Predictors	Estimates	CI	p
(Intercept)	2032.17	−1533.35–5597.70	0.264
enjoy	705.50	71.87–1339.14	0.029
fitness	−76.00	-821.97–669.97	0.842
appearance	466.48	−213.06–1146.02	0.178
Usertype [intervention]	937.28	−1802.33–3676.89	0.502
Random Effects			
σ2	16906787.76		
τ00 Userid	10058695.31		
ICC	0.37		
N Userid	22		
Observations	800		
Marginal R2/Conditional R2	0.034/0.395		

Table 5 shows no significant difference between the control and intervention groups concerning their daily steps and motives. But, the result shows that overall a significant correlation between daily steps and enjoyment $F(1,794.98) = 4.78$, $p = 0.029$, $\eta 2 = 0.675$ (enjoy), $\eta 2 = 0.006$ (fitness), $\eta 2 = 0.257$ (appearance).

7 Discussion

This study evaluates the MoM app, a mobile intervention designed to promote physical activity behavior through personalized and adaptive strategies, measured by daily step counts. Two groups were assessed: the intervention group using the MoM app with a motivation model and the control group using a simpler version without personalization. The study includes a two-week baseline and a six-week treatment period to investigate both within-group (time) and between-group effects.

Results show that the MoM app, integrating a motivation model, effectively increases daily step counts, leading to a healthier lifestyle. The intervention group showed a

52.7% increase in daily steps, compared to 4.1% in the control group, supporting the hypothesis that motivation-based adaptations enhance behavior change. This finding provides insight into how motivation works in digital interventions and highlights its potential in behavior change systems [16].

The app's motivation model, based on reward prediction error, utilized three main motives—fitness, enjoyment, and appearance. Weekly surveys allowed the app to adapt strategies based on user responses. Enjoyment was significantly correlated with daily steps, while fitness and appearance were not. This suggests that different reward types may affect behavior differently, and further research could explore the relationship between various motives and physical activity outcomes.

8   Conclusion

This study investigates how digital interventions can effectively incorporate behavior change components—techniques like goal-setting, feedback, and incentives—along with mechanisms of action such as motivation. The findings show that an explicit model of motivation enhances the personalization and effectiveness of interventions. Modeling motivation as part of digital health tools offers a promising approach to fostering healthy behaviors. Future research should explore and model other mechanisms that could further support long-term behavior change.

References

1. Hekler, E.B., et al.: Advancing models and theories for digital behavior change interventions. Am. J. Prev. Med. **51**(5), 825–832 (2016)
2. Carey, R.N., et al.: Behavior change techniques and their mechanisms of action: a synthesis of links described in published intervention literature. Ann. Behav. Med. **53**(8), 693–707 (2019)
3. Taj, F., Klein, M.C.A., van Halteren, A.: Digital health behavior change technology: bibliometric and scoping review of two decades of research. JMIR mHealth and uHealth **7**(12), e13311 (2019). https://doi.org/10.2196/13311
4. Taj, F., Klein, M.C.A., Van Halteren, A.: Motivating machines: the potential of modeling motivation as MoA for behavior change systems. Information **13**(5), 258 (2022). https://doi.org/10.3390/info13050258
5. Verharen, J.P.H., Adan, R.A.H., Vanderschuren, L.J.M.J.: How reward and aversion shape motivation and decision making: a computational account. Neuroscientist **26**(1), 87–99 (2020)
6. Scholten, H., et al.: Behavioral trainings and manipulations to reduce delay discounting: a systematic review. Psychon. Bull. Rev. **26**(6), 1803–1849 (2019)
7. Michie, S., West, R.: A Guide to Development and Evaluation of Digital Behaviour Change Interventions in Healthcare. Silverback Publishing (2016)
8. Ryan, R.M., et al.: Intrinsic motivation and exercise adherence. Int. J. Sport Psychol. **28**(4), 335–354 (1997)
9. Adams, M.A.: A Pedometer-Based Intervention to Increase Physical Activity: Applying Frequent, Adaptive Goals and a Percentile Schedule of Reinforcement. University of California, San Diego (2009)
10. Tyagi, P.: Pragmatic Flutter: Building Cross-Platform Mobile Apps for Android, iOS, Web & Desktop. CRC Press (2021)

11. Hoffman, L.: Longitudinal Analysis: Modeling within-Person Fluctuation and Change. Routledge (2015)
12. de Haan-Rietdijk, S., Kuppens, P., Hamaker, E.L.: What's in a Day? A Guide to Decomposing the Variance in Intensive Longitudinal Data. Front. Psychol. 7 (2016)
13. Barr, D.J., et al.: Random effects structure for confirmatory hypothesis testing: keep it maximal. J. Mem. Lang. **68**(3), 255–278 (2013)
14. Bates, D., et al.: Fitting linear mixed-effects models using lme4. J. Stat. Softw. **67**(1), 1–48 (2015)
15. Schielzeth, H., et al.: Robustness of linear mixed-effects models to violations of distributional assumptions. Methods Ecol. Evol. **11**(9), 1141–1152 (2020)
16. Michie, S., et al.: From theory-inspired to theory-based interventions: a protocol for developing and testing a methodology for linking behaviour change techniques to theoretical mechanisms of action. Ann. Behav. Med. **52**(6), 501–512 (2018)

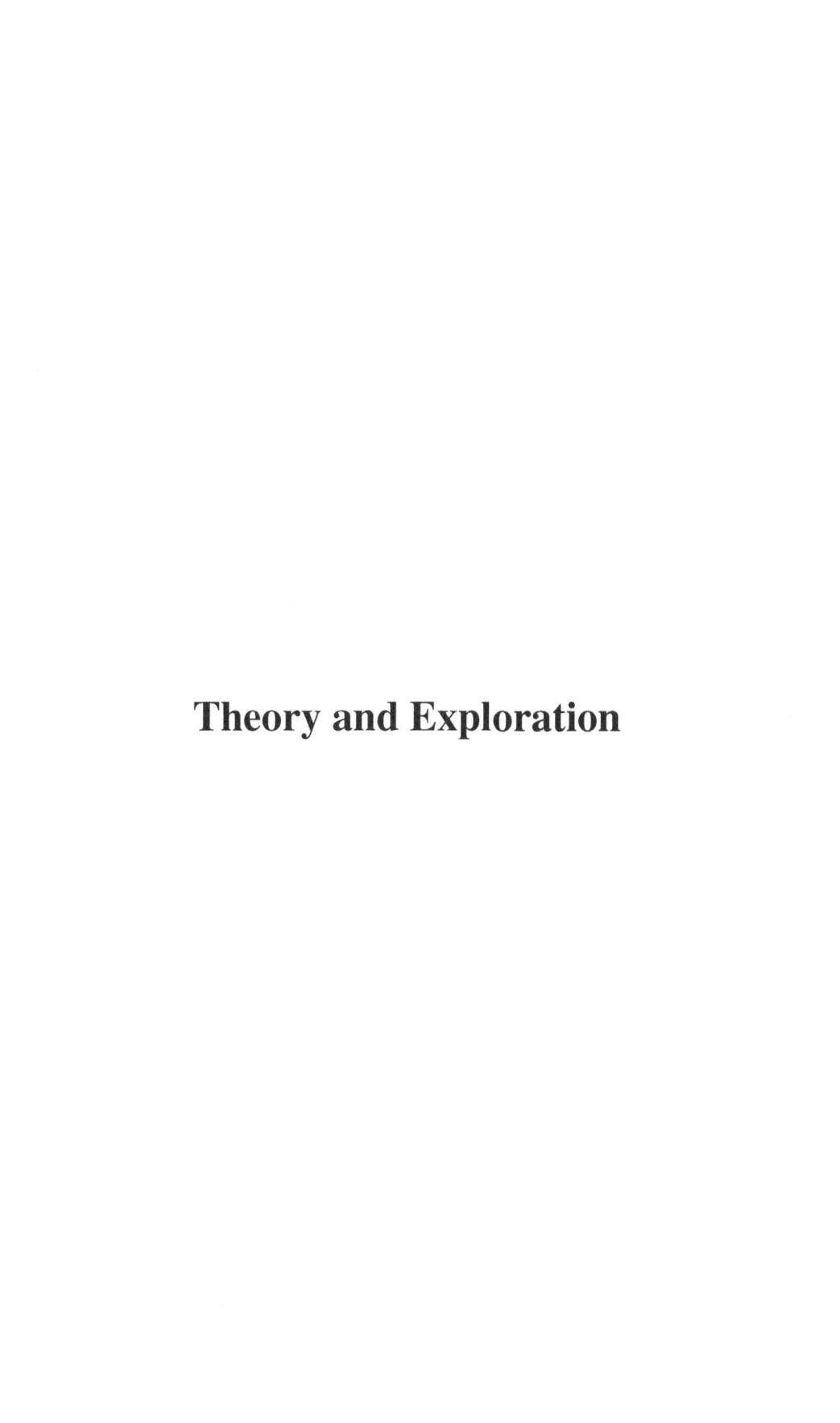

Theory and Exploration

Exploring the Potential and Limitations of Large Language Models to Control the Behavior of Embodied Persuasive Agents

Christian Corrò$^{(\boxtimes)}$ ⓘ and Luca Chittaro ⓘ

Human-Computer Interaction Lab, Department of Mathematics, Computer Science and Physics, University of Udine, Via Delle Scienze 206, 33100 Udine, Italy
{christian.corro,luca.chittaro}@uniud.it

Abstract. Interactive agents are an essential element of many persuasive applications. Their design and development have so far required extensive human effort to model their appearance and behavior. However, recent advances in the generative capabilities of Large Language Models (LLMs) might pave the way to build persuasive agents capable of autonomous, open-ended interactions without requiring the traditional investment in agent development. In this paper, we investigate the creation of an LLM-based embodied agent aimed at interacting with users in real-time to coach them in performing slow and deep breathing. In the approach we followed, the LLM uses a text-based context to generate a composition of predefined behaviors for interacting with the user through both verbal and nonverbal communication. The text-based context provided to the LLM described essential details, like the user's respiratory rate, to monitor the exercise. Information about actual user's breathing was provided to the LLM-model through a physiological sensor. The LLM-based breathing coach managed to follow the exercise structure and generated believable contingent behavior compositions. However, as we describe in the paper, building and evaluating the system allowed to highlight limitations of using only LLMs to create agents capable of real-time user interactions. The identified limitations suggest a need for hybrid approaches.

Keywords: Persuasive agent · LLM-based agent · Breathing coach · Embodied agent · Intelligent virtual agent · Real-time human-agent interaction

1 Introduction and Motivation

Interactive agents are an essential element of many persuasive applications, ranging from education to health interventions [1–4]. Persuasive agents can effectively guide user behavior, foster sustained engagement, and personalize interventions, thereby enhancing motivation and adherence [5–7]. Their design and development have so far required extensive human effort to model their appearance and behavior. This is primarily because they have been developed using complex handcrafted rule-based systems, such as finite-state machines and frame-based dialogue management systems [3], which are time-consuming to create. Moreover, these rule-based systems often lack the flexibility to

© The Author(s), under exclusive license to Springer Nature Switzerland AG 2025
K. T. Win et al. (Eds.): PERSUASIVE 2025, LNCS 15711, pp. 61–73, 2025.
https://doi.org/10.1007/978-3-031-94959-3_5

handle unstructured or novel user inputs beyond their pre-defined rules and scenarios, limiting their ability to engage in dynamic, naturalistic conversations or respond to unexpected user behavior, hindering their effectiveness in real-world applications [3]. However, recent advances in the generative capabilities of Large Language Models (LLMs), can pave the way to build persuasive agents capable of autonomous, open-ended interactions without requiring the traditional investment in agent development. LLMs are artificial intelligence models capable of generating credible, human-like, contextually appropriate text [8]. A particularly remarkable aspect of these models is their unprecedented ability to handle language semantics [8]. These models are trained on a large body of text data and operate using an autoregressive approach, i.e., they generate text by using preceding tokens (words fragments) to predict the most probable subsequent token. The architectural characteristics of LLMs (see [9]), coupled with an extensive number of parameters, which are values learned during training that define how the model processes inputs, lead to the emergence of complex behaviors in handling language semantics [8]. This enables them not only to perform complex tasks of text understanding and generation, but also to function as social agents capable of engaging in complex interactions with humans [10, 11]. LLMs can be prompted to mimic a personality, retain memory of previous interactions, and adaptively respond to social stimuli [11, 12]. LLMs are able to display persuasive capabilities comparable to those of humans [11], they can generate persuasive messages across various contexts, often matching or even surpassing the persuasiveness of human-authored content [13]. Although these findings are raising concerns about the application of LLMs to misinformation campaigns and manipulations of public discourse [11], LLMs can offer novel opportunities for building more robust and effective persuasive agents for positive purposes, such as user's health.

Recent studies are focusing on leveraging the generative capabilities of LLMs to build intelligent agents capable of autonomous, open-ended interactions [10, 14, 15]. Given a goal to achieve, these LLM-based agents autonomously decompose the goal into a sequence of tasks [16]. Each task is then translated by the LLM into a sequence of executable atomic actions chosen from a predefined set of actions provided by the system designer. Although the space of possible actions to complete a task is confined to the predefined set, the underlying LLM still offers significant flexibility: it determines how to decompose the goal, devises a plan, and generates the sequence of atomic actions the agent should perform. This process allows to take advantage of the powerful generative capabilities of LLMs, while ensuring that the agent cannot perform any action outside of those prespecified, thus preventing aberrant behavior [17]. While this approach is showing promise for constructing intelligent agents with robust context-based interaction capabilities [14], the efficiency of the process of goal decomposition, planning, and construction of sequences of atomic actions is negatively affected by the latency of LLMs. This issue is further exacerbated by the necessity of employing prompt engineering techniques, such as Chain of Thought (CoT) [18], ReAct [19], or Reflexion [20], to achieve optimal performance from the LLM in generating outputs. The core idea of these techniques involves having the LLM explicitly articulate in natural language, across various stages, what could be the best outcome, simulating reasoning [21]. These staged approaches are important because they guide the LLM to systematically process information, enhance its understanding of complex queries, and generate more accurate and coherent responses. Unfortunately, the latency in generating a sequence of executable atomic actions may hinder real-time interaction with an LLM-based agent, raising questions about the feasibility of using only LLMs in controlling the behavior of persuasive agents that need to interact in real-time with users.

To investigate these challenges, we have created an LLM-based interactive embodied persuasive agent within the health domain. Specifically, we have focused on a breathing coach to train users in performing slow and deep breathing. The objective of this paper is twofold: *(1) to assess the feasibility* of using an LLM-based approach for creating a breathing coach capable of real-time interaction, and *(2) to assess the appropriateness* of the LLM's generated behaviors in relation to the user's context, training goals and the persuasive strategies adopted.

In this paper we define a breathing coach as an intelligent virtual agent that provides personalized guidance and support to users in learning and practicing breathing techniques. We have chosen to build a breathing coach because it allows for the definition of a limited set of atomic actions and operates within a context that does not require the agent to have fast reaction times, thereby mitigating the inevitable issue of generation latency in LLMs. Compared to the other breathing coach proposed in the literature [22], the novelty of our approach lies in the radical paradigm shift in the creation process of the breathing coach. We explored the transition from a *rule-based* agent paradigm, where the agent behaviors are triggered by rules hardcoded by the system designer (for example, to have the breathing coach provide verbal feedback if the respiratory rate is above or below a predefined threshold) to a completely different paradigm based on a LLM.

2   The LLM-Based Embodied Breathing Coach

The design of the system for constructing the breathing coach was inspired by a virtual agent in a different area [14] that is capable of interacting with the virtual environment of Minecraft, a popular sandbox game, by performing action sequences for tasks specific to the game, such as autonomous navigation, resource gathering, and tool crafting. These sequences are generated through an iterative process involving two LLMs, focusing on goal decomposition and planning across multiple stages. To minimize latency due to multiple stages of generation, our system employs instead a single LLM. Goal decomposition, planning and behavior selection are performed through a single stage of Zero-Shot-CoT technique [23], which uses CoT without providing the LLM with examples. Moreover, rather than generating a sequence of actions for interacting with the virtual environment, in our approach the LLM generates a composition of predefined behaviors for interacting with the user through both verbal and nonverbal communication. Therefore, multiple behaviors can be combined and executed in parallel.

The core idea is to delegate the LLM to decide which among the set of available behaviors the embodied agent can perform, are most suited to the current goal and context. As shown in Fig. 1, our system comprises different components organized into a pipeline that can be concisely described as follows. The first stage of the pipeline gathers gathering multimodal user inputs, specifically respiratory signals and spoken utterances.

The respiratory signals are passed to a physiological signals processor, which extracts the current respiratory rate and depth, and translates them into textual descriptions that are then added to the evolving text-based context. Simultaneously, user's speech is converted to text through a speech-to-text module, enabling the system to capture and process spoken interactions. For instance, when the agent asks users for their name, user's spoken response is transcribed into text and added to the *text-based context*, allowing the agent to address users using their name during the exercise. All the textual inputs are combined with high-level instructions (the *system prompt*) and the collection of predefined behaviors (the *behavior library*). This combined information is fed into the *Behavior Composer LLM*, which determines the most suitable set of behaviors to achieve the current training goals (e.g., guiding the user in adopting a slower and/or deeper breathing pattern). The LLM outputs a *behavior composition*, specifying which behaviors to execute and in what sequence. Finally, the *Agent Behavior Executor* uses the behavior composition to execute the behaviors of the breathing coach. Throughout this process, the pipeline loops back, updating the text-based context with new physiological data, allowing the system to adaptively refine the coaching strategy as the user progresses.

The system was developed in Unity version 2021.3.14f1. The 3D model of the agent was built with Ready Player Me. We used the OpenAI API for the LLM, specifically we used the *gpt-3.5-turbo-0125* and *gpt-4–0125* models (2023). API calls were made directly in Unity using a dedicated library. For both speech-to-text and text-to-speech, we used Azure Speech Services. The system was run in immersive virtual reality on a Meta Quest Pro headset. For audio output and microphone input, we used Sony WH-1000XM4 over-ear headphones. To acquire the user's breathing signal, we used Thought Technology hardware (ProComp Infinity encoder with an abdominal expansion/contraction sensor).

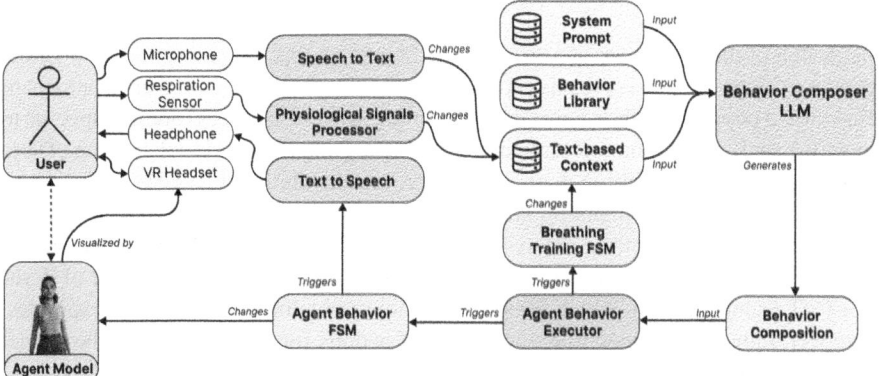

Fig. 1. Overview of the Breathing Coach architecture.

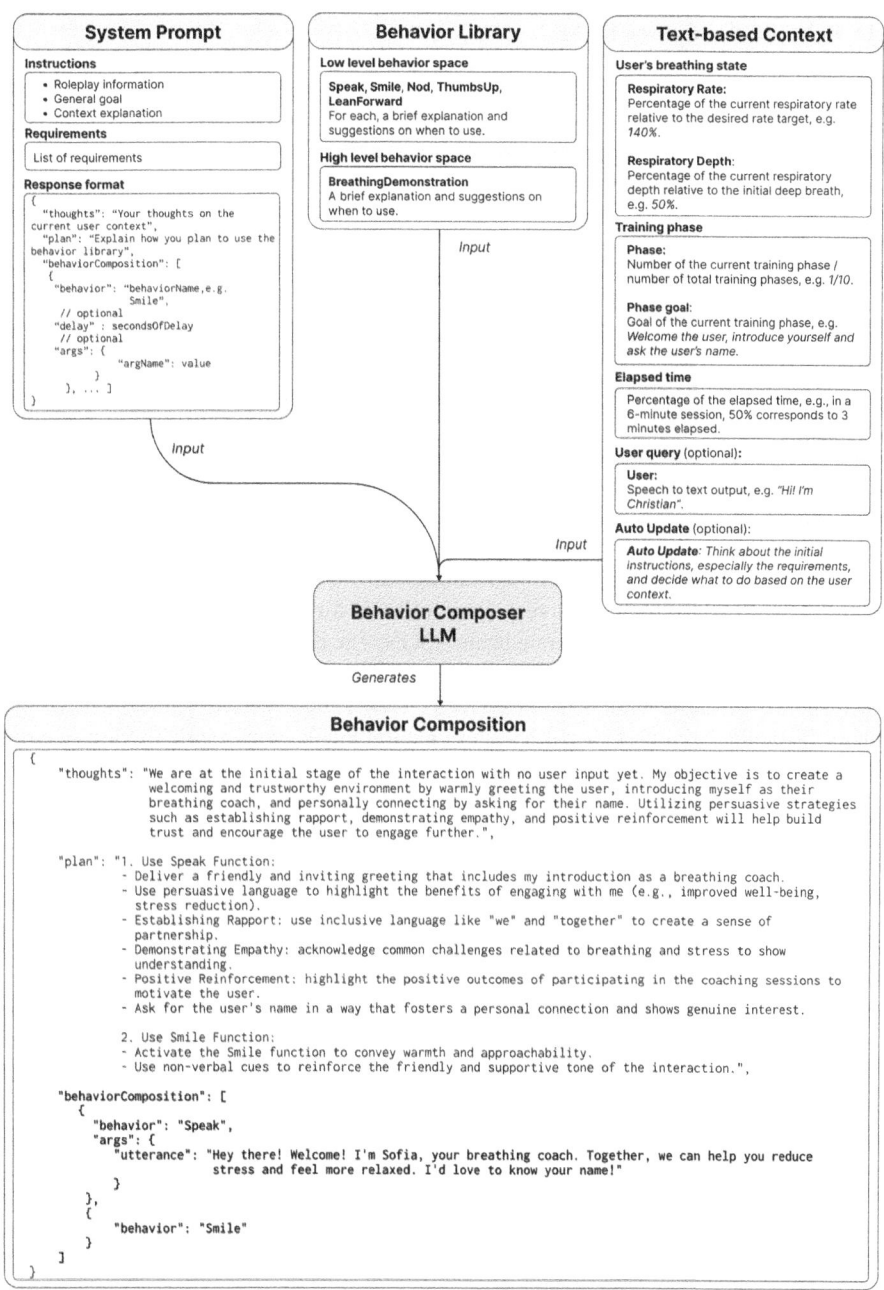

Fig. 2. Details of the input provided to the Behavior Composer LLM, and an example of a Behavior Composition generated by GPT 4.

2.1 Behavior Composer LLM

The pivotal component of the system is the Behavior Composer LLM, that determines the behavior of the breathing coach. The generation of a behavior composition is significantly influenced by the system prompt, the text-based context, and the behavior library. Figure 2 shows the details of the input provided to the Behavior Composer LLM, and an example of a Behavior Composition generated by GPT 4.

System Prompt. The system prompt provides the fundamental information to guide the LLM to generate believable behavior compositions. It includes information regarding the roleplay scenario, the overall goal, the context explanation, the requirement list, and the response format. The roleplay and overall goal information we provided in the tests described in this paper was: "*You are a breathing coach named Sofia. The overall goal is to train the user in a technique of slow and deep breathing, precisely the 5–7-3 technique, which involves 5 s of inhaling, 7 s of exhaling, and a 3-s pause.*". A crucial element of the prompt is the numbered list of requirements that the LLM must adhere to when generating the response. A sample of these requirements includes statements such as "*1 - Think step by step.*", "*6 - You can only use the functions available in the behavior library.*" and "*10 - You must follow the training phase goal.*". The prompt concludes by requiring the LLM to generate its responses in JSON format. Through OpenAI's JSON mode, the LLM consistently generated valid JSON. The response format forces the LLM to reason before generating the behaviors composition following the CoT technique. The response format schema is: {Thoughts, Plan, Behavior Composition}, where "Thoughts" requires the LLM to use natural language to explicitly describe the current context, "Plan" requires the LLM to explain how the system will use the behavior library based on the context, and "Behavior Composition" contains the behaviors that the persuasive agent will execute. System prompt construction, particularly the requirements section, was an iterative process in which requirements were added or modified to guide the generation of desired behavior compositions. Once the prompt was finalized, it was used consistently for the tests.

Text-Based Context. The text-based context provided to the LLM included five key components to monitor and guide the training progress: (i) textual information about user's respiratory rate and depth, used to monitor the user's physiological state throughout the session; (ii) goal of the training phase, as the session was organized into several phases, each with a specific goal to provide guidance to the LLM in generating behavior compositions coherent with a breathing training session. This included both the current phase number relative to the total, for example "1/4," and the corresponding goal, such as "*Welcome the user, introduce yourself, and ask for the user's name*"; (iii) elapsed time, provided to track session duration and to enable the agent to conclude the session once the predefined duration was reached; (iv) user query, which was incorporated into the context through a continuous speech recognition system when users speak; and (v) the auto-update message "*Think about the initial instructions, especially the requirements, and decide what to do based on the context*", which was inserted into the text-based context after 10 s of coach inactivity, enabling the LLM to re-evaluate and adapt to the updated context.

Behavior Library. The behavior library is a textual list of behaviors that are allowed to the breathing coach. Behaviors are described by a behavior name, a brief description of what happens when the behavior is performed, and a suggestion of its usage. The library is organized into two categories: *low-level behavior space* and *high-level behavior space*. The low-level behavior space contains behaviors that can be combined with each other, including "Speak" (Fig. 3a), "Smile", "Nod", "Thumbs Up" and "Lean Forward". The high-level behavior space contains behaviors that allow to automate series of complex movements, such as the Breathing Demonstration, which guides users through an entire breathing cycle, illustrating both inhalation and exhalation timing (Figs. 3b and c). Additionally, the Behavior Composer LLM can autonomously transition to subsequent training phases upon determining that the objectives of the current phase have been achieved, using the "Next Training Phase" action.

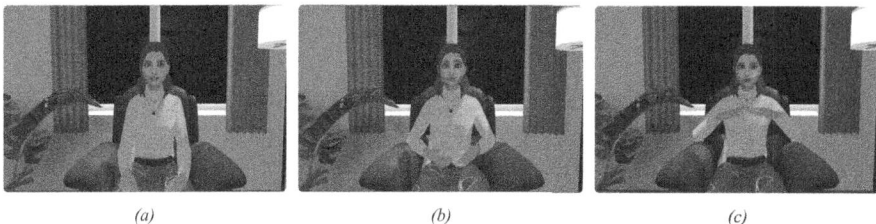

    (a)   *(b)*   *(c)*

Fig. 3. Screenshots of a breathing training session with the Breathing Coach from the user's viewpoint. The sequence shows the Breathing Coach: *(a)* welcoming the user and asking for his/her name; *(b)* demonstrating the duration of the inhalation phase, guiding the user on how long to breathe in; *(c)* demonstrating the duration of the exhalation phase, guiding the user on how long to breathe out.

2.2 Agent Behavior Executor

The Agent Behavior Executor processes the textual information generated by the LLM and triggers the corresponding animations for the embodied agent. Upon receiving the behavior composition from the Behavior Composer LLM, the Agent Behavior Executor activates states in two multilayer Finite State Machines (FSMs): the Agent Behavior FSM and the Breathing Training FSM. The Agent Behavior FSM encapsulates all behaviors from the behavior library, acting as an interface for triggering and orchestrating behavior executions. Each state within this FSM corresponds to a specific animation. For example, if the behavior composition is {Speak("Hello, I am Sofia!"), Smile, LeanForward}, it will sequentially activate the Speak state, initiating the speech animation and text-to-speech output, along with the Smile and LeanForward states. Thus, the choice of how to manipulate the FSM states is not hardcoded but is entirely delegated to the LLM. The Breathing Training FSM governs the sequence of breathing training phases, which the system uses to update the text-based context as the user progresses through the phases of the training.

3 Evaluation

To evaluate the system, we conducted 20 coaching sessions, 10 with the GPT 3.5 model and 10 with the GPT 4 model. Each session lasted up to 6 min, resulting in a total of 240 behavior compositions (120 for each model). GPT-3.5 exhibits lower generation latency [24], providing faster responses, whereas GPT-4, though slower, performs better on benchmarks on language understanding tasks such as the SuperGLUE benchmark [24], demonstrating better context understanding. By using both models, we aimed to explore the trade-off between *generation latency* and the *appropriateness of generated behavior compositions* in relation to the specific training phase goal and the user context. An a priori power analysis was conducted using G*Power version 3.1.9.7 [25] to determine the minimum sample size required. The required sample size to achieve 80% power for detecting a medium effect, at a significance criterion of $\alpha = .05$, was $N = 128$ for a two tailed independent t-test. Thus, the obtained sample size of $N = 240$ is adequate. All statistical analyses were conducted with Jamovi version 2.6.2.

3.1 Measures

1. *Generation Latency* measures the time in milliseconds required to produce the behavior compositions. It is calculated as the average time required for a behavior composition.
2. *Behavioral Alignment Score* (BAS) serves as a quantitative measure assessing the appropriateness of generated behavior compositions in relation to the specific training phase goal and the user context. The behavior composition, along with the training goal and the user context, was logged for each generation. Similarly to [26] each log was then evaluated through expert evaluation by two independent raters using a 5-point scale (1 = "not at all" to 5 = "very much") based on the question: "Is the behavior composition appropriate in relation to the training phase goal and the user context?" The BAS score is then calculated by averaging these ratings. To ensure the consistency of the evaluations, the inter-rater reliability was calculated using Cohen's kappa. The Cohen's kappa value obtained was $\kappa = 0.68$, indicating substantial agreement between the raters [27].
3. *Successful Termination* measures the percentage of training sessions that successfully conclude within the designated time frame. It is used to assess how well the system adheres to time constraints and completes the training process as intended.

4 Results and Discussion

The results, shown in Fig. 4, indicate a trade-off between the generation latency and the appropriateness of the behavior compositions generated. GPT 3.5 is faster in providing a response ($M = 2.45$, $SD = 0.18$) compared to GPT-4 ($M = 6.01$, $SD = 0.36$),t(238) $= -34.70$, p < .001. However, GPT 4 is more proficient at using context as reflected in its higher BAS score ($M = 3.25$, SD $= 0.32$) compared to GPT-3.5 ($M = 2.24$, *SD* $= 0.72$), $t(238) = -3.93$, p < .001, thereby generating believable contingent behavior compositions that are consistent with both the context and the training phases. For example, the breathing coach initially introduced itself and asked for the users' names, correctly waiting for a response, and was also able to correctly provide feedback on users' progress during the breathing exercise. These findings align with broader observations on LLM-driven systems, showing that while more advanced models (e.g., GPT-4) tend to produce richer, context-aware outputs, they do so at the expense of higher latency [28]. The 3.5 model exhibited an early termination problem: despite explicit instructions in the prompt, it did not always consider the elapsed time to conclude the training session and prematurely ended it. Moreover, although GPT 3.5 was the faster model, it still exhibited considerable latency, exacerbated by the need to employ prompting techniques like CoT. The generation of behavior compositions is time-consuming, thus significantly limiting the viability of the LLM-based approach in building a breathing coach capable of interacting in real-time with the user. The identified limitations suggest a need for hybrid approaches, where the capabilities of LLMs are used in conjunction with other components, including rule-based systems. These observations are consistent with a broader trend in the artificial intelligent (AI) field, where *compound AI systems* are emerging [29]. These systems address complex tasks by combining multiple interacting components, each specialized for specific sub-tasks. For instance, a hierarchical language agent proposed in [30] combines a proficient LLM for high-level reasoning (referred to as Slow Mind) with lightweight models (referred to as Fast Mind) and rule-based policies for fast, real-time execution of actions, demonstrating the effectiveness of hybrid approaches in reducing latency while maintaining context-aware behavior. In the case of the breathing coach, for instance, a rule-based system could deterministically manage corrective feedback, e.g., when users' respiratory rate exceeds a threshold, the system would instruct them to slow down, while session management and persuasive verbal interactions, such as motivational support, could be delegated to the LLM. In a broader perspective, the LLM could handle high-level reasoning on the context, while rule-based systems could help to swiftly react to different stimuli that require a quick response.

We encountered two additional challenges that must be addressed in future work: *inappropriate feedback* and *hallucinations*. First, particularly with the 3.5 model, we observed occasional instances ($n = 28$) of inappropriate feedback, particularly where the model inappropriately employed positive reinforcement instead of delivering corrective guidance, thus undermining the coaching objective. For example, in one case the user was breathing too quickly, and feedback was needed to slow him down. However, the LLM not only overlooked this corrective feedback but actually praised the user's performance despite the error. Upon inspecting the behavior composition logs, which detail the model's reasoning for choosing specific behaviors, we found entries like: "*The user is breathing too quickly. However, giving negative feedback at this moment could discourage them from continuing the exercise; it is better to use a confidence-boost strategy to keep the user motivated by telling he's doing a great job*". This suggests that while LLMs can play the role of a persuasive coach, they sometimes rely on out-of-context persuasive techniques. This issue aligns with broader concerns in the literature regarding the dual potential of LLMs to both enhance and undermine informational integrity through persuasive strategies [31]. On one hand, LLMs possess the capability to motivate and engage users effectively by providing encouraging feedback, which can enhance user adherence and overall experience. On the other hand, inappropriate feed-back can reduce the effectiveness of interventions and potentially lead to unintended negative outcomes, such as decreased user trust or engagement [11]. Understanding of the context and the persuasion capabilities of LLMs is improving as these models become more advanced [32]. Consequently, such inappropriate behaviors might see a reduction in future iterations of the models.

Hallucinations, where the model invents or distorts information, are the second crit-ical issue identified. Hallucination instances were observed in $n = 36$ behavior com-positions generated for GPT-3.5, and $n = 19$ for GPT-4. For instance, in one case the LLM informed the user, "*Your heart rate has dropped significantly, indicating excellent relaxation*" despite not having access to any real-time heart rate data. This fabricated feedback could mislead the user and compromise the reliability of the coaching system. Hallucinations pose a significant risk in persuasive applications, as users may uncriti-cally accept off-topic or inaccurate guidance [28]. This problem is well-documented in the literature and remains an unresolved challenge [28]. Research has begun to explore various techniques to mitigate hallucinations. For instance, retrieval-augmented gener-ation (RAG) approaches provide the LLM with verified external data sources to anchor responses [33], while reinforcement learning from human feedback (RLHF) helps align outputs with user expectations [34]. Two additional strategies could help mitigate this problem. First, rather than relying exclusively on Zero-Shot CoT prompting as in this study, it is possible to provide the model with detailed, carefully designed examples of possible interactions. Second, fine-tuning on domain-specific data (e.g., training proto-cols) can reduce the likelihood of misleading or erroneous outputs, aligning the model's responses more closely with the intended coaching context.

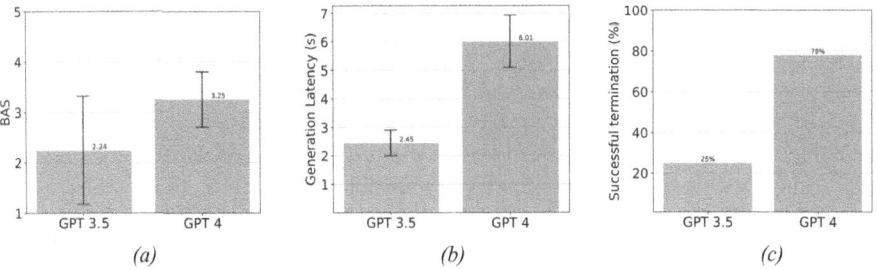

Fig. 4. (a) Mean generation latency, (b) mean behavioral alignment score, and (c) successful termination percentage for each LLM model used.

5   Limitations and Future Work

While our study shows the potential of LLMs in creating an embodied breathing coach, several limitations must be acknowledged. First, the sample size of 20 training sessions (10 with GPT-3.5 and 10 with GPT-4) is relatively small, which may limit the generaliz-ability of our findings. Second, our study was restricted to the single domain of breathing training, which may not reflect the broader applicability of LLM-based agents in other persuasive contexts. Future research should explore the versatility of this approach across various domains to determine its generalizability and to identify any domain-specific challenges or opportunities. Third, another limitation concerns the predefined behavior library used in our system. While this library ensures that the agent operates within predefined behaviors, the limited number of implemented behaviors may restrict the range of interactions and hinder the ability to generate more sophisticated behavior compositions. Expanding the behavior library could enhance the adaptability of the agent and its effectiveness in diverse scenarios. Lastly, our evaluation metrics are limited. Incorporating additional quantitative measures, such as user satisfaction, engagement, credibility and objective performance indicators, would provide a more comprehensive assessment of the effectiveness of the agent and user experience. Our future work will concentrate on leveraging LLMs for reasoning on the context and high-level planning, while employing rule-based systems for executing behaviors swiftly. Additionally, we plan to incorporate more granular measures regarding the capabilities of LLMs in generating persuasive behavior compositions composed of a richer behavior library comprising both verbal and non-verbal elements, such as facial expressions and posture. We also plan to explore more recent and faster models, as well as open models.

6 Conclusions

In this paper, we investigated the creation of an LLM-based embodied agent aimed at interacting with users in real-time to coach them in performing slow and deep breathing by generating behavior compositions. While the LLM-based approach demonstrated effectiveness in generating persuasive behavior compositions, it also revealed significant challenges, including latency, inappropriate feedback, and hallucinations. These issues highlight the limitations of relying solely on LLMs for real-time interactions in persuasive applications. Our findings suggest the necessity of adopting hybrid approaches that leverage the strengths of both LLMs and rule-based systems.

Disclosure of Interests.   The authors have no competing interests to declare that are relevant to the content of this article.

References

1. Fogg, B.J.: Persuasive Technology: Using Computers to Change What We Think and Do. Morgan Kaufmann Publishers, Amsterdam; Boston (2003)
2. Cassell, J., Sullivan, J., Scott, P. (eds.): Embodied Conversational Agents. MIT Press, Cambridge, Mass (2000)
3. Laranjo, L., et al.: Conversational agents in healthcare: a systematic review. J. Am. Med. Inform. Assoc. **25**, 1248–1258 (2018). https://doi.org/10.1093/jamia/ocy072
4. Provoost, S., Lau, H.M., Ruwaard, J., Riper, H.: Embodied conversational agents in clinical psychology: a scoping review. J. Med. Internet Res. **19**, e6553 (2017). https://doi.org/10.2196/jmir.6553

5. Bickmore, T.W., Picard, R.W.: Establishing and maintaining long-term human-computer relationships. ACM Trans. Comput.-Hum. Interact. **12**(2), 293–327 (2005). https://doi.org/10.1145/1067860.1067867

6. Provoost, S., et al.: Improving adherence to an online intervention for low mood with a virtual coach: study protocol of a pilot randomized controlled trial. Trials **21**, 860 (2020). https://doi.org/10.1186/s13063-020-04777-2

7. Mercado, J., Espinosa-Curiel, I.E., Martínez-Miranda, J.: Embodied conversational agents providing motivational interviewing to improve health-related behaviors: scoping review. J. Med. Internet Res. **25**, e52097 (2023). https://doi.org/10.2196/52097

8. Wei, J., et al.: Emergent Abilities of Large Language Models. http://arxiv.org/abs/2206.07682, (2022). https://doi.org/10.48550/arXiv.2206.07682

9. Vaswani, A., et al.: Attention is all you need. Advances in neural information processing systems. 30 (2017)

10. Park, J.S., O'Brien, J., Cai, C.J., Morris, M.R., Liang, P., Bernstein, M.S.: Generative agents: interactive simulacra of human behavior. In: Proceedings of the 36th Annual ACM Symposium on User Interface Software and Technology, pp. 1–22. Association for Computing Machinery, New York (2023). https://doi.org/10.1145/3586183.3606763

11. Breum, S.M., Egdal, D.V., Gram Mortensen, V., Møller, A.G., Aiello, L.M.: The persuasive power of large language models. Proc. Int. AAAI Conf. Web Soc. Media **18**, 152–163 (2024). https://doi.org/10.1609/icwsm.v18i1.31304

12. Wang, L., et al.: A survey on large language model based autonomous agents. Front. Comput. Sci. **18**, 186345 (2024). https://doi.org/10.1007/s11704-024-40231-1

13. Karinshak, E., Liu, S.X., Park, J.S., Hancock, J.T.: Working with AI to persuade: examining a large language model's ability to generate pro-vaccination messages. Proc. ACM Hum.-Comput. Interact. **7**(CSCW1), 1–29 (2023). https://doi.org/10.1145/3579592

14. Zhu, X., et al.: Ghost in the Minecraft: Generally Capable Agents for Open-World Environments via Large Language Models with Text-based Knowledge and Memory, (2023). https://doi.org/10.48550/arXiv.2305.17144

15. Wang, Z., Cai, S., Chen, G., Liu, A., Ma, X.S., Liang, Y.: Describe, explain, plan and select: interactive planning with LLMs enables open-world multi-task agents. In: Advances in Neural Information Processing Systems, vol. 36 (2024)

16. Huang, W., Abbeel, P., Pathak, D., Mordatch, I.: Language models as zero-shot planners: extracting actionable knowledge for embodied agents. In: Proceedings of the 39th International Conference on Machine Learning, pp. 9118–9147. PMLR (2022)

17. Crouse, M., etal.: Formally Specifying the High-Level Behavior of LLM-Based Agents

18. Wei, J., et al.: Chain-of-thought prompting elicits reasoning in large language models. Adv. Neural. Inf. Process. Syst. **35**, 24824–24837 (2022)

19. Yao, S., Zhao, J., Yu, D., Du, N., Shafran, I., Narasimhan, K., Cao, Y.: ReAct: Synergizing Reasoning and Acting in Language Models. International Conference on Learning Representations (ICLR). (2023)

20. Shinn, N., Cassano, F., Gopinath, A., Narasimhan, K., Yao, S.: Reflexion: Language agents with verbal reinforcement learning. In: Advances in Neural Information Processing Systems, vol. 36 (2024)

21. Huang, W., et al.: Inner Monologue: Embodied Reasoning through Planning with Language Models (2022)

22. Shamekhi, A., Bickmore, T.: Breathe deep: a breath-sensitive interactive meditation coach. In: Proceedings of the 12th EAI International Conference on Pervasive Computing Technologies for Healthcare, pp. 108–117. ACM, New York NY USA (2018). https://doi.org/10.1145/3240925.3240940

23. Kojima, T., Gu, S.S., Reid, M., Matsuo, Y., Iwasawa, Y.: Large language models are zero-shot reasoners. Adv. Neural. Inf. Process. Syst. **35**, 22199–22213 (2022)

24. Wang, A., et al.: SuperGLUE: A Stickier Benchmark for General-Purpose Language Understanding Systems. In: Advances in Neural Information Processing Systems. Curran Associates, Inc. (2019)

25. Faul, F., Erdfelder, E., Lang, A.-G., Buchner, A.: G*Power 3: a flexible statistical power analysis program for the social, behavioral, and biomedical sciences. Behav. Res. Methods **39**, 175–191 (2007). https://doi.org/10.3758/BF03193146

26. Beck, S., Kuhner, M., Haar, M., Daubmann, A., Semmann, M., Kluge, S.: Evaluating the accuracy and reliability of AI chatbots in disseminating the content of current resuscitation guidelines: a comparative analysis between the ERC 2021 guidelines and both ChatGPTs 3.5 and 4. Scand J. Trauma Resusc. Emerg. Med. (2024). https://doi.org/10.1186/s13049-024-01266-2

27. Cohen, J.: A coefficient of agreement for nominal scales. Educ. Psychol. Measur. **20**, 37–46 (1960). https://doi.org/10.1177/001316446002000104

28. Bommasani, R., et al.: On the Opportunities and Risks of Foundation Models. ArXiv. (2022). https://doi.org/10.48550/arXiv.2108.07258

29. Gupta, R., et al.: The Shift from Models to Compound AI Systems. http://bair.berkeley.edu/blog/2024/02/18/compound-ai-systems/

30. Liu, J., Yu, C., Gao, J., Xie, Y., Liao, Q., Wu, Y., Wang, Y.: LLM-powered hierarchical language agent for real-time human-AI coordination. In: Proceedings of the 23rd International Conference on Autonomous Agents and Multiagent Systems. pp. 1219–1228. International Foundation for Autonomous Agents and Multiagent Systems, Richland, SC (2024)

31. Carrasco-Farre, C.: Large Language Models are as persuasive as humans, but how? About the cognitive effort and moral-emotional language of LLM arguments, (2024). https://doi.org/10.48550/arXiv.2404.09329

32. Esin, D., Lovitt, L., Alex, T., Stuart, R., Jack, C., Ganguli, D.: Measuring the Persuasiveness of Language Models. https://www.anthropic.com/news/measuring-model-persuasiveness

33. Lewis, P., et al.: Retrieval-augmented generation for knowledge-intensive NLP tasks. In: Proceedings of the 34th International Conference on Neural Information Processing Systems, pp. 9459–9474. Curran Associates Inc., Red Hook, NY, USA (2020)

34. Ouyang, L., et al.: Training language models to follow instructions with human feedback (2022). https://doi.org/10.48550/arXiv.2203.02155

Insights into the Design of Ethical and Trustworthy Persuasive Technologies

Parinda Rahman[✉] and Ifeoma Adaji

The University of British Columbia, Okanagan Campus, Kelowna, Canada
parinda1@student.ubc.ca, ifeoma.adaji@ubc.ca

Abstract. Persuasive technologies drive behavioral changes across domains like healthcare, education, and e-commerce but face ethical challenges around consent, autonomy, privacy, and transparency. This study explores ethical design considerations in Human-Computer Interaction through expert focus groups and interviews. The study provides guidelines for the design of ethical and trustworthy persuasive technology. Key findings highlight the need for clear consent mechanisms, visual aids to reduce consent fatigue, customizable notifications to enhance autonomy, and transparent communication with algorithmic clarity. Participants also emphasized the importance of mechanisms for rectifying user errors and promoting equitable navigation. These insights offer practical guidance for fostering trust and ethical engagement, with future research needed to explore diverse demographics and long-term effectiveness.

Keywords: persuasive design · ethics · trust · persuasive technologies

1 Introduction

Advancements in technology and increasing digitalization have transformed interactions with information systems and smart technologies. AI-driven recommendations on platforms like Amazon and Netflix, along with personalized notifications from wearables, significantly influence human behavior [55]. This transformation is driven by persuasive system design (PSD), which integrates elements to influence user attitudes and behaviors without coercion [19]. PSD is widely applied in healthcare, education, and e-commerce to encourage desired behaviors [34].

However, persuasive technologies also raise ethical concerns. While they can promote beneficial behaviors, they may exploit cognitive biases and manipulate decision-making through unethical practices like "dark patterns" [24,32]. Such tactics can coerce users into unintended actions, leading to negative outcomes such as financial loss and diminished trust [35,60]. Despite growing awareness, there is a lack of actionable frameworks for ethical PSD [36]. Existing literature emphasizes transparency, consent, and privacy but lacks concrete guidelines for designers [22]. Users' perceptions of ethicality directly influence trust and adoption of persuasive technologies [2,44].

© The Author(s), under exclusive license to Springer Nature Switzerland AG 2025
K. T. Win et al. (Eds.): PERSUASIVE 2025, LNCS 15711, pp. 74–88, 2025.
https://doi.org/10.1007/978-3-031-94959-3_6

Ethicality in persuasive technologies includes fairness, non-manipulation, privacy, and autonomy. Users trust systems that respect agency, provide transparency, and avoid deceptive tactics [28,58]. Emerging regulations highlight the urgency of addressing these concerns [11,39]. However, translating ethical principles into concrete design features remains challenging due to varying ethical considerations across domains and demographics [29,31].

This research explores design considerations for ethical and trustworthy persuasive systems, focusing on transparency, autonomy, consent, and privacy by answering the overarching research question: "*what design considerations should be included in persuasive systems for an ethical and trustworthy persuasive design*". The paper's specific research questions build on ethical concerns identified in Rahman & Adaji's systematic literature review [45].

- **RQ1:** What design features enhance consent to improve users' ethical perception and trust?
- **RQ2:** What design features enhance user autonomy to improve users' ethical perception and trust?
- **RQ3:** What design features improve data privacy and security to enhance users' ethical perception and trust?
- **RQ4:** What design features improve transparency to enhance users' ethical perception and trust?

By answering these questions, this study aims to bridge literature gaps and contribute to ethical design practices and industry standards.

2 Related Work

Persuasive technologies influence behavior through techniques like gamification, gamblification, and digital nudging. Ethical game design fosters autonomy and competence [7,16], but lacks actionable guidelines for ethical implementation. Conversely, gamblified elements raise concerns about addictive behaviors [33]. Digital nudging subtly steers choices, sometimes undermining autonomy [3,57]. These issues-spanning autonomy, privacy, and consent-lead to trust concerns and psychological harm [62].

Existing frameworks like Value-Sensitive Design (VSD) and Participatory Design embed ethical values into design [20,37], yet lack specific guidance for persuasive systems. VSD does not translate values into concrete design practices, while Participatory Design emphasizes inclusion without addressing dark patterns. This study complements these frameworks by developing actionable guidelines addressing autonomy, privacy, informed consent, and transparency.

3 Methodology

This qualitative study used semi-structured interviews and focus groups with HCI professionals to explore ethical considerations in persuasive system design.

3.1   Participant Recruitment and Sampling

Participants were recruited via professional networks, academic institutions, and industry contacts, targeting HCI professionals with at least three years of experience in persuasive technology, UX design, and ethics. Two focus group sessions were held and six one-on-one interviews were conducted to accomodate scheduling conflicts. The study was approved by Behavioural Research Ethics Board of the Unviersity of British Columbia, Okanagan campus. Table 1 summarizes participant demographics.

3.2   Data Collection

Interviews and focus groups (90 min each) explored ethical concerns in persuasive technology through open-ended questions:

– **Consent**: Discussion surrounding design considerations as well as examples of terms and conditions interfaces were discussed.
– **Transparency**: What level of transparency is expected regarding data usage? Examples of well- and poorly-implemented transparency were discussed.
– **User Autonomy**: What features promote or restrict autonomy? How should systems balance influence and control?
– **Privacy and Security**: What concerns exist regarding personal data collection and how should persuasive designs reflect these?

3.3   Data Analysis

Data were transcribed and analyzed using thematic analysis. Two independent researchers conducted coding, identifying themes inductively and deductively. Key themes included transparency, autonomy, consent fatigue, and privacy concerns. Coding discrepancies were resolved through consensus discussions, with a third researcher mediating if necessary to ensure consistency.

3.4   Addressing Biases

To mitigate recruitment biases, professionals from academia, industry, and design disciplines were included. However, as participants were HCI professionals, their perspectives may not fully reflect end-user concerns. Future research should expand participant pools to include end-users for validation in real-world contexts. This study ensures a robust, expert-driven exploration of ethical issues while acknowledging its limitations.

4   Results

4.1   RQ1: Consent

Clarity and Understandability in Language and Communication. Participants in the study emphasized the importance of clarity and comprehensibility in language for obtaining meaningful consent within persuasive systems.

Table 1. Participant information and experience.

Group	ID	Role	Education	Experience
Focus Group 1	P1	HCI Researcher	Human-Computer Interaction	3 years
Focus Group 1	P2	UX Researcher and Game Designer	Psychology and Neuroscience	14 years
Focus Group 1	P3	HCI Researcher and VR Developer	Computer Science	2 years
Focus Group 1	P4	HCI Researcher and VR Developer	Internet of Things	2 years
Focus Group 1	P5	UX/UI Developer	UI/UX Design	2 years
Focus Group 2	P6	Product Manager	Computer Science and Engineering	2 years
Focus Group 2	P7	HCI Researcher	Computer Science and Engineering	2 years
Focus Group 2	P8	HCI Researcher	Computer Science and Engineering	2 years
One-on-One Interview	P9	Product Designer	UX and Interaction Design	5 years
One-on-One Interview	P10	UX Designer	Digital Communication and Multimedia	2 years
One-on-One Interview	P11	UX Developer	Mathematics	10 years
One-on-One Interview	P12	Senior Product Designer	Business Administration	5 years
One-on-One Interview	P13	HCI Researcher	Computer Science	3 years
One-on-One Interview	P14	Product Manager	Computer Science and Engineering	2 years

They noted that consent language should be easily understood by an average user, emphasizing that consent mechanisms should offer flexibility and personalization options. This aligns with prior literature suggesting that when users share an understanding of a system's persuasive intent and perceive value in the persuasion, they are more inclined to engage with the system [10]. One participant described the necessity of flexibility in consent mechanisms:

I think it should be well spelled out... I think consent shouldn't be a compulsory field, but rather permission that is flexible and easily understood. It should be broken down clearly so users realize there's no harm in using a particular feature (P2).

Participants further underscored the need for concise and clear communication to prevent disengagement. A participant articulated this concern, stating:

Another thing that comes to mind is clarity in the copywriting. Some merchants make it intentionally long, which discourages users from reading. We want to keep it as concise as possible.(P4)

This highlights the significance of brevity and transparency to support informed decision-making, while also mitigating perceptions of manipulation. At the same time, participants expressed some skepticism, suggesting that full transparency might occasionally reduce the system's effectiveness in persuading users to complete target actions. Zhang et al. emphasize that transparent presentation of goals, methods, and risks within persuasive interventions is critical for building trust [37]. Similarly, Cemiloglu et al. found that users perceive systems as more ethical when the system's intended outcomes align with their expectations and strategies [12]. In the context of persuasive health applications, risk literacy emerges as a vital component in fostering user trust [17]. Risk literacy refers to an individual's ability to understand, interpret, and make informed decisions about risks in various contexts. It involves assessing probabilities, weighing potential consequences, and making reasoned judgments to navigate uncertain situations effectively [17]. Participants suggested incorporating strategies to inform users about the persuasive elements embedded in the app. These insights align with findings by Benner et al., who observed that transparent communication within applications can enhance users' ethical perception of the system [5].

Visual Information Presentation. Visual information presentation is crucial for enhancing clarity and understanding in persuasive systems, particularly when conveying consent and data usage. Participants noted that design features like checklist-style bullet points and color coding can improve users' understanding of consent-related information. This aligns with previous research highlighting "consent fatigue", where users consent without fully understanding due to poorly presented information [48]. To address this, participants recommended using visual aids like short-form videos to enhance users' risk literacy and build trust. Such multimedia elements simplify complex information, improve comprehension, and support ethical perception by clarifying data practices [21]. Participants also noted that vulnerable groups, such as older adults and those with accessibility needs, may be more susceptible to manipulative designs. This emphasizes the need for ethical visual communication to reduce the impact of dark patterns and ensure transparency in user choices [18]. Effective visual communication can mitigate these negative effects, reinforcing ethical design practices [59] [50]. The following extract reflects this.

> Or maybe explaining what they're collecting in forms of like short videos could also help. I think short-form videos could also help. OK, this is the data that we're collecting and maybe present it in a nice, presentable manner that could help in user gain trust. Another option is to visualize what they're doing with the data (P6).

This suggestion highlights the potential of engaging multimedia formats to communicate complex data practices more effectively. Implementing strategies such as short videos or data visualizations could not only improve user comprehension but also empower users by making data collection processes more transparent, ultimately fostering greater trust in the persuasive system. Previous studies, particularly in medicine have identified that the use of videos for consent information is effective [25, 27]. While these visual aids are likely to increase user awareness of a system's intent, further research is needed to explore their impact on adoption rates and the overall effectiveness of persuasive messaging.

Design Considerations. Some of the design suggestions made by the participants when providing consent within persuasive systems are summarized below.

- Use short-form videos to visualize the usage of data.
- Use keyworded consent forms with words in bold or colors to highlight the persuasive strategy used.

– Use bullet points with potential buttons and toggle options to allow for permissions and then use an alternative button to redirect to the full terms and conditions.
– Have visualizations of what the data is being used for,
– By the creation and usage of a standardized rating system, persuasive products could be labeled with symbols or letters to indicate levels of data usage, privacy, and potential persuasive strategies, similar to movie ratings. This system would provide users with at-a-glance information, promoting informed decision-making.

4.2 RQ 2: Autonomy

Choice of Users in Navigating the System. Participants expressed concerns that persuasive systems frequently restrict user autonomy through specific design tactics, such as making unsubscribing or opting-out processes intentionally challenging to navigate, thereby encouraging continued use. This aligns with Reactance Theory [9], which suggests that perceived restrictions on freedom can provoke adverse reactions [46]. Participants noted that increasing user access to information and allowing genuine choice in navigating the system could enhance agency and reduce resistance, supporting Self-Determination Theory [15], which emphasizes that autonomy and voluntary choice foster user trust and engagement. This finding is supported by the work of Sanchez et al. [50] where participants who were UX experts reported that choice in navigating a system increases user agency. The following extract reflects on this.

> *Like it doesn't give the users freedom to it gives the users freedom to cancel the subscription. But in some cases users forget to cancel and there is no reminder or option. That's a kind of strategy for user to renew that subscription over time[...] but I think there are also some like a good strategy example is that they will give you a notification before that subscription or that free trial is is failed (P9).*

A recurring issue was systems restricting user choice by making beneficial options less accessible, raising concerns about manipulative design through intentional friction. For example, a subscription service may make cancellation difficult by burying it in obscure menus or requiring multiple steps, discouraging users from opting out. Providers may do this to maximize profits, increase engagement, or nudge users toward certain behaviors, often leveraging dark patterns. While this benefits the provider, it can come at the expense of user autonomy and transparency. Participants debated whether such tactics were equally questionable across contexts, contrasting e-commerce platforms with user-centered applications like Duolingo, which focus on goals like language learning. This echoes ethical concerns from Nudge Theory [57] and the Capability Approach [52], which advocate for systems that enhance user capabilities and freedom of choice. Autonomy in design was seen as critical for trust, particularly in high-stakes contexts like financial transactions, where options to undo or seek support after errors are essential. However, some participants worried that extensive autonomy might dilute persuasive intent and reduce engagement. Self-nudging principles [47] address this balance, suggesting user-defined safeguards to maintain persuasion while preserving agency.

> *if there is any payment-related issue involved, there should be an option to remove my card or like to add my card. It should be like one simple step (P2).*

> *I mean, if you don't click on this button you cannot go to the next page and that is aggressive. So you could just like you could include buttons like them being able to skip (P4)*

From a design perspective, participants advocated for accessible UI features, such as adjustable font sizes and audio or visual cues, particularly to support older users or those with specific accessibility needs. Eight out of fourteen participants emphasized that customization in persuasive systems could allow users to select their preferred level of influence, aligning with Self-Determination Theory's focus on autonomy-supportive environments that respect users' preferences and enhance engagement [54].

Furthermore, participants identified that user's should have the choice to customize preferences. This is consistent with the tailoring principle used in many persuasive technologies [42]. However, the persuasive principle of prompting may cause annoyance and users perceive the system to be unethical when they are unable to modify the frequency of the notification.

> *OK, if I go beyond this, then I want to get some notification. Otherwise I don't want to get notification the person has to have that autonomy over the system, that if I want to pause the notification for a certain period of time (P8)*

Design Considerations. Some of the design suggestions made by the participants to improve autonomy within persuasive systems are summarized below.

- Allow users to customize notification frequency and the level of persuasive messaging to suit their personal preferences.
- Ensure that user-beneficial options are easily accessible by avoiding the use of smaller or grayed-out buttons that obscure these options.
- Gather user feedback after interactions with key features, especially those designed to persuade or guide users toward specific actions.
- Send reminders via notifications for time-sensitive actions, such as the end of a free trial, to ensure users are well-informed and can make proactive choices.
- Minimize friction in opting out of features or actions, making the process as straightforward as possible to respect user autonomy.
- Offer users the option to defer actions, providing flexibility and accommodating users who may want to revisit choices at a later time.

4.3   RQ3: Data Privacy and Security

Selective Data Sharing and Flexibility. Participants highlighted that persuasive systems often function within interconnected networks, where data sharing aids in algorithm optimization and product development, consistent with previous research [31]. They emphasized the need for mechanisms that allow users to selectively share or opt out of sharing sensitive data and to download shared data for reassurance, fostering trust. This aligns with findings [49] that user autonomy over data sharing reduces exploitation and enhances agency. These insights are rooted in Decisional Autonomy Theory, which advocates for empowering users to make informed decisions [63]. Systems enabling selective data sharing and retrieval uphold ethical design principles, reducing coercion and enhancing trust. Integrating such mechanisms addresses ethical concerns and promotes user-centered design in persuasive systems. The following extracts reflect these findings.

> *They can probably add what kind of data you're collecting and maybe you have the option to opt out of some data points (P12).*

> *Making it easy to download your data if you wanna know what sort of data they have collected and delete it. If you decide to just be done with it knowing that you have that option that's also a kind of a way that reassures the users as well (P9).*

The following extract suggests that not only should users be provided the option to change the privacy settings but the system should also provide the users guidelines on how that action can be done.

> *So one of the key features that can be included to ensure data privacy is and security is giving the users an option to change it at anytime they want and that needs to be available in the settings option or in the help center. There needs to be direct directions that where they can, how they can turn it off or if it can be turned off or not (P3).*

Communication. A key theme across all participants was the importance of clear communication regarding data usage and privacy policies in persuasive systems. Participants emphasized that systems should explicitly inform users about data collection and its use in persuasive strategies to build trust and avoid concerns about manipulation. This aligns with Communication Privacy Management (CPM) Theory, which highlights the importance of individuals controlling their private information and understanding its sharing [43]. Clear privacy policies empower users to make informed decisions, enhancing trust and supporting autonomy. Gamification was suggested as an effective strategy for communicating these practices, consistent with Boucca et al. [8].

> *Like educating the user on how they're using the data and sort of gamifying it. Like maybe they have a certain set of flashcards or lessons that you know*

if you just read through they will give you like a $3.00 gift voucher or $5.00 gift voucher like something like that can be an interesting addition when the a company wants to collect data or educate users (P11).

Design Considerations

- Easy options to delete or to download the data that was shared
- Using a gamified approach or using monetary incentives to inform the user about data usage
- Add the details of the certifications or protocols on data privacy and security that the system uses

4.4 RQ4: Transparency

Clear Communication for Ensuring the User's Decision-Making. Participants emphasized that transparent communication is vital in persuasive systems. The system should clearly inform users about the type and extent of data being collected. The use of accessible and precise language was highlighted as a key factor in fostering trust and facilitating user understanding. This aligns with the Transparency and Control Framework (TCF), which underscores the importance of providing users with clear, accessible information through simple and understandable language. Such practices not only build trust but also empower users to make informed decisions [41].

And I definitely think copywriting is one thing that is one kind of design consideration that should be made (P1).

Participants emphasized the need for tailoring communication in persuasive systems to meet the needs of different user groups, reducing the risk of alienating vulnerable users. Personalized communication can address issues of dissatisfaction, as noted by Sattarov et al., where vulnerable users struggle to understand persuasive technologies [51]. The Digital Divide Theory further highlights disparities in technology access and usability, leading to inequitable experiences [61]. By implementing personalized strategies, persuasive systems can enhance inclusivity, trust, and usability, ensuring equitable and effective experiences for diverse users.

So things that oh, they can sign up with a particular maybe accounts like we can sign up with Twitter. This is important as we (younger people) can sign up just as easily compared to older people. Yeah. So I want to just like define the kind of audience based on whatever future use or what to persuade them to use (P13).

Participants emphasized transparency as crucial for trust in persuasive systems. They noted that deceptive design-such as presenting choices that are overridden by algorithms-leads to perceptions of unethical manipulation. For instance, if outcomes seem random but are biased, trust diminishes. This aligns with Binns

[6], who highlights the ethical risks of deceptive algorithms. Ensuring transparency and avoiding manipulative design are key to fostering trust in persuasive technologies.

> *When I'm doing a lottery, I get the maximum benefit every time, how can I trust it? I think if you are showing me the lottery option then show me that ok like you use some random algorithm. Just don't go for the maximum one always (P13).*

Moreover, participants identified that many persuasive systems should provide algorithmic transparency in deciding how the recommendations or strategies in the persuasive system are made. It was highlighted that even if users do not have the ability to understand the algorithm, there should be transparency about the algorithm. Annay et al. explore the concept of algorithmic transparency and emphasize its limitations while highlighting the need for ethical considerations in system design [1].

> *I think users don't have the capacity to judge the algorithms that are used, but they deserve to know (P11).*

Design Considerations. Some of the suggested design considerations are as follows.

– Option to get reviews from the user for each of the aspects like customer support or certain product features
– Recommendation algorithms to be clearly explained
– Clarity in the use of language in persuasive messaging
– Make certain actions more noticeable and give the user more freedom through having options like a secondary button
– Ensure diverse user representation in datasets and tailor interventions for fairness and accessibility.
– Prioritize non-monetary benefits like personalization and inclusion, ensuring transparency in user choices.

5   Discussion

This study provides critical insights into ethical and trustworthy persuasive technology design, focusing on consent, autonomy, data privacy, and transparency. It highlights key ethical dilemmas and proposes strategies for balancing persuasion with user rights and trust.

5.1   Consent and Communication

Participants highlighted consent fatigue due to lengthy and complex consent forms, aligning with prior research [13]. Users prefer concise, visually enhanced consent dialogs [30]. A key contribution is a standardized rating system for data privacy, inspired by blockchain applications [53], which requires further exploration in persuasive systems. Future studies should assess the effectiveness of such rating systems in real-world applications and explore alternative ways of presenting consent information to minimize fatigue while ensuring comprehension.

5.2   Autonomy and User Choice

Manipulative design practices create an unequal choice burden, undermining autonomy, as highlighted by Hassan et al. [26]. While customization aids autonomy [38], excessive options can overwhelm users, shifting usability responsibility onto them. A balance between system defaults and user control is necessary. Industry-standard rating systems, such as MARS [56], provide a model for evaluating persuasive systems. Regulatory frameworks like IARC, PEGI, and ESRB [4] could inform the development of standardized rating approaches for persuasive technologies. Additionally, the role of adaptive systems that dynamically adjust based on user preferences should be explored further to enhance autonomy while minimizing cognitive burden.

5.3   Transparency and Persuasion

Transparency is critical for trust, as reflected in frameworks like TCF [41]. However, transparency may reduce persuasion effectiveness [23]. Gamification could balance transparency with engagement, aligning persuasive goals with user values [16]. More research is needed to identify which gamification techniques can effectively balance transparency while maintaining persuasive impact. Future work should examine how different transparency levels affect user decision-making and long-term engagement in persuasive systems.

5.4   Ethical Perception and Trustworthiness

Trust in persuasive technologies depends on user control, company reputation, and system flexibility. The ability to reverse actions aligns with Nielsen's usability heuristics [40]. Allowing users to modify self-set goals prevents entrapment and fosters engagement [48]. Trust also varies by company, as seen in user perceptions of brands like Apple and Meta. Research by Sanchez et al. [49] highlights the role of company reputation in digital trust, particularly in financial transactions. Further research is necessary to assess how corporate transparency, privacy policies, and ethical design practices influence long-term user trust and system adoption.

5.5   Regulatory and Broader Considerations

Regulatory frameworks, such as GDPR [14], must evolve to address the complexity of persuasive technologies. Designers should follow ethical standards, particularly in sensitive domains like healthcare and finance. Cross-disciplinary collaborations among HCI researchers, ethicists, and policymakers are crucial. While this study relies on expert focus groups, future research should incorporate broader participant samples [61]. Emerging technologies like AI and XR introduce new ethical challenges, including algorithmic bias and diminished user agency [1]. Iterative prototyping and user studies can help refine ethical design principles. Additionally, policymakers should consider mechanisms for auditing persuasive technologies to ensure compliance with ethical guidelines and prevent manipulative practices.

6   Conclusion

This study highlights key considerations for ethical persuasive technologies, emphasizing consent, autonomy, transparency, and data privacy. Addressing consent fatigue, manipulative design, and algorithmic opacity fosters trust and ethical engagement. Future research should explore diverse contexts and validate these recommendations through real-world implementations to ensure inclusive and effective system design. Furthermore, ongoing assessments of ethical design principles through empirical studies will be necessary to adapt to technological advancements and evolving user expectations.

References

1. Ananny, M., Crawford, K.: Seeing without knowing: limitations of the transparency ideal and its application to algorithmic accountability. New Media Soc. **20**(3), 973–989 (2018)
2. Baldwin, R.: From regulation to behaviour change: giving nudge the third degree. Mod. Law Rev. **77**(6), 831–857 (2014)
3. Barev, T.J., Janson, A.: Towards an integrative understanding of privacy nudging–systematic review and research agenda (2019)
4. Baumel, A., Faber, K., Mathur, N., Kane, J.M., Muench, F.: Enlight: a comprehensive quality and therapeutic potential evaluation tool for mobile and web-based ehealth interventions. J. Med. Internet Res. **19**(3), e82 (2017)
5. Benner, D., Schöbel, S.M., Janson, A., Leimeister, J.M.: How to achieve ethical persuasive design: a review and theoretical propositions for information systems. AIS Trans. Hum.-Comput. Interact. **14**(4), 548–577 (2022)
6. Binns, R., Van Kleek, M., Veale, M., Lyngs, U., Zhao, J., Shadbolt, N.: 'It's reducing a human being to a percentage' perceptions of justice in algorithmic decisions. In: Proceedings of the 2018 CHI Conference on Human Factors in Computing Systems, pp. 1–14 (2018)
7. Blohm, I., Leimeister, J.M.: Gamification: design of it-based enhancing services for motivational support and behavioral change. Bus. Inf. Syst. Eng. **5**, 275–278 (2013)
8. Bouça, M.: Mobile communication, gamification and ludification. In: MindTrek, pp. 295–301 (2012)
9. Brehm, J.W.: A theory of psychological reactance (1966)

10. Burr, C., Cristianini, N., Ladyman, J.: An analysis of the interaction between intelligent software agents and human users. Mind. Mach. **28**(4), 735–774 (2018)
11. California Secretary of State: Qualified statewide ballot measures (2020). https://www.sos.ca.gov/elections/ballot-measures/qualified-ballot-measures.   Accessed 2024
12. Cemiloglu, D., Gurgun, S., Arden-Close, E., Jiang, N., Ali, R.: Explainability as a psychological inoculation: building resistance to digital persuasion in online gambling through explainable interfaces. Int. J. Hum.–Comput. Interact. 1–19 (2023)
13. Choi, H., Park, J., Jung, Y.: The role of privacy fatigue in online privacy behavior. Comput. Hum. Behav. **81**, 42–51 (2018)
14. Council, N.C.: Deceived by design, how tech companies use dark patterns to discourage us from exercising our rights to privacy. Norwegian Consumer Council Report (2018)
15. Deci, E.L., Ryan, R.M.: Intrinsic Motivation and Self-determination in Human Behavior. Springer, Cham (2013)
16. Deterding, S., Dixon, D., Khaled, R., Nacke, L.: From game design elements to gamefulness: defining gamification. In: Proceedings of the 15th International Academic MindTrek Conference: Envisioning Future Media Environments, pp. 9–15 (2011)
17. DeWalt, D.A., Boone, R.S., Pignone, M.P.: Literacy and its relationship with self-efficacy, trust, and participation in medical decision making. Am. J. Health Behav. **31**(1), S27–S35 (2007)
18. Drew, L., et al.: Designing the interface between research, learning and teaching. Des. Res. Q. **2**(3), 1–5 (2007)
19. Fogg, B.J., Hreha, J.: Persuasive technology (2012)
20. Friedman, B.: Human Values and the Design of Computer Technology, no. 72. Cambridge University Press (1997)
21. Garcia-Retamero, R., Cokely, E.T.: Designing visual aids that promote risk literacy: a systematic review of health research and evidence-based design heuristics. Hum. Factors **59**(4), 582–627 (2017)
22. Gasser, R., Brodbeck, D., Degen, M., Luthiger, J., Wyss, R., Reichlin, S.: Persuasiveness of a mobile lifestyle coaching application using social facilitation. In: IJsselsteijn, W.A., de Kort, Y., Midden, C., Eggen, B., van den Hoven, E. (eds.) PERSUASIVE 2006. LNCS, vol. 3962, pp. 27–38. Springer, Heidelberg (2006). https://doi.org/10.1007/11755494_5
23. Gheorghiu, A.V., Roman, V., Petruca, I.: Influence, persuasion, influence peddling, lobby and decision transparency in public institutions. Int. J. Commun. Res. **11**(3), 209–222 (2021)
24. Gray, C.M., Kou, Y., Battles, B., Hoggatt, J., Toombs, A.L.: The dark (patterns) side of UX design. In: Proceedings of the 2018 CHI Conference on Human Factors in Computing Systems, pp. 1–14 (2018)
25. Hall, E.W., et al.: Use of videos improves informed consent comprehension in web-based surveys among internet-using men who have sex with men: a randomized controlled trial. J. Med. Internet Res. **19**(3), e64 (2017)
26. Hassan, L., Hamari, J.: Gameful civic engagement: a review of the literature on gamification of e-participation. Gov. Inf. Q. **37**(3), 101461 (2020)
27. Hood, C.A., Hope, T., Dove, P.: Videos, photographs, and patient consent. BMJ **316**(7136), 1009–1011 (1998)
28. Huda, M.: Empowering application strategy in the technology adoption: insights from professional and ethical engagement. J. Sci. Technol. Policy Manag. **10**(1), 172–192 (2019)

29. Jacobs, N.: Two ethical concerns about the use of persuasive technology for vulnerable people. Bioethics **34**(5), 519–526 (2020)

30. Koch, S., Altpeter, B., Johns, M.: The {OK} is not enough: a large scale study of consent dialogs in smartphone applications. In: 32nd USENIX Security Symposium (USENIX Security 2023), pp. 5467–5484 (2023)

31. Kühler, M.: Exploring the phenomenon and ethical issues of AI paternalism in health apps. Bioethics **36**(2), 194–200 (2022)

32. Luguri, J., Strahilevitz, L.J.: Shining a light on dark patterns. J. Legal Anal. **13**(1), 43–109 (2021)

33. Macey, J., Hamari, J.: Gamcog: a measurement instrument for miscognitions related to gamblification, gambling, and video gaming. Psychol. Addict. Behav. **34**(1), 242 (2020)

34. Maedche, A., et al.: AI-based digital assistants: opportunities, threats, and research perspectives. Bus. Inf. Syst. Eng. **61**, 535–544 (2019)

35. Mathur, A., et al.: Dark patterns at scale: findings from a crawl of 11k shopping websites. Proc. ACM Hum.-Comput. Interact. **3**(CSCW), 1–32 (2019)

36. Mathur, A., Kshirsagar, M., Mayer, J.: What makes a dark pattern... dark? Design attributes, normative considerations, and measurement methods. In: Proceedings of the 2021 CHI Conference on Human Factors in Computing Systems, pp. 1–18 (2021)

37. Muller, M.J., Druin, A.: Participatory design: the third space in human–computer interaction. In: Human Computer Interaction Handbook, pp. 1125–1153. CRC Press (2012)

38. Murmann, P., Karegar, F.: From design requirements to effective privacy notifications: empowering users of online services to make informed decisions. Int. J. Hum.-Comput. Interact. **37**(19), 1823–1848 (2021)

39. U.S.S.D.F. for Nebraska: Senators introduce bipartisan legislation to ban manipulative dark patterns (2019). http://www.fischer.senate.gov/public/index.cfm/2019/4/senators-introduce-bipartisan-legislation-to-ban-manipulative-dark-patterns

40. Nielsen, J.: Enhancing the explanatory power of usability heuristics. In: Proceedings of the SIGCHI Conference on Human Factors in Computing Systems, pp. 152–158 (1994)

41. Nissenbaum, H.: A contextual approach to privacy online. Daedalus **140**(4), 32–48 (2011)

42. Oyebode, O., Alqahtani, F., Orji, R.: Exploring for possible effect of persuasive strategy implementation choices: towards tailoring persuasive technologies. In: International Conference on Persuasive Technology, pp. 145–163. Springer, Cham (2022)

43. Petronio, S.: Boundaries of Privacy: Dialectics of Disclosure. Suny Press (2002)

44. Purpura, S., Schwanda, V., Williams, K., Stubler, W., Sengers, P.: Fit4life: the design of a persuasive technology promoting healthy behavior and ideal weight. In: Proceedings of the SIGCHI Conference on Human Factors in Computing Systems, pp. 423–432 (2011)

45. Rahman, P., Adaji, I.: Ethics in persuasive technologies: a systematic literature review. In: Proceedings of the International Conference on Mobile and Ubiquitous Multimedia, pp. 106–118 (2024)

46. Rains, S.A., Turner, M.M.: Psychological reactance and persuasive health communication: a test and extension of the intertwined model. Hum. Commun. Res. **33**(2), 241–269 (2007)

47. Reijula, S., Hertwig, R.: Self-nudging and the citizen choice architect. Behav. Public Policy **6**(1), 119–149 (2022)

48. Royakkers, L., Timmer, J., Kool, L., van Est, R.: Societal and ethical issues of digitization. Ethics Inf. Technol. 1–16 (2018). https://doi.org/10.1007/s10676-018-9452-x

49. Sánchez-Adame, L.M., Monroy-Rodríguez, G., Mendoza, S., Decouchant, D., Mateos-Papis, A.P.: Framework for ethically designed microtransactions in the metaverse. IEEE Access (2023)

50. Sánchez Chamorro, L., Bongard-Blanchy, K., Koenig, V.: Ethical tensions in UX design practice: exploring the fine line between persuasion and manipulation in online interfaces. In: Proceedings of the 2023 ACM Designing Interactive Systems Conference, pp. 2408–2422 (2023)

51. Sattarov, F., Nagel, S.: Building trust in persuasive gerontechnology: user-centric and institution-centric approaches. Gerontechnology **18**(1) (2019)

52. Sen, A.: Development as Freedom Knopf. New York (1999)

53. Shaker, M., Shams Aliee, F., Fotohi, R.: Online rating system development using blockchain-based distributed ledger technology. Wirel. Netw. **27**(3), 1715–1737 (2021). https://doi.org/10.1007/s11276-020-02514-w

54. Sheldon, K.M., Elliot, A.J.: Goal striving, need satisfaction, and longitudinal well-being: the self-concordance model. J. Pers. Soc. Psychol. **76**(3), 482 (1999)

55. Skjuve, M., Haugstveit, I.M., Følstad, A., Brandtzaeg, P.: Help! is my chatbot falling into the uncanny valley? An empirical study of user experience in human-chatbot interaction. Hum. Technol. **15**(1), 30–54 (2019)

56. Stoyanov, S.R., Hides, L., Kavanagh, D.J., Zelenko, O., Tjondronegoro, D., Mani, M.: Mobile app rating scale: a new tool for assessing the quality of health mobile apps. JMIR Mhealth Uhealth **3**(1), e3422 (2015)

57. Thaler, R.H.: Nudge: Improving Decisions About Health. Wealth and Happiness/Yale (2008)

58. Timmer, J., Kool, L., van Est, R.: Ethical challenges in emerging applications of persuasive technology. In: MacTavish, T., Basapur, S. (eds.) PERSUASIVE 2015. LNCS, vol. 9072, pp. 196–201. Springer, Cham (2015). https://doi.org/10.1007/978-3-319-20306-5_18

59. Tufte, E.R.: The visual display of quantitative information. J. Healthcare Qual. (JHQ) **7**(3), 15 (1985)

60. Tuncer, R., Sergeeva, A., Bongard-Blanchy, K., Distler, V., Doublet, S., Koenig, V.: Running out of time (RS): effects of scarcity cues on perceived task load, perceived benevolence and user experience on e-commerce sites. Behav. Inf. Technol. **43**(11), 2281–2299 (2024)

61. Van Deursen, A., Van Dijk, J.: Internet skills and the digital divide. New Media Soc. **13**(6), 893–911 (2011)

62. Weinmann, M., Schneider, C., Brocke, J.: Digital nudging. Bus. Inf. Syst. Eng. **58**, 433–436 (2016)

63. WsrN, I.: Privacy and Freedom. by Alan F. Westin, p. 487. Atheneum Publishers, New York (1967) 10.00

Effect of Competitive and Cooperative Learning Contexts in Controversial Information Search: Preliminary Results

Cheyenne Dosso[1]([⊠]), Mohamed Benlamine[2], Tiffany Morisseau[3], Christophe Heintz[4], and Jean-Sébastien Vayre[5]

[1] University Côte d'Azur, LAPCOS, Nice, France
cheyenne.dosso@univ-cotedazur.fr
[2] Higher Colleges of Technology, Dubai, United Arab Emirates
mbenlamine@hct.ac.ae
[3] University Paris Cité, LAPEA, Paris, France
tiffany.morisseau@u-paris.fr
[4] Central European University, Vienna, Austria
heintzc@ceu.edu
[5] University Côte d'Azur, GREDEG, Nice, France
jean-sebastien.vayre@univ-cotedazur.fr

Abstract. Context. Information and Communication Technologies (e.g., search engines, AI) disseminate a large volume of information, the quality of which can vary, particularly when the search topics are controversial. To manage both the quantity and quality of the information they process, users must adopt effective search strategies while maintaining epistemic vigilance. **Objectives.** This study examines the effects of the learning context (cooperation vs. competition) on search strategies (exploration-exploitation), online epistemic vigilance, as well as knowledge gain and attitude change regarding the controversial topic of animal protein consumption (meat, milk, eggs). **Method.** Forty-seven participants have currently taken part in the study, with data collection still ongoing. Twenty-six participants were assigned to the competition condition (preparing a debate), and twenty-one to the cooperation condition (preparing a discussion). All participants had 20 min to search for information to prepare for their respective exchanges. **Results.** The main findings show that a cooperative context leads users to pursue mastery goals, prompting them to adopt deeper content exploitation strategies and acquire more knowledge by the end of the search compared to individuals in a competitive context. Those in the competitive context tend to explore more, learn more superficially, pursue performance goals, and more frequently re-exploit the same content in their queries to find arguments that corroborate their viewpoint. Surprisingly, competitors still shift their attitudes toward animal suffering following the information search, whereas cooperators tend to polarize their initial attitudes on this issue. **Conclusion.** This study has implications for the domain of traditional ICTs and generative AI as persuasive technologies.

Keywords: Persuasive technology · exploration-exploitation strategies · epistemic vigilance · achievement goals · cooperation-competition · controversial topic

© The Author(s), under exclusive license to Springer Nature Switzerland AG 2025
K. T. Win et al. (Eds.): PERSUASIVE 2025, LNCS 15711, pp. 89–104, 2025.
https://doi.org/10.1007/978-3-031-94959-3_7

1 Introduction

To address the deterioration of global democracy over the last decade, with increasing criticism of traditional media outlets [1], users are turning to Information and Communication Technologies (ICTs) to make democratic and political decisions on often divisive and controversial topics (e.g., climate change, legality of abortion, immigration, wars, consumption habits). General search engines like Google and generative AIs like ChatGPT have become persuasive tools that can influence users' attitudes and behaviors through shared information content [2]. However, this content consists of an overwhelming amount of information with highly variable quality (i.e., informational disorder), making human-ICT interactions ineffective for learning purposes [3] and contributing to misinformation, the proliferation of conspiracy theories, and the broader "information war" [4]. For instance, recent years have been marked by a series of crises and events (e.g., the 2016 U.S. presidential election, the January 6, 2021 Capitol insurrection, Brexit, the COVID-19 pandemic) that have raised questions about the neutrality of the internet and social media in the dissemination of information [5]. One of the main drivers of this manipulation of information is the highly competitive international landscape of political discourse within democratic digital societies (e.g., the power and influence of certain lobbies, associations, and coalitions [6, 7] which may lead individuals to compromise the neutrality and objectivity of the information they disseminate in service of competition [8]. From the perspective of users processing information shared online, a competitive context can lead to more superficial learning outcomes that serve performance goals, rather than fostering deeper learning outcomes aligned with mastery goals, typically associated with cooperative contexts [9].

In addressing this societal challenge, this preliminary study aims to understand how different learning contexts (competitive vs. cooperative) impact users' information search strategies, their epistemic vigilance regarding the sources and content they process, their knowledge acquisition, and their attitude change regarding a controversial topic (i.e., the consumption of animal proteins). From an applied perspective, this study sheds new light on persuasion and communication strategies driven by either competition or cooperation, paving the way for the development of innovative systems for managing controversy and persuasion.

1.1 Information Search Activity

The cognitive activity of information search (IS) through a search engine involves users navigating three cyclical and iterative stages to achieve their learning goals [10]:

(1) **Planning/(Re)planning:** This stage involves the development of an initial mental representation of the goal, based on mapping the task requirements, the characteristics of the learning context, and the activation of prior knowledge and metacognitive knowledge in working memory regarding the topic and search strategies to be employed. The goal is then translated into keywords and submitted as a query to the search engine.

(2) **Evaluation and Selection of Search Engine Results Pages (SERPs):** Here, the user mentally compares the content of the result pages with their mental representation of the learning goal to decide which results to select for more in-depth processing.

(3) **Processing and In-Depth Reading of Documents:** This phase focuses on under-standing and extracting information from sources (e.g., websites, blogs, social media) to integrate it into long-term memory as knowledge.

In a complex informational environment like the Web, which is characterized by its richness (i.e., vast quantity) and variety (i.e., diverse and sometimes controversial or contradictory arguments and perspectives), the cognitive cost of IS activity—including comprehending content [11] and assessing the epistemic quality of information [12] — is particularly high. To navigate this complexity, users must engage in effective search strategies.

1.2 Information Search Strategies

To manage the volume of information they process and learn efficiently, users employ different strategies that allow them to either explore or exploit the search space [10, 13]. The exploration strategies involve broad navigation of SERPs to cover a wider search space, identify new areas for investigation, and acquire a basic but diverse understand-ing of a topic directly from the SERP interface [14]. Users formulate queries that are thematically and semantically distant from one another [10]. In other words, exploration tends to result in more superficial understanding, yielding general knowledge [15]. The exploitation strategies entail more focused navigation along specific paths of informa-tion, processing documents in greater depth to gain complex, conceptual knowledge about a targeted topic. Queries submitted to the search engine are thematically and semantically closer to one another. Exploitation generally leads to a deeper understand-ing of a topic, where the more time a user spends reading a document, the more their knowledge increases after the search [16, 17].

While exploration and exploitation strategies aid users in navigating the vast infor-mational landscape of the Web, they must also exercise epistemic vigilance regarding the credibility of sources and the reliability of their content.

1.3 Epistemic Vigilance

According to [18], epistemic vigilance model, users begin by evaluating the plausibility of information [19] through a mental comparison of their prior knowledge and beliefs with information encountered online. This process determines the perceived coherence of the content.

Richter and Maier [20] refer to this as Epistemic Monitoring in their Two-Steps Model, where users assess the coherence, validity, and reliability of information based on their prior knowledge and beliefs. They propose that users engage in more controlled evaluations of information inconsistencies only when specific conditions are met, such as high epistemic motivation (i.e., the desire to obtain a more accurate representation of reality), sufficient knowledge of the topic, and adequate cognitive resources to engage in information control strategies through multiple document reading [21].

When evaluating source credibility, the Elaboration Likelihood Model (ELM) by [22] posits that users' motivation and knowledge levels determine whether source char-acteristics (e.g., expertise, benevolence) are assessed in-depth. Within digital contexts and human-system interactions, these theoretical models are explored through sourcing skills, which refer to the ability to evaluate online sources and content critically. These skills support epistemic self-regulation when interacting with diverse information from multiple documents shared by varied sources [23, 24]. However, the extent to which users engage in controlled epistemic vigilance and effective search strategies can depend on their learning context and search goals.

1.4 Search Context and Goals: Cooperation-Mastery vs. Competition-Performance

According to the Purposeful Reading Theory [25], users select their reading, processing, and evaluation strategies based on their initial mental representation of the task at hand and the learning context in which they are situated. For instance, [26, 27] show that a context conducive to high-level learning—such as performing tasks for academic purposes rather than personal or leisure activities—leads users to engage in deeper search strategies and to be more attentive when evaluating controversial information.

Social Interdependence Theory [28, 29] distinguishes between two types of learning contexts. Competition involves obstructing others' actions, thereby complicating the achievement of shared goals through interpersonal rivalry. Cooperation, in contrast, entails facilitating others' actions to enable group success through collective effort. While competition drives individuals to impose their viewpoints and pursue defense-oriented [30] and performance-oriented goals (emphasizing social comparison and demonstrating competence), cooperation enhances individuals' motivation to engage in a deeper understanding of diverse perspectives to achieve mastery goals [9, 29, 31]. Furthermore, cooperation fosters greater epistemic vigilance regarding the diversity of communicated information [32, 33], whereas in competitive contexts, individuals are more susceptible to confirmation bias, reinforcing their preexisting attitudes and viewpoints regardless of the actual quality of the information [34, 35].

2   Current Study

In today's highly competitive digital society, users engage in daily information seeking (IS) to acquire knowledge and make informed decisions about their well-being and lives in general. The present study aims to understand how competitive and cooperative learning contexts influence individual motivations to pursue mastery versus performance goals during IS on controversial topics. More specifically, if the IS context affects users' search and learning strategies as well as their level of epistemic vigilance [25–27], then a competitive context, where individuals pursue performance goals, should lead to more superficial strategies (exploration). In this scenario, the objective is to impose one's viewpoint and amass supporting arguments without achieving a deep understanding of the topic [29, 34, 35]. Conversely, cooperation, which encourages individuals to pursue mastery goals, should promote deeper strategies (exploitation), fostering a comprehensive understanding of various arguments while enhancing epistemic vigilance [32, 33]. In this regard, three general hypotheses were investigated:

Hypothesis 1: A content exploitation strategy, representing mastery goals, will be more prevalent in cooperative contexts, while content exploration, reflecting performance goals, will dominate in competitive contexts.

Hypothesis 2: Epistemic vigilance will be stronger in cooperative settings than in competitive ones due to differing motivations for source evaluation.

Hypothesis 3: Cooperative contexts will lead to greater knowledge gains and more significant attitude changes than competitive contexts.

To test these hypotheses, the study employed a between-subjects design with the independent variable "learning context" (cooperation vs. competition), assessed across 14 dependent variables detailed in Sect. 3.4.

3 Method

3.1 Participants

A total of 47 participants took part in this study, all of whom were students at a French University from the first to the third year, representing a wide range of disciplines. Twenty-six participants were assigned to the competition condition, while twenty-one were assigned to the cooperation condition.

In the competition condition, the average age of the students was 20.88 years ($SD = 4.52$), with ages ranging from 18 to 42 years. Fourteen were male and twelve were female. In the cooperation condition, the average age of the students was 20.38 years ($SD = 2.29$), with ages ranging from 18 to 25 years. Eight participants were male, and thirteen were female.

Given that knowledge and skills in IS are known to influence the search and navigation strategies employed by users [36], a series of independent samples t-tests were conducted on several variables assessing IS knowledge and skills. The aim was to ensure that there were no significant differences on these variables between the competition group and the cooperation group. In line with this expectation, no significant differences were found between the two groups in terms of: the total number of years using the Internet ($t(45) = -0.715$; $p > .05$), self-rated knowledge in information seeking (4- point Likert scale; $t(45) = 0.372$; $p > .05$), and the total score on the Information Seeking Self-Efficacy scale ([37]; $t(45) = 1.24$; $p > .05$).

Finally, since prior knowledge on the search topic is also known to affect search and navigation strategies, the total score obtained by participants in both groups on the pre – IS MCQs was compared. No significant difference was found between the two groups ($t(45) = 0.964$; $p > .05$).

3.2 Topic and Tasks

To investigate the research objective within the context of controversy, the topic of animal protein consumption was selected. Both groups of participants were tasked with preparing either a competitive debate or a cooperative discussion in the post-IS phase on the topic of animal protein consumption. Specifically, participants were required to search the internet for up to 20 min to prepare for their exchanges. All participants had complete freedom in their IS activities, with no restrictions on the web content they accessed. To maintain ecological validity, participants were instructed to search for information as they would in their everyday lives. The learning context (competition vs. cooperation) was manipulated solely through task instructions: (1) Search for information to prepare for a competitive debate on animal protein consumption, or (2) Search for information to prepare for a cooperative discussion on animal protein consumption.

3.3 Protocol

The entire experimental protocol was previously approved by the Research Ethics Committee of the University where the researchers are based. The overall experimental protocol for this study consists of four main phases: (1) pre-experimentation phase (i.e., recruitment, signing of the informed consent form, completion of the pre-questionnaire online via the Lime Survey platform), (2) experimentation phase dedicated to IS sessions on the Internet, (3) experimentation phase dedicated to debates/discussions, and (4) post-experimentation phase (i.e., debriefing, compensation €30).

It is important to note that data collection for this study is still ongoing, and this paper focuses on the research objectives and analyses related to the second phase of experimentation, which involves IS sessions in preparation for the third phase (competitive debate or cooperative discussion in groups of 2 to 4 participants). As a result, this study will benefit from future submissions, particularly concerning the third phase of the experimental protocol, which will not be detailed in this paper.

3.4 Measures

In total, 14 dependent variables (DVs) were developed according to four categories: (a) Exploration-Exploitation strategies; (b) Epistemic Vigilance; (c) Factual Learning; and (d) Attitudes.

Exploration-Exploitation strategies. To describe the **navigation behaviors** employed by participants during their search session, we calculated: the proportion of navigational exploration **(DV1)** and the proportion of time spent on navigational exploration **(DV2).**

For **DV1,** we calculated the total number of all new SERPs (Search Engine Results Pages) and new documents (e.g., websites, online PDFs, blogs, articles, etc.) visited based on the search logs to determine the total number of new URLs accessed by participants during the search session. We then created a measure of navigational exploration proportion by dividing the total number of new SERPs visited by the total number of new URLs visited (SERPs + documents). Thus, the sum of the proportion of navigational exploration and the proportion of navigational exploitation equals 1.

For **DV2,** we calculated the total time spent on new SERPs and new documents based on the search logs to determine the total time spent on new URLs during the search session. The proportion of time spent on navigational exploration was then calculated by dividing the total time spent on new SERPs by the total time spent on new URLs (SERPs + documents). Thus, the sum of the proportion of time dedicated to navigational exploration and navigational exploitation equals 1.

To understand the **thematic learning strategies (exploration-exploitation)** employed by participants during their search session, three dependent variables were developed: the proportion of thematic exploration (DV3), the proportion of thematic exploitation (DV4), and the proportion of thematic re-exploitation (DV5). After extracting all the queries produced by participants from the search logs, a human annotation method for the queries was implemented following the approach described in [10, 38]. Two independent annotators coded 10% of queries produced by the sample as exploration (1), exploitation (2), re-exploitation (3). The Cohen's Kappa coefficient was 71%, translating a correct agreement between annotators. After discussing the points of divergence, a single annotator completed coding the remaining queries of the sample.

For each participant, we first summed the total number of queries produced during the search session. Next, we divided the total number of exploration queries by the total number of all queries to calculate DV3. The same operation was repeated for the total number of exploitation queries (DV4) and the total number of re-exploitation queries (DV5). Thus, the sum of DV3, DV4, and DV5 equals 1.

Epistemic Vigilance. To determine the extent to which participants recognize, recall, and evaluate online sources and information content, four dependent variables were developed from the post-RI questionnaire.

For **DV6**, the proportion of recognized sources, participants were asked to indicate whether they remembered each document they visited during their search by responding to the question: "Do you remember this information source?" with the response options "Yes" or "No." After calculating the total number of documents visited, the total number of information sources marked as "Yes" by the participants was divided by the total number of documents visited. In this way, the sum of the proportion of recognized sources and the proportion of unrecognized sources equals 1.

For **DV7** (Mean Score of Expertise Source Evaluation) and **DV8** (Mean Score of Benevolence Source Evaluation), participants were required to evaluate each information source they remembered using a 10-item scale. The response options consisted of a 7-point Likert scale ranging from "Strongly Disagree" to "Strongly Agree". Five items were dedicated to evaluating the source's level of expertise, and five items to assessing the source's benevolence. DV7 was calculated by summing the total evaluations of the five expertise items and dividing it by the total number of recognized sources (coded as "Yes"). Similarly, DV8 was calculated by dividing the total evaluations of the five benevolence items by the total number of recognized sources.

Regarding **DV9** (Mean Number of Recalled Arguments), participants were tasked with recalling as many arguments as possible that were presented by the information sources they had consulted and remembered. DV9 is calculated by dividing the total number of recalled arguments by the total number of sources recognized by the participant.

Factual Learning. Through **DV10**, we sought to determine the participants' gain in factual knowledge regarding animal protein consumption between the pre- and post-IS phases. DV10 corresponds to the difference in total scores between the post-test (T2) and the pre-test (T1).

Attitudes. Through four dependent variables, we aimed to determine the extent and direction of changes in participants' attitudes concerning various controversial aspects related to animal protein consumption: scientific knowledge and health **(DV11)**, animal suffering and consumption habits **(DV12)**, animal suffering and slaughterhouse violence **(DV13)**, and political decisions and ecology **(DV14).**

In both the pre- and post-IS phases, participants were required to complete attitude scales with two items per controversial topic, rating their positions on a 9-point bipolar scale ranging from (-4) "Strongly Disagree" to (4) "Strongly Agree," with the midpoint labeled as "Neither Agree nor Disagree," coded as 0. The more positive the attitudes, the more the participant favored meat consumption, while more negative attitudes indicated a preference for a meat-free diet.

For each of our four dependent variables related to attitudes (DV11, DV12, DV13, and DV14), we calculated an attitude change/reinforcement index as follows (Fig. 1):

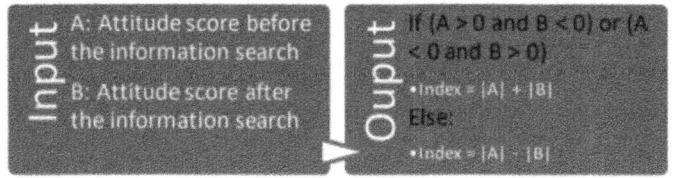

Fig. 1. Attitude change/reinforcement index calculation

The attitude change/reinforcement index can be explained as follows. First, we took the attitude scores from before (A) and after (B) the IS. We then calculated the absolute values of both scores to neutralize the signs. If there was a polarity change (i.e., a shift from positive to negative or vice versa), the index was calculated by summing the absolute values of A and B, indicating a significant shift in attitude. If there was no polarity change, the index was calculated by subtracting the absolute value of B from A, reflecting either reinforcement or a slight adjustment of the initial attitude. A positive index suggests a change in attitude, while a negative index indicates a reinforcement of the initial attitude.

4 Results

4.1 Assumption Check and Statistical Models

To investigate the three hypotheses, independent samples t-tests were conducted across the fourteen dependent variables described previously. Each dependent variable was tested for the assumption of normality (Shapiro's test) and homogeneity of variances (Levene's test). When these assumptions were violated, Welch's correction was applied to the t-test. For all analyses, the learning context (competition vs. cooperation) was the between-subjects factor. All t-test results are presented in Table 1 and all means (*SD*) are presented in Table 2.

Table 1. Summary of t-test results for the learning context (competition vs. cooperation) on all dependent variables

Measure	$t(df)$	t	p	d
Navigation behaviors				
DV1: Proportion of navigational exploration	(45)	.358	n.s	
DV2: Proportion of time spent on navigational exploration	(43.4)*	−2.148	<.05	−.629
Thematic learning				
DV3: Proportion of thematic exploration	(41.9)*	−.418	n.s	
DV4: Proportion of thematic exploitation	(40.6)*	−.809	n.s	
DV5: Proportion of thematic re-exploitation	(37.7)*	2.077	= .05	.589
Epistemic vigilance – Sources recognition and evaluation				
Measure	$t(df)$	t	p	d
DV6: Proportion of recognized sources	(36.5)*	.840	n.s	
DV7: Mean score of expertise source evaluation	(26.6)*	1.221	n.s	
DV8: Mean score of benevolence source evaluation	(24.8)*	1.419	n.s	
Epistemic vigilance – Contents and arguments recalled				
DV9: Mean number of recalled arguments	(42.2)*	−.843	n.s	
Factual learning				
DV10: Factual knowledge gain	(45)	−2.21	< .05	−.648
Attitudes changes				
DV11: Change in Attitude Toward Science and Health (SSA)	(45)	.371	n.s	
DV12: Change in Attitude Toward Animal Suffering and Consumption Habits (VAHC)	(39.5)*	1.15	n.s	

(*continued*)

Table 1. (*continued*)

Measure	$t(df)$	t	p	d
DV13: Change in Attitude Toward Animal Suffering and Slaughterhouse Violence (VASA)	(37.5)*	2.65	< .05	.751
DV14: Change in Attitude Toward Politics and Ecology (EP)	(43)*	.405	n.s	

Note. * *Welch's correction, n.s.* (not significant).

4.2 Learning Context (Cooperation vs. Competition)

Information Search Strategies (Navigational and Thematic Exploration-Exploitation). As indicated in Table 1, the learning context has a significant effect on the proportion of time participants spent engaging in navigational content exploration ($p < .05$). Specifically, Table 2 shows that participants in the competition condition dedicated more time to initiating new paths of search and examining SERPs (navigational exploration) than those in the cooperation condition. Participants in the cooperation condition spent more time deeply reading the documents they accessed and to more thoroughly process a targeted path of search (navigational exploitation).

Regarding thematic learning, Table 1 highlights that only the proportion of thematic re-exploitation is significant ($p = .05$). In the competition condition, participants tend to reuse previously generated queries more often during their search sessions and to investigate redundant learning objectives (re-exploitation) to a greater extent than in cooperative settings. In conclusion, hypothesis 1 is only partially confirmed.

Epistemic Vigilance (Sources and Contents). Regarding the variables related to epistemic vigilance (sources and arguments), the analyses revealed no significant differences for all variables. Hypothesis 2 is definitively not confirmed.

Factual Knowledge Gain and Attitudes Changes As shown in Table 1, the learning context has a significant effect on factual knowledge gain ($p < .05$). Referring to Table 2, it is observed that cooperative context leads to a greater amount of factual learning than the competitive context. This part of H3 is validated.

Regarding attitude changes, Table 1 shows a significant effect of learning context on attitudes toward animal suffering and violence in slaughterhouses (DV13; $p < .05$). Participants who cooperate tend to strengthen their pre-existing attitudes on the issue, while those who compete are more likely to change their attitudes post-IS. This part of H3 is partially confirmed.

Table 2. Means and standard deviation for all dependent depending on learning context (competition vs. cooperation)

Measure	Competition		Cooperation	
	M	SD	M	SD
Navigation behaviors				
DV1: Proportion of navigational exploration	.56	.16	.55	.16
DV2: Proportion of time spent on navigational exploration	.40	.25	.25	.24
Thematic learning				
DV3: Proportion of thematic exploration	.74	.18	.76	.19
DV4: Proportion of thematic exploitation	.17	.17	.21	.19
DV5: Proportion of thematic re-exploitation	.08	.14	.02	.07
Epistemic vigilance – Sources recognition and evaluation				
DV6: Proportion of recognized sources	.82	.23	.75	.30
DV7: Mean score of expertise source evaluation	26.5	3.14	24.5	6.93
DV8: Mean score of benevolence source evaluation	28.4	2.73	26.03	7.11
Epistemic vigilance – Contents and arguments recalled				
DV9: Mean number of recalled arguments	1.62	1.43	2	1.49
Factual learning				
DV10: Factual knowledge gain	.23	3	2.1	2.72
Attitudes				
DV11: Change in Attitude Toward Science and Health (SSA)	1.65	3.72	1.24	3.94
DV12: Change in Attitude Toward Animal Suffering and Consumption Habits (VAHC)	1.85	3.06	.71	3.58
DV13: Change in Attitude Toward Animal Suffering and Slaughterhouse Violence (VASA)	1.39	3.81	−.86	1.82
DV14: Change in Attitude Toward Politics and Ecology (EP)	.58	4.46	.14	2.85

5   Discussion, Limitations and Conclusion

This study aims to identify the effects of the learning context (cooperation vs. competition) on search strategies (exploration-exploitation strategies), online epistemic vigilance, knowledge gain and attitude changes. In line with the purposeful reading theory, the learning context in which an information search (IS) takes place determines the strategies employed as well as the level of epistemic vigilance toward information sources [25–27].

Hypothesis 1 was partially confirmed: when participants were in a cooperative context, they dedicated more time to in-depth document processing (navigational exploitation), whereas their counterparts in a competitive context spent more time exploring SERPs (exploration). These findings align with social interdependence theory [29], which suggests that cooperation fosters deeper learning by encouraging individuals to engage with multiple perspectives (mastery goal). In contrast, competition leads to more superficial learning, as the primary objective is to impose one's viewpoint on others to achieve a performance goal. Notably, participants in the competitive condition reformulated queries with similar content (thematic re-exploitation) more frequently than those in the cooperative condition. This supports previous findings indicating that competition reinforces confirmation bias [34, 35]. Indeed, competitors searched for semantically similar information, suggesting that their goal was to find supporting arguments rather than diverse perspectives to effectively defend their stance during the debate phase (performance goal).

However, the pursuit of performance goals proved detrimental to knowledge acquisition, as individuals in competitive conditions learned less than those in cooperative conditions (confirming this part of Hypothesis 3). Consistent with prior research showing that greater time spent processing documents (deep exploitation) leads to increased knowledge gain at the end of an IS session [16, 17], participants in the cooperative condition exhibited greater knowledge acquisition, as they spent more time engaging with the documents than those in the competitive condition.

In addition, although the differences in the effects of cooperation and competition on attitudes are not always statistically significant, the information searches conducted by participants in cooperative contexts tend to be more morally relevant, particularly concerning ethical and social acceptability. In contrast to competition, these searches promote the development of more positive and benevolent attitudes toward ethical issues related to animal suffering. On the competition side, the result concerning attitude change is both surprising and intriguing: competitors exhibit a shift in their attitudes toward animal suffering after the IS phase. This result aligns with cognitive dissonance theory [39] and the "meat paradox" [40], in which a conflict arises between people's positive attitudes toward animals and their meat consumption. A recent study [41] found that exposure to information about animal welfare and meat consumption triggers cognitive dissonance, which, while not necessarily altering behavior, increases motivation to avoid meat. In our study, repeated exposure to arguments in favor of both animal welfare and meat consumption among competitors seeking to defend their dietary habits may have induced dissonance, leading to attitude adjustments. This suggests that interactions with ICT can be persuasive and influence ethical attitudes, even in performance-oriented learning contexts.

Regarding epistemic vigilance, Hypothesis 2 was not confirmed, neither for sources nor for arguments. Concerning sources, it is possible that the learning context alone is insufficient to explain epistemic vigilance. Notably, the Integrated Framework of Multiple Texts (IF-MT) proposed in [42] builds on previous model of purposeful reading [25] and examines the role of cognitive-affective variables, such as individuals' pre-existing attitudes toward a topic, in their strategies for evaluating and integrating contradictory content. As explained in [43], when individuals have weak pre-existing attitudes, they tend to engage in more superficial content evaluations, whereas those with strong pre-existing attitudes are more critical and attentive to the quality of the content they read. Future analyses will need to consider this variable. Regarding argument recall, this measure was likely not representative enough of epistemic vigilance to be observed. Particularly, as data collection is ongoing, we will develop a post hoc annotation grid for arguments that will allow us to determine the extent to which the recalled arguments are polarized, moderate, or neutral and to link these to the evaluations made by the users.

To conclude, these initial results, which represent a first step towards more extensive future analyses, highlight the importance of the external learning context (cooperation vs. competition) in motivating mastery goals that lead to greater learning and performance goals that result in more superficial learning. This has significant implications for the field of traditional ICTs and generative AI. Indeed, future research should explore conversational modes between AI and users, based on competition or cooperation, in the context of controversial topics, and examine their effects on persuasion and attitude change in users. For example, one could imagine a generative AI that uses attack and defense strategies to express a viewpoint on a controversial topic, which would be less receptive to the exchange of knowledge and divergent viewpoints, as would be the case in a more cooperative exchange mode. As the study suggests, the competitive mode, which may have induced more cognitive dissonance, led to a shift in attitudes toward animal suffering. On the other hand, cooperative individuals maintained more moral attitudes. It is crucial to determine the extent to which certain modes of persuasion (competitive vs. cooperative) can lead users to adopt more moral attitude changes on controversial topics.

Acknowledgments. This work has been supported by the French government, through the UCA-JEDI Investments in the Future project managed by the National Research Agency (ANR) with the reference number ANR-15-IDEX-01. This study was performed in the Cocolab (MSHS Sud-Est – Université Côte d'Azur). The authors greatly acknowledge the Cocolab (Complexity and Cognition Lab, USR3566, Université Côte d'Azur – CNRS) and its staff.

Disclosure of Interests. The authors have no competing interests to declare that are relevant to the content of this article.

References

1. Papada, E., et al.: Defiance in the face of autocratization: Democracy report 2023. V-Dem Working Paper (2023). https://papers.ssrn.com/sol3/papers.cfm?abstract_id=4560857
2. Ghofrani, T.: The impact of new media technologies on persuasive communication in the time of global crisis. Int. J. Technol. Manag. **94**(3/4), 419–435 (2024). https://doi.org/10.1504/ijtm.2024.136420
3. Collins-Thompson, K., Hansen, P., Hauff, C.: Search as Learning. Dagstuhl Seminar Reports **7**(2), 135–162 (2017). https://doi.org/10.4230/DagRep.7.2.135
4. Benkler, Y., Faris, R., Roberts, H.: Network Propaganda. Oxford University Press eBooks (2018). https://doi.org/10.1093/oso/9780190923624.001.0001

5. Watts, D.J., Rothschild, D.M., Mobius, M.: Measuring the news and its impact on democracy. Proc. Natl. Acad. Sci. U.S.A. (2021). https://doi.org/10.1073/pnas.1912443118
6. Brulle, R.J.: Networks of opposition: A structural analysis of U.S. Climate change counter-movement coalitions 1989–2015. Sociol. Inquiry **91**(3), 603–624 (2019). https://doi.org/10.1111/soin.12333
7. Willis, R., Curato, N., Smith, G.: Deliberative democracy and the climate crisis. WIREs Climate Change (2022). https://doi.org/10.1002/wcc.759
8. Boullier, D.: Comment sortir de l'emprise des réseaux sociaux. L'ère du réchauffement médiatique. Le Passeur (2020)
9. Darnon, C., Muller, D., Schrager, S.M., Pannuzzo, N., Butera, F.: Mastery and performance goals predict epistemic and relational conflict regulation. J. Educ. Psychol. **98**(4), 766–776 (2006). https://doi.org/10.1037/0022-0663.98.4.766
10. Dosso, C., Tamine, L., Paubel, P., Chevalier, A.: Navigational and thematic exploration–exploitation trade-offs during web search: effects of prior domain knowledge, search contexts and strategies on search outcome. Behav. Inform. Technol. **43**(10), 2232–2258 (2023). https://doi.org/10.1080/0144929X.2023.2242514
11. Salmerón, L.: Search interfaces and learning about controversial topics. In: Proceedings of the 1st International Workshop on Search as Learning with Multimedia Information, pp. 1–2 (2019). https://doi.org/10.1145/3347451.3356729
12. Szegőfi, Á., Heintz, C.: Institutions of epistemic vigilance: the case of the newspaper press. Soc. Epistemol. **36**(5), 613–628 (2022). https://doi.org/10.1080/02691728.2022.2109532
13. Hardy, J.H., III., Day, E.A., Arthur, W., Jr.: Exploration-exploitation tradeoffs and information-knowledge gaps in self-regulated learning: implications for learner controlled training and development. Hum. Resour. Manag. Rev. **29**(2), 196–217 (2019). https://doi.org/10.1016/j.hrmr.2018.07.004
14. Dosso, C., Chevalier, A., Tamine, L., Paubel, P., Salmerón, L.: People also ask: How does this tool affect exploration-exploitation strategies with regard to prior domain knowledge and search context? An eye-tracking study. . Appl. Ergonom. **121**, 104367 (2024). https://doi.org/10.1016/j.apergo.2024.104367
15. Collins-Thompson, K., Rieh, S.Y., Haynes, C.C., Syed, R.: Assessing learning outcomes in web search. In: Proceedings of the Conference on Human Information Interaction and Retrieval (CHIIR'16), pp. 163–172 (2016). https://doi.org/10.1145/2854946.2854972
16. Gadiraju, U., Yu, R., Dietze, S., Holtz, P.: Analyzing knowledge gain of users in informational search sessions on the web. In: Proceedings of the Conference on Human Information Interaction and Retrieval (CHIIR'18), pp. 2–11 (2018). https://doi.org/10.1145/3176349.3176381
17. Pardi, G., von Hoyer, J., Holtz, P., Kammerer, Y.: The role of cognitive abilities and time spent on texts and videos in a multimodal searching as learning task. In: Proceedings of the Conference on Human Information Interaction and Retrieval (CHIIR'20), pp. 378–382 (2020). https://doi.org/10.1145/3343413.3378001
18. Sperber, D., et al.: Epistemic vigilance. Mind Lang. **25**(4), 359–393 (2010). https://doi.org/10.1111/j.1468-0017.2010.01394.x
19. Mercier, H., Sperber, D.: The enigma of reason. Harvard University Press, Cambridge (2017). https://doi.org/10.4159/9780674977860
20. Richter, T., Maier, J.: Comprehension of multiple documents with conflicting information: a two-step model of validation. Educ. Psychol. **52**(3), 148–166 (2017). https://doi.org/10.1080/00461520.2017.1322968
21. Maier, J., Richter, T.: Fostering multiple text comprehension: how metacognitive strategies and motivation moderate the text-belief consistency effect. Metacogn. Learn. **9**(1), 51–74 (2014). https://doi.org/10.1007/s11409-013-9111-x

22. Petty, R.E., Cacioppo, J.T.: The Elaboration Likelihood Model of Persuasion. Springer, New York (1986)

23. Brante, E.W., Strømsø, H.I.: Sourcing in text comprehension: a review of interventions targeting sourcing skills. Educ. Psychol. Rev. **30**(3), 773–799 (2018). https://doi.org/10.1007/s10648-017-9421-7

24. Mason, L., Boldrin, A., Ariasi, N.: Searching the Web to learn about a controversial topic: are students epistemically active? Instr. Sci. **38**, 607–633 (2010)

25. Rouet, J.F., Britt, M.A., Durik, A.M.: RESOLV: Readers' representation of reading contexts and tasks. Educ. Psychol. **52**(3), 200–215 (2017). https://doi.org/10.1080/00461520.2017.1329015

26. Schoor, C., et al.: Readers' perceived task demands and their relation to multiple document comprehension strategies and outcome. Learn. Individ. Differ. **88**, 102018 (2021). https://doi.org/10.1016/j.lindif.2021.102018

27. Schoor, C., Rouet, J.F., Britt, M.A.: Effects of context and discrepancy when reading multiple documents. Read. Writ. **36**(5), 1111–1143 (2023). https://doi.org/10.1007/s11145-022-10321-2

28. Deutsch, M.: A theory of cooperation and competition. Hum. Relat. **2**(2), 129–152 (1949). https://doi.org/10.1177/001872674900200204

29. Johnson, D.W., Johnson, R.T.: Cooperation and Competition: Theory and Research. Interaction Book Company, Edina (1989)

30. Hart, W., Albarracín, D., Eagly, A.H., Brechan, I., Lindberg, M.J., Merrill, L.: Feeling validated versus being correct: a meta-analysis of selective exposure to information. Psychol. Bull. **135**(4), 555–588 (2009). https://doi.org/10.1037/a0015701

31. Dweck, C.S.: Motivational processes affecting learning. Am. Psychol. **41**(10), 1040–1048 (1986). https://doi.org/10.1037/0003-066X.41.10.1040

32. Lees, D., Djordjevic, A.: Curiosity, collaboration and co-creation: using Grand Challenges to develop employability and tackle 21st Century problems. Br. J. Guid. Couns. **52**(1), 119–132 (2024). https://doi.org/10.1080/03069885.2024.2304716

33. Sinha, T., Bai, Z., Cassell, J.: A new theoretical framework for curiosity for learning in social contexts. In: Lavoué, É., Drachsler, H., Verbert, K., Broisin, J., Pérez-Sanagustín, M. (eds.) EC-TEL 2017. LNCS, vol. 10474, pp. 254–269. Springer, Cham (2017). https://doi.org/10.1007/978-3-319-66610-5_19

34. De Dreu, C.K., van Knippenberg, D.: The possessive self as a barrier to conflict resolution: effects of mere ownership, process accountability, and self-concept clarity on competitive cognitions and behavior. J. Pers. Soc. Psychol. **89**(3), 345–357 (2005). https://doi.org/10.1037/0022-3514.89.3.345

35. Postmes, T., Spears, R., Cihangir, S.: Quality of decision making and group norms. J. Pers. Soc. Psychol. **80**(6), 918–930 (2001)

36. Smith, C.L.: Domain-independent search expertise: a description of procedural knowledge gained during guided instruction. J. Am. Soc. Inf. Sci. **66**(7), 1388–1405 (2015). https://doi.org/10.1002/asi.23272

37. Rodon, C., Meyer, T.: Self-efficacy about information retrieval on the web across all domains: a short measure in French and English. Behav. Inform. Technol. **37**(5), 430–444 (2018). https://doi.org/10.1080/0144929x.2018.1449252

38. Dosso, C., Moreno, J. G., Chevalier, A., Tamine, L.: COST: An annotated data collection for complex search. In: Proceedings of the 30th ACM International Conference on Information & Knowledge Management (CIKM'21), pp. 4455–4464. ACM, New York (2021). https://doi.org/10.1145/3459637.3481998

39. Festinger, L.: A Theory of Cognitive Dissonance. Stanford University Press (1957). https://doi.org/10.1515/9781503620766

40. Dowsett, E., Semmler, C., Bray, H., Ankeny, R.A., Chur-Hansen, A.: Neutralising the meat paradox: cognitive dissonance, gender, and eating animals. Appetite **123**, 280–288 (2018). https://doi.org/10.1016/j.appet.2018.01.005

41. Weingarten, N., Lagerkvist, C.: Can images and textual information lead to meat avoidance? The mediating role of cognitive dissonance. Food Qual. Prefer. **104**, 104747 (2022). https://doi.org/10.1016/j.foodqual.2022.104747

42. List, A., Du, H., Wang, Y., Lee, H.Y.: Toward a typology of integration: examining the documents model framework. Contemp. Educ. Psychol. **58**, 228–242 (2019). https://doi.org/10.1016/j.cedpsych.2019.03.003

43. Anmarkrud, Ø., Bråten, I., Florit, E., Mason, L.: The role of individual differences in sourcing: a systematic review. Educ. Psychol. Rev. **34**(2), 749–792 (2021). https://doi.org/10.1007/s10648-021-09640-7

The Heuristic Evaluation of Manipulative Interfaces

Frank Lewis[✉][iD] and Julita Vassileva[iD]

University of Saskatchewan, Saskatoon, SK S7N 5C9, Canada
`fbl773@usask.ca`

Abstract. Deceptive Design, also known as "Dark Patterns", manipulates users through interface design that exploits cognitive biases, psychology, and design standards to extract money, data, or attention. As governments act against such practices, it is crucial to distinguish them from benevolent design approaches like Persuasive Technology, which aims to influence user behavior positively. By condensing the past decade of Dark Pattern taxonomies with Straussian Grounded Theory (SGT), we have created a set of five heuristics diagnostic of manipulative design. We present the results of a small study using these heuristics and propose that our heuristic evaluation (HE) process can enhance the assessment of Persuasive Technology.

1 Introduction

Persuasive technology (PT), Persuasive Systems Design (PSD), and Behaviour Change Support Systems (BCSS) represent design paradigms that seek to encourage, enable, facilitate, or otherwise influence user behaviour and perception *for their betterment*. However, there is another design paradigm that seeks these goals, but with less benevolent aims. "Deceptive Design" [3], a paradigm which uses "Dark Patterns" (DPs) with the to exploit users for their resources (i.e. money, time, data) [13] to the benefit of the designer. PT has been exempt from such classification since its inception when BJ Fogg included the caveat "without coercion or deception" [8], however this exemption may not be PT designers' to make.

Intentions aside, the complicated mix of contextual factors, UI/UX principles, and user cognition can lead to systems designed with good intentions being perceived as manipulative, as well as systems designed to manipulate users as benign. As government organizations and UI/UX practitioners begin to crackdown on such issues [6,7], we offer another tool in the effort to distinguish well-intentioned best-practice design from manipulative ploys that mascaraed as beneficial to maximize the extraction of user resources. Continuing our previous work [12] to unify and relate DPs, we have developed five heuristics tailored to the identification, classification, and description of manipulative interactions and tested their abilities through the heuristic evaluation (HE) of five interfaces with varied design elements in persuasive, manipulative, and neutral contexts.

K. T. Win et al. (Eds.): PERSUASIVE 2025, LNCS 15711, pp. 105–116, 2025.
https://doi.org/10.1007/978-3-031-94959-3_8

This paper presents our HE process, the derivation of our five heuristics, and the results of our HE. With this, we hope to contribute an effective and intuitive method of evaluation to the growing PT evaluation ecosystem that allows users to enjoy the benefits of persuasive systems, without experiencing negative consequences - intended or otherwise.

2   Background and Related Works

2.1   Dark Patterns

First defined in 2010 by then practitioner (now researcher) Harry Brignull, Dark Patterns (DPs) were described as "User interfaces that have been designed to trick users into doing things that they would not have otherwise done" [3]. They are distinct from anti-patterns in that they are *intentionally added* to interfaces with the goal of causing said effects in order to create interactions that disproportionately benefit designers. Another distinction between anti-patterns and DPs is that the former are much easier to *perceive*. When users encounter an anti-pattern, they become conscious of the negative impacted it has on their experience. While DPs can do the same, their effectiveness may also depend on concealment, often implemented through the same mechanisms that contribute to a seamless, intuitive, and genuinely helpful UI design. This overlap in design principles is at the root of what complicates efforts identify DPs.

Although contemporary literature is shifting towards a higher-level conceptualization of DPs [10], early work in the field focused on identifying surface-level design elements (patterns) as "Dark", leading to a series of exhaustive taxonomies being proposed independently from numerous domains. This is a problematic approach as it a) cannot scale with changing design paradigms and advancing technological capabilities, and b) lacks the contextual factors required to distinguish malignant from benevolent designs.

As a design paradigm that seeks to influence, enable, and support specific user actions/inactions, PT shares more in common with Deceptive Design than perhaps any other design paradigm. As stated previously stated, the caveat "Without coercion or deception" [8] has protected PT from such labels, but we argue that coercion, deception, and manipulation are potential user experiences *regardless* of designer intention and thus *are not the designer's to exclude*. Intentions aside, if interactions are not designed with care, even benevolent designers could create systems that are *perceived* as malignant - regardless of the system's true purpose.

While our work is not the first to address the distinction between DD and PSD, Growing government concern over the negative effects of social technology makes this distinction paramount. As such, our proposed evaluation could represent a meaningful contribution to the growing PT-evaluation ecosystem.

2.2   Evaluation and Persuasive Technology

While different domains may employ different methods of system evaluation, one low-cost, effective, accessible, and adaptable UI/UX evaluation method comes in the form of *Heuristic Evaluation* (HE).

Pioneered by Jakob Nielsen, Rolf Molich, and Don Norman [14], HE involves an individual performing a series of system tasks while with respect to a set of evaluation-criteria ("Heuristics") followed by a meeting with other evaluators to discuss and resolve heuristic infractions.

While NNgroup's (Nielsen/Norman group) ten usability heuristics are considered the standard, many researchers have created their own heuristics, tailored to the nuances of their respective application domains. [11,16] to achieve stronger evaluations that account for domain nuances. We believe that HE can also be applied to discern manipulative interactions from benevolent paradigms such as PT.

Evaluation Methods in Persuasive Technology. In 2020, Nyström and Stibe, proposed a modification to Stibe et al.'s earlier work defining the "Intention/Outcome Matrix" to include a nested "Visibility/Darkness Matrix" [17] which qualifies DPs on 2 axes: *Visibility* (ranging from "visible" to "invisible") and *Darkness* (Ranging from "'dark" to "grey"). Though useful in describing DPs through PT concepts, we believe that "darkness" must be described in greater detail if we are to meaningfully address DPs.

In 2024, Ahuja and Kumar [2], mapped "problematic design practices" to the design layers of an interface. This produced a corpus of 48 design elements coded by layer, element, behaviour design factor (Motivation, Ability, Trigger) [9], and finally how the design might threaten *autonomy*. This framework brings a valuable locative tool to the table that also reveals normative considerations surrounding PT design.

Aside from identifying problematic PT, other evaluation methods, such as the one proposed by Agyei et al. [1] strive to evaluate a system's persuasive potential from the outset of its design by having experts analyze the design specifications of a system, with respect to the PSD model [15]. If, as their findings suggest, persuasive potential can be determined as soon as the design phase, why not *manipulative* potential? Although our heuristics were intended for the evaluation of full-fidelity interfaces, they are just as applicable at other stages of UI/UX design.

Finally, we would like to note Clausen et al.'s call for a multi-faceted, and inclusive evaluation process in the design of a PT [5]. We hope to answer this call, and add our HE process to the growing PT evaluation ecosystem.

3   Methodology

Traditionally, HE involves a group of participants grading an interface/interaction against a set of predetermined evaluation criteria (heuristics) as individuals before consolidating their evaluations and forming a plan of action to address the issues identified [14]. Following this methodology, we had a group of five students with experience in HE evaluate five tasks on five different interfaces against our manipulative design heuristics. This section covers the origin and details of our heuristics, the five tasks we asked participants to undertake, and our recruitment/data collection processes.

3.1 Generating The Heuristics

Table 1. The five manipulative design heuristics

H1	**Inadequate Comprehensibility of Information:**
	The interface manipulates users by presenting information that is either too complex or too numerous for fair evaluation
H2	**Inadequate Validity of Information:**
	The interface manipulates users by presenting invalid or intentionally biased information
H3	**Inadequate Availability/Disclosure of Information:**
	The design manipulates users by hiding, removing, or (alternatively) highlighting certain elements in the interface encouraging the forfeiture of their resources
H4	**Absence of Appropriate Friction:**
	The path of least resistance leads to the unnecessary forfeit of user resources/disproportionately benefits the designer
H5	**Presence of Inappropriate Friction:**
	The design manipulates users by introducing undue friction in certain interactions

Completing our 2024 research [12] which applied Straussian Grounded Theory (SGT) [18] to code a condensed set of known DPs, we arrived at a core category of *friction* and suggest this phenomenon as diagnostic of manipulative intent or at least *perceived* manipulative intent. Our research suggests that DPs utilize friction to target user cognition (dubbed *cognitive friction*) and/or user agency (dubbed *agency friction*). The former can be further specified into issues of information *comprehensibility*, information *validity*, and information *availability* while the latter is simply split between *present* (i.e. user agency is restricted), and *absent* (i.e. user agency is less/unrestricted). These five sub-categories of friction are what lead to the definition of the heuristics described in Table 1.

3.2 The Tasks

Collected "in the wild" during our SGT process [12] as examples/validation, the tasks contain examples of interfaces we consider manipulative, benign, and persuasive. Participants were not given any particular order to conduct the tasks, but were encouraged to complete Task 5 sooner as it was required for the group evaluation.

Table 2. Evaluation task sources, objectives, and design paradigms

Task	Source	Objective	Design Paradigm
T1	JSTOR	Configure your cookies.	Manipulative
T2	Niiwin	Download the eBook.	Persuasive
T3	GitLab	Delete the branch.	Frictive (Benign)
T4	Fictional Café	Connect to the Wifi.	Manipulative
T5	Amazon.ca	Cancel the Amazon Prime subscription.	Manipulative

3.3 Conduct

Our study received approval from The University of Saskatchewan's Behavioural Research Ethics Board (Application 4770) and was conducted on August 12th, 2024. A group of five masters students with were recruited via personal invitation by the first author based on their experience with HE and were compensated with $20 gift cards for their participation. The study took two hours to complete consisting of a one-hour individual analysis, a ten-minute recess, a 45-minute group evaluation of the final task, and a five-minute follow-up questionnaire. This paper focuses on the *individual analysis* portion of the study.

The **individual assessment** phase had participants independently evaluate the five tasks depicted in Table 2 with respect to the heuristics described in Table 1. Participants were instructed to describe the infractions they found as well as any potential effects they may have on users on sticky-notes color coded to the heuristic they concerned and place the notes related to a task in the provided bag bearing the task's number. During the ten minute recess, these bags were collected, shuffled, and re-organized into five sets of five, each set containing now anonymized evaluations of tasks one to four as Task 5 bags were removed for the group analysis.

The **group assessment** phase picked up immediately after and involved the creation of an affinity diagram with the notes generated during the fifth task. Here participants were guided with the objective to "Describe the goals of the interface and the measures it took to actualize those goals". This process made it impossible to identify individual participants which in turn made eliminated the possibility of running the same analyses that we were able to run on the other tasks. For this reason, and lack of relevance, the results from this phase are excluded from the study, though task five data pertaining to the individual assessment remains where possible.

Once the study had completed, the anonymized evaluations were collected and digitally transcribed to a database for analysis.

4   Results

After transcription we had collected a total of 178 Notes, 157 of which were valid, 22 of which were discarded because they a) did not constitute an infraction (e.g. Commending GitLab on a good UI) or b) described an interaction caused due to construct error (i.e. describe an issue due to our firewall). Of the valid notes, 131 described *infractions* and 26 described *effects*. To accomodate the six cases where participants had recorded an infraction and an effect on the same note six additional effect-type notes were added. To accomodate unmarked effect-type notes 21 notes were re-classified as effects, making the final note count **163** (Table 3).

Table 3. Summary of infractions (Infr.) and effect (Eff.) notes generated for Task's 1–5 by Heuristics 1–5

Heuristic Flag Breakdown by Task							
	H1	H2	H3	H4	H5	Total	
						Infr.	Eff.	Σ
T1	10	5	9	13	12	28	21	49
T2	9	12	8	2	8	26	13	39
T3	1	0	0	0	2	3	0	3
T4	6	10	7	3	5	25	6	31
T5	6	9	9	1	16	28	13	41
Infr.	21	23	24	12	30			
Eff.	11	13	9	7	13			
Σ	32	36	33	19	43			**163**

To evaluate our heuristics and the effectiveness of the HE process in detecting/describing DPs and manipulative interfaces, a master-key of "core infractions" was created prior to analysis such that participant results could be scored against it as well as their peers. This allowed the calculation of the following metrics:

Naive Inter Coder Agreement - the proportion of actual to possible agreement events regarding whether or not a flag was raised, ignorant to *why* it was raised (Eqs. 1 and 2).

Precision - The percentage of core infractions flagged as a violation *regardless of* heuristic correctness (Eq. 3).

Accuracy - The percentage of core infractions flagged as a violation of the *correct* heuristic *as dictated by the key* (Eq. 4).

Aggregated Accuracy - The percentage of core infractions flagged as a violation of the *correct* heuristic *when considering the entire group as a single evaluator* (Eq. 5).

$$\%Agreement_{H_x} = \frac{max(Reported_{H_x}, \neg Reported_{H_x})}{\# of\, Evaluations} \tag{1}$$

$$\%Agreement_{T_x} = \frac{\sum_{H=1}^{5} max(Reported_H, \neg Reported_H)}{Possible\, Agreements} \tag{2}$$

Table 4. Naive ICA by task/heuristic and overall, as per Eqs. 1 and 2

Naive Inter Coder Agreement by Task				
	Task 1	Task 2	Task 3	Task 4
H1	1.0	0.8	0.8	0.8
H2	0.6	1.0	1.0	0.8
H3	0.6	0.6	1.0	0.8
H4	1.0	0.6	1.0	0.8
H5	0.8	1.0	0.8	0.6
Overall	0.8	0.8	0.92	0.76

4.1 Accuracy, Precision, and Aggregated Accuracy

Precision, accuracy, and aggregated accuracy are metrics that describe how well participants were able to classify/identify *specific* infractions present in the tasks, according to the answer key created by the first author. While ICA tells us how well participants agree on *which* heuristics were/were-not violated, these statistics tell us how well they agree on *what constitutes an infraction* (precision) and how accurately their evaluations are according to our key (accuracy) (Table 4).

$$Precision_{T_x} = \frac{\sum_{I=0}^{n} was\_found(I)}{n} \tag{3}$$

$$Accuracy_{T_x} = \frac{\sum_{I=0}^{n} where\, H_{E_I} = H_{Key_I}}{N} \tag{4}$$

$$Agg.Accuracy_{T_x} = \frac{\sum_{I=0}^{n} where\, H_{T_I} = H_{K_I}}{N} \tag{5}$$

where: T_x = Task [1,4], H = Heuristic [1,5], E = Evaluator [A,E], n = # of infractions in task T_x, I = Infraction $[1, n]$, K = Answer Key, and N = # of possible matching classifications according to K (Table 5).

Table 5. Breakdown of evaluation precision, accuracy (Acc.), and aggregated accuracy (Agg. Acc.) for Infractions (Infr.) in tasks 1–4.

Evaluation Accuracy and Precision by Task								
Task	Total Infr.	Infr. Identified	Flags Raised	Accurate Flags	Agg. Acc. Flags	Summary Precision	Accuracy	Agg. Acc
T1	9	9	32	16	8	1.0	0.5	0.89
T2	5	5	14	9	4	1.0	0.64	0.8
T3	0	N/A	2	0	0	N/A	0	0
T4	8	5	14	4	3	0.62	0.29	0.37
						$\bar{x}$		
Σ	22	19	62	29	15	0.87	0.36	0.51

5   Discussion

When observing the infractions reported (Fig. 2), the profile for T2 was most similar to T4's (the WiFi-connection form). This could be because both represent a *Forced Enrolment* [13]. Both utilize *cognitive friction* type infractions (Information comprehension, validity, and availability) over *agency restricting* types of friction. Infractions of the former type cite the non-functional download button, unclear requirements, overwhelming text, and mailchimp's external privacy policy. Infractions of the latter describe the forfeiture of their email as prerequisite to obtaining the book. T4 is similar in that evaluators reported unclear form requirements, a non-functional "Continue" button, inability to access the privacy policy, and covert data-collection for cognitive-friction infractions plus a forced subscription/hidden alternative connection mode as agency friction infractions. Additionally, T2 and T4 used similar elements to implement their forced subscription pattern, though T2 had far higher precision and accuracy when identifying this. 3/5 evaluators flagged it correctly in T2 compared to 1/5 in T4 where only 2/5 evaluators identified it *at all*. Both reported unclear form-requirements: in T2 this was concerning the "indicates required" note being absent from some required fields, in T4 the evaluators reported validity infractions concerning the undisclosed fact that the whole form must be filled out to grant access (potentially because the form technically *isn't required*) (Fig. 1).

Finally, we noticed our method lack the ability to describe *positive* uses of friction. Unlike NNgroup's [14] heuristics, ours look for instances where interactions *meet* the criteria rather than instances where they *do not*. By focusing on what not to do, we may have missed opportunities to highlight instances where friction is applied to the benefit of the user. As an example, both T1 (involving cookie configuration) and T2 contained "overwhelming text" as a core infraction. However, in T2, the text utilizes reciprocity [4] by framing the collection of email/data as a compensation for the development of the book. As such, T2 seems to be *informing* users as well as persuading. Additionally, when loading into T2, the first perceptible element is this explanatory paragraph, and the

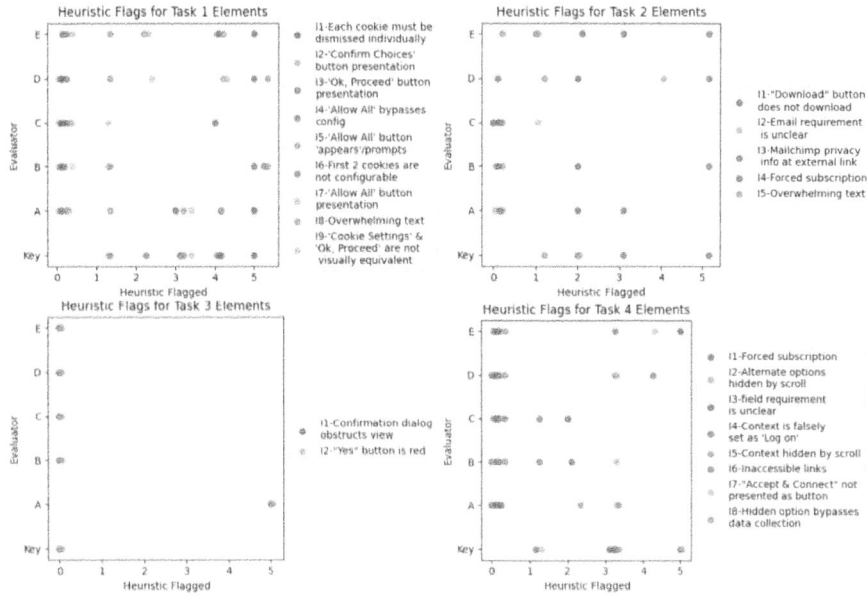

Fig. 1. UI elements commonly reported by evaluators plotted against heuristics. The Y axis denotes the participant Id and the X axis, the heuristic flagged. $X = 0$ indicates that no infraction was reported.

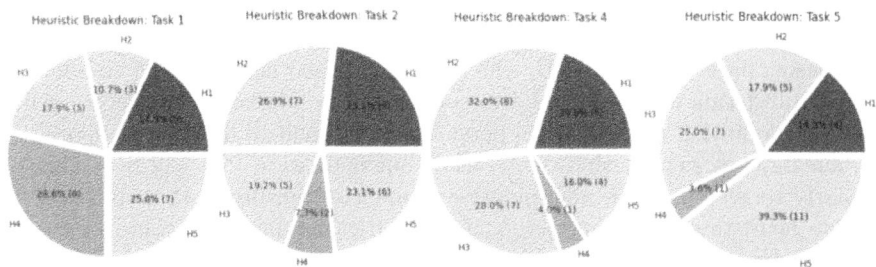

Fig. 2. Heuristic infractions by task for tasks containing manipulative elements.

form cannot be accessed unless users scroll past it. Comparing this to T4 where users first encounter a form, and underneath it, a hidden option that *bypasses* the form, are clear measures that the designers of T2 took to respect and inform users which our heuristics failed to capture.

6   Threats to Validity

There are two threats to validity concerning our participants. First, because they were personally recruited, and known by the first author, bias could have been introduced to their evaluations based on personal relations. We believe this to be mitigated as all participants were trained researchers familiar with the importance of research integrity and their relation to the first author did not constitute a power-relationship. The second is that although HE produces a lot of data, and is effective in aggregated groups of roughly five evaluators, more participants would extend value of our findings beyond an exploratory proof-of-concept.

There were also two threats to construct validity. One occurring during Task 2 when some participants found an interaction path that led to an unknown page outside of our firewall which prevented the stylesheets from loading causing it to look less professional. Although the facilitating researcher was alerted addressed this matter during the evaluation, it may have negatively impacted T2's evaluation. The second concerns the general lack of effort made by the researchers to conceal the identity of the platforms being evaluated (i.e. GitLab, Amazon, JSTOR, etc.) which may have led participants to evaluate the interfaces based on pre-existing opinions of the brands.

7   Conclusion and Future Work

In conclusion, to assist in the classification and identification DPs, we used Straussian Grounded Theory to reduce dark patterns to their a common element and derived heuristics from the resulting subcategories of *friction*. We believe that our heuristics, could help distinguish manipulative uses of friction from design paradigms like PSD, which employ similar elements, but to different ends. To test this we conducted and compared the heuristic evaluations of five interfaces following manipulative, persuasive, and neutral design paradigms.

Our findings suggest that, while using our heuristics, PTs will be evaluated similarly to systems with manipulative tendencies. Future work would seek to include heuristics describing *helpful* uses of friction such that complex strategies to influence users for the better are not overlooked or mistaken for having manipulative intent and to include PT experts in future studies using the same heuristics.

Finally, even considering our proposed methods inability to distinguish between the design paradigms, we believe that its ability to identify and classify manipulative interactions and stakeholder-inclusive nature could make it a valuable addition to the PT evaluation ecosystem.

Acknowledgments. This research was supported by NSERC through the Discovery Grant Program RGPIN-2021-03521 to the second author.

Disclosure of Interests. The authors have no competing interests to declare that are relevant to the content of this article.

References

1. Agyei, E., Kekkonen, M., Oinas-Kukkonen, H.: Evaluating the persuasive potential from software design specifications. In: Baghaei, N., Ali, R., Win, K., Oyibo, K. (eds.) Persuasive Technology, pp. 15–25. Springer, Cham (2024)
2. Ahuja, S., Kumar, J.: Layered analysis of persuasive designs: a framework for identification and autonomy evaluation of dark patterns. In: Gray, C.M. (ed.) Proceedings of the Workshop Mobilizing Research and Regulatory Action on Dark Patterns and Deceptive Design Practices (DDPCHI 2024) CHI Conference on Human Factors in Computing Systems (CHI 2024), Honolulu, HI, USA, 11–16 May 2024. CEUR Workshop Proceedings, vol. 3720. CEUR-WS.org (2024). https://ceur-ws.org/Vol-3720/paper1.pdf
3. Bringnull, H.: What are darkpatterns? (2010). https://www.darkpatterns.org
4. Cialdini, R.B.: The science of persuasion. Sci. Am. **284**(2), 76–81 (2001)
5. Clausen, S., Marx, J., Mirbabaie, M., Stieglitz, S.: From dark patterns to digital sludging: mapping the ethical debate on controversial persuasive system design. In: 43rd International Conference on Information Systems - ICIS 2022, pp. 1–9. Kopenhagen, Dänemark (2022). https://aisel.aisnet.org/icis2022/soc_impact_is/soc_impact_is/11. https://fis.uni-bamberg.de/handle/uniba/95731
6. Lupiáñez-Villanueva, F., et al.: Behavioural study on unfair commercial practices in the digital environment – dark patterns and manipulative personalisation – Final report. Publications Office of the European Union (2022). https://doi.org/10.2838/859030
7. Federal Trade Commission: Bringing dark patterns to light (2022). https://www.ftc.gov/reports/bringing-dark-patterns-light
8. Fogg, B.J.: Persuasive technology: using computers to change what we think and do. Ubiquity **2002**, 5 (2002). https://doi.org/10.1145/764008.763957
9. Fogg, B.: A behavior model for persuasive design. In: Proceedings of the 4th International Conference on Persuasive Technology, Persuasive 2009. ACM, New York (2009). https://doi.org/10.1145/1541948.1541999
10. Gray, C.M., Santos, C.T., Bielova, N., Mildner, T.: An ontology of dark patterns knowledge: foundations, definitions, and a pathway for shared knowledge-building. In: Proceedings of the 2024 CHI Conference on Human Factors in Computing Systems, CHI 2024. ACM, New York (2024). https://doi.org/10.1145/3613904.3642436
11. Lam, D., Sajjanhar, A.: Heuristic evaluations of cultural heritage websites. In: 2018 Digital Image Computing: Techniques and Applications (DICTA), pp. 1–6. IEEE (2018)
12. Lewis, F., Vassileva, J.: Seeing in the dark: revealing the relationships, goals, and harms of dark patterns. In: Gray, C.M. (ed.) Proceedings of the Workshop Mobilizing Research and Regulatory Action on Dark Patterns and Deceptive Design Practices (DDPCHI 2024) CHI Conference on Human Factors in Computing Systems (CHI 2024), Honolulu, HI, USA, 11–16 May 2024. CEUR Workshop Proceedings, vol. 3720. CEUR-WS.org (2024). https://ceur-ws.org/Vol-3720/paper8.pdf
13. Mathur, A., et al.: Dark patterns at scale: findings from a crawl of 11k shopping websites. Proc. ACM Hum. Comput. Interact. **3**(CSCW), 81:1–81:32 (2019)
14. Nielsen, J.: Enhancing the explanatory power of usability heuristics. In: Proceedings of CHI, pp. 152–158 (1994)
15. Oinas-Kukkonen, H., Harjumaa, M.: Persuasive systems design: key issues, process model, and system features. Commun. Assoc. Inf. Syst. **24**(1), 28 (2009)

16. Paz, F., Paz, F.A., Arenas, J.J., Rosas, C.: A perception study of a new set of usability heuristics for transactional web sites. In: Karwowski, W., Ahram, T. (eds.) Intelligent Human Systems Integration, pp. 620–625. Springer, Cham (2018)
17. Stibe, A., Cugelman, B.: Persuasive backfiring: when behavior change interventions trigger unintended negative outcomes. In: Meschtscherjakov, A., De Ruyter, B., Fuchsberger, V., Murer, M., Tscheligi, M. (eds.) Persuasive Technology, pp. 65–77. Springer, Cham (2016)
18. Strauss, A., Corbin, J.: Basics of Qualitative Research. Sage Publications (1990)

Digital Persuasion: Understanding the Impact of Online Influencers on Public Opinion

Omran Berjawi[1]([✉])(iD), Rida Khatoun[2](iD), and Giuseppe Fenza[3](iD)

[1] IMT School for Advanced Studies Lucca, 55100 Lucca, LU, Italy
`omran.berjawi@imtlucca.it`
[2] Institut Polytechnique de Paris, 91120 Palaiseau, France
`rida.khatoun@telecom-paris.fr`
[3] University of Salerno, 84084 Fisciano, SA, Italy
`gfenza@unisa.it`

Abstract. The studying of opinion dynamics and its propagation within social networks is crucial for addressing a wide range of challenges, including political polarization, public health, and marketing strategies. In this work, we study the problem of opinion dynamics by proposing a framework based on Friedkin-Johnsen (FJ) to identifies influential users and study their impact on dynamics opinions of community. The FJ model assume each individual have two opinions: initial and expressed. Through a series of initial opinion manipulation experiments, the proposed framework assesses the impact of influential versus random users on the overall community opinion. The proposed framework is validated using a tweet dataset representing the U.S. presidential election. The results shows that influencers with highest influencing score, significantly shift the overall community opinion. Moreover, the results shows that the impact of influencers not limited to direct neighbors, but beyond it, to their neighbors of neighbors. This study demonstrates how digital influencers on social media can shape public opinion regarding a subject or cause.

Keywords: Friedkin-Johnsen Model · Opinion Dynamics · Social Networks · Persuasion · Influencers · Sentiment Analysis

1 Introduction

Social media platforms have grown tremendously and changed the way we communicate, exchange ideas, and form opinions. They have become a space through which any individual can express their opinions on any issue and anywhere in our world without any obstacles, which has led to their use as a sharpened tool in various aspects, including political discourse, consumer behaviors, and public health campaigns [11]. To understand the mechanisms of individuals' opinion formation and how it is reshaped, it is significant to understand the relation

© The Author(s), under exclusive license to Springer Nature Switzerland AG 2025
K. T. Win et al. (Eds.): PERSUASIVE 2025, LNCS 15711, pp. 117–127, 2025.
https://doi.org/10.1007/978-3-031-94959-3_9

between the intrinsic factors (e.g., pre-existing beliefs) and extrinsic influences (e.g., influencers, and media exposure). An important factor in this relationship is the role of influential users on reshaping opinions, and behaviors of their audience within their networks [6]. For instance, celebrities can play a significant role in public opinion during election campaigns. In the U.S. presidential election of 2020, figures like Dwayne "The Rock" Johnson and Taylor Swift allocated their platforms to promote voter participation and share their political beliefs. In 2024, Taylor Swift and Jennifer Lopez have publicly endorsed Kamala Harris, while Donald Trump has garnered support from prominent figures such as Elon Musk, Kid Rock, and Hulk Hogan.

Various recent works have proposed various methods to identify influencers and study their relationship with opinion dynamics. For instance, the factors that influence the spread of opinion have been investigated in [15]. Other researchers investigated this relationship through optimizing opinion dynamic models [13]. Some studies modify the user opinions in a graph [17], while other approaches optimize the average opinion in the FJ [9]. More recent studies show the effectiveness of mathematical models in studying opinion dynamics within social networks. Among these models, the Friedkin-Johnsen (FJ) model [7] has provided a foundational framework for studying opinion dynamics and has been confirmed by a sustained line of experiments [16]. The FJ model simulates how opinions evolve through iterative interactions between individuals' intrinsic beliefs and the expressed views of their neighbors. While the FJ model has been extensively applied in theoretical and empirical studies, its application to identifying influential users and simulating the impact of targeted opinion manipulation remains an area with significant potential for further exploration.

In this context, we study the mechanisms of opinion dynamics within the social network graph by proposing an approach based on the FJ model. Specifically, this study focuses on the role of influencers and how manipulating their opinions can affect public opinion. By utilizing a publicly available dataset from Kaggle [10], which includes tweets collected during the U.S. presidential election of 2020, we demonstrate that interactions between certain influencers and various tweeters can change the opinions and convictions of the latter. The primary contributions of this research are threefold:

- Influencer identification: Identify and rank influential users within communities by interpreting the influence matrix from the FJ model at equilibrium.
- Sentiment manipulation: Examine the impact of influencers on overall opinion by manipulating the initial opinions of influential users versus random users.
- Propagation analysis: Analysis of the users most affected by the manipulation, who are directly related (neighbors) to the influencers or indirectly related (neighbors of neighbors).

This paper is organized as follows: In Sect. 2, an overview of the existing literature on opinion dynamics models was discussed. Section 3 details the approach used in this research. The experimental results are presented in Sect. 4. Finally, Sect. 5 summarizes the key contributions and concludes the paper.

2   Related Works

The study on the opinion dynamic within online communities have become an hot topic, specifically, understand how opinion change and evolve between individuals. This section present the works the deal with these phenomena.

Okawa et al. [12] proposed a hybrid method that integrates opinion dynamics models with deep learning techniques to enhance the predictive accuracy of opinion dynamics models. Zhou et al. [18] used user past opinions, their context, neighbours opinions, as input to neural network to predict the user opinion. Other researches aimed in analyzing the role of influencers within social network. Arruda et al. [1] study the how influencers behavior increase the intensity of echo chamber. In the same context, Galante et al. [8] focused on how influencers' content spreading the emergence of echo chambers.

In another line of research, other studies extend of the FJ model. For instance, Jia et al. [14] examined the evolution of social influence within the FJ framework, highlighting how individuals' susceptibility to influence changes over time. [3] proposed a extension of the FJ model, including a dynamic network structure in which connections are added or removed over time according to recommendations from the network. [2] utilized FJ model for analyzing how people's opinions propagate through social networks and how influencers can affect these dynamics.

In same context, several studies employ the FJ model to analyze equilibrium opinions in social networks. Biondi et al. [4] extract the conditions that FJ model induces opinion polarization in social networks by analyzing equilibrium opinions. In a similar vein, Zhou et al. [16] interpreting equilibrium opinions of nodes through absorbing random walks to address challenges posed by signed relationships, such as the absence of doubly stochastic properties in the fundamental matrix.

Zhang [13] provides a valuable contribution by addressing the problem of opinion optimization in directed social networks using the FJ model. Their work focuses on minimizing and maximizing the average equilibrium opinion by modifying the internal opinions of selected K nodes to 0 and 1. Building on their approach, this work extends the use of the fundamental matrix Ω. Specifically, the fundamental matrix was used to identify influential users whose opinions impact the equilibrium state of the network. Our contribution complements their work by shifting the focus from optimization strategies to influencer identification and manipulation analysis. This approach provides a deeper understanding of the structural dynamics of opinion propagation and highlights the role of influencers in shifting sentiment changes by comparing the effects of targeted interventions at influential nodes to random interventions.

3   Methodology

This section describes in detail the employed methodology to study the opinion dynamics within social networks. The complete methodology is composed as follows: data preparation, graph construction & community detection, and opinion dynamics modeling. The subsequent subsections outline each component in detail.

3.1 Data Preparation

First as preliminary data processing, the data used in this work consists of tweets shared by users within a social network. On Twitter, the interaction among users extend beyond static relationships (e.g., followers or friends), it consists of various content-based engagement such as mentions, replies, and retweets. The data preparation phase consists of the following steps:

- Interaction Extraction: This step aims to extract the mention engagement within a tweet to represent the interaction between users, if one user mentions another user in their tweet, the frequency of mentions between users was calculated. These frequencies are associated as weights of interactions, reflecting the strength of influence between users.
- Sentiment Analysis: This steps focuses on measuring the user emotional stance on a specific topic through user tweets. For this purpose, the RoBERTa pre-trained model was employed to determine the sentiment polarity, ranging from negative to positive. The average sentiment score for each user was calculated and used as their initial opinion, providing a quantitative measure of the user's overall stance.

3.2 Graph Construction and Community Detection

This component involves constructing a directed interaction graph, $G = (V, E)$, to represent user interactions. Here, $V = \{v_1, v_2, \cdots, v_n\}$ denotes the set of users, and E represents the edges between users. The edges are created between two users if one mentioned the other in their tweets, with edge weights $a_{(v_i, v_j)}$ assigned as the frequency of mentions from v_i to v_j. Once the network is constructed, the Louvain method [5], a modularity-based optimization algorithm, was employed to detect communities within the network.

3.3 Opinion Dynamics Modeling

This phase represents the core of this research, which employs FJ model to simulate opinion dynamics. The FJ model assumes that each node in the network is characterized by two types of opinions: an initial opinion s_i and an expressed opinion $x_i(t)$ at any given time t. The initial opinion s_i represents the individual's inherent stance on a specific topic, expressed as a value in the range $[-1, 1]$, where $s_i = -1$ indicates complete opposition to the topic, and $s_i = 1$ denotes full support. Importantly, s_i remains constant throughout the process. In contrast, the expressed opinion $x_i(t)$ evolves over time, influenced by interactions with other users in the social network. The progression of these expressed opinions at $(t + 1)$ is governed by the following equation:

$$x_i(t + 1) = \frac{s_i + \sum_{j \in N(i)} a_{ij} x_j(t)}{1 + \sum_{j \in N(i)} a_{ij}} \tag{1}$$

Here, a_{ij} represents the weight of the interaction between v_i and v_j, and $N(i)$ denotes the set of neighbors of v_i.

In this study, the FJ model was applied to the constructed graph. The average sentiment score (see Sect. 3.1) was used as s_i, while the weights of the connections between users were represented by a_{ij}. The model iteratively updates each user's $x_i(t)$ until the opinions converge, which means that each individual has stabilized into a fixed opinion. This process reaches a steady state represented by the equilibrium vector

$$\mathbf{x} = (I + L)^{-1} . s \tag{2}$$

where I is the identity matrix, and L is the Laplacian matrix.

The matrix $(I + L)^{-1}$, also known as the fundamental matrix [9], summarizes the structural relationships within the network, reflecting how the interactions and initial opinions of individuals shape the final steady-state opinions. This formulation allows us to reveal how much initial opinion of each node influences other nodes' opinions and, conversely, how each node's opinion is influenced by the opinions of others in the network.

Influence Identification. We define influencers as those whose opinions significantly impact the opinions of others. This step is aimed at detecting and ranking the influential users by extracting their influence scores $InScore_i$ through the following equation:

$$InScore_i = \frac{1}{n} \sum_{j=1}^{n} \omega_{ij} \tag{3}$$

where ω_{ij} are the fundamental matrix elements at the i-th row and the j-th column of the matrix.

This score quantifies the influence of user i on the equilibrium opinions of the network. A higher $InScore_i$ indicates that user i has a high impact on the users final opinions. Using this score, users were ranked to identify key influencers within the community.

Opinion Manipulation. To study the impact of influencers on overall opinion, two sentiment manipulations was performed to assess how modifying the initial opinions of influential users, as compared to random users, affects the overall community sentiment. The two types of manipulation simulations are as follows:

- Positive Manipulation: In this simulation, the initial opinions s_i of the targeted user were set to $+1$, indicating a strongly positive sentiment.

– Negative Manipulation: In the second simulation, the initial opinions s_i were
  set to -1, reflecting a strongly negative sentiment.

For each simulation, the FJ model was running to calculate a new set of
equilibrium opinions, x_i. To study the changes in opinion of influencers versus
random users, the average equilibrium opinion, denoted as $Avg(z)$, was calculated, which capture the overall change in network sentiment.

4   Experiments and Results

This section detailed the experiments performed and present the result obtained
from this work. First the influential users within community were identified and
ranked. Following by studying their roles in shifting community opinion via
manipulation their initial opinion.

4.1   Dataset

In this work, a publicly available dataset was employed from Kaggle [10], which
contains more than 1.7 million tweets collected during the 2020 U.S. election and
spans over one month. The dataset includes valuable metadata for each user, such
as the number of followers, likes, retweets, and other engagement metrics. This
dataset was selected due to its relevance in examining opinion dynamics within
the context of a political event and allowing for a deeper analysis of user activity
and interaction.

4.2   Influencer Identification

The influencer identification approach outlined in Subsect. 3.3 was applied in
this experiment to detect the influential users. We ranked the top 15 influencers
based on their $InScore$, and split them into three distinct batches:

– Batch 1: Top 5 influencers.
– Batch 2: Influencers ranked 6–10.
– Batch 3: Influencers ranked 11–15.

The purpose of distributing influencers users to several batches is to analyze
the impact of $InScore$ on opinion dynamics. To validate the effectiveness of the
proposed approach in identifying the influencers, we compared the results with
the normalized centrality metric [2], which is used to identify influencers.

The results, as summarized in Table 1, detect the top 15 influencers within the
network. It reveal that the FJ model successfully detected the same influential
users as the normalized centrality metric method. Moreover, the FJ model shows
its efficacy in ranking them by assigning $InScore$ to each user.

Additionally, the correlation between $InScore$ and the user engagements
(total number of retweets, number of tweets, and follower count) of the identified influencers was investigated. As seen in Table 1, the correlation shows that

Table 1. Detected Influencers

Rank	User	Batch	Influence Score	Retweets (Sum)	Number of Tweets	Followers Count
1	RealJamesWoods	Batch 1	0.8908	109251	8	2,685,154
2	w_terrence	Batch 1	0.8805	42741	15	1,188,925
3	Varneyco	Batch 1	0.8523	4800	55	663,854
4	Rasmussen_Poll	Batch 1	0.7605	2505	52	358,137
5	JudicialWatch	Batch 1	0.7009	42773	87	1,843,739
6	EpochTimes	Batch 2	0.5169	3232	36	319,635
7	trish_regan	Batch 2	0.4883	3152	6	737,555
8	WayneDupreeShow	Batch 2	0.3430	1385	20	504,846
9	Styx666Official	Batch 2	0.2417	417	6	90,474
10	realTrumpForce	Batch 2	0.1662	12682	88	87,096
11	RealMattCouch	Batch 3	0.1549	730	10	439,534
12	JoeTalkShow	Batch 3	0.1159	12369	110	107,473
13	Wizard_Predicts	Batch 3	0.1155	1967	57	12,659
14	Out5p0ken	Batch 3	0.1088	12	6	27,476
15	MarkSimoneNY	Batch 3	0.1001	13579	97	193,717

there is a positive correlation between $InScore$ and Follower Count, as well as $InScore$ and Retweets (Sum). It highlights that influencers with higher follower counts and retweet engagements are associated with high $InScore$, while on the other hand, the number of tweets generated by influencers does not directly contribute to a user's influence.

These results indicate that some users engagement levels do not necessarily represent their influence, even if there is a large number of tweets. In contrast, some engagements, like the number of followers and retweets, have more meaning when studying their relation to the influence of the user.

4.3   Sentiment Manipulation

This experiment aims to investigate the impact of sentiment manipulation on the overall dynamic of community opinion. Specifically, we compare the opinion at equilibrium after simulating the positive and negative manipulation on the influential users versus random users.

The results demonstrate that the top influencers (Batch 1) exerted a significantly stronger influence on the network's equilibrium opinion than lower-ranked influencers (Batch 2 and Batch 3) or random users. Specifically, as shown in Fig. 1a (top row) and Table 2, positive sentiment manipulation on Batch 1 resulted in a significant rise in the average network opinion, from -0.3932 to 0.0866, whereas negative sentiment interventions amplified polarization by reducing the average opinion from -0.3932 to -0.5857.

For Batch 2, the results in Fig. 1b show a rise in the average network opinion for positive manipulation, from -0.3932 to -0.3408, whereas negative sentiment manipulation reduces the average opinion from -0.3932 to -0.429. On the other

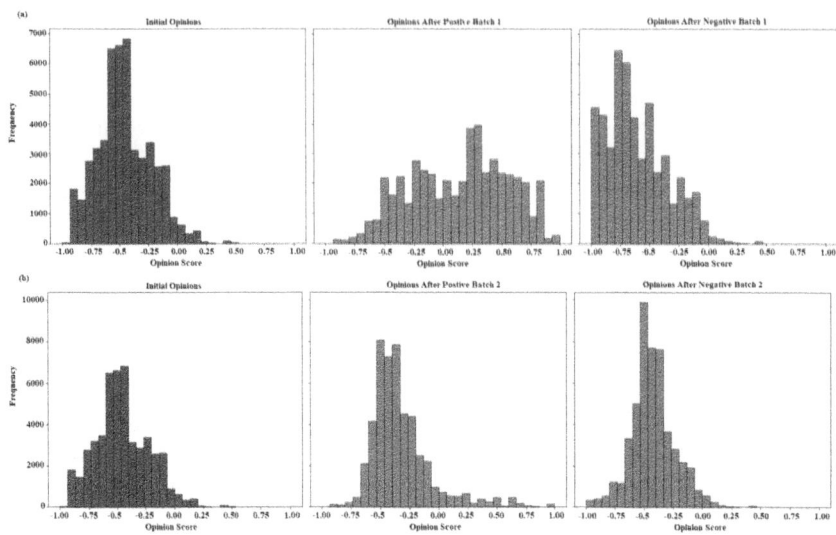

Fig. 1. A comparison of opinion distributions before and after positive and negative manipulation for Batch 1 and Batch 2.

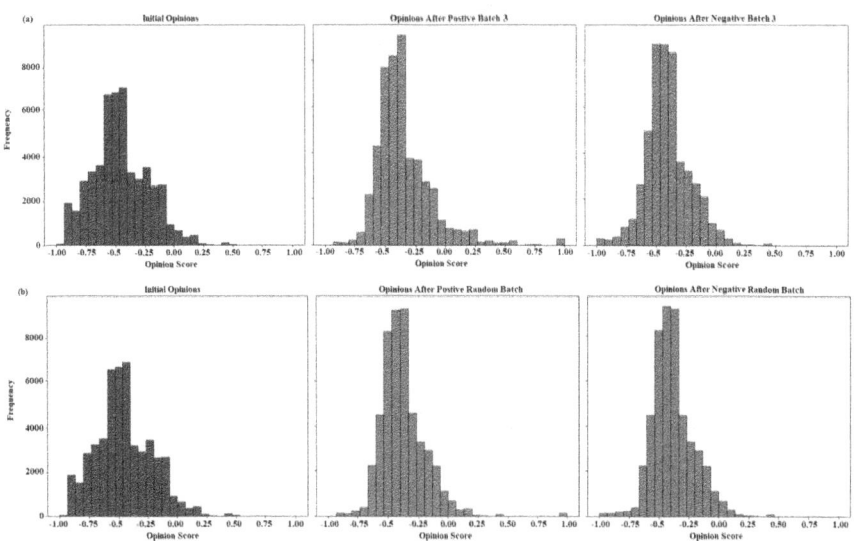

Fig. 2. A comparison of opinion distributions before and after positive and negative manipulation for Batch 3 and random Batch.

hand, for Batch 3, as shown in Fig. 2a and Table 2, there are minor changes in the average sentiment for both types of manipulation.

Finally, the last batch, which represents the random users, shows a negligible impact on the overall sentiment. As depicted in Figs. 2b (bottom row), and Table 2, for positive manipulation, the average opinion for both manipulation types provides negligible shifts in the network's average opinion, which suggests their limited roles. From -0.3932 to -0.3904 and from -0.3932 to -0.3940, respectively.

Based on the above results, the findings support the hypothesis that influential users exhibit a clear ability to influence community opinion more effectively than other users, whether by amplifying positive emotions or exacerbating negative emotions. As observed, there is a strong relation between *InScore* and the ability to shift the overall opinion of the community. When the *InScore* increases, the opinion-shifting impact increases. Specifically, those with higher *InScores* were able to induce significant changes in the community's sentiment, both in positive and negative directions. These results underline the importance of identifying and ranking influential users based on their influence score, as their influence score plays a crucial role in the impact on overall opinion of the community.

Table 2. Equilibrium Opinion Changes by Batch

Batch	Original Opinion	Positive Manipulation	Negative Manipulation
Batch 1	-0.3932	0.0866	-0.5857
Batch 2	-0.3932	-0.3408	-0.4291
Batch 3	-0.3932	-0.3647	-0.4120
Random Batch	-0.3932	-0.3904	-0.3940

4.4   Propagation Analysis

Table 3. Top 10 Affected Users for Positive/Negative Manipulation

	Direct Connection		Indirect Connection	
	Batch 1	Batch 2	Batch 1	Batch 2
Positive Intervention	7	8	3	2
Negative Intervention	6	9	4	1

After detecting the influencers and studying the relation between manipulating the initial opinion of influencers and its impact on the overall opinion of the community, we study how the influence propagate within the network. The propagation analysis investigates how opinion changes spread through the network through analyzing who the most affected users are by the opinion manipulation simulation.

This experiment examined the top 10 most affected users for Batch 1 and Batch 2 influencers, who were identified as having the most substantial impact on the community's collective sentiment, whether these users are directly connected to the influencers or influenced indirectly through neighbors of neighbors. As shown in Table 3, we have seen a consistent pattern in the spread of sentiment changes for Batch 1 influencers. Both direct and indirect connections to the influencers are impacted by the two types of sentiment manipulation. The most impacted users are the influencers' neighbors; however, the impact also reached the indirect connections, demonstrating that the influencers can spread their influence through the network. On the other hand, for Batch 2, for both manipulations, most impacted users are the influencers' neighbors, in which 8 out of 10 for positive and 9 out of 10 for negative are the directed neighbors.

In summary, regardless of the type of manipulation (positive or negative), the experiments provide valuable understanding into who is most affected by opinion manipulation. The findings validate that manipulating the initial opinion of the top influencer users (Batch 1) not limited to their neighbours, rather, it extends to neighbour of neighbours and, ultimately, to the broader community. In contrast, manipulating the initial opinion of Batch 2 influencers is more confined to their direct neighbors. These results suggest that as the influencer score increases, the influencer's impact expands beyond their immediate network to indirectly connected users and, eventually, to the overall network.

5   Conclusion

This paper proposes a framework based on the FJ model to study the opinion dynamics within online communities. The proposed approach identifies the influential users and their impact on community opinion by analyzing the effects of manipulating their initial opinions, and examines how targeted manipulation of influential users can propagate through the network. The findings show that, in contrast to more traditional approaches, the suggested approach may identify influencers and rank them according to their influence score. The findings also highlight the fact that users with higher influence ratings have a significant impact on shifting opinions in the community and that their power extends beyond their immediate neighbors to include indirect relationships. In future research directions, the manipulation of opinion in real time may be investigated, in addition to validating the approach across different social network platforms.

References

1. de Arruda, H.F., Oliveira, K.A., Moreno, Y.: Echo chamber formation sharpened by priority users. iScience **27**(11) (2024)

2. Berjawi, O., Cavaliere, D.: Dynamic analysis of influencer impact on opinion formation in social networks. In: Web Information Systems Engineering–WISE 2024 PhD Symposium, Demos and Workshops: WEB-for-GOOD 2024, AIWDA 2024, SWIFT-AG 2024, and Demos, Doha, Qatar, 2–5 December 2024, Proceedings, p. 394. Springer, Cham (2024)

3. Bhalla, N., Lechowicz, A., Musco, C.: Local edge dynamics and opinion polarization. In: Proceedings of the Sixteenth ACM International Conference on Web Search and Data Mining, pp. 6–14 (2023)

4. Biondi, E., Boldrini, C., Passarella, A., Conti, M.: Dynamics of opinion polarization. IEEE Trans. Syst. Man Cybern. Syst. **53**(9), 5381–5392 (2023)

5. Blondel, V.D., Guillaume, J.L., Lambiotte, R., Lefebvre, E.: Fast unfolding of communities in large networks. J. Stat. Mech: Theory Exp. **2008**(10), P10008 (2008)

6. Erikson, R.S., Tedin, K.L.: American Public Opinion: Its Origins, Content, and Impact. Routledge (2019)

7. Friedkin, N.E., Johnsen, E.C.: Social influence and opinions. J. Math. Sociol. **15**(3–4), 193–206 (1990)

8. Galante, F., Vassio, L., Garetto, M., Leonardi, E.: Modeling communication asymmetry and content personalization in online social networks. Online Soc. Netw. Media **37**, 100269 (2023)

9. Gionis, A., Terzi, E., Tsaparas, P.: Opinion maximization in social networks. In: Proceedings of the 2013 SIAM International Conference on Data Mining, pp. 387–395. SIAM (2013)

10. Hui, M.C.: Us election 2020 tweets (2020). https://www.kaggle.com/datasets/manchunhui/us-election-2020-tweets. Accessed 16 Jan 2025

11. Khanom, M.T.: Using social media marketing in the digital era: a necessity or a choice. Int. J. Res. Bus. Soc. Sci. (2147-4478) **12**(3), 88–98 (2023)

12. Okawa, M., Iwata, T.: Predicting opinion dynamics via sociologically-informed neural networks. In: Proceedings of the 28th ACM SIGKDD Conference on Knowledge Discovery and Data Mining, pp. 1306–1316 (2022)

13. Sun, H., Zhang, Z.: Opinion optimization in directed social networks. In: Proceedings of the AAAI Conference on Artificial Intelligence, vol. 37, pp. 4623–4632 (2023)

14. Tian, Y., Wang, L.: Opinion dynamics in social networks with stubborn agents: an issue-based perspective. Automatica **96**, 213–223 (2018)

15. Zhan, M., Kou, G., Dong, Y., Chiclana, F., Herrera-Viedma, E.: Bounded confidence evolution of opinions and actions in social networks. IEEE Trans. Cybern. **52**(7), 7017–7028 (2021)

16. Zhou, X., Sun, H., Xu, W., Li, W., Zhang, Z.: Friedkin-Johnsen model for opinion dynamics on signed graphs. IEEE Trans. Knowl. Data Eng. (2024)

17. Zhou, X., Zhang, Z.: Opinion maximization in social networks via leader selection. In: Proceedings of the ACM Web Conference 2023, pp. 133–142 (2023)

18. Zhu, L., He, Y., Zhou, D.: Neural opinion dynamics model for the prediction of user-level stance dynamics. Inf. Process. Manag. **57**(2), 102031 (2020)

Design and Solutions

LifeLink: The Design and Evaluation of an mHealth App for Caregivers Supporting Individuals with Suicidality

Smriti Jha⬤, Gerry Chan$^{(\boxtimes)}$⬤, and Rita Orji⬤

Faculty of Computer Science, Dalhousie University, Halifax, NS, Canada
gerry.chan@dal.ca

Abstract. In this paper, we report on a user study with 50 participants in-the-wild, followed by a semi-structured interview with 20 participants after a week of using an app designed for caregivers of individuals experiencing suicidal thoughts, called *LifeLink*. The app was designed iteratively following a user-centered design approach involving caregivers. Results show that *LifeLink* is user-friendly, elicits a positive user experience and effectively empowers caregivers. The use of the features was found to be persuasive in influencing caregiver behaviors toward supporting individuals experiencing suicidal thoughts. Our research findings contribute to advancing knowledge regarding the development of persuasive technology designed for suicide prevention, focusing on creating user-friendly, impactful tools that deliver a positive user experience.

Keywords: Digital Well-being · Mobile Health (mHealth) · Mental Health · Persuasive Technology · Suicide Prevention

1 Introduction

Suicide is defined as the "intentional ending of one's own life" [1]. The devastating effects of suicide are far-reaching, impacting not only the individual who dies by suicide but also their loved ones and caregivers [2, 3]. Despite seeking help from a wide array of sources, research suggests that caregivers constantly face unique and significant hurdles, including difficulties in accessing timely support systems and the overwhelming impact of personal mental health struggles on their ability to provide care [4]. The advances in mobile health (mHealth) applications or apps, offers a promising path toward improving healthcare, particularly for supporting behavior change and ensuring that patients follow established treatment pathways [5]. However, research shows that a key area of ongoing concern is the extent to which these apps effectively meet the particular needs of caregivers [6].

In this paper, we present the design, development, and evaluation of the effectiveness of a persuasive mHealth app called *LifeLink* that was purposefully designed to support caregivers of individuals experiencing suicidal thoughts. *LifeLink* was developed iteratively and incrementally using a user-centered design approach [7] to ensure that it is

K. T. Win et al. (Eds.): PERSUASIVE 2025, LNCS 15711, pp. 131–146, 2025.
https://doi.org/10.1007/978-3-031-94959-3_10

tailored to the user's preferences, as well as persuasive design principles [8] while incorporating evidence-based techniques to support caregivers. Despite the ongoing development and increasing availability of mHealth tools aimed at preventing suicide, studies show that there is a considerable lack of research investigating their effectiveness in lowering suicide-related outcomes [9]. Existing studies also show that apps aimed at suicide prevention and follow-up for individuals at risk could be more effective if they were developed with active input from caregivers [10]. Although informative, the efficacy of suicide prevention apps is under-researched, particularly for caregivers supporting individuals with suicidality. As such the goal of this research is to evaluate the effectiveness of *LifeLink* for supporting caregivers of individuals experiencing suicidal thoughts.

We conducted a one-week study involving 50 participants in-the-wild, followed by a semi-structured interview with 20 participants to answer the research question: "To what extent did using the *LifeLink* application generate a positive experience for caregivers?" The overall results of our study demonstrate that *LifeLink* is a usable application that offers positive user experience and is perceived as an effective tool for promoting behavior change. These results offer valuable insights into novel approaches for designing mHealth applications that promote health and well-being, as well as digital health interventions that aim to reduce the severity of suicidal thoughts.

We contribute to the field of Human-Computer Interaction (HCI) and persuasive technology in three ways. Firstly, we designed a mHealth app to help caregivers who are supporting individuals experiencing suicidal ideation. Secondly, we provide both quantitative and qualitative insights for improving the design of mHealth apps for caregivers who are in the process of helping individuals reduce the severity of suicidal thoughts. Thirdly, based on our results, we offer practical recommendations for designing mHealth apps.

2   Background and Related Work

2.1   Suicide

The damaging effects of suicide are far-reaching, impacting not only the individual who takes their own life but also causing significant trauma and grief within their community and among their loved ones [11]. While the act of suicide itself might appear as an escape from reality [12], the causal pathway to lethal suicidal behavior is manifested in a series of stages [13]. To prevent suicide, it is essential to have a clear understanding of the different stages of suicide and underlying risk factors that predict suicide. Previous research has identified risk factors that are most strongly associated with suicide and their impact on developing technological interventions for suicide prevention [14]. Several factors were statistically associated with suicide such as adverse life events, past suicide attempts, low education level, loneliness or high isolation, depression, family history of suicide, and sexual trauma. Understanding risk factors that are modifiable can be helpful for the development of technologies for suicide prevention.

2.2   mHealth Apps for Suicide Prevention

Recent review of existing literature suggests that there has been a rapid increase in the use of mHealth apps for suicide prevention because they are easy to use, may encourage honest reporting on sensitive issues, and could reduce stigma more than face-to-face methods [15–17]. For example, SafePlan [18], is a mental health support and safety planning app that was designed and evaluated by students and clinicians in Ireland. The researchers reported that the app was well received with respect to user confidentiality and interface design being key features of interest. More recently, BriteSide [19], a self-guided smartphone app for adults experiencing suicidal ideation, included safety planning and check-in features, as well as distraction (a bubble-popping game) and calming (guided mindfulness recordings) activities to reduce suicidal thoughts. Study results showed that the severity of psychological distress was significantly reduced in the intervention condition after having access to the app for six (6) weeks. In one more study involving 129 psychiatric patients compared the effects of using a psychotherapy-based app called LifeApp'tite [20], both with and without the addition of standard clinical therapeutic interventions. The findings of the study indicated a less pronounced reduction in self-reported suicide risk among participants in the treatment plus app group when compared to other groups after the intervention period.

Despite the many positive results reported showing that these apps are generally well-received and effective at reducing suicidal ideation, there is some research suggesting that technology-based suicide prevention remains understudied and the many that are available provide limited interactive features [21]. For example, in a recent systematic review, Melia et al. [9] reported that mHealth apps are useful for individuals at elevated risk of suicide or self-harm, including a reduction in depression, psychological distress, and self-harm, and an increase in coping self-efficacy. In another systematic review, Jha et al. [14] found that there is scope to use persuasive strategies in suicide prevention apps to make them persuasive and tailored to the individual.

Furthermore, although many mHealth apps for suicide prevention exist (e.g., Safe-Plan [18], Backup [22], ibobbly [23]), there is limited research to examine the design of such apps and their efficacy in addressing the unique mental health needs of caregivers supporting individuals with suicidal ideation. Furthermore, very few studies focus on evaluating the user experience and persuasive strategies employed in suicide prevention apps [24, 25]. As such, this research aims to fill this gap by designing and evaluating an app specifically for caregivers of individuals experiencing suicidal thoughts and insight into effective strategies, resources, and support systems to help them manage their roles while ensuring the safety and well-being of the individuals in their care.

3   LifeLink App Development and Design

3.1   System Design

LifeLink was developed using Android Studio [26], with the Dart programming language and Flutter framework for fast and flexible UI development. The backend was powered by Firebase [27], utilizing Firebase Auth for secure user authentication, Cloud Firestore for real-time database management, Crashlytics for monitoring and resolving app crashes, and Firebase Storage for handling user-generated content. Flutter Animation was used to create smooth, visually appealing transitions and animations.

3.2 Development of Features and User Interface Design

The development of *LifeLink* was iterative and incremental. We first conducted a brainstorming session with 12 researchers, each with at least 15 years of experience across various disciplines, including psychiatry, persuasive computing, health center leadership, and community leadership in suicide prevention. These experts represented a range of organizations from across Canada. After gathering their insights and feedback, we proceeded with sketching low-fidelity wireframes (Fig. 1) and then developed a high-fidelity interactive prototype (Fig. 2). The low-fidelity wireframes were used to collect the needs and perspectives of caregivers of individuals experiencing suicidal thoughts on using a mobile app for managing their own mental health and well-being. The high-fidelity prototype was evaluated for ease of navigation and the clarity of features. *LifeLink* was continuously refined using the comments received about improving the design reaching the final design of a fully developed and functional app (Fig. 3).

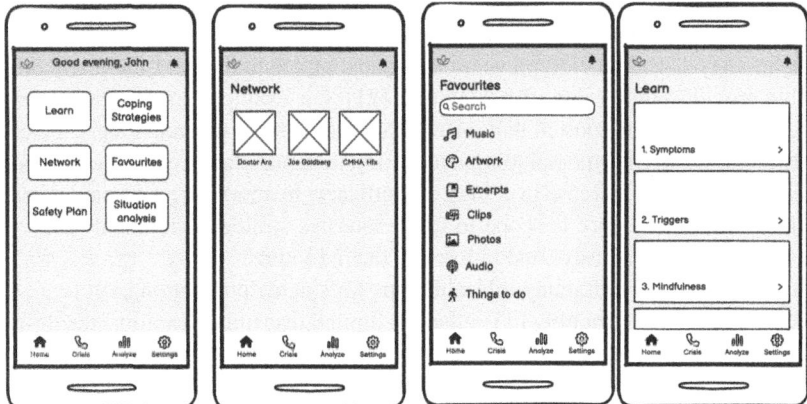

Fig. 1. Low-fidelity wireframes in the initial stages of developing the *LifeLink* app.

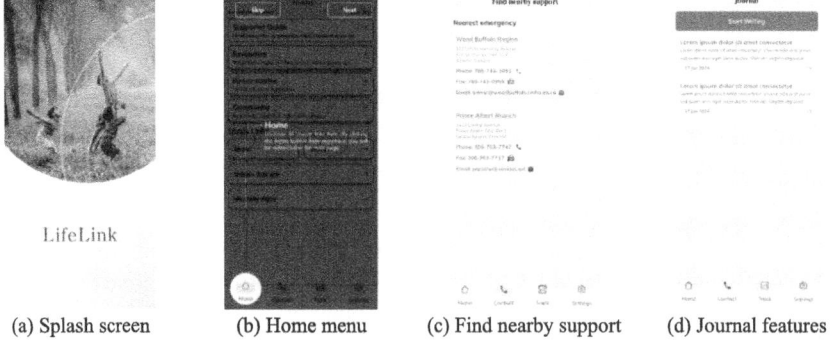

(a) Splash screen   (b) Home menu   (c) Find nearby support   (d) Journal features

Fig. 2. High-fidelity prototypes while developing the *LifeLink* app.

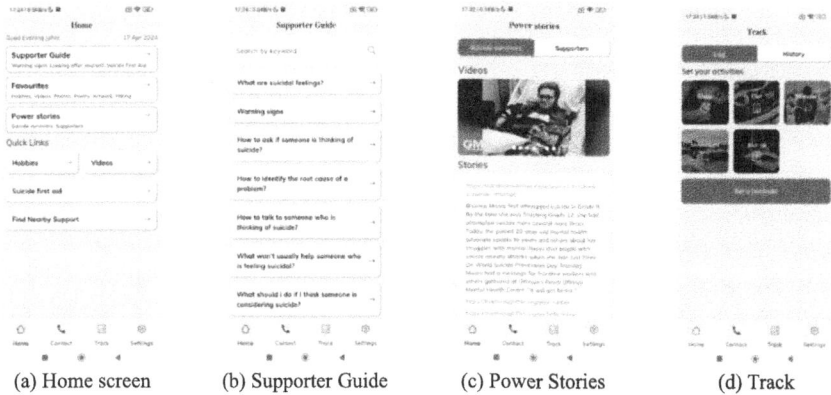

(a) Home screen   (b) Supporter Guide   (c) Power Stories   (d) Track

Fig. 3. Fully developed and functional version of the *LifeLink* user interface and features.

The features incorporate ideas gathered from evaluation of the prototype, as well as recommendations from existing reviews showing that persuasive strategies are a promising tool that can be used for designing suicide prevention apps [6, 14]. Particularly, the design was informed by the Persuasive Systems Design (PSD) model [8]. We implemented 11 persuasive strategies (Table 1) as app features from the PSD model, and some examples of the fully developed version of the UI are shown in Fig. 3.

Among the many features in *LifeLink*, there are three core features: (1) Supporter Guide, (2) Power Stories, and (3) Track. The **Supporter Guide** (Fig. 3b) aligns with the principle of "verifiability" [8] by providing users with verified information about various topics related to suicide and suicide prevention via outside sources. Users can search for a topic by entering any keyword. Users can also visit the information source on the web by clicking the hyperlink below each page. This feature helps caregivers in finding information about different topics related to suicide prevention. **Power Stories** (Fig. 3c) aligns with the principle of "simulation" [8] and is where users can browse 'Videos' and 'Stories' of real-life 'Suicide survivors' and 'Supporters'. This feature helps caregivers in knowing how people in similar situations overcome their situation. **Track** (Fig. 3d) aligns with the principle of "self-monitoring" [8] and is where users can track their 'Sleep', 'Diet, 'Stressors', 'Movement' or 'Journal' their thoughts. Users can see their daily and monthly sleep records, as well as visualize their daily calorie intake. Users can also select from different causes of stress and log their movements and journal to reflect on their day.

Table 1. Implementation of features based on the PSD model [8].

Persuasive Strategy	Description	Feature Implementation
Tunneling	The app should guide users in attitude or behavior change process by providing means for action	Guided walkthrough of main features on the "Home" screen, upon signing up
Personalization	The app should offer personalized content and services for individual users	Personalized greetings on the "Home" screen based on user's time zone; personalized breakdown of logged data in History tab within Track
Rehearsal	The app should provide means for rehearsing target behavior	Access to suicide prevention support resources using "find nearby support" within Contact. Instantly seek professional help via call or chat by accessing provincial resources
Reduction	The app should reduce steps users take when performing target behavior	Breakdown of suicide prevention information into searchable topics within Supporter Guide; categorization of Favorite, Hobbies and support resources within Find Nearby Support
Tailoring	The app should provide tailored information for user groups	Province-specific nearby support centers within Contact
Customization	The app should provide customizable abilities based on user preference	Adding trusted contacts; theme customization; notification settings; account deletion
Simulation	The app should provide means for observing link between cause and effect for users' behavior	Videos of real-life suicide supporters and survivors in Power Stories
Real-world feel	The app should provide information about the organization or actual people behind its content and services	About Us section within Settings provided developer information, privacy policy, information about the app
Verifiability	The app should provide means to verify accuracy of app content via outside sources	Source links for Supporter Guide content, Power Stories and support resources within Contact
Self-monitoring	The app should provide means for users to track their performance or status	Tracking well-being through Sleep, Diet, Movement, Stressors, and Journaling; History feature for progress review within Track

(continued)

Table 1. (*continued*)

Persuasive Strategy	Description	Feature Implementation
Liking	The app should have a look and feel that appeals to users	Illustrations for Hobbies; sample images in Artwork and Photos

4   User Study Design

To evaluate the perceived persuasiveness of the features and usability of *LifeLink,* we used a mixed-methods user study approach. Both quantitative and qualitative data were collected for analysis. The evaluation consisted of four steps: (1) complete a pre-study questionnaire, (2) use *LifeLink* for one week (7 days), (3) complete a post-study questionnaire, and (4) participate in an optional semi-structured interview. Given the sensitive nature of the topic, extra precautions were taken to support potentially triggered participants. At the beginning of the survey and interview, participants were provided with a list of supportive resources, including suicide hotlines for adults, young adults, and a support service directory. Furthermore, the interviewer was safeTALK certified, a suicide response training offered by the Canadian Mental Health Association and developed by LivingWorks Canada [28].

4.1   Recruitment and Procedures

Recruitment occurred through partnerships, professional networks, local mailing lists, word of mouth, sharing circles, and social media platforms. We partnered with Roots of Hope Nova Scotia [29] to support recruitment and conducted an online seminar to create awareness and familiarize people with participation procedures. After receiving ethics clearance from our university ethics board, recruitment of participants commenced. We recruited caregivers of individuals experiencing suicidal thoughts to evaluate the app. Participants were required to be 16 years or older, live in Canada, be proficient in English, own an Android device, and have supported or are supporting an individual experiencing suicidal thoughts. Participants who met the inclusion criteria were invited to proceed with the following four-step procedure:

Step 1: After reading the consent form and understanding the nature of their participation, participants completed a demographics questionnaire about their age, gender, and level of education.

Step 2: After completing Step 1, participants were provided with a link to download *LifeLink* and asked to use it for 7 days.

Step 3: After 7 days, participants completed a post-study questionnaire that evaluated their experience with using the app. The questionnaire consisted of validated measurement instruments that have been commonly used in HCI research to assess user preferences. In particular, usability was evaluated using the System Usability Scale (SUS) developed by Lewis and Sauro [30]. The SUS consists of 10 items and has been used to evaluate a wide range of products and applications, including mHealth apps [31, 32]. In addition to usability, participants were asked to rate their overall experience of the app.

Participants completed the short version of the User Experience Questionnaire Short (UEQ-S) [33]. The UEQ-S is a 7-point semantic differential scale (-3 = most negative anchor value (e.g., "boring") to $+3$ = most positive anchor value (e.g., "exciting")) and has been widely used in HCI research [34]. Participants also rated the persuasiveness of the 11 persuasive strategies implemented in *LifeLink* on a scale (4 items) developed by Drozd et al. [35]. This scale has been validated and employed in many studies including Orji et al. [36]. Participants indicated their level of agreement on a 5-point Likert scale (1 = strongly disagree to 5 = strongly agree).

Step 4: Interested participants took part in an optional semi-structured interview. Interviews were conducted online and took approximately 20 minutes.

4.2 Data Analysis

Out of 247 pre-test survey responses, 74 were valid, and 63 were complete (answered all questions and passed attention checks). Fifty participants completed both the pre-test and post-test surveys, forming the final pool for the online survey. As such, data analysis was performed on the final sample of 50 responses. The sample size was informed by relevant literature on evaluating mobile-based interventions for suicide prevention and is considered adequate for evaluating users' perspectives on a suicide prevention app [37, 38], given the number of features investigated. Twenty (20) out of the 50 participants also participated in an optional semi-structured interview. Results were analyzed using both quantitative and qualitative data analysis techniques. Quantitative data collected in the questionnaire were analyzed using descriptive statistics to first explore the data, followed by one-sample t-tests to determine whether the subjective ratings significantly differed from the neutral midpoint of the scales (3 on a 5-point Likert scale). Qualitative interview data were analyzed using a thematic analysis approach.

5 Results

5.1 Participant Demographics

The demographics of our study population are shown in Table 2. In general, most participants fall in the age bracket of 26–35 years old (38%), most of the participants were cis women (46%) while for academic qualification, the majority held a master's or doctoral degree (44%).

5.2 Quantitative Results

Overall, SUS scores were reported to provide an overview of the usability of *LifeLink*. The SUS revealed an average score of 72.08 ($SD = 18.32$), indicating that the overall usability of the app is "above average" [39]. This suggests that there is still room for improving the app. Furthermore, results of a one-sample t-test indicated that users' SUS ratings are statistically significant, ($t(49) = 5.05, p = 0.001$), ($M = 3.70, SD = 0.98$).

Next, we analyzed the scores collected from the UEQ-S. Results showed that scores generally leaned toward the positive spectrum of the scale, $M = 1.415$ ($SD = 1.284$).

Table 2. Participants' demographic information ($N = 50$).

Characteristics	Frequency (%)
Age	16–18: 6%, 19–25: 28%, 26–35: 38%, 36–45: 18%, 46–55: 6%, over 56: 2%, prefer not to say: 2%
Gender identity	Cis man: 38%, Cis woman: 46%, trans woman: 2%, non-binary: 6%, agender: 2%, Gender non-conforming: 2%, Prefer not to say: 4%
Education level	Less than high school: 2%, high school: 12%, college diploma: 12%, bachelor's degree: 30%, master's or doctoral degree: 44%

A one-sample t-test showed that the scores were statistically significant ($t(49) = 3.39$, $p = 0.001$). The overall score was higher than 0.8, which meant that the app elicited a positive user experience. The benchmark results from the UEQ Data Analysis Tool [40] showed that the overall user experience score was "Good" (the evaluated product is among the best 10% of results) suggesting a positive evaluation from users (Fig. 4).

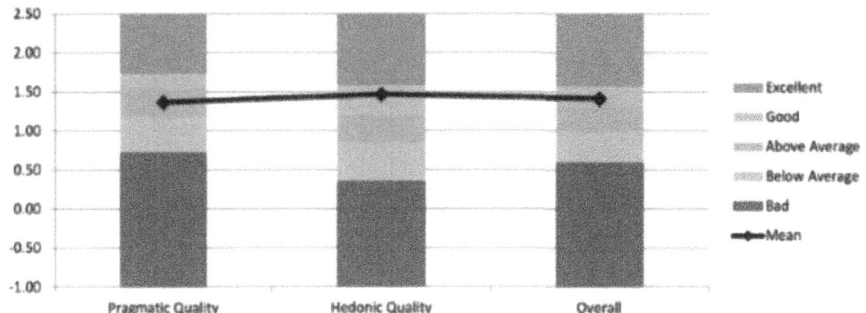

Fig. 4. Comparison of results of LifeLink's user experience with benchmark data to understand the relative quality of our app as compared to other products.

Finally, we analyzed the persuasiveness of the 11 persuasive strategies implemented in *LifeLink* by first plotting the mean scores followed by performing a one-sample t-test on the perceived persuasive scale data against a neutral rating of 3. Results (Fig. 5) shows that the mean score of perceived persuasiveness for all 11 persuasive strategies (tunneling, personalization, rehearsal, reduction, customization, simulation, real-world feel, verifiability, self-monitoring, liking) was higher than the neutral score of 3 (red middle dashed line). To further evaluate whether the persuasiveness of the strategies, we conducted the one-sample t-test on the scores collected from the perceived persuasiveness scale [35] on a mid-point of 3. As shown in Table 3, all 11 persuasive strategies were perceived to be significantly persuasive ($p = 0.001$) suggesting that all the strategies are persuasive or effective for supporting an individual experiencing suicidal thoughts.

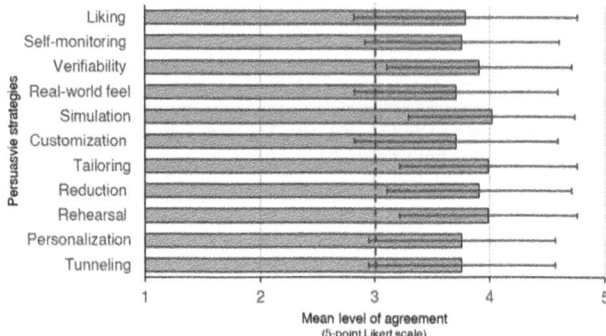

Fig. 5. A bar chart showing the mean results for perceived persuasiveness of *LifeLink* features and overall, on a 5-point (1 = strongly disagree to 5 = strongly agree) Likert scale. The red broken indicates the neutral rating of 3.

Table 3. Descriptive statistics and one-sample t-test results for the 11 persuasive strategies implemented in *LifeLink* ($N = 50$).

	Descriptive statistics		One-sample t-test			
Strategies	*M*	*SD*	*t*	*df*	*p*	Cohen's *d*
Tunneling	3.76	0.81	6.64	49	.001	0.81
Personalization	3.76	0.81	6.64	49	.001	0.81
Rehearsal	3.99	0.77	9.10	49	.001	0.77
Reduction	3.91	0.80	8.03	49	.001	0.80
Tailoring	3.99	0.77	9.10	49	.001	0.77
Customization	3.71	0.88	5.73	49	.001	0.88
Simulation	4.02	0.72	9.99	49	.001	0.72
Real-world feel	3.71	0.88	5.73	49	.001	0.88
Verifiability	3.91	0.80	8.03	49	.001	0.80
Self-monitoring	3.76	0.84	6.47	49	.001	0.84
Liking	3.79	0.97	5.75	49	.001	0.97
Overall	3.85	0.72	8.31	49	.001	0.72

5.3   Qualitative Results

To gain a more detailed understanding of users' experiences and views about *LifeLink* we conducted semi-structured interviews. Of the 50 participants who used the app for the full week and completed the post-study questionnaire, 20 participants volunteered to participate in Step 4 – the optional, semi-structured interview. A thematic analysis [41] was conducted using ATLAS.ti [42], a qualitative data analysis software to organize and uncover patterns in the collected data. Interview recordings were transcribed and Braun and Clarke's [43] six phase approach was used to analyze the qualitative interview data

[44] which involved: (1) familiarizing oneself with the data, (2) generating initial codes, (3) searching for themes, (4) reviewing themes, (5) defining and naming themes, and (6) writing up the report. Using an inductive approach [45], our aim was to establish clear links between the evaluation and identify key themes that emerged from participants' responses regarding their interest in, overall perception of, and experiences with *LifeLink*. Our analysis revealed four themes as discussed in the subsequent sections. The extracts are presented with minor spelling and grammatical corrections.

Theme 1: Emotional and Visual Engagement through Artistic Expression enhanced users' well-being. The poetry and artwork features were appreciated for providing an emotionally soothing space. Users felt that these features enhanced their sense of well-being and engagement. For example, one participant said "*I really liked the poetry feature... It had that surprise element in it. I think I haven't seen anything like that in any other application*" [P47], while another participant said "*I really like the poems and adding arts feature. This felt good*" [P50]. This suggests that the use of features that allowed users to express their artistic talents can elicit positive feelings.

Theme 2: The opportunity to listen to others makes me feel less isolated. The "Power Stories" feature was appreciated by participants, as it provided a sense of community and understanding. Hearing from others who had gone through similar experiences helped users feel less isolated and more connected to others facing similar challenges. This was evident when one participant said "*It (the app) gave guidance towards some of the problems. I felt that when I use that app every day, there's less negativity. If I like read or see the power stories and all like supporters' stories, the next day, it gives me more positivity around the society and makes me realize that others are also struggling and it's not only me*" [P24]. This suggests that use of the "Power Stories" feature can cultivate a sense of community allowing caregivers to feel supported and understand that they are not facing their challenges alone.

Theme 3: The self-care and activity tracking features are valuable because they help to better understand and improve myself. Many participants valued the ability to track their personal well-being through features like sleep, stress, diet, and hobbies. The app allowed users to monitor aspects of their health, with some users appreciating how the tracking helped them gain insight into their behaviors and identify areas for improvement. For example, a participant said "*I tried the movement, I just said, let me try to pop in exercise I do daily like for me, I like walking. This is a nice one to track how well you're exercising and getting enough exercise, which makes it very important for the body and mind, at this point in time. I was also particularly interested in sleeping and dieting things. Personally, I just wanted to see how well I'm doing because I find it difficult to sleep because I have this routine of almost overworking myself*" [P04], while a different participant said "*it (Track) made me realize that if I have some weak point, I need to take care of myself first before helping somebody else. So, if I'm not well, I'm not going to be any of any help to someone who is having suicidal thoughts. It helped me in keeping track of my mental health*" [P47]. Collectively, this suggests that the use of the app helps caregivers realize their own mental health and keep thriving to improve themselves so they can better help others.

Theme 4: The ability to customize my preferences helps me to reflect on my experiences as a caregiver. Several participants mentioned the ability to customize the app's experience, such as adjusting to dark mode, tracking personal hobbies, or storing positive content. For example, one participant said *"When I opened the app it opened in light mode. I immediately switched to dark mode and I'm glad that the app has a dark mode theme on it because everything I use, I prefer dark mode. I like that the app sort of fits well within the theme that I use, as it's easy on the eyes"* [P05], whereas another participant said *"The hobbies was a really nice thing because I was kind of thinking about it and it feels to me like a positive place for documenting your behaviors, which can be like a positive reinforcement of the good things that you are actually doing, as hobbies are like happy things. So sometimes if you're feeling down, having a place where those things all are is just really nice"* [P08]. These comments suggest that the app can offer a "safe space" for caregivers to reflect and document their progress helping to reflect on their own experiences and finding what they enjoy.

6 Discussion

This study investigated the effectiveness of *LifeLink* specifically designed for caregivers supporting individuals with suicidal thoughts. In general, our quantitative results showed that the app was usable, elicited a positive user experience, and the features were perceived to be persuasive. Furthermore, qualitative results suggest that *LifeLink* was helpful for caregivers, enabling them to gain a deeper understanding of themselves, feeling more connected to others, and encouraging more thoughtful reflection on their personal experiences as they engaged with the various features in the app.

6.1 Implications for Design

Based on our findings, we offer four key recommendations for researchers and mHealth application developers. These recommendations are intended to guide the design of solutions aimed at suicide prevention, with a particular focus on supporting caregivers who assist individuals experiencing suicidal thoughts.

Design Recommendation 1: Promote self-care by tracking personal habits. Continuous tracking and encouraging sustained engagement have been shown to be an important aspect of shaping users' behavior change in mHealth apps [46]. We observed that many participants found the features tracking sleep, stress levels, dietary intake, and hobbies to be particularly valuable for monitoring their personal well-being. As such, we recommend tracking personal habits (e.g., sleep, diet, exercise) and helping users understand their mental and physical well-being and promoting self-care. Tracking can be particularly useful for caregivers and individuals managing their mental health, providing a sense of control and structure in daily life. For example, the app can help users plan routines, give feedback on progress, and motivate them to keep on improving themselves. However, while tracking features are beneficial, it is important to consider concerns regarding data security, privacy measures, and ethical considerations, particularly when dealing with sensitive caregiver information. Tracking features like sleep, stress levels, and diet collect personal and sensitive data. When implementing such features, robust data encryption protocols must be used to protect users' sensitive health information. Likewise, tracking sensitive information such as mental health status or caregiving activities requires careful ethical considerations. The app should provide safeguards to prevent discrimination, stigmatization, or unintended harm. For example, caregivers tracking their well-being might be vulnerable to burnout or stress, and the app should provide ethical guidance on interpreting the data and how it could impact users emotionally. In addition, data anonymization can help mitigate risks of identifying users in datasets used for research, ensuring a balance between useful insights and the privacy of the individual.

Design Recommendation 2: Integrate personal stories and community-driven content to provide emotional support. Sharing stories with others who have similar experiences is a valuable way to gain emotional support, which includes expressions of understanding, care, and compassion from those who share similar experiences [47]. Many participants found that connecting with others who had similar experiences provided them with a sense of community and reduced feelings of isolation. Thus, we recommend integrating personal stories and community-driven content as they can offer emotional support and validation, reducing feelings of isolation. These stories can foster a sense of hope and resilience among users, helping them feel more confident while supporting others, as well as managing their own struggles. For example, the app can organize stories around common themes or emotions such as anxiety, grief, and mental health struggles. This will likely help users find relatable stories and connect with others who are facing similar situations.

Design Recommendation 3: Encourage users to reflect and document their progress. Personalization in mental health apps can enhance user engagement by making the app feel more individualized and meaningful [48, 49]. Our results showed that the ability to personalize the app's experience allowed users to create a "safe space" for them to reflect and document their progress. Thus, we recommend that apps allow users to adjust settings or store personal content that empowers them to take ownership of their mental health journey. For example, the app can prompt users to set personal mental health goals such as practicing gratitude, meditation, or completing therapy exercises. This can provide a sense of accomplishment as users document and track their achievements.

Design Recommendation 4: Enable users to express their artistic creativity to increase positive feelings. Beyond research showing that features such as practicing gratitude and mindfulness exercises can cultivate positive emotions and positive thinking [50], our results further suggest that features that allow users to express their artistic talents can also elicit positive feelings. Thus, we suggest integrating more artistic and creative outlets, such as allowing users to contribute their own artwork or poetry, can foster a deeper emotional connection. Providing personalized poetry recommendations or creative prompts based on the user's emotional state could make mHealth apps more interactive and adaptive.

6.2 Limitations and Directions for Future Work

While the study presented some interesting results, it is important to acknowledge some limitations. Most of our participants were from Western countries, which could introduce geographical and cultural biases. Therefore, our findings may not be generalizable to all populations. Future studies evaluating the app with broader populations and larger sample size, including people from different cultural or socio-economic backgrounds can provide more insights on the app's generalizability. Moreover, we evaluated the app usage short-term (one week). Thus, a longer follow-up would provide insights into sustained engagement and the long-term impact on caregivers' mental well-being.

7 Conclusion

To summarize, we explored how mobile-based apps can be better designed to support caregivers of individuals experiencing suicidal thoughts. Designing mental health technologies for and with caregivers is crucial, as they face unique challenges while dealing with suicidality. We designed *LifeLink*, a persuasive mHealth app to support caregivers of individuals experiencing suicidal thoughts. *LifeLink* was developed following an iterative and incremental approach considering user feedback and persuasive design principles to support caregivers. The findings increase our knowledge of the multiple perspectives, needs, and difficulties encountered by caregivers assisting individuals contemplating suicide, thereby providing a better understanding of how the design of mHealth apps can be adapted to effectively meet the unique requirements and lived realities of caregivers. This research emphasizes the critical need for app design that not only actively supports the roles and responsibilities of caregivers but also prioritizes their well-being and offers readily accessible resources during times of urgent need.

Acknowledgements. This research was undertaken, in part, thanks to funding from the Canada Research Chairs Program. We acknowledge the support of the Natural Sciences and Engineering Research Council of Canada (NSERC) through the Discovery Grant. The research is conducted as part of the Dalhousie University Persuasive Computing Lab.

References

1. Turecki, G., et al.: Suicide and suicide risk. Nat. Rev. Dis. Prim. **5**, 74 (2019)
2. Jain, F.A.: Commentary on suicide in family caregivers: State of the field. J. Am. Geriatr. Soc. (2024)
3. O'Dwyer, S.T., et al.: Suicidality in family caregivers of people with long-term illnesses and disabilities: a scoping review. Compr. Psychiatry. 110 (2021)
4. Micol, V.J., et al.: Stress in caregivers of youth hospitalized for suicide ideation or attempt. Behav. Ther. (2024)
5. Rowland, S.P., et al.: What is the clinical value of mHealth for patients? npj Digit. Med. 3 (2020)
6. Jha, S., et al.: Can your smartphone save a life? a systematic review of mobile-based interventions for suicide prevention. Int. J. Hum. Comput. Interact. (2024)
7. Norman, D.A., Draper, S.W.: User centered system design. User Centered Syst. Des. (1986)
8. Oinas-Kukkonen, H., Harjumaa, M.: Persuasive systems design: Key issues, process model, and system features. Commun. Assoc. Inf. Syst. **24**, 485–500 (2009)
9. Melia, R., et al.: Mobile health technology interventions for suicide prevention: Systematic review. JMIR mHealth uHealth. 8 (2020)
10. Castillo-Sánchez, G., et al.: Suicide prevention mobile apps: descriptive analysis of apps from the most popular virtual stores. JMIR mHealth uHealth. 7 (2019)

11. Cerel, J., et al.: The impact of suicide on the family. Crisis **29**, 38–44 (2008)

12. Suicide as an Escape From the Self | Psychology Today Canada

13. Van Orden, K.A., et al.: The interpersonal theory of suicide. Psychol. Rev. **117**, 575–600 (2010)

14. Jha, S., et al.: Identification of risk factors for suicide and insights for developing suicide prevention technologies: a systematic review and meta-analysis. Hum. Behav. Emerg. Technol. (2023)

15. Gryglewicz, K., et al.: Translating suicide safety planning components into the design of mHealth App features: systematic review. JMIR Ment. Heal. 11 (2024). https://doi.org/10.2196/52763

16. Braciszewski, J.M.: Digital technology for suicide prevention. Adv. Psychiatry Behav. Heal. **1**, 53–65 (2021)

17. Yu, T., et al.: Effectiveness of internet-based cognitive behavioral therapy for suicide: a systematic review and meta-analysis of RCTs. Psychol. Heal. Med. **27**, 2186–2203 (2022)

18. O'Grady, C., et al.: A mobile health approach for improving outcomes in suicide prevention (SafePlan). J. Med. Internet Res. 22 (2020)

19. Josifovski, N., et al.: Efficacy of BrighterSide, a self-guided app for suicidal ideation: randomized controlled trial. JMIR Ment. Heal. 11 (2024)

20. O'Toole, M.S., et al.: Testing an app-assisted treatment for suicide prevention in a randomized controlled trial: effects on suicide risk and depression. Behav. Ther. **50**, 421–429 (2019)

21. De la Torre, I., et al.: Mobile apps for suicide prevention: review of virtual stores and literature. JMIR mHealth uHealth. 5 (2017)

22. Pauwels, K., et al.: BackUp: development and evaluation of a smart-phone application for coping with suicidal crises. PLoS One. 12 (2017)

23. Tighe, J., et al.: Ibobbly mobile health intervention for suicide prevention in Australian indigenous youth: a pilot randomised controlled trial. BMJ Open. 7 (2017)

24. Reen, J., et al.: Saving life and keeping privacy: a study on mobile apps for suicide prevention and privacy policies. Lect. Notes Comput. Sci. 13213 LNCS, 190–207 (2022)

25. Wilks, C.R., et al.: User engagement and usability of suicide prevention apps: systematic search in app stores and content analysis. JMIR Form. Res. 5 (2021)

26. Download Android Studio and SDK tools, https://developer.android.com/studio. Last accessed 05 March 2025

27. Google Analytics for Firebase, https://firebase.google.com/docs/analytics. Last accessed 05 March 2025

28. LivingWorks: LivingWorks safeTALK, https://livingworks.net/training/livingworks-safetalk/. Last accessed 05 March 2025

29. ROOTS OF HOPE NS, https://rootsofhopens.com/. Last accessed 05 March 2025

30. Lewis, J.R., Sauro, J.: The factor structure of the system usability scale. Lect. Notes Comput. Sci. 5619 LNCS, 94–103 (2009)

31. Isaković, M., Sedlar, U., Volk, M., Bešter, J.: Usability pitfalls of diabetes mHealth apps for the elderly. J. Diabetes Res. 2016 (2016)

32. Santoso, I.S., et al.: Effectiveness of gamification in mHealth apps designed for mental illness. Proceeding - 2021 2nd Int. Conf. ICT Rural Dev. IC-ICTRuDev 2021 (2021)

33. Laugwitz, B., Held, T., Schrepp, M.: Construction and evaluation of a user experience questionnaire. Lect. Notes Comput. Sci. 5298 LNCS, 63–76 (2008)

34. Schankin, A., Budde, M., Riedel, T., Beigl, M.: Psychometric properties of the user experience questionnaire (UEQ). Conf. Hum. Factors Comput. Syst. - Proc. (2022)

35. Drozd, F., Lehto, T., Oinas-Kukkonen, H.: Exploring perceived persuasiveness of a behavior change support system: A structural model. Lect. Notes Comput. Sci. 7284 LNCS, 157–168 (2012)

36. Orji, R., et al.: Modeling the efficacy of persuasive strategies for different gamer types in serious games for health. User Model. User-Adap. Inter. **24**, 453–498 (2014)

37. Morgiève, M., et al.: A digital companion, the emma app, for ecological momentary assessment and prevention of suicide: Quantitative case series study. JMIR mHealth uHealth. 8 (2020)

38. McManama O'Brien, K.H., et al.: A pilot study of the acceptability and usability of a smartphone application intervention for suicidal adolescents and their parents. Arch. Suicide Res. **21**, 254–264 (2017)

39. Bangor, A., Kortum, P., Miller, J.: Determining what individual SUS scores mean: adding an adjective rating scale. J. Usability Stud. **4**, 114–123 (2009)

40. Schrepp, M., Hinderks, A., Thomaschewski, J.: Construction of a benchmark for the user experience questionnaire (UEQ). Int. J. Interact. Multimed. Artif. Intell. **4**, 40 (2017)

41. Braun, V., Clarke, V.: Thematic analysis. In: APA handbook of research methods in psychology, Vol 2: Research designs: Quantitative, qualitative, neuropsychological, and biological, pp. 57–71. American Psychological Association, Washington (2012)

42. Hwang, S.: Utilizing qualitative data analysis software: A review of Atlas. ti. Soc. Sci. Comput. Rev. **26**, 519–527 (2008)

43. Braun, V., Clarke, V.: Using thematic analysis in psychology. Qual. Res. Psychol. **3**, 77–101 (2006)

44. Mihas, P.: Qualitative research methods: approaches to qualitative data analysis. Int. Encycl. Educ. Ed. 302–313 (2023)

45. Thomas, D.R.: A general inductive approach for analyzing qualitative evaluation data. Am. J. Eval. **27**, 237–246 (2006)

46. Miyamoto, S.W., et al.: Tracking health data is not enough: a qualitative exploration of the role of healthcare partnerships and mhealth technology to promote physical activity and to sustain behavior change. JMIR mHealth uHealth. 4 (2016)

47. Bradshaw, J., et al.: Kindness, listening, and connection: patient and clinician key requirements for emotional support in chronic and complex care. J. Patient Exp. 9 (2022)

48. Chan, G., et al.: Feeling moodie: insights from a usability evaluation to improve the design of mHealth Apps. Int. J. Hum. Comput. Interact. (2023)

49. Eaton, C., et al.: User engagement with mHealth interventions to promote treatment adherence and self-management in people with chronic health conditions: a systematic review (Preprint). J. Med. Internet Res. (2023)

50. Uribe, F.A.R., et al.: Effectiveness of an app-based intervention to improve well-being through cultivating positive thinking and positive emotions in an adult sample: study protocol for a randomized controlled trial. Front. Psychol. 14 (2023)

Bridging Research and Practice in Persuasive Mobile Stress Management Apps: A 21-Year Comparative Analysis and Novel Design Framework

Mona Alhasani$^{(\boxtimes)}$ ⓘ, Oladapo Oyebode ⓘ, and Rita Orji ⓘ

Faculty of Computer Science, Dalhousie University, Halifax, NS B3H 4R2, Canada
{mona.alhasani,oladapo.oyebode,rita.orji}@dal.ca

Abstract. Mobile health (mHealth) apps have gained recognition as effective means of delivering interventions for managing stress, offering accessible and scalable alternatives to traditional therapies. However, from a persuasion standpoint, there is a notable gap in the literature regarding the design and effectiveness of mobile-based behaviour change apps for stress management over the years. Therefore, we conduct a comparative analysis to explore trends in persuasive mobile apps for stress management (PMAS) in the literature and in the wild from 2003 to 2024 (21 years). Specifically, we identify the most frequently used persuasive strategies in PMAS design, including their operationalization and effectiveness. Additionally, we compare the persuasive strategies employed in the academic literature and those in commercial apps, as well as examine the therapeutic frameworks for intervention design, target audience, evaluation methods, and effectiveness of PMAS in reducing stress. Based on our findings, we developed a two-stage framework for designing effective PMAS and offer recommendations for future research to address identified gaps.

Keywords: Persuasive interventions · stress management · mobile apps · comparative analysis · conceptual framework · design recommendations

1 Introduction

The pervasive impact of stress on mental and physical health has become a global concern. Mental stress has been linked to chronic illnesses [1], reduced productivity [2], and an overall decline in quality of life [3]. Traditional stress management interventions, such as face-to-face psychotherapy and workshops, are effective but often limited by accessibility, cost, and scalability [4]. Mobile health (mHealth) app interventions have emerged as promising solutions, offering scalable, convenient, and cost-effective alternatives. Moreover, mHealth apps address barriers such as geographical limitations, mental health stigma, and shortages of qualified professionals [4]. mHealth apps have gained traction as platforms for stress management over the years, offering features such as stress tracking, guided mindfulness exercises, cognitive behavioural therapy (CBT), and positive reinforcement mechanisms [5]. By incorporating evidence-based therapeutic frameworks, including CBT and mindfulness-based stress reduction, these apps provide structured methods to alleviate stress [6]. Beyond accessibility, mHealth apps utilize persuasive strategies to engage users, promote adherence to healthy behaviours, and enhance the overall user experience, thereby supporting stress management practices [7]. Despite the growing recognition of mHealth apps for stress management, gaps remain in understanding the persuasive strategies that drive their design and implementation.

While these apps incorporate evidence-based frameworks and persuasive features, comprehensive analysis of the trends shaping their development and strategies for promoting user engagement and behaviour change is limited, particularly in the literature [8]. To the best to our knowledge, this is the first study to initiate this research method by systematically comparing the persuasive strategies documented in academic literature with those implemented in real-world apps within the persuasive technology field. This comparison is essential to uncover potential disparities in the selection and implementation of persuasive techniques, which may influence the effectiveness and user adoption of persuasive mobile apps for stress management (PMAS). Without such insights, it remains unclear whether research-focused approaches align with real-world practices or how persuasive strategies can be optimized to improve their outcomes. Therefore, this work aims to address the following research questions: **RQ1**: What are the trends in persuasive mobile apps for stress management, and how effective are PMAS?, **RQ2**: What are the most implemented persuasive strategies, and how are they operationalized?, **RQ3**: What are the similarities and differences between persuasive strategies implemented in the academic literature versus real-world apps?, **RQ4**: How can we design a framework to guide the development of effective and credible persuasive stress management apps?, and **RQ5**: What gaps exist in the literature, and what recommendations can guide the future development of persuasive apps for stress management?

2 Persuasion Frameworks and Persuasive Strategies

Persuasive technology refers to interactive computing systems intentionally designed to ethically influence users' attitudes and behaviours [9]. These systems aim to promote positive behaviour changes, such as adopting healthy habits or reducing harmful ones, by leveraging psychological and behavioural principles to motivate and support users effectively [10, 11]. One foundational framework in this field is the Fogg Behaviour Model (FBM) [12], which identifies three essential conditions required for a person to perform a target behaviour: (i) sufficient motivation, (ii) the ability to perform the behaviour, and (iii) the presence of a trigger. These three factors must occur simultaneously for the behaviour to take place. In addition, the FBM outlines seven persuasive strategies—*reduction, tunneling, tailoring, suggestion, self-monitoring, surveillance, and conditioning*—that guide the design of behaviour change or persuasive technologies. Building on FBM, Oinas-Kukkonen et al. [11] proposed the Persuasive Systems Design (PSD) model, a comprehensive framework for embedding persuasive features into systems to drive behavioural and attitudinal changes. The PSD framework organizes 28 persuasive strategies into four categories. The *Primary Task Support* category includes strategies that assist users in achieving their main goals. The *Dialogue Support* category focuses on providing feedback, such as notifications or suggestions, to engage and motivate users. The *System Credibility Support* category highlights techniques that enhance system trustworthiness to increase its persuasive potential. Lastly, the *Social Support* category encompasses strategies that enable user interaction or collaboration to foster desired behaviours. Table 1 outlines the PSD framework's four categories, detailing the strategies in each group. Another popular framework is the Behavior Change Techniques Taxonomy (BCTT) [13], which offers a detailed classification of strategies for behaviour change. The BCTT includes techniques such as *goal setting, feedback, self-monitoring, social comparison, and reinforcement*. These strategies provide granular insights into designing interventions that effectively influence behaviour. We apply these well-established frameworks to identify persuasive strategies implemented in mobile apps for stress management. By leveraging both the PSD framework and the BCTT, we systematically and comparatively examine a wide range of strategies to ensure wider coverage and analysis.

Table 1. Persuasive strategies included the PSD categories [11]

Primary Task Support	Dialogue Support	System Credibility Support	Social Support
Reduction	Praise	Trustworthiness	Social learning
Tunneling	Rewards	Expertise	Social comparison
Tailoring	Reminders	Surface credibility	Normative influence
Personalization	Suggestion	Real-world feel	Social facilitation
Self-monitoring	Similarity	Authority	Cooperation
Simulation	Liking	Third-party endorsements	Competition
Rehearsal	Social role	Verifiability	Recognition

3   Materials and Methods

To address our research questions, we conducted a systematic quantitative content analysis using a modified coding scheme validated by Orji et al. [9]. This scheme categorizes data into themes such as study year, therapies, designs, target audiences, persuasive strategies, and their effectiveness, facilitating accessibility for designers, researchers, and decision-makers. It was chosen for its alignment with our focus on persuasive strategies and proven reliability in similar contexts [14].

3.1   Search Strategy and Eligibility Criteria

The inclusion criteria required articles to be published in English between 2003 and 2024 (post-Fogg's foundational work in 2002) and to discuss persuasive technology design, evaluation, or both for stress management. We conducted a systematic search across six databases—ACM Digital Library, Scopus, PubMed, IEEE, Springer, and EBSCO-Host—and supplemented this with Google Scholar to ensure comprehensive coverage. These databases were selected to capture studies on stress management interventions in domains such as health informatics, behavioural science, and human-computer interaction (HCI). We also reviewed the reference lists of selected articles to identify additional relevant studies. The search query included combinations such as ("stress" OR "stress management") AND ("Behavior Change Technology" OR "Persuasive Technology") AND ("web" OR "mobile" OR "VR" OR "AR" OR "Mixed Reality"). This ensured a comprehensive coverage of established and emerging technologies used in stress management interventions. The initial search yielded 1,860 unique articles. Titles and abstracts were screened to exclude studies on non-digital interventions or those not focused on persuasive technology. This process retained 107 studies. After a full-text review of intervention types and platforms, 49 studies focusing on mobile apps for stress management were included in the final analysis. The identification process is summarized in Fig. 1.

4   Results

Our analysis of existing PMAS revealed some interesting trends and insights.

This section addresses **RQ1** by presenting the trends of PMAS from reviewed studies, including trends by year and country, therapies used in their development, target audiences, evaluation methods, and their effectiveness in reducing stress. Then, it delves into the most frequently implemented persuasive strategies in designing PMAS and how they were operationalized in the reviewed studies (**RQ2**). Finally, it answers **RQ3** by comparing the similarities and differences between persuasive strategies implemented in the reviewed studies and real-world apps.

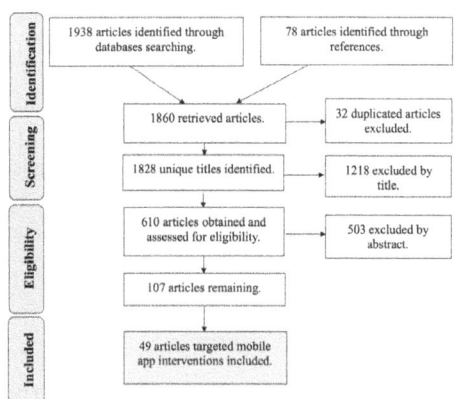

Fig. 1. PRISMA flow diagram depicting the study selection process workflow [15].

4.1 Types of Persuasive Mobile Apps for Stress Management

It is important to highlight that some studies employed more than one technology. Among the 49 studies on persuasive mobile apps analyzed, ten studies incorporated wearable sensors [16–25] to capture stress through bio-signals, emphasizing physiological monitoring. Five studies utilized games [21, 26–29] to enhance user engagement and promote stress reduction. Similarly, two studies leveraged virtual reality (VR) [17, 27] to deliver immersive and interactive stress management experiences. Additionally, two studies [25, 30] integrated a smartwatch app to provide multi-device support, and one study [16] created a mobile and web-based omnichannel platform. The remaining 33 studies implemented only mobile apps without integrating additional technologies.

4.2 Persuasive Mobile App for Stress Management by Year and Country

The distribution of PMAS shows fluctuating activity across the years. Singular studies were documented in 2011, 2013, 2015, and 2016, with limited activity in earlier years. However, a noticeable increase occurred from 2017 onward, with two studies in 2017 and 2018, followed by a rise in 2019 (five studies) and 2020 (seven studies). In 2021, five studies were conducted, and this upward trend continued with seven studies in 2022, eight in 2023, and nine in 2024, reflecting sustained and growing interest in this area over the past decade. Globally, the distribution of these studies highlights their international reach, as shown in Fig. 2. The United States (USA) leads significantly with eleven studies, followed by South Korea, New Zealand, Australia, the Netherlands, and India, each contributing three studies. Canada and China each contributed two studies, while other countries, including Germany, Italy, and others, contributed one study each.

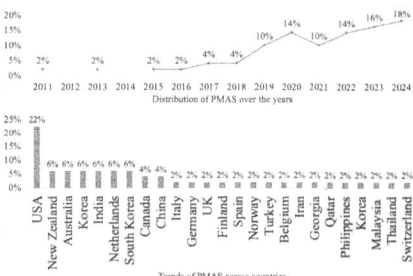

Fig. 2. Trends of persuasive mobile apps for stress management by year and country.

4.3 Evidence-Based Therapies in Persuasive Stress Management Apps Design

Figure 3 highlights evidence-based therapies in PMAS. Among the 49 studies, 39 reported specific therapies for intervention design, while 10 did not report any therapeutic approach. Frequently used therapies include Mindfulness-Based Stress Reduction (MBSR) and Cognitive Behavioral Therapy (CBT), reported in 18 and 9 studies, respectively. Positive Psychology Exercises (PPE) were used in 6 studies, and

Compassion-Focused Therapy and Mindfulness-Based Cognitive Therapy (MBCT) were each employed in 4 studies. Additionally, some studies reported the use of less common therapies, such as Laughter Therapy and Brainwave Entrainment Therapy, each utilized in 1 study, showcasing the variety of approaches in intervention design.

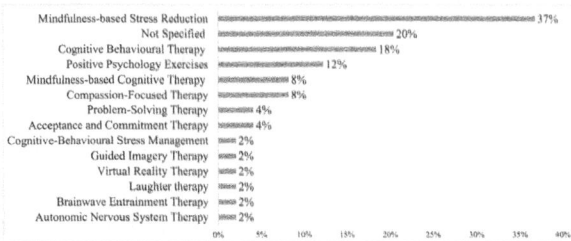

Fig. 3. Evidence-based therapies used to develop persuasive apps for stress management.

4.4   Methods, Study Design, and Target Audience

The methodologies employed to evaluate PMAS varied across the reviewed studies. Mixed methods (combining qualitative and quantitative approaches) were used in 15 studies (38%). Quantitative methods alone were the most common, and they were used in 33 studies (59%), with tools like surveys/questionnaires and wearable sensors dominating data collection methods. Qualitative approaches, such as interviews, were the least used, with only one study (3%) focusing solely on design usability. Interestingly, 27 studies (55%) utilized randomized controlled trials (RCTs) with control groups, while 22 studies (45%) did not. We further examined the diversity of target audiences in these interventions. As shown in Fig. 4, the reviewed studies addressed a wide range of populations. Most studies focused on adults (96%), with 16 studies (33%) targeting adults in general and the remaining studies targeting specific adult subgroups. University students were the most frequently studied subgroup, appearing in 8 studies (16%). Employees and office workers were the focus of 5 studies (10%), while 4 studies (8%) addressed individuals with post-traumatic stress disorder (PTSD). Healthcare providers (e.g., physicians and nurses), women (including pregnant and nursing women), and military personnel or veterans were each represented in 3 studies (6%). Other populations, such as teachers, men, cancer patients/survivors, and drivers, were each the focus of 1 study (2%). Limited attention was given to adolescents (2%), children (2%), or the elderly (0%).

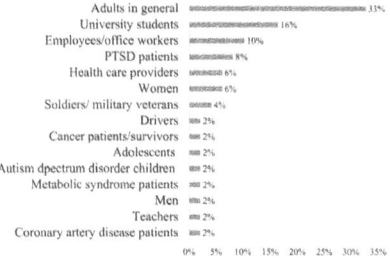

Fig. 4. Demographics targeted by persuasive mobile app for stress management.

4.5 Persuasive Strategies Employed in Mobile Apps for Stress Management

Figure 5 highlights the diverse range of persuasive strategies utilized in PMAS. Among the 49 reviewed studies, 40 employed multiple strategies, while only 9 relied on a single strategy. *Self-monitoring* was the most commonly used, appearing in 33 studies (67%), followed by *reminders* in 21 studies (43%) and *tunneling* (35%) in 17 studies. *Personalization* and *goal setting* were also notable, featured in 11 (22%) and 6 (12%) studies, respectively. In contrast, strategies like *social learning* and *punishment* were infrequently employed, with only 2 and 1 studies utilizing them. Table 2 provides a detailed summary of how each strategy was implemented based on the intervention descriptions.

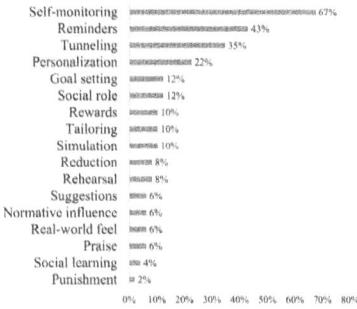

Fig. 5. Persuasive strategies employed in the mobile app for stress management.

4.6 Overall Effectiveness of Persuasive Stress Management Apps Based on the Evaluation Outcomes

We categorized the effectiveness of PMAS in the reviewed studies based on their ability to meet the design goals outlined by the authors. This approach, used in prior systematic reviews [9], allows for synthesizing outcomes from studies with diverse methodologies. PMAS were categorized as follows: Effective (fully achieved stress reduction goal), Partially Effective (mixed evaluation results showing partial achievement of stress reduction goals), Neutral (no significant or positive outcomes), and Not Specified (design evaluation only without reporting stress or physiological outcomes). Figure 6 summarizes our findings: Of 49 reviewed studies, 30 (61%) were Effective, 10 (21%) were Partially Effective, 3 (6%) were Neutral, and 6 (12%) did not report effectiveness.

Table 2. Persuasive strategies employed in reviewed studies and how they were implemented.

Persuasive strategy	How it was implemented in the literature apps	Studies	Total
Self-monitoring	Graphical/Visual representation	[16, 18, 19, 21, 22, 24, 30–40]	17
	Textual representation	[16, 19, 21, 32, 37, 38, 41–47]	13
	Numerical representation	[5, 45, 46, 48–51]	10
Reminders	Push notifications	[18, 19, 22, 30, 31, 33, 34, 36, 40–42, 44, 52–59]	20
	Email	[49]	1
Simulation	Visual effect	[26, 28]	2
	Audio effect	[20, 23, 29]	3
Personalization	Personalized intervention based on user preferences (Subjectively)	[22, 30, 32, 33, 35, 37, 53, 60]	8
	Personalized intervention based on user data (Objectively)	[20]	1
	Personalized feedback based on user experience and progression	[41, 55]	2
Tunneling	Order-based guidance	[5, 16, 23, 35, 38, 53, 56–59, 61–63]	13
	Voice-based guidance	[20]	1
	Visual-based guidance	[17, 25, 29]	3
Social role	Text-based communication with experts/chatbot	[16, 28, 32, 55]	4
	Text-based communication with friends	[41]	1
	Voice-based communication with experts	[31]	1
Rewards	Leaves, branches, or flowers	[26, 40]	2
	Points	[21, 60]	2
	Badges	[26]	1
Goal setting	List of goals	[16, 40]	2
	Goals in a calendar	[33]	1
	Step count	[19]	1
	Session number	[30, 38]	2
Rehearsal	Visual/Video tutorial	[30, 63]	2
	Text instruction	[24, 42]	2

(continued)

Table 2. (*continued*)

Persuasive strategy	How it was implemented in the literature apps	Studies	Total
Suggestion	Recommendation for adjustments	[21]	1
	Recommendation for practicing	[40, 47]	2
Tailoring	Tailored game to specific group	[58, 60]	2
	Tailored resources based on location/mental status	[27, 44, 52]	3
Real-world feel	Contact us	[16, 35, 47]	3
Reduction	Quick Access Information/ book appointment	[32, 47]	2
	Coping Mechanisms List	[33]	1
	Editable Template	[40]	1
Punishment	Loose a life, and the game resets	[21]	1
Normative influence	Social community/peer support	[28, 42, 54]	3
Social learning	List of peer coping mechanisms	[33]	1
	Social community (peer learning)	[40]	1
Praise	Encouragement feedback (text)	[24, 26, 29]	3

Effectiveness of Persuasive Stress Management Apps Based on Persuasive Strategies. To ensure a focused analysis, we excluded the six studies in the "Not Specified" category that did not report on the effectiveness of their interventions. The effectiveness of the apps was then assessed based on their implemented persuasive strategies, as summarized in Fig. 7. Among the dominant strategies, *self-monitoring* demonstrated 68% effectiveness, with 32% partially effective in reducing stress. Similarly, apps employing *reminders* showed 70% effectiveness and 20% partial effectiveness. Strategies such as *social role* and *rewards* reported effectiveness rates of 67% and 60%, respectively. *Goal-setting* and *personalization* each demonstrated 50% effectiveness; however, both *personalization* and *rewards* also reported 20% ineffectiveness. *Simulation* emerged as the most effective strategy, with 80% of apps showing full effectiveness and 20% partial effectiveness. Notably, less frequently implemented strategies, including *suggestions, praise, punishment*, and *real-world feel*, reported 100% effectiveness or partial effectiveness. In contrast, apps employing the *tailoring* strategy were the least effective, with 50% deemed ineffective in reducing stress.

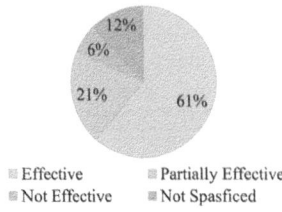

Fig. 6. Effectiveness of persuasive stress management apps by the study outcomes.

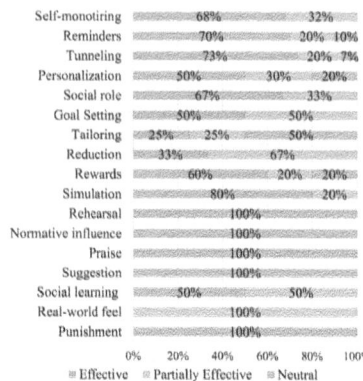

Fig. 7. Comparative effectiveness based on persuasive strategies.

4.7 Comparing Persuasive Strategies Operationalized in the Literature and Real-World Apps

This section builds on prior research exploring persuasive strategies implemented in stress management mobile apps available in app stores (n = 150) using the PSD model [64]. Apps were extracted from Google Play and Apple's App Store using the following search query: ("stress" AND ("management" OR "monitoring" OR "detection" OR "mindfulness" OR "meditation" OR "breathing" OR "relaxation" OR "prevention")). We compare the strategies identified in that paper with those we identified in the academic literature in the current paper (see Sect. 4.5). Our findings highlight both similarities and differences (See Fig. 8). Both contexts prioritize *self-monitoring*, with 51% of real-world apps and 67% of reviewed studies employing this strategy. The next dominant strategy in both contexts is *reminder*, which is operationalized in 36% of real-world apps and 43% of apps in the reviewed studies. Other frequently used strategies in both contexts include *tailoring, rewards, reduction,* and *personalization,* but in varying degrees. Specifically, *personalization* is more dominant in real-world apps, with 81% coverage, compared to only 22% coverage of reviewed studies. Strategies categorized under System Credibility Support are also employed in real-world apps. These include *trustworthiness* (39%), *expertise* (26%), *authority* (11%), *verifiability* (9%), *surface credibility* (6%), and *third-party endorsements* (4%). In addition to credibility-focused strategies, real-world apps also employ strategies like *competition* (1%), *recognition* (2%), and *social facilitation* (5%), which are social support strategies, as well as the *similarity* strategy (4%). Yet, *the tunneling* strategy is more dominant in the literature (35%), distinguishing it from real-world apps (7%).

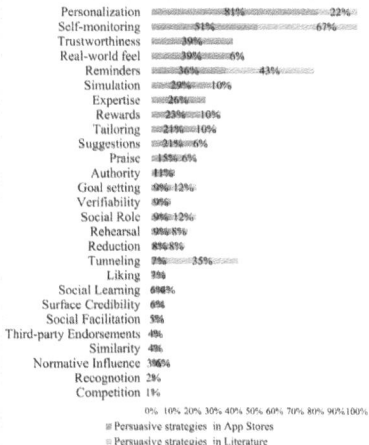

Fig. 8. Persuasive strategies employed in real-world apps versus apps in reviewed studies.

5 Discussion

This systematic and comparative review showed that 80% of studies designing PMAS rely heavily on evidence-based therapeutic frameworks for stress reduction, especially Mindfulness-Based Stress Reduction (MBSR) and Cognitive Behavioral Therapy (CBT). These findings align with previous research [65], highlighting CBT and MBSR as effective approaches for stress reduction. Positive Psychology Exercises, including gratitude practices and breathing techniques, were also commonly integrated, reinforcing their value in digital stress interventions [66]. Additionally, some apps employed less common therapies, such as laughter therapy [26] and VR therapy [27], which have been shown to be effective in managing stress based on our results. Furthermore, our findings on persuasive strategies operationalized in PMAS reveal key trends in implementation approaches and effectiveness, providing insights for future mobile app interventions. While most studies incorporated multiple strategies, research indicates no direct correlation between the number of strategies used and the overall effectiveness of the intervention [67]. Notably, each strategy was often implemented in diverse ways, as shown in Table 2, offering valuable guidance for researchers seeking to optimize strategy implementation. Among the strategies, *self-monitoring* emerged as the most frequently implemented and found to be effective by most studies. This underscores its critical role in helping users to be aware of stress occurrence and triggers and effectively track progress toward stress mitigation [68]. In line with our findings, research has shown that *self-monitoring* is the most implemented strategy in persuasive health and wellness interventions [9]. *Reminder*, which is the next dominant and effective strategy based on our findings, has the potential to sustain user engagement [69]. Strategies like *tunnelling* and *goal setting* also effectively guided user behaviour [11]. Less commonly implemented strategies, such as *praise*, *punishment*, *social learning*, and *real-world feel*, were reported to be effective or partially effective, suggesting untapped potential for further exploration. Although employed in five studies, *tailoring* was found to be ineffective in most of the studies. While most apps in the reviewed studies tailored content based on user characteristics (e.g., location or mental state), tailoring could be further enhanced by dynamically adapting content to users' literacy levels or the specific needs of groups such as different age groups, genders, or stress types like academic, work, or financial stress.

5.1 Two-Stage Framework for Designing Persuasive Stress Management Apps

This section introduces a two-stage framework inspired by our findings to guide the design of effective stress management apps for persuasive app designers, mental health practitioners, and researchers (**RQ4**). Our comparative analysis of persuasive strategies in academic literature-based apps and real-world apps from app stores highlighted key differences: academic apps prioritize evidence-based strategies for stress reduction, while real-world apps incorporate credibility-enhancing strategies, such as authority and verifiability, to build trust. This distinction reflects the broader audience, long-term adoption goals, and trust-building needs of real-world apps, especially given the sensitivity of stress management. In contrast, academic apps primarily focus on developing effective, evidence-based interventions before commercialization. Based on these insights, we propose a framework for designing persuasive stress management apps: Stage 1 emphasizes integrating evidence-based strategies during development to ensure effectiveness, while Stage 2 focuses on enhancing credibility and fostering user engagement post-launch (Fig. 9).

Stage 1: App Design Using Evidence-Based Strategies. The first stage integrates evidence-based strategies from our review findings to develop effective stress management apps. This phase ensures the app addresses core user needs while leveraging the most widely implemented and effective persuasive strategies (See Sect. 4.6.1). To guide designers, we created a recommended pool of strategies to serve as a foundation for effective interventions. Key strategies include *self-monitoring*, where users track stress levels, habits, and triggers, providing real-time feedback for informed decision-making; *reminders*, offering context-aware notifications to maintain engagement with stress-reducing activities; and *personalization*, tailoring content and interventions to users' stress levels, preferences, and progress. The use of *tunneling*, providing step-by-step guidance for stress management activities, is also crucial, along with *rewards* and non-competitive incentives like virtual achievements to encourage positive behaviour. Simplifying tasks through *reduction* and offering *rehearsal* materials for stress relief techniques can reduce cognitive load and enhance usability. *Simulation* allows users to observe the impact of their behaviour on stress levels, while *goal-setting* helps users manage stress and track progress. *Normative influence* encourages positive actions by showcasing effective stress management behaviours, and incorporating a *social role*, such as virtual assistance or expert communication, provides users with guidance and professional support.

Stage 2: Enhancing Credibility in the App Marketplace. In the second stage, the focus shifts to optimizing the app for broader dissemination in commercial app stores, long-term use and adoption, and trust building. While strategies such as social comparison and recognition are implemented in app store apps, they are avoided here due to the potential negative impact on stressed individuals. Research has shown a positive correlation between perceived competition and mental health issues [70], making these strategies less suitable for stress management apps. Instead, we recommend strategies that prioritize trust, credibility and engagement. These include emphasizing the app's ***trustworthiness*** by clearly communicating its evidence-based foundation and scientific validity, showcasing the ***expertise*** of qualified mental health professionals involved in its development, and incorporating endorsements from reputable organizations or certifications to validate its quality. ***Verifiability*** ensures transparency by providing references to the research and methodologies supporting the app's content while creating a ***real-world feel*** that allows users to communicate directly with the developers for feedback, fostering authenticity and trust. Additionally, system-generated ***suggestions*** and ***praise*** for achievements guide users toward stress-reducing behaviours and further enhance engagement. These two strategies are frequently implemented in real-world apps, and based on our literature review findings, they demonstrate a potential for stress reduction (Fig. 9).

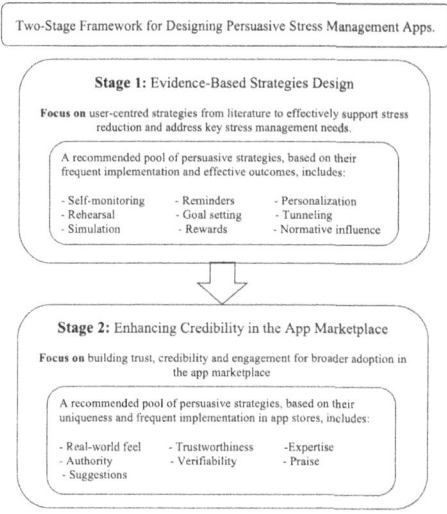

Fig. 9. The two-stage framework for designing persuasive mobile apps for stress management.

5.2 Gaps and Future Research Directions for PMAS

Our findings reveal significant gaps in the current literature. Based on these gaps, we offer recommendations to drive progress and explore potential research avenues in advancing Human-Computer Interaction and persuasive technology for stress management mobile apps (**RQ5**).

Recommendation 1: Research on PMAS is largely focused on developed nations, creating a digital divide (See Sect. 4.2). Therefore, *future studies should close this gap by considering diverse cultural, geographical, and socio-economic factors that shape* *stress experiences and coping strategies* [71]. Research has shown that culturally tailored interventions can enhance relevance, effectiveness, and overall well-being [72].

Recommendation 2: The predominant focus of PMAS is on emotion-based coping strategies, utilizing mindfulness, mindful breathing, and gratitude exercises to alleviate stress-related negative emotions [73]. Conversely, only 6% of studies explore coping strategies for addressing underlying stressors to resolve or mitigate them [73]. This imbalance highlights a critical research gap (See Sect. 4.3), underscoring *the need to investigate and expand proactive, problem-solving approaches to stress management mobile app interventions.*

Recommendation 3: The primary focus of PMAS has been on adults, with a notable gap in research targeting adolescents, the elderly, and children (See Sect. 4.4). This highlights the need for more inclusive studies. Future research *should prioritize the design and development of persuasive stress management apps tailored to these underrepresented age groups.*

Recommendation 4: The literature on PMAS often lacks detailed descriptions of the persuasive strategies employed, including their implementation methods and specific examples. This gap makes it challenging for researchers and practitioners to understand or replicate these designs. Future *research should address this by adopting structured reporting formats—such as tables, figures, or lists* (similar to Sect. 4.5)—*to clearly document the strategies used and their application within intervention designs.*

6 Conclusion

Our review highlights the diverse and evolving landscape of PMAS. Evidence-based therapies, such as MBSR and CBT, were frequently used, emphasizing their importance in intervention design. The studies primarily focused on adults, with students as a secondary target group. Persuasive strategies, such as self-monitoring and reminders, were commonly employed in both real-world and literature-based apps, though notable differences in strategy prioritization emerged between these contexts. Based on these findings, we propose a two-stage framework for designing effective persuasive stress management apps. We offer recommendations to address gaps in literature-based apps and guide future research. There are some limitations to this study. The restriction to English-language papers may have excluded relevant non-English studies, suggesting that future reviews should consider broader language inclusion. Additionally, the search strategy may have overlooked studies using alternative terminology like "persuasive systems" or regional spelling variations like "behaviour" vs. "behavior", indicating the need for more inclusive search terms in future research.

References

1. Larzelere, M.M., Jones, G.N.: Stress and Health. Primary Care - Clinics in Office Pract. **35**, 839–856 (2008). https://doi.org/10.1016/j.pop.2008.07.011

2. Timotius, E., Octavius, G.S.: Stress at the workplace and its impacts on productivity: a systematic review from industrial engineering, management, and medical perspective. Indus. Eng. Manage. Sys. **21**, 192–205 (2022)
3. Babapour, A.-R., Gahassab-Mozaffari, N., et al.: Nurses' job stress and its impact on quality of life and caring behaviors: a cross-sectional study. BMC Nurs. **21**, 75 (2022)
4. Greenwood, H., Krzyzaniak, N., et al.: Telehealth Versus Face-to-face Psychotherapy for Less Common Mental Health Conditions: Systematic Review and Meta-analysis of RCT (2022)
5. Bear, K.A., Barber, C.C., et al.: The impact of a mindfulness app on postnatal distress. Mindfulness (N Y). (2022). https://doi.org/10.1007/s12671-022-01992-7
6. Loo Gee, B., Griffiths, K.M., et al.: Effectiveness of mobile technologies delivering ecological momentary Interventions for stress and anxiety: a systematic review. J. Am. Med. Inform. Assoc. **23**, 221–229 (2016)
7. Oyebode, O., Ndulue, C., et al.: Persuasive Mobile Apps for Health and Wellness: A Comparative Systematic Review. Springer International Publishing (2020)
8. Alhasani, M., Mulchandani, D., et al.: A systematic review of persuasive strategies in stress management apps. BCSS@PERSUASIVE, p. 2662 (2020)
9. Orji, R., Moffatt, K.: Persuasive technology for health and wellness: State-of-the-art and emerging trends. Health Informatics J. **24**, 66–91 (2018)
10. Orji, R.: Why are persuasive strategies effective? exploring the strengths and weaknesssses of socially-oriented persuasive strategies. In: Lecture Notes in Computer Science, Lecture Notes in Artificial Intelligence and Lecture Notes in Bioinformatics). Springer Verlag (2017)
11. Oinas-kukkonen, H., Harjumaa, M.: Persuasive Systems Design: Key Issues, Process Model, and System Features. Communications of the Association for Information Systems 24 (2009)
12. Fogg, B.J., Fogg, G.E.: Persuasive Technology: Using Computers to Change What We Think and Do. Morgan Kaufmann, San Francisco, USA (2003)
13. Michie, S., Richardson, M., et al.: The behavior change technique taxonomy (v1) of 93 hierarchically clustered techniques: building an international consensus for the reporting of behavior change interventions. Ann. Behav. Med. **46**, 81–95 (2013)
14. Aldenaini, N., Alqahtani, et al.: Trends in Persuasive Technologies for Physical Activity and Sedentary Behavior: A Systematic Review (2020)
15. Liberati, A., Altman, D.G., et al.: The PRISMA statement for reporting systematic reviews and meta-analyses of studies that evaluate health care interventions. J. Clin. Epidemiol. 62 (2009)
16. Lappalainen, P., Kaipainen, et al.: Feasibility of a personal health technology-based psychological intervention for men with stress and mood problems: RCT. J Med Internet Res. 15 (2013)
17. Soyka, F., Leyrer, M., et al.: Enhancing stress management techniques using virtual reality. Proceedings of the ACM Symposium on Applied Perception, SAP **2016**, 85–88 (2016)
18. Patlar Akbulut, F., Ikitimur, B., Akan, A.: Wearable sensor-based evaluation of psychosocial stress in patients with metabolic syndrome. Artif. Intell. Med. **104**, 101824 (2020)
19. Smith, E.N., Santoro, E., et al.: Integrating wearables in stress management interventions: promising evidence from a randomized trial. Int. J. Stress Manag. (2019)
20. Zepf, S., El Haouij, et al.: Studying personalized just-in-time auditory breathing guides and potential safety implications during simulated driving. UMAP 2020 - Proceedings of the 28th ACM Conference on User Modeling, Adaptation and Personalization, pp. 275–283 (2020)
21. Zafar, M.A., Ahmed, B., et al.: Gaming away stress: using biofeedback games to learn paced breathing. IEEE Trans. Affect. Comput. **11**, 519–531 (2020)
22. Elvitigala, D.S., Scholl, P.M., et al.: StressShoe: A DIY Toolkit for just-in-time personalised stress interventions for office workers performing sedentary tasks. In: Proceedings of Mobile-HCI 2021 - ACM International Conference on Mobile Human-Computer Interaction: Mobile Apart, MobileTogether. Association for Computing Machinery, Inc (2021)

23. Min, B., Park, H., et al.: The effectiveness of a neurofeedback-assisted mindfulness training program using a mobile app on stress reduction in employees: randomized controlled trial. JMIR Mhealth Uhealth **11**, e42851 (2023)

24. Choi, Y.-J., Cho, D.-H., et al.: Feasibility of a mobile app for traumatic stress management using neurofeedback-based meditation and binaural beat music: a pilot randomized controlled trial. Digit Health. **10** (2024)

25. Son, C., Hegde, S., et al.: Use of a mobile biofeedback app to provide health coaching for stress self-management: pilot quasi-experiment. JMIR Form Res. **7**, e41018 (2023)

26. Deshpande, G., Chanda, S.: Laughter as a controller in a stress buster game. PervasiveHealth '20: 14th EAI International Conference on Pervasive Computing Technologies for Healthcare (2020)

27. De Asis, K.M.R., Guillem, E.J.P., et al.: Serenity: a stress-relieving virtual reality application based on philippine environmental variables. ACM Proceeding Series. 155–159 (2020)

28. Orji, J., Chan, G., et al.: SmileApp: The Design and Evaluation of an mHealth App for Stress Reduction Through Artificial Intelligence and Persuasive Technology. Presented at the (2024)

29. Jeong, H., Yoo, J.H., Goh, M., Song, H.: Deep breathing in your hands: designing and assessing a DTx mobile app. Front Digit Health. 6 (2024)

30. Wallace, T., Morris, J.T., et al.: Implementation of a mobile technology-supported diaphragmatic breathing intervention in military mTBI with PTSD. J. Head Trauma Rehabilit. **37**, 152–161 (2022)

31. Reid, S.C., Kauer, S.D., et al.: A mobile phone application for the assessment and management of youth mental health problems in primary care: Health service outcomes from a randomised controlled trial of mobiletype. BMC Fam Pract. 14 (2013)

32. Kuhn, E., Kanuri, N., et al.: A randomized controlled trial of a smartphone app for posttraumatic stress disorder symptoms. J. Consult. Clin. Psychol. **85**, 267–273 (2017)

33. Lee, K., Cho, H., et al.: Toward Future-Centric Personal Informatics: Expecting Stressful Events and Preparing Personalized Interventions in Stress Management. Conference on Human Factors in Computing Systems – Proceedings, pp. 1–13 (2020)

34. Fuller-Tyszkiewicz, M., Richardson, B., et al.: Efficacy of a smartphone app intervention for reducing caregiver stress: randomized controlled trial. JMIR Ment Health. 7 (2020)

35. Borosund, E., Mirkovic, J., et al.: A stress management app intervention for cancer survivors: design, development, and usability testing. JMIR Form Res. **2**, 1–16 (2018)

36. DiNardo, M.M., Greco, C., et al.: Effects of an integrated mindfulness intervention for veterans with diabetes distress: a randomized controlled trial. BMJ Open Diabetes Res Care. 10 (2022)

37. Demirel, S., Roke, Y., et al.: Assessing the effectiveness of STAPP@Work, a self-management mobile app, in reducing work stress and preventing burnout: single-case experimental design study. J. Med. Internet Res. **26**, e48883 (2024)

38. Valinskas, S., Nakrys, et al.: Sensa mobile app for managing stress, anxiety, and depression symptoms: pilot cohort study. JMIR Form Res. **7**, e40671 (2023)

39. Yoopat, P., Thoicharoen, P., et al.: Assessment of work-related stress utilizing the find my stress mobile application among university students and adult workers amidst the COVID-19 pandemic. J. Bodyw. Mov. Ther. **39**, 415–422 (2024)

40. Alhasani, M., Orji, R.: Promoting stress management among students in higher education: evaluating the effectiveness of a persuasive time management mobile App. Int. J. Hum. Comput. Interact. (2024)

41. Hwang, H., Kim, S.M., et al.: The efficacy of a smartphone-based app on stress reduction: randomized controlled trial. J. Med. Internet Res. **24**, 1–16 (2022)

42. Zhang, H., Zhang, A., et al.: A brief online mindfulness-based group intervention for psychological distress among chinese residents during COVID-19: a pilot randomized controlled trial. Mindfulness (N Y). **12**, 1502–1512 (2021)

43. Chu, A., Rose, T.M., et al.: Evaluating the effects of a mindfulness mobile application on student pharmacists' stress, burnout, and mindfulness. Am. J. Health Syst. Pharm. **79**, 656–664 (2022)
44. Fiol-DeRoque, M.A., Serrano-Ripoll, et al.: A mobile phone-based intervention to reduce mental health problems in health care workers during the COVID-19 pandemic (PsyCovidApp): Randomized controlled trial. JMIR Mhealth Uhealth. 9 (2021)
45. Carissoli, C., Villani, et al.: Does a meditation protocol supported by a mobile application help people reduce stress? suggestions from a controlled pragmatic trial. Cyberpsychology, Behavior, and Social Networking 18 (2015)
46. Xu, H., Eley, R., Kynoch, et al.: Effects of mobile mindfulness on emergency department work stress: a randomised controlled trial. EMA - Emergency Medicine Australasia **34**, 176–185 (2022)
47. Rakshitha, V.S., Mahadevi, M., et al.: Student stress buster: mobile app testing and solutions for anxiety and depression. In: 2023 12th International Conference on Advanced Computing (ICoAC), pp. 1–8. IEEE (2023)
48. Jallo, N., Thacker, L.R., et al.: A stress coping app for hospitalized pregnant women at risk for preterm birth. MCN The American Journal of Maternal/Child Nursing. **42**, 257–262 (2017)
49. Bostock, S., Crosswell, A.D., et al.: Mindfulness on-the-go: effects of a mindfulness meditation app on work stress and well-being. J. Occup. Health Psychol. **24**, 127–138 (2019)
50. Hwang, W.J., Jo, H.H.: Evaluation of the effectiveness of mobile app-based stress-management program: a randomized controlled trial. Int. J. Environ Res. Public Health. 16 (2019)
51. Shreekumar, A., Vautrey, P.-L.: Managing Emotions: The Effects of Online Mindfulness Meditation on Mental Health and Economic Behavior (2022)
52. Barber, C.C., Singh, S., et al.: PositivelyPregnant: Using guided prompts in a stress-management app for pregnant women. 2–6 (2018)
53. Kranenburg, L.W., Gillis, J., et al.: The effectiveness of a nonguided mindfulness app on perceived stress in a nonclinical Dutch population: randomized controlled trial. JMIR Ment Health. **9**, 1–9 (2022)
54. Weis, R., Ray, S.D., et al.: Mindfulness as a way to cope with COVID-19-related stress and anxiety. Couns. Psychother. Res. **21**, 8–18 (2021). https://doi.org/10.1002/capr.12375
55. Ulrich, S., Lienhard, N., et al.: A chatbot-delivered stress management coaching for students (MISHA App): pilot randomized controlled trial. JMIR Mhealth Uhealth **12**, e54945 (2024)
56. Zhao, C., Zhao, Z., et al.: Efficacy and acceptability of mobile application-delivered acceptance and commitment therapy for posttraumatic stress disorder in China: A randomized controlled trial. Behav. Res. Ther. **171**, 104440 (2023)
57. Boszko, M., Krzowski, B., et al.: Impact of AfterAMI mobile app on quality of life, depression, stress and anxiety in patients with coronary artery disease: open label. Randomized Trial. Life. **13**, 2015 (2023)
58. Wielgosz, J., Walser, R.D., et al.: Clinical benefits of self-guided mindfulness coach mobile app use for veterans with posttraumatic stress disorder: A pilot randomized control trial. Psychol Trauma. (2024)
59. Borjalilu, S.: The efficacy of Persian Version of Mindfulness-Based Stress Management app (Aramgar) for college's mindfulness skills and perceived stress. Int. J. Islamic Educ. Psychol. 4 (2023)
60. Carlier, S., Van Der Paelt, S., et al.: Using a serious game to reduce stress and anxiety in children with autism spectrum disorder. ACM International Conference Proceeding Series. 452–461 (2019)
61. Duraimani, S.: A Cross-sectional and longitudinal study of the effects of a mindfulness meditation mobile application platform on reducing stress and anxiety. Int. J. Yoga. 12 (2019)

62. Callahan, C., Kimber, J., et al.: The Real-World Impact of App-Based Mindfulness on Headspace Members With Moderate and Severe Perceived Stress. JMIR Mhealth Uhealth. 12 (2024)

63. Dantes, G.R., Asril, N.M., et al.: Brief Mobile App–Based Mindfulness Intervention for Indonesian Senior High School Teachers: Protocol for a Pilot Randomized Controlled Trial. JMIR Res Protoc

64. Alhasani, M., Mulchandani, D., et al.: A systematic and comparative review of behavior change strategies in stress management Apps. Front. Public Health 10, 1 (2022)

65. Abbasi, F., Shariati, K., et al.: Comparison of the Cognitive Behavioral Therapy and Mindfulness-Based Stress Reduction: Reducing Anxiety Symptoms. In Press, Womens Health Bull (2018)

66. Goodmon, L.B., Middleditch, A.M., et al.: Positive psychology course and its relationship to well-being, depression, and stress. Teaching of Psychology 43 (2016)

67. Alhasani, M., Orji, R.: Exploring Trends, Pitfalls, and Future Directions in Digital Behaviour Change Interventions for Managing Student Stress. Int. J. Hum. Comput. Interact. 1–20 (2024)

68. Alhasani, M., Oyebode, O., et al.: SereneMind: design and evaluation of a persuasive mobile app for managing stress among adults. In: 2023 IEEE 11th International Conference on Serious Games and Applications for Health (SeGAH). IEEE (2023)

69. Morrison, L.G., Hargood, C., et al.: The effect of timing and frequency of push notifications on usage of a smartphone-based stress management intervention. PLoS One. 12 (2017)

70. Dqg, G., Ri, L., Dgglwlrqdo, R.U., et al. Competition, Anxiety, and Depression in the College Classroom : Variations by Student Identity and Field of Study (2016)

71. Kuo, B.C.H., Soucie, K.M., et al.: The mediating role of cultural coping behaviours on the relationships between academic stress and positive psychosocial well-being outcomes. Int. J. Psychol. 53, 27–36 (2018)

72. Hirsh, J.B., Kang, S.K., et al.: Personalized persuasion: tailoring persuasive appeals to recipients' personality traits. Psychol. Sci. 23, 578–581 (2012)

73. Kaye, M., McIntosh, D., et al.: Stress: The Psychology of Managing Pressure. New York (2017)

Designing Behavior Change Support Systems for Recovery from Addictions: Mapping Software Features with Counseling Strategies

Hasan Selkan Taskan🆔 and Harri Oinas-Kukkonen(✉)🆔

University of Oulu, 90570 Oulu, Finland
`harri.oinas-kukkonen@oulu.fi`

Abstract. Addiction is one of the most important health issues around the world. It affects individuals, families, and societies while traditional approaches struggle with relapse and drop-out rates, accessibility problems, and aftercare support. However, behavior change support systems can offer substantial support by integrating evidence-based counseling strategies with Persuasive Systems Design. This paper presents a framework for mapping psychological approaches (Cognitive Behavioral Therapy, Motivational Interviewing, Minnesota Model, Contingency Management, and Family/Couples Therapies) with specific Persuasive Systems Design principles. This approach fills the gap between treatment and technology by showing how counseling strategies and persuasive software features can support addiction recovery together at different stages of recovery.

Keywords: Information Systems · Persuasive Systems Design · Addiction · Counseling

1 Introduction

Addiction is a serious public health threat impacting millions of individuals, families, and communities around the world. In 2019 alone, alcohol and other psychoactive substances caused 3.2 million deaths worldwide. Despite these alarming numbers, traditional addiction treatment approaches struggle with high relapse rates, limited reach, insufficient aftercare support, and high drop-out rates [1–4]. An individual's journey from the beginning of addiction treatment to full recovery requires continuous support to reach long-term behavior change [4]. With today's digital developments, information systems make it possible to provide solutions that support individuals throughout their recovery journey. Using different information systems approaches gives users personalized, easy-to-access, and effective solutions [5]. For instance, Behavior Change Support System (BCSS) is an interactive, technological solution designed specifically to help people adopt a certain attitude or behavior without coercion or deception [6]. These types of systems benefit both users by improving the outcomes of treatments, and professionals by providing invaluable support [6, 7]. Despite this potential, their development is hindered by the multidisciplinary complexity between information systems

K. T. Win et al. (Eds.): PERSUASIVE 2025, LNCS 15711, pp. 165–175, 2025.
https://doi.org/10.1007/978-3-031-94959-3_12

and intervention approaches [8]. Therefore, the main objective of this study is to seek a deeper understanding about how to effectively implement psychotherapies for addiction treatment in BCSSs.

2 Background

2.1 Persuasive Systems Design

Persuasive Systems Design (PSD) provides a structured approach for designing systems that influence behaviors and attitudes without any coercion or deception [9]. It explains persuasive software features in four categories: Primary Task Support (PRIM), Dialogue Support (DIAL), System Credibility Support (CRED), and Social Support (SOCI). The PRIM category simply helps users to perform targeted tasks more effectively; the DIAL category facilitates the interaction between the system and users to keep them engaged; the CRED support enhances the system's believability to increase its persuasiveness; and the SOCI category uses social influence to motivate users for change [9]. PSD also has proven particularly valuable in health-related interventions, including addiction treatment [10]. It provides a clear framework for integrating persuasive features for professionals from various fields. In web-based addiction treatment settings, PSD features, especially PRIM features like personalization, simulation, self-monitoring, and reduction, are often used to enhance motivation and engagement and monitor changes [10–13].

2.2 Psychological Approaches to Addiction Recovery

The World Health Organization specifically recommends five different approaches for addiction treatment: Cognitive Behavioral Therapy, 12-step Approaches, Motivational Interviewing / Motivational Enhancement Therapy, Contingency Management, and Family/Couples Therapies [1]. They all encompass a combination of empirically supported, widely used, and theoretically grounded approaches [14–19] Although the World Health Organization calls for further research on the 12-step concept, it does not specify a particular model for it [20]. Therefore, we included the Minnesota Model as it is one of the most widely used and established among the 12-step approaches [10, 21, 22]. Also, MI/MET are included together as MI is basically a broader therapeutic approach to MET [23]. Abbreviation of "MI" will be used to refer to both approaches moving forward for simplicity.

Cognitive Behavioral Therapy (CBT) is a form of psychotherapy that focuses on identifying and then shaping problematic thought patterns. It adopts a structured and goal-oriented approach. It also uses strategies such as functional analysis, cognitive restructuring, behavioral activation, problem-solving, skills training, and homework to help users achieve healthier behaviors and treatment outcomes [18, 24, 25].

Motivational Interviewing (MI) and Motivational Enhancement Therapy (MET) share a client-centered counseling approaches aiming to enhance intrinsic motivation for change. MI is a broader therapeutic approach, while MET focuses on feedback, assessments, and change plans. Both rely on structured, conversational strategies to help clients resolve ambivalence about their unhealthy behaviors. Their key components include enhancing motivation, addressing ambivalence, supporting self-efficacy, empathy, reflective listening, affirmations, summarizing, drawing out change talk, and readiness to change [26–28].

Minnesota Model (MM) is a multidisciplinary, holistic approach that integrates physical, emotional and mental aspects of addiction treatment. It views addiction as a chronic disease that needs lifelong management and focuses on long-term recovery by emphasizing the importance of total abstinence, responsibility, peer support, and meeting participation. It also uses evidence-based practices such as psychoeducation, and involvement of family members and centralizes the model into shared responsibility [29, 30].

Contingency Management (CM) is a behavioral intervention that uses tangible rewards to reinforce positive behavioral changes. It links specific target behaviors with incentives for their recurrence by using behavioral reinforcement, operant conditioning, incentives, and individualized goals derived from behavioral principles [31, 32].

Family/Couples Therapies (FCT) is a psychological approach that treats families as a whole system and aims to improve communication between individuals. It seeks to improve the functioning of relationships and understand relationship dynamics by offering various solutions to conflicts between individuals, such as psychoeducation or a supportive role [33, 34].

2.3 Developing the Conceptual Framework

Mapping PSD features and psychological approaches provides a practical way to more effectively utilize evidence-based counseling strategies in BCSS. To ensure the quality and rigor of our taxonomy, we followed an iterative process. First, we reviewed addiction-specific psychotherapy manuals and guidelines, listing the strategies found in each psychological approach [24–26, 28–33]. After identifying the strategies, matching PSD features were recognized by the researchers. Each of the constructs was carefully analyzed to determine which PSD features can most fittingly be operationalized within a BCSS. PSD features were categorized into "main" and "additional" based on a systematic evaluation of the alignment between each feature and the core therapeutic goals of psychological approaches. Features were classified as "main" when they directly supported the key constructs of approaches, and "additional" when they provided complementary roles to enhance treatment's overall efficacy. Only the mappings that reached full consensus among researchers were included in the final taxonomy. It is also important to note that different psychological approaches can share the same PSD features as we did not categorize the features as approach-specific.

3   Findings

3.1   Psychological Approaches as Persuasive Software Features

The systematic organization of counseling strategies ensures a clear understanding of how they can be used to achieve behavior change in a digital environment. Tables 1 and 2 provide specific and actionable PSD features that align with various counseling strategies from five different models. Across all five approaches, certain PSD features appear more frequently than others. These patterns suggest that while certain PSD features can support a wide range of counseling strategies, others serve more targeted purposes within specialized psychological approaches. For example, REM, SMO, PRA, SMU, and PER

Table 1. Main PSD Features for the Psychological Approaches

CBT	MI	MM	CM	FCT
PRIM: RED: Simplify cognitive exercises into manageable steps SMO: Provide tools to track progress on goals, for example, reduced craving or abstinence SMU: Visualize potential outcomes of individuals' actions PER: Personalize cognitive and behavioral tasks to match individual triggers REH: Provide means for exercising refusal skills, coping mechanisms, etc.	**PRIM:** SMO: Let users track goals and behaviors to amplify ambivalence and realize barriers PER: Adapts sessions immediately after "change talk" to each user's stated ambivalence	**PRIM:** REH: Allow users to practice scenarios and responses SMU: Show impact of addiction on family relations	**PRIM:** SMU: Show outcomes of the behaviors PER: Customize reward structures to address each user's goals and relapse triggers SMO: Allow users to track progress toward their goals	**PRIM:** REH: Practice responses to relapse scenarios SMU: Show the impact of family relations on addiction
DIAL: SUG: Give recommendations to teach strategies to reduce stress	**DIAL:** SRO: Use virtual social agents for empathetic conversations PRA: Acknowledge user progress to increase confidence SUG: Bring up reasons for change	**CRED:** TRU: Share and listen first-hand real-life experiences EXP: Incorporate content from trusted sources	**DIAL:** REW: Give virtual rewards for achieving milestones REM: Encourage goal completion by sending notifications PRA: Give positive feedback for achieving milestones	**DIAL:** SRO: Provide means to teach families effective ways to express emotions and listen each other
		SOCI: SLE: Enables users to observe and learn from peers COO: Provide means for collaborative discussions with peers		**SOCI:** SLE: Teaching conflict resolution techniques and letting family members share with each other SFA: Provide means for collaborative exercises REC: Highlight achievements within the family

Note: RED: Reduction; SMO: Self-monitoring; SMU: Simulation; PER: Personalization; REH: Rehearsal; REM: Reminders; PRA: Praise; SUG: Suggestion; EXP: Expertise; SRO: Social Role; REC: Recognition; SFA: Social Facilitation; COO: Cooperation; REW: Rewards; SLE: Social Learning.

were identified as main or additional features in four to five approaches. REH, REC, and SLE were also observed in three approaches. By contrast, features like REW were highly specific as it is only observed in the Contingency Management approach that relies on tangible incentives. These findings provide a foundation for discussing how these alignments can inform the design of more effective, engaging, and multidisciplinary digital solutions.

3.2 Counseling Strategies as Persuasive Software Features

CBT's focus on modifying unhelpful thought processes and behaviors makes the PRIM features particularly important. For instance, reduction (RED) helps break complex cognitive restructuring exercises into smaller, easier-to-understand steps. Self-monitoring (SMO) lets users track their ongoing awareness of maladaptive thoughts or behaviors. Meanwhile, functional analysis fits well with the simulation (SMU) principle as it helps users to observe the link between cause and effect regarding their behavior in a safe environment. Personalization (PER) ensures each user's targets are relevant to their situation, which supports CBT's individualized assignments and goal setting. Finally, behavioral

Table 2. Additional PSD Features for the Psychological Approaches

CBT	MI	MM	CM	FCTs
PRIM: TAI: Tailor content to segments of users through their behavioral or systems usage patterns TUN: Guide users through focused cognitive restructuring exercises	**PRIM**: TAI: Adjust content to user's readiness to change SMU: Visualize the consequences of current and alternative behaviors	**PRIM**: SMO: Let users track emotional, physical and mental progress	**CRED**: TRU: Inform users on clear, reliable reward systems	**PRIM**: PER: Personalize communication exercises to family-specific needs
DIAL: REM: Send notifications to practice coping strategies during high-risk situations PRA: Give positive feedback for achieving therapy goals	**DIAL**: REM: Notify users to revisit goals for change	**DIAL**: REM: Highlight the importance of meetings and peer support PRA: Let users have personal insights fostering mutual support	**SOCI**: SLE: Share success stories to inspire other users	**DIAL**: SUG: Inform families about upcoming high-risk periods

(*continued*)

Table 2. (*continued*)

CBT	MI	MM	CM	FCTs
CRED: EXP: Give resources for skills training	**SOCI**: REC: Highlight user achievements to inspire further action	**SOCI**: SFA: Highlight active peer and family participation in recovery REC: Publicly celebrate user milestones		**CRED**: AUT: Include guidelines to help healthy roles and prevent over-dependence

Note: SMO: Self-monitoring; SMU: Simulation; PER: Personalization; TAI: Tailoring; TUN: Tunneling, REM: Reminders; PRA: Praise; SUG: Suggestion; EXP: Expertise; SRO: REC: Recognition; TRU: Trustworthiness; SFA: Social Facilitation; AUT: Authority; SLE: Social Learning

activation can be easily mimicked by using the rehearsal (REH) principle to reintroduce prior pleasant activities and encourage engagement in positive activities. On the other hand, additional features, like tailoring (TAI), tunneling (TUN), reminders (REM), praise (PRA), and expertise (EXP), may still be helpful but are not as central to CBT's core strategies even if they provide support the counseling process.

Since MI focuses on internal motivation and shapes the counseling around readiness to change, DIAL features are important in capturing an empathetic tone needed to resolve ambivalence. For instance, social role (SRO) can be used to express empathy to show understanding of individuals' perspectives as a virtual social agent or counselor interface. PRA and suggestions (SUG) also can serve as key tools for immediate reinforcement to change when the "change talk" comes. Similarly, SMO and PER can play crucial roles in matching each user's readiness level and tracking behaviors and personal goals, as well as aligning interventions with each user's level of motivation. Additional features like REM on the other hand can be used, for instance, to prompt goal reflection or session attendance but not as fundamental to MI's essential mechanism of empathy and self-discovery. Similarly, TAI can segment users by their specific barriers or readiness levels, SMU can simulate future scenarios if no change occurs, and REC can highlight each user's achievements to build better confidence. However, these four features stay complementary to the MI's understanding of psychological intervention.

In the MM, the SOCI category seems to be more dominant, which is also in line with its principles. For example, including social learning (SLE) seems to be a practically effective way of benefiting from peer support strategies. Cooperation (COO) lets users collaborate on digital tasks while sharing and discussion ideas to improve collective accountability which reflects the idea of shared responsibility and community bonding. Beyond the social aspect, REH also is crucial for practicing scenarios like refusing substance offers or managing social pressure in recovery-focused and supportive contexts, while EXP and trustworthiness (TRU) build trust in the treatment setting by reassuring users that the program's materials come from reputable sources and derive directly from real-life experiences. Additionally, SMU as a main feature aligns with MM's holistic approach and lets us emphasize the family idea in the recovery process. It could model how addiction affects family dynamics where users see or experience how behaviors like neglect or financial strain impact loved ones. In addition to these features, SMO, REM, PRA, social facilitation (SFA), and REC complement MM's holistic approach by including several ways for providing support. For example, with the ongoing reflection coming from the SMO, it can help individuals to sense that the progress is meaningful, even small wins. Similarly, in terms of REC and PRA, the system can feature a "Milestone Wall" where users can share achievements, and motivational experiences to create a collective atmosphere.

In addition, CM heavily relies on incentives and behavioral conditioning. It centers on the principle of reinforcing positive behaviors with tangible rewards, which makes rewards (REW), PRA, and PER the most defining features. These features help reinforce desired actions, such as submitting screenings or attending sessions, by directly linking them to benefits particularly meaningful to the user. Also, SMO lets users keep an eye on their progress toward the goals that trigger rewards, while SMU helps them see the benefits of meeting these behavioral milestones. On the other hand, TRU has a supportive role in ensuring that all users are aware of the objective rewards system, while SLE can create a digital environment where people are rewarded socially to encourage the same positive behaviors.

Lastly, since FCTs view the entire family as interconnected, DIAL and SOCI features become important to promote healthier communication and conflict resolution. For example, with the social role (SRO), a psychoeducation can be delivered by structured conversations. Also, SLE lets family members observe each other's experiences while SFA extends this dynamic by guiding them to do tasks together. Additionally, REH is likewise fundamental for practicing real-life scenarios, like handling stressors. On the other hand, PER improves the intervention by adapting it to each family's unique experiences and roles, while SUG helps families become aware of high-risk periods and learn what to do in those situations. Authority (AUT) also supports the psychoeducation given by offering a powerful guideline or maybe a figure.

4   Discussion

This study provides a blueprint for translating foundational addiction treatment strategies into persuasive software features guided by the PSD framework. By doing this, we aimed to bridge the conceptual gap between the practical realities of information system design and the underpinnings of psychological approaches. While PSD has strong theoretical roots in behavioral and persuasive communication theories, the explicit alignment with established addiction treatments is less commonly documented [9].

The scientific literature clearly shows the positive impact of persuasive technologies on user engagement and adherence [10, 35]. On the other hand, addiction treatment settings have historically struggled with maintaining patient involvement over time, a factor critical to achieving meaningful clinical outcomes [4, 36]. However, different persuasive software features, particularly REM, have already proven to extend sustained participation [12, 37, 38]. These features, when grounded in evidence-based counseling strategies, can enhance their meaning clinically by facilitating long-term behavioral change in a structured environment. Our study also suggests that particular PSD features are being overlooked in health interventions. For example, while REH is found in three out of five different psychological approaches recommended for addiction, the literature shows that it is not commonly used in these types of settings [10]. Therefore, the mapping of PSD features to psychological strategies is important in order to identify gaps in practice.

A critical dimension of our framework also lies in its potential to enhance both the treatment and follow-up phases of recovery. Conventional treatment models often focus on in-person sessions, which, unfortunately, leave individuals without sufficient guidance once these sessions end [4]. Mapping the PSD features with counseling strategies lets us see which features can be used in intense treatment periods, follow-up periods, or both. For example, CBT counseling strategies such as relapse prevention planning can be operationalized through the REH feature during the intensive treatment and remain available long after the initial treatment session with, for instance, SMO and REM. Similarly, in MI, the structured use of REM, SUG, and PER ensures that a user's digital environment continually reinforces motivation which allows an easier transition from intensive treatment to follow-up treatment reducing the risk of relapses.

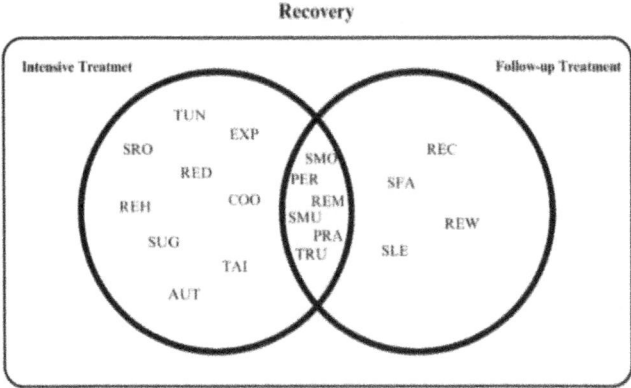

Fig. 1. Identified Features' Distribution within the Addiction Recovery Process

As a result, systematically integrated BCSS can serve as a continuous companion through all the stages of the recovery journey. As can be seen in Fig. 1, when the PSD features identified in the five psychological approaches are divided into intensive treatment, follow-up treatment and both, the PSD features corresponding to intensive treatment are more prevalent than follow-up treatment. This may be due to the fact that intervention approaches are mostly focused on in-person meetings as mentioned earlier. However, while the literature does not allow for a clear distinction of PSD features between intensive treatment and follow-up treatment for now, this classification can be used as a hypothetical starting point for their use in contexts where they can be most impactful.

This framework also must be considered with certain caveats. While the distinction between intensive treatment and follow-up support aligns with established clinical research, practical applications often need ongoing adjustment. Moreover, thorough empirical testing is crucial to confirm how well this approach works in real-world scenarios. It is recommended that future digital interventions use this framework as a base, with iterative improvements and testing for effectiveness.

5   Conclusion

This study presents a foundation for designing information systems targeting recovery from addiction problems. It has a novel approach that uses important strategies of the counseling models recommended by the World Health Organization and translates these strategies into a practically applicable form using PSD features in a guided manner. This approach bridges the gap between user-centered digital design and evidence-based counseling practices for creating effective interventions. This will provide a critical step toward advancing digital health solutions tailored to addiction recovery by aligning psychological principles with persuasive technology.

Acknowledgments. This study has received funding from the Research Council of Finland under decision 351670 with theme "Persuasive digital health interventions: Software features as key predictors for successful prevention and treatment of overweight, obesity, metabolic syndrome and cardiovascular diseases".

Disclosure of Interests. The authors have no competing interest to declare.

References

1. World Health Organization: Global status report on alcohol and health and treatment of substance use disorders. Geneva: World Health Organization; Licence: CC BY-NC-SA 3.0 IGO (2024)
2. Brorson, H.H., Arnevik, E.A., Rand-Hendriksen, K., Duckert, F.: Drop-out from addiction treatment: a systematic review of risk factors. Clin. Psychol. Rev. **33**(8), 1010–1024 (2013). https://doi.org/10.1016/j.cpr.2013.07.007
3. Kabisa, E., Biracyaza, E., Habagusenga, J.D., Umubyeyi, A.: Determinants and prevalence of relapse among patients with substance use disorders: case of Icyizere psychotherapeutic centre. Substance Abuse Treatment, Prevention, and Policy **16**(1), 13 (2021). https://doi.org/10.1186/s13011-021-00347-0
4. Lappan, S.N., Brown, A.W., Hendricks, P.S.: Dropout rates of in-person psychosocial substance use disorder treatments: a systematic review and meta-analysis. Addiction **115**(2), 201–217 (2020). https://doi.org/10.1111/add.14793
5. Mohr, D.C., Burns, M.N., Schueller, S.M., Clarke, G., Klinkman, M.: Behavioral intervention technologies: Evidence review and recommendations for future research in mental health. Gen. Hosp. Psychiatry **35**(4), 332–338 (2013)
6. Oinas-Kukkonen, H.: Behavior change support systems: a research model and agenda. In: Ploug, T., Hasle, P., Oinas-Kukkonen, H. (eds.) PERSUASIVE 2010, LNCS, vol. 6137, pp. 1–3. Springer, Berlin, Heidelberg (2010). https://doi.org/10.1007/978-3-642-13226-1_3

7. Kazemi, D.M., Borsari, B., Levine, M.J., Li, S., Lamberson, K.A., Matta, L.A.: A systematic review of the mHealth interventions to prevent alcohol and substance abuse. J. Health Commun. **22**(5), 413–432 (2017)
8. Mohr, D.C., Weingardt, K.R., Reddy, M., Schueller, S.M.: Three problems with current digital mental health research… and three things we can do about them. Psychiatr. Serv. **68**(5), 427–429 (2017)
9. Oinas-Kukkonen, H., Harjumaa, M.: Persuasive systems design: key issues, process model, and system features. Communications of the Association for Information Systems **24**, Article 28 (2009). https://doi.org/10.17705/1CAIS.02428
10. Kelders, S.M., Kok, R.N., Ossebaard, H.C., Van Gemert-Pijnen, J.E.: Persuasive system design does matter: a systematic review of adherence to web-based interventions. J. Med. Internet Res. **14**(6), e152 (2012). https://doi.org/10.2196/jmir.2104
11. Theopilus, Y., Al Mahmud, A., Davis, H., Octavia, J.R.: Persuasive strategies in digital interventions to combat internet addiction: a systematic review. Int. J. Med. Informatics **195**, 105725 (2024). https://doi.org/10.1016/j.ijmedinf.2024.105725
12. Oyebode, O., Orji, R.: Persuasive strategy implementation choices and their effectiveness: Towards personalised persuasive systems. Behaviour & Information Technology **42**(13), 2176–2209 (2022). https://doi.org/10.1080/0144929X.2022.2112612
13. Lehto, T., Oinas-Kukkonen, H.: Persuasive features in web-based alcohol and smoking interventions: a systematic review of the literature. J. Med. Internet Res. **13**(3), e46 (2011). https://doi.org/10.2196/jmir.1559
14. Kelly, J.F., Humphreys, K., Ferri, M.: Alcoholics anonymous and other 12-step programs for alcohol use disorder. Cochrane Database of Systematic Reviews **2020**(3), CD012880 (2020). https://doi.org/10.1002/14651858.CD012880.pub2
15. O'Farrell, T.J., Fals-Stewart, W.: Behavioral couples therapy for alcoholism and drug abuse. Guilford Press (2006)
16. Anderson, D.J., McGovern, J.P., DuPont, R.L.: The origins of the Minnesota model of addiction treatment—a first person account. J. Addict. Dis. **18**(1), 107–114 (1999)
17. Higgins, S.T., Budney, A.J., Bickel, W.K., Foerg, F., Donham, R., Badger, G.J.: Incentives improve outcome in outpatient behavioral treatment of cocaine dependence. Arch. Gen. Psychiatry **51**(7), 568–576 (1994)
18. Beck, A.T., Wright, F.D., Newman, C.F., Liese, B.S.: Cognitive Therapy of Substance Abuse. Guilford Press (1993)
19. Miller, W. R., Rollnick, S.: Motivational Interviewing: Preparing People to Change Addictive Behavior. Guilford Press (1991)
20. World Health Organization: Mental Health Gap Action Programme (mhGAP) guideline for mental, neurological and substance use disorders. Geneva: World Health Organization (2023). https://www.who.int/publications/i/item/9789240084278. Accessed 16 January 2024
21. Meil, M., Mills, J.A. (eds.): Addictions - Diagnosis and Treatment. IntechOpen (2021). https://doi.org/10.5772/intechopen.91534
22. Van Wormer, K., Davis, D.: Addiction Treatment: A Strengths Perspective, 4th edn. Cengage, Boston (2018)
23. Guydish, J., Jessup, M., Tajima, B., Manser, S.T.: Adoption of motivational interviewing and motivational enhancement therapy following clinical trials. J. Psychoact. Drugs Suppl. **6**, 215–226 (2010). https://doi.org/10.1080/02791072.2010.10400545
24. Cully, J.A., Dawson, D.B., Hamer, J., Tharp, A.L.: A provider's guide to brief cognitive behavioral therapy. Department of Veterans Affairs, South Central Mental Illness Research, Education, and Clinical Center (MIRECC) (2020)
25. Carroll, K.M.: A cognitive-behavioral approach: treating cocaine addiction. Therapy manuals for drug addiction. National Institute on Drug Abuse (1998). NIH Publication Number 98–4308

26. Substance Abuse and Mental Health Services Administration (SAMHSA): Using motivational interviewing in substance use disorder treatment (TIP 35). SAMHSA (2021). Retrieved from https://store.samhsa.gov
27. Miller, W.R., Rollnick, S.: Motivational Interviewing: Helping People Change. 3rd edn. Guilford Press (2013)
28. Miller, W.R., Zweben, A., DiClemente, C., Rychtarik, R.: Motivational Enhancement Therapy Manual: A Clinical Research Guide for Therapists Treating Individuals with Alcohol Abuse and Dependence (Project MATCH Monograph Series, Vol. 2). Government Printing Office (1992)
29. Nowinski, J., Baker, S., Carroll, K. M.: Twelve-step facilitation therapy manual: a clinical research guide for therapists treating individuals with alcohol abuse and dependence. National Institute on Alcohol Abuse and Alcoholism. Project MATCH Monograph Series. NIH Publication No. 94–3722 (1999)
30. Spicer, J.: Minnesota model: the evolution of the multidisciplinary approach to addiction recovery. Hazelden Educational Materials (1993)
31. Lynch, M., Cowie, M., Wallace, A., Ethier, A., Hodgins, D.C.: Contingency management implementation manual. University of Calgary (2023)
32. Petry, N.M.: A clinician's guide for implementing contingency management programs. University of Connecticut Health Center (2001)
33. Substance Abuse and Mental Health Services Administration (SAMHSA): Substance use disorder treatment and family therapy (TIP 39). SAMHSA (2020). Retrieved from https://store.samhsa.gov
34. Keitner, G.I., Heru, A.M., Glick, I.D.: Clinical manual of couples and family therapy. American Psychiatric Publishing, Inc (2010)
35. Idrees, A.R., Kraft, R., Mutter, A., Baumeister, H., Reichert, M., Pryss, R.: Persuasive technologies design for mental and behavioral health platforms: a scoping literature review. PLOS Digital Health 3(5), e0000498 (2024). https://doi.org/10.1371/journal.pdig.0000498
36. Dacosta-Sánchez, D., González-Ponce, B.M., Fernández-Calderón, F., Sánchez-García, M., Lozano, O.M.: Retention in treatment and therapeutic adherence: How are these associated with therapeutic success? An analysis using real-world data. Int. J. Methods Psychiatr. Res. 31(4), e1929 (2022). https://doi.org/10.1002/mpr.1929
37. Webb, T.L., Joseph, J., Yardley, L., Michie, S.: Using the internet to promote health behavior change: a systematic review and meta-analysis of the impact of theoretical basis, use of behavior change techniques, and mode of delivery on efficacy. J. Med. Internet Res. 12(1), e4 (2010). https://doi.org/10.2196/jmir.1376
38. Fry, J.P., Neff, R.A.: Periodic prompts and reminders in health promotion and health behavior interventions: Systematic review. J. Med. Internet Res. 11(2), e16 (2009). https://doi.org/10.2196/jmir.1138

Investigation of the Eye Donor Aust App's Persuasiveness

Waraporn Chumkasian[1]([envelope]) [iD], Constantinos Petsoglou[2] [iD],
Elena Vlahu-Gjorgievska[1] [iD], and Khin Than Win[1] [iD]

[1] University of Wollongong, Wollongong, NSW 2522, Australia
wc817@uowmail.edu.au
[2] University of Sydney, Sydney, NSW 2006, Australia

Abstract. Previous studies have shown that providing donation education through smartphone applications (apps) significantly enhances knowledge and improves users' attitudes. In this study, two hundred forty participants were surveyed to determine the perceived persuasiveness of the Eye Donor Aust app. SPSS software was employed to test the correlations between demographic variables and analyze data distribution, and Structural Equation Modeling was created to explore the multivariate causal relationships among constructs. The findings indicate that three PSD principles (Credibility Support, Dialogue Support, and Social Support) significantly enhanced the app's persuasiveness, while participants' age and gender were significantly associated with the app's persuasiveness. These findings can inform the development of high-quality educational apps employing PSD principles that effectively persuade users.

Keywords: Perceived Persuasiveness · Eye Donation App · Persuasive System Design

1 Introduction

The World Health Organisation (WHO) recently reported that approximately 4.2 million people suffer from corneal blindness, a condition that can be treated with corneal transplantation [1]. Corneal transplantation is one of the most common surgeries, with over 180,000 cases performed worldwide each year, resulting in improved vision for recipients [2]. However, corneal transplantations are not possible without cornea donations. In Australia, the demand for cornea grafts has been increasing yearly, but donations have not increased at the same rate.

Attitude plays a significant role in establishing positive consent for eye donation from potential donors and their key family members [3]. It also has a substantial relationship with donation knowledge [4]. Positive attitudes enhance donation awareness, which can change public behavior [5].

Previous studies have shown multiple barriers to eye donation, including a lack of awareness, negative attitudes, and knowledge of the donation procedure [3]. Educating the public about eye donation is an effective way to foster a favorable attitude and

K. T. Win et al. (Eds.): PERSUASIVE 2025, LNCS 15711, pp. 176–187, 2025.
https://doi.org/10.1007/978-3-031-94959-3_13

encourage people to donate their eyes [6]. It corrects misconceptions about the donation procedure, raises awareness about donation [6], and promotes it as a noble act [7]. Mobile health applications (apps) have also increased rapidly in recent years. These apps are used in health promotion and education [8], as well as in the self-management of consumers, e.g., for asthma [9], heart failure [10], mental health[11], physical activity [12] weight management [13], and breastfeeding education [14].

The Eye Donor Aust app is an educational tool designed to enhance knowledge about eye donation, shift attitudes, and boost users' awareness [15]. It contains essential eye donation education using plain language and multimedia to enhance users' learning. The seven eye donation eligibility questions are another way to educate users and provide easy access for registering if they agree. The users can send instant messages to inform them of their wish to become eye donors to their next of kin.

The app was developed following the Persuasive System Design (PSD) principles [16]. The persuasive features used in the app design help to motivate users to achieve the goals of behavior change effortlessly by dividing the app's content into categories, presenting the endorsements of trustworthy organizations, and providing options for users to share, exchange information, or receive support provided on the national organ donation registration's website and its social media. The app's PSD strategies are presented in Table 1.

Table 1. Overview of the Eye Donor Aust's Persuasive Strategies and Implementation [15].

Persuasive strategies	Implementations
Primary Task Support	Reduction: the app divides content into sections that are easy to understand Tunelling: guiding users to access different information sections based on their navigation Tailoring: the reading text feature and flexible text size to assist users with visual impairment
Dialogue Support	Similarity: the recipient's video testimonial helps users understand the value of eye donation to the recipient Social roles: the religious statement helps users reflect on their beliefs regarding eye donation Liking: the app employs multimedia and colour-coded content in the design, making it visually appealing
Credibility Support	Third-party endorsement: the app displays the logos of the organizations that endorsed the app, such as The Eye and Tissue Bank, Universities, and NSW Health Expertise: the app informs users that a domain expert developed it Verifiability: the app provides links to reliable content sources
Social Support	Social facilitation: the app provides options to inform next of kin of the wish to become an eye donor, and the users can share this app with their friends

The Eye Donor Aust app benefits users by overcoming donation barriers and improving awareness; however, the persuasive design mechanism that influences users remains unclear. Evaluating persuasiveness is challenging because it is time-consuming and costly, and ethical issues may arise in some cases [17]. Some earlier studies have investigated users' perceived persuasiveness of the mHealth applications [18, 19]. In this study, we examine the influence of the PSD constructs on the users' perceived persuasiveness and attitudes towards the Eye Donor Aust app.

2   Theoretical Background and the Research Model

The Eye Donor Aust app was developed based on the Design Science Research (DSR) adopting Persuasive System Design (PSD), consisting of three iterative design and development cycles. Its development is based on mapping the meta-requirements (based on a literature review, user surveys, and consultation with field experts) into design requirements. The PSD constructs used to develop the app are as follows.

Primary Task Support construct, including the Reduction, Tunneling, and Tailoring principles, simplifies complex behaviors into manageable tasks. Reducing users' cognitive burdens enhances their effectiveness and may improve the behavior's benefit-to-cost ratio [20].

Dialogue Support construct guides the implementation of computer-human dialogue to motivate and assist users in engaging with the app, thereby enhancing its persuasive power [16]. It can also bolster users' confidence, leading to behavioral changes such as increasing donation knowledge and improving donation awareness [20]. Since the app includes video testimonials from organ recipients and religious messages regarding eye donation, users should find this feature relevant. Therefore, this construct is essential in an eye donation app design [12].

Credibility Support can significantly impact users' engagement with the target behavior [21]. It shares a similar concept to trust, enabling app users to follow instructions easily and thereby achieve the app's goals. This approach helps build users' trust and makes the app more compelling [12, 16].

Social Support construct supports individuals' collaboration in a group by identifying shared goals and achieving objectives through action. This leads to positive outcomes such as increased commitment, a willingness to adopt sustainable behavior, and improved performance [21, 22].

Since **Attitudes** are crucial factors influencing potential donors to increase eye donation awareness [6], understanding which PSD constructs impact users' attitudes will benefit the future design of eye donation initiatives.

Additionally, the study examines the PSD constructs contributing to **Perceived Persuasiveness** and Attitudes while evaluating the relationships among these constructs. The hypotheses are formulated as follows.

H1: Primary task support is positively related to Dialogue support.

H2: Primary task support is positively related to Social support.

H3: Dialogue task support is positively related to Attitudes.

H4: Dialogue task support affects perceived Persuasiveness.

H5: Dialogue task support is positively related to Credibility support.

H6: Credibility support affects perceived Persuasiveness.

H7: Credibility support is positively related to Social support.

H8: Social support is positively related to perceived Persuasiveness.

3   Research Method

The study was conducted from September to October 2024. Ethics approval was obtained from the Southeastern Sydney Local Health District. The setting of the study was at two Outpatient Eye Clinics in a tertiary hospital in Sydney. Only the individuals who met the inclusion criteria (were willing to participate in the study, were able to consent, and could install the Eye Donor Aust app) participated in the study. The participants were asked to complete a hardcopy questionnaire and return it in the prepared envelope by post within two weeks of using the app.

The SPSS computer program was used to examine the correlation between the demographic variables and the user's Perceived Persuasiveness, including assessing the data descriptively and in terms of distribution. The Partial Least Squares Structural Equation Modelling (PLS-SEM) explored factors influencing users' Perceived Persuasiveness and Attitudes.

The questionnaire comprised three parts. The first part included questions regarding participants' demographic information. The second part contained questions examining users' perceived persuasiveness, adapted from prior studies [17, 19, 21–23] and the third part included questions about users' attitudes toward eye donation (Table 2). Participants were asked to rate their agreement with the statements on a seven-point scale.

Table 2. The Questionnaires

Categories	Statements	Ref:
Primary Task Support	The Eye Donor Aust app provided eye donation information divided into categories that made it **easy** for me to learn.	[17]
	The app **provided** me with comprehensive information related to cornea transplantation.	[19]
	I found the **text to audio** option helpful.	[17]
	I found the option in the app to **change text size** helpful	[17]
Dialog Support	The **video testimonials** from previous organ recipients helped me to understand the benefits of eye donation.	[17]
	The **religious statements** presented in the app allowed me to reflect on my beliefs/understanding of eye donation.	[24]
	The **color-coded content** in the app is attractive.	[24]
	The app included **images** related to eye donation that are visually appealing.	[24]
Credibility Support	I think the Eye Donor Aust app is a **credible resource** (supported by expert organizations, NSW Eye and Tissue Bank, and Sydney Eye Hospital).	[17]
	I think the Eye Donor Aust app is a **trustworthy resource** developed by domain experts.	[17]
	I think the Eye Donor Aust app provided **verified content** form different sources (including web links to national organ donation website DonateLife and its social media.	[17]
Social Support	The Eye Donor Aust app provided the option to **inform my next of kin** about my decision to become an eye donor.	[22]
	The Eye Donor Aust app provided the **option to share** the app with my friends.	[19]
Persuasiveness to intention to become an eye donor	The Eye Donor Aust app is personally **relevant** to me.	[17]
	The Eye Donor Aust app **enhanced** my knowledge about eye donation.	[17]
	The Eye Donor Aust app provided me with the information regarding eye donation that **I need to know** before deciding to become an eye donor.	[19]
	The **eligibility quiz** within the app is helpful in my decision to become an eye donor.	[17]
Attitude	For me to register or continue to be registered as an Eye Donor is **GOOD**.	[25]
	For me to register or continue to be registered as an Eye Donor is **VALUABLE**.	
	For me to register or continue to be registered as an Eye Donor is **POSITIVE**.	
	For me to register or continue to be registered as an Eye Donor is **FAVOURABLE**.	
	For me talk to my family, partner or close friend about my donation decision is **GOOD**.	
	For me talk to my family, partner or close friend about my donation decision is **VALUABLE**.	
	For me talk to my family, partner or close friend about my donation decision is **FAVOURABLE**.	
	For me talk to my family, partner or close friend about my donation decision is **POSITIVE**.	

4 Results

Based on the results, the odds ratios were reported with a 5% margin of error, assumed $p = 0.05$, with a 95% confidence level. The sample size of 240 participants, 110 males and 130 females, was considered adequate [26]. The demographic information of the participants is presented in Table 4. The participants were between 16 and 75 years old, and the mean age of males and females was 42.8 ±16.5 and 46.9 ±17.3, respectively.

When examining the relationship between the constructs and demographic variables, the study found that the app's perceived persuasiveness significantly correlates with participants' age and gender, at $p = .027$ and $.001$, respectively, and both relationships are positive (Table 3). However, the Pearson correlation shows that the strength of the relationship between Perceived Persuasiveness and age and gender is considered a weak but significant correlation (values ranging from 0.10 to 0.39) [27]. The older participants regarded the app as beneficial and relevant, even though previous research suggests that increased age can lead to reduced app usage due to physical and mental decline [28]. Gender also significantly correlates with users' perceived persuasiveness; the analysis found that the R^2 values for males and females regarding users' perceived persuasiveness were acceptable, with females scoring slightly higher. This indicated that females perceived the app's usefulness more positively than males.

Table 3. Correlations of PSD Constructs and Demographic Information

	Pearson Correlation	Sig. (2-tailed)	95% Confidence Intervals (2-Tailed)	
			Lower	Upper
Perceived Persuasiveness - Gender	.207	.001	.083	.325
Perceived Persuasiveness - Age	.143	.027	.016	.264

A comparison of the constructs overall, using the description in SPSS, reveals that nearly all constructs have a mean score higher than the neutral score of four ($p < 0.001$), except for the Social Support construct. This indicates a consensus among participants on five constructs that are effective influencers of behavior change to varying degrees. Credibility Support emerged as the most influential construct (mean 6.22, SD 0.804), while Social Support was the lowest score (3.11, SD 0.402). The data distribution exhibited negative skewness, indicating that most participants rated the construct highly, with only a few scoring low. Additionally, the results indicate positive Kurtosis, suggesting that the scores for all constructs are concentrated around the mean, reflecting widespread agreement among participants regarding the influence of these constructs. The Kolmogorov-Smirnov and Shapiro-Wilk tests were conducted with values less than .001, confirming that the data for all constructs are not normally distributed (see Table 7). The Average Variance Extracted (AVE) was evaluated to verify that the study's convergent validity was statistically valid, with each construct demonstrating a value greater than 0.5. Internal reliability and validity were evaluated by examining Cronbach's alpha, the composite reliability (rho_a), and (rho_c) of each item. Each item was valued between 0.794 and 0.961, indicating that response values for each participant across all questions were consistent and acceptable to an excellent level. The Fornell-Larcker criterion helps determine whether the convergent and discriminant validity of the measurement model is established. The square root of a construct's average variance extracted (AVE) in this study was greater than the correlation between the construct and another construct. Results were considered acceptable in the Heterotrait-Monotrait ratio of correlations (HTMT) assessment, as all constructs had values less than 0.9.

Table 4. Significance Testing Results of the Structural Model Path Coefficients

	Path Coefficients	t statistics	p values	95% Confidence Intervals	Significance p<0.05
Credibility S -> Attitudes	0.196	1.834	0.067	(-0.027, 0.395)	No
Credibility S -> Perceived Persuasiveness	0.233	2.007	0.045	(0.021, 0.475)	Yes
Credibility S -> Social P	0.400	4.364	0.000	(0.221, 0.574)	Yes
Dialogue P -> Attitudes	0.215	2.040	0.041	(0.000, 0.411)	Yes
Dialogue P -> Credibility P	0.677	14.933	0.000	(0.573, 0.751)	Yes
Dialogue P -> Perceived Persuasiveness	0.292	2.985	0.003	(0.091, 0.477)	Yes
Perceived Persuasiveness -> Attitudes	-0.049	0.434	0.664	(-0.269, 0.183)	No
Primary TS -> Attitudes	-0.033	0.300	0.764	(-0.264, 0.169)	No
Primary TS -> Dialogue S	0.756	21.278	0.000	(0.672, 0.816)	Yes
Primary TS -> Perceived Persuasiveness	-0.129	1.263	0.207	(-0.325, 0.071)	No
Primary TS -> Social S	0.324	3.510	0.000	(0.143, 0.502)	Yes
Social S -> Attitudes	0.096	0.975	0.329	(-0.098, 0.291)	No
Social S -> Perceived Persuasiveness	0.419	5.127	0.000	(0.261, 0.582)	Yes

The SmartPLS program examined the relationship between constructs and the app users' perceived persuasiveness and attitudes by creating the constructs and calculating the path coefficient and its significance (Table 4). The study found that only the Dialogue Support construct significantly affects Attitudes. Three constructs, Credibility Support, Dialogue Support, and Social Support, significantly impact perceived persuasiveness. Relationships among the constructs were also identified (Fig. 1). Dialogue Support is related substantially to Credibility Support, and the Credibility Support construct is significantly associated with Social Support. Primary Task Support significantly affects both Dialogue Support and Social Support.

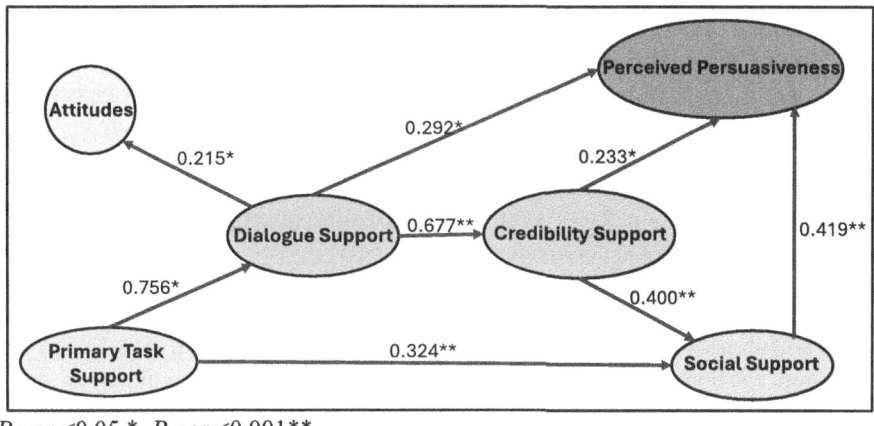

$P=$ or <0.05 *, $P=$ or <0.001**

Fig. 1. Structural Model Path Coefficients

5   Discussion

All hypotheses in the current study were significant, leading to rejecting the null hypotheses.

The current study found that older participants perceived the app as valuable and useful ($p = 0.027$). However, older individuals face obstacles that can discourage app usage, including negative attitudes toward technology, lack of trust, limited technological skills, and declining mental and physical abilities [29, 30]. To help older users effectively utilize and maximize the benefits of these applications, the apps must be designed to meet their needs and assist in overcoming the challenges associated with use. To overcome these challenges, our app includes features such as adjustable font sizes and text-to-speech capabilities to help users with vision impairments read or listen to the content. The color-coded content also helps users easily follow the group content.

Additionally, the study revealed that females tend to perceive the app's value and persuasiveness as slightly greater than males. This finding contrasts with another study suggesting that males have a more positive attitude toward using new technology, including apps, and perceive more value in them than females [30]. However, since females generally show greater interest in seeking health information, this interest may lead them to find the app more valuable than males [30]. The result also aligns with Oyibo et al.'s findings [37], which indicated that female app users perceived higher persuasiveness and experienced greater positive expected outcomes, increased engagement, and a higher likelihood of achieving the app's goals in behavior change.

The study found that three PSD constructs, Credibility Support, Dialogue Support, and Social Support, significantly influenced users' Perceived Persuasiveness. This may be attributed to the differing nature of the persuasive app or intervention. In comparison, all PSD constructs affected the users' perceived Persuasiveness in the study involving the web-based intervention for weight loss [20]. In contrast, another study utilizing the gamified persuasive system found that only Dialogue Support significantly impacted users' Perceived Persuasiveness [21].

Credibility Support received the highest scores for the most persuasive construct in this study. Displaying symbols and informing participants about trusted organizations such as Sydney Eye Hospital and endorsing the app could enhance the persuasive power of the app. Reliability and trustworthiness are key concerns for consumers seeking online health information [31]. Therefore, emphasizing and implementing this construct in health app design could contribute to its success.

The Social Support construct affects the users' Perceived Persuasiveness, motivating them to engage through social learning, social comparison, or competition [12]. The app connects with national organ donation on Facebook and other social media platforms to promote eye donation awareness and app engagement [15], making it easy to share. Participants in this study scored lower in social support than in any other constructs, despite numerous studies indicating that social media, such as Facebook, boost organ donation registration among living donor candidates [32]. This could be due to the fact that the study took place in eye clinics, where participants included patients with vision impairment. Furthermore, a quarter of the participants (n = 63) were elderly aged 60 and over; almost a quarter faced challenges in using the internet or accessing social media, compounded by physical limitations such as dexterity issues or cognitive decline [33]. These factors may lead older participants to perceive less value in using apps to receive Social Support, thereby finding limited social benefits when making decisions about eye donation.

The Dialogue Support construct significantly influenced users' attitudes in this study ($\beta = 0.215$, p = 0.041). The eye donation app employs PSD strategies based on the similarity principle, which helps users empathize with the recipient's feelings. The social roles principle enables users to reflect on their religious beliefs and eye donation, while the Liking principle enhances the app's visual appeal [15]. This finding is congruent with the study of Shevchuk, Degrimenci, and Oinass-Kukkonen [21], which showed that Dialogue Support facilitated and created an overall favorable attitude toward the system, resulting in this principle's significant impact on the perceived persuasiveness of the app that encourages users to sustainable behavior.

In the current study, the users' Perceived Persuasiveness did not significantly influence any other constructs, similar to the findings by Beerlage-de-Jong et al. [19]. This can be explained by the fact that it is the outcome, not a component of Persuasive mode.

This study's limitations include using a convenience sample, which may have introduced some selection bias affecting the results. Participants were recruited from a specific demographic, including eye patients, caregivers, and hospital visitors at eye clinics. Consequently, their perspectives may not accurately reflect the general population's views, leading to limited generalizability.

6 Conclusion

In this study, we presented a path model illustrating the PSD constructs that influence app users' perceptions of persuasiveness and attitudes. The analysis indicated that three PSD constructs (Dialogue Support, Credibility Support, and Social Support) contribute to users' Perceived Persuasiveness. Only the Dialogue Support construct has a significant effect on users' Attitudes. Older participants found the app more valuable and relevant than younger participants, similar to how females rated it slightly higher than males. These findings highlight the importance of customizing the design of a donation app based on PSD constructs. Additional research is needed on users' perceptions of persuasiveness regarding other organ donation apps.

Acknowledgement. The first author would like to thank Dr. Gunasekaran, the staff at the Sydney/Sydney Eye Hospital's eye clinics, and the participants.

Disclosure of Interests. There is no conflict of interest to disclose.

References

1. World Health Organisation: World report on vision (2025)
2. Ali del Barrio, J., et al.: Corneal transplantation after failed grafts: Options and outcomes. Surv Ophthalmol **66**, 20–40 (2021)
3. Chumkasian, W., et al.: Prevalence and predictors of knowledge and attitudes toward eye donation among the general population: a systematic review. Cornea **42**, 520–528 (2023)
4. Xulu-Kasaba, Z., Mashige, K., Naidoo, K.: Knowledge, attitudes and practices of eye health among public sector eye health workers in South Africa. Int. J. Environ. Res. Public Health **18**, 12513 (2021)
5. Grunig, J.E.: Image and substance: From symbolic to behavioral relationships. Public Relations Review **19**, 121–139 (1993)
6. Williams, A.M., Muir, K.W.: Awareness and attitudes toward corneal donation: challenges and opportunities. Clinical Ophthalmology 1049–1059 (2018)
7. Parija, S., Chakraborty, K., Sahu, D.P.: A study on knowledge, attitude, and practice about eye donation among medical students and healthcare professionals at a tertiary hospital in Eastern India. Indian J. Ophthalmol. **71**, 3513–3520 (2023)
8. Mosa, A.S.M., Yoo, I., Sheets, L.: A systematic review of healthcare applications for smartphones. BMC Med. Inform. Decis. Mak. **12**, 1–31 (2012)
9. Almutairi, N., Vlahu-Gjorgievska, E., Win, K.T.: mHealth Asthma Management App's Content Creation, Stakeholders' Values and Design Features. International Journal of Human–Computer Interaction 1–17 (2024)
10. Creber, R.M.M., Maurer, M.S., Reading, M., Hiraldo, G., Hickey, K.T., Iribarren, S.: Review and analysis of existing mobile phone apps to support heart failure symptom monitoring and self-care management using the Mobile Application Rating Scale (MARS). JMIR Mhealth Uhealth **4**, e5882 (2016)
11. Guracho, Y.D., Thomas, S.J., Almutairi, N., Win, K.T.: Persuasive system design features for mobile mental health applications. In: Persuasive Technology, pp. 116–132. Springer Nature Switzerland (2024)

12. Matthews, J., Win, K.T., Oinas-Kukkonen, H., Freeman, M.: Persuasive technology in mobile applications promoting physical activity: a systematic review. J. Med. Syst. **40**, 1–13 (2016)

13. Vlahu-Gjorgievska, E., Mulakaparambil Unnikrishnan, S., Win, K.T.: mHealth applications: A tool for behaviour change in weight management. Connecting the System to Enhance the Practitioner and Consumer Experience in Healthcare 158–163 (2018)

14. Meedya, S., et al.: Developing and testing a mobile application for breastfeeding support: the Milky Way application. Women and Birth **34**, e196–e203 (2021)

15. Chumkasian, W., et al.: Design and Development of mHealth App: Eye Donor Aust. In: International Conference on Persuasive Technology, pp. 75–88. Springer (2024)

16. Oinas-Kukkonen, H., Harjumaa, M.: Persuasive systems design: Key issues, process model, and system features. Commun. Assoc. Inf. Syst. **24**, 28 (2009)

17. Thomas, R.J., Masthoff, J., Oren, N.: Can i influence you? development of a scale to measure perceived persuasiveness and two studies showing the use of the scale. Frontiers in Artificial Intelligence **2**, 24 (2019)

18. Almohanna, A.A.S., Vlahu-Gjorgievska, E., Meedya, S., Win, K.T.: Evaluating user perceptions of the persuasive system design in a breastfeeding mHealth app: a cross-sectional study. Behaviour & Information Technology 1–25 (2024)

19. Beerlage-de Jong, N., Kip, H., Kelders, S.M.: Evaluation of the perceived persuasiveness questionnaire: user-centered card-sort study. J. Med. Internet Res. **22**, e20404 (2020)

20. Drozd, F., Lehto, T., Oinas-Kukkonen, H.: Exploring perceived persuasiveness of a behavior change support system: a structural model. In: Persuasive Technology. Design for Health and Safety: 7th International Conference, PERSUASIVE 2012, Linköping, Sweden, June 6–8, 2012. Proceedings 7, pp. 157–168. Springer (2012)

21. Shevchuk, N., Degirmenci, K., Oinas-Kukkonen, H.: Adoption of gamified persuasive systems to encourage sustainable behaviors: Interplay between perceived persuasiveness and cognitive absorption. In: International Conference on Information Systems ICIS 2019 Proceedings, Dec 15–18, Munich, Germany. Association for Information Systems (Year)

22. Lehto, T., Oinas-Kukkonen, H.: Explaining and predicting perceived effectiveness and use continuance intention of a behaviour change support system for weight loss. Behaviour & Information Technology **34**, 176–189 (2015)

23. Oyibo, K., et al.: Perceived persuasive effect of behavior model design in fitness apps. In: Proceedings of the 26th Conference on User Modeling, Adaptation and Personalization, pp. 219–228 (Year)

24. Lehto, T., Oinas-Kukkonen, H., Drozd, F.: Factors affecting perceived persuasiveness of a behavior change support system (2012)

25. Hyde, M.K., White, K.M.: Disclosing donation decisions: the role of organ donor prototypes in an extended theory of planned behaviour. Health Educ. Res. **24**, 1080–1092 (2009)

26. Jhantasana, C.: Should a rule of thumb be used to calculate PLS-SEM sample size. Asia Social Issues **16**, e254658–e254658 (2023)

27. Schober, P., Boer, C., Schwarte, L.A.: Correlation coefficients: appropriate use and interpretation. Anesth. Analg. **126**, 1763–1768 (2018)

28. Batis, A.A., Albarrak, A.: Preferences and features of a blood donation smartphone app: a multicenter mixed-methods study in Riyadh, Saudi Arabia. Computer Methods and Programs in Biomedicine Update **1**, 100005 (2021)

29. Rasche, P., et al.: Prevalence of health app use among older adults in Germany: national survey. JMIR Mhealth Uhealth **6**, e8619 (2018)

30. Van Elburg, F.R.T., Klaver, N.S., Nieboer, A.P., Askari, M.: Gender differences regarding intention to use mHealth applications in the Dutch elderly population: a cross-sectional study. BMC Geriatr. **22**, 449 (2022)

31. Win, K.T., Roberts, M.R., Oinas-Kukkonen, H.: Persuasive system features in computer-mediated lifestyle modification interventions for physical activity. Inform. Health Soc. Care **44**, 376–404 (2019)

32. Bramstedt, K.A., Cameron, A.: Beyond the billboard: the Facebook-based application, donor, and its guided approach to facilitating living organ donation. Am. J. Transplant. **17**, 336–340 (2017)

33. Talib, M.: Use of e-health communication to improve social wellbeing in older adults: a Structured literature review (2023)

MyHealthCore: Towards a Community-Engaged HIV Prevention Persuasive mHealth App for Black Communities in Canada

Kaminda Natasha Musumbulwa$^{(\boxtimes)}$, Gerry Chan , Oladapo Oyebode ,
and Rita Orji

Faulty of Computer Science, Dalhousie University, Halifax, NS, Canada
kaminda.musumbulwa@dal.ca

Abstract. Black communities in Canada are disproportionately affected by HIV, comprising 24.6% of new cases despite representing only 4.3% of the population. Systemic barriers such as stigma, racial bias, and inadequate access to culturally responsive health services contribute to this disparity. This study engages Black community members and HIV service providers to inform the design and development of a culturally responsive mHealth app for HIV prevention. Guided by community-based research and user-centered design principles, focus group discussions explored preferences for content, functionality, and design of an HIV prevention app. Data collected from focus groups identified five overarching themes: (1) general health concerns, (2) cultural responsiveness, (3) HIV prevention needs, (4) mHealth application preferences, and (5) culturally responsive information needs. Participants emphasized the importance of addressing stigma, providing multilingual options, and ensuring privacy and security. Preferences for app features included geolocation for testing centers, interactive risk assessments, and engaging educational content. The study highlights the critical need for integrating cultural relevance, user-centered design, and robust privacy measures into mHealth apps.

Keywords: HIV prevention · Black communities · mobile health (mHealth) · cultural responsiveness · user-centered design · community-based research (CBR) · HIV stigma · health equity · persuasive technology

1 Introduction

Nearly 2,000 people in Canada were newly diagnosed with HIV in 2022 [1]. This represents a 38% increase in new HIV diagnoses since 2020. Though disaggregated data is not collected uniformly – for example, the provinces of Québec and Manitoba did not submit data in 2021 – existing data demonstrates that Black communities continue to be disproportionately impacted by HIV [1]. In 2021, it was estimated that Black communities account for 4.3% of Canada's total population [2]. They did, however, account for 24.6% of new HIV cases in Ontario in the previous year [3]. Despite being identified as one of the five population groups with higher rates of HIV, there were no national estimates of new cases for Black people [4].

© The Author(s), under exclusive license to Springer Nature Switzerland AG 2025
K. T. Win et al. (Eds.): PERSUASIVE 2025, LNCS 15711, pp. 188–200, 2025.
https://doi.org/10.1007/978-3-031-94959-3_14

The ongoing disparity of HIV incidence amongst Black people is linked to multi-level systemic barriers that leave communities without access to culturally appropriate and responsive health services [5]. Black communities remain underserved in the areas of health research and health service delivery, which is a vital aspect of developing and delivering effective HIV prevention interventions [6]. Effective HIV prevention interventions for Black communities are those that respond to their systemic risk for HIV associated with their lived experiences of structural racism, multiple dimensions of stigma, and the social determinants of health [7]. To address this issue and promote early engagement in the HIV care cascade, innovative and culturally responsive interventions are needed [3].

The present study aims to inform the design and development of a culturally responsive mHealth HIV prevention application tailored to meet the unique needs of Black communities. Guided by a community-engaged approach, this work integrates insights from community members and HIV care service providers in Canada to co-design a relevant mobile health solution. By prioritizing clinical accuracy and culturally informed design, this study highlights the intersection between addressing systemic health disparities leveraging technological innovation, emphasizing the critical role of community engagement in developing technologies for key populations [8]. Our methodology is grounded in prior research on digital health tools for HIV prevention showing a willingness amongst Black communities in Canada to access HIV prevention content using mHealth apps [9].

In this research, we contribute to the ongoing efforts exploring technology-based interventions for HIV prevention in underserved populations by answering the following question: *"What factors influence the acceptability or reluctance of Black communities to use an mHealth app for HIV prevention, and how can their perspectives be integrated into its culturally responsive design and development?"* Our work offers three contributions to the fields of persuasive technology and designing for underrepresented communities. First, we identify key cultural, informational, and technological considerations for engaging Black communities in HIV prevention. Second, we provide empirical evidence on the acceptability and usability of mHealth solutions among Black community members and service providers. Third, we present actionable design strategies for addressing systemic health disparities through culturally responsive and user-centered mHealth applications. Together, these findings have implications for future research and the deployment of health interventions targeting other marginalized populations.

2   Background and Related Work

2.1   HIV Stigma and Cultural Responsiveness in HIV Care

HIV stigma has been shown to impede effective diagnosis, prevention, care, and treatment of HIV by reducing access to points of care [10]. It is a complex, intersectional issue and refers to the processes of devaluing, labeling, and stereotyping based on one's HIV status and leading to the loss of social status and experiences of discrimination and othering [11]. The compounded experiences of racism, sexism, homophobia, transphobia, along with conservative cultural norms and religious values make HIV stigma a considerable barrier for the Black community in Canada, is diverse including people of

African descent, with varying ethnic, cultural, gender, religious, and linguistic experiences [5, 12]. As a result, discussing HIV and sexual health is highly stigmatized. Many myths surrounding sex and the transmission, prevention, and treatment of HIV persist in the Black community [10].

Given the experiences of structural racism and stigma, it is important that HIV interventions for Black communities be culturally responsive. Cultural responsiveness in healthcare refers to the ability of a provider or system to center patient experiences and understandings of health that are influenced by their unique cultural lenses [13]. This shifts the emphasis from the views of healthcare professionals, which may be attached to harmful unconscious biases that are embedded in the oppressive ideals of the healthcare system [13]. Embracing cultural responsiveness in HIV healthcare may look like acknowledging the barriers diverse patients may face when accessing health services instead of focusing on their individual health behaviors [14]. In the Black community, this can be applied by implementing interventions that account for their cultural beliefs, norms, and values [14].

2.2 mHealth as a Platform for HIV Prevention Interventions

Increasingly, mHealth apps are being adopted to address the various health needs of diverse communities [15]. mHealth apps support the accessibility and dissemination of health information across large geographic areas [15] as they can address health service delivery gaps across the HIV care cascade [16]. Using mHealth apps for HIV prevention can provide easy, continuous access to sexual health information without the barriers to accessing standard healthcare such as proximity to and availability of health services [15]. When designed with access to peer networks, mHealth apps can support improved health literacy, self-efficacy, and self-management of one's health, especially in specific Black groups [17]. For example, Black women are more likely to use mobile phones to search for health information [18]. This presents an opportunity to explore the effect among other Black groups including men, youth, and gender-diverse people.

2.3 Persuasive Technology for Health Behaviour Modification

Persuasive technology (PT) refers to the integration of digital tools to influence user behavior and attitudes without coercion [34]. The growing use of smartphones and wearable devices has created opportunities for PT to increase users' motivation and drive behavioral change. Persuasive design frameworks, such as those proposed by Oinas-Kukkonen and Harjumaa, categorize persuasive system principles into four main groups: (1) primary task support, (2) dialogue support, (3) system credibility support, and (4) social support [35].

In the absence of HIV-prevention specific solutions tailored to Black communities in the Canadian context, the exploration of existing mHealth solutions such as the *Don't Die* app [33] can inform the adoption of validated persuasive strategies. The app serves as a notable example of digital innovation for health behavior modification, employing several persuasive strategies to engage and motivate users. Primary task support is evident in the app's self-monitoring feature, which tracks user health metrics and reinforces progress toward health goals [35]. Self-monitoring has been recognized as a powerful tool for sustaining behavior change by increasing self-awareness and accountability [35]. Additionally, dialogue support is implemented through the app's reward mechanisms, where users receive personalized feedback and incentives based on their daily scores, reinforcing engagement and adherence to healthier behaviors [35]. Incorporating similar persuasive strategies into future HIV prevention mHealth solutions presents the potential to develop an engaging app for users that can address the existing barriers to health care access for Black communities and the promote uptake of traditional HIV prevention methods.

3   Exploratory Study Design

To gather input on the perspectives and attitudes of Black community members and HIV service providers towards using an mHealth app for HIV prevention, our exploratory study utilized a qualitative approach. The study is modelled after a similar HIV app design and development procedure for Black women living in metro-Atlanta [15].

3.1   Community-Based Research (CBR)

Using the principles of CBR, including collaboration and co-learning will ensure that the community's perspectives are reflected in the final app [19]. CBR approaches are used in HIV research as they promote the recognition of contributors to disparate HIV outcomes including the social determinants of health by affected populations [19]. Incorporating CBR principles increases the potential for a research process that is equitable to participants and respects them as members of the research team, rather than mere research subjects [19]. Research done with the meaningful engagement of community members ensures that resulting interventions adequately explore community knowledge [20].

3.2   Study Population and Recruitment

This study was reviewed and approved by our institutional ethics board. We recruited 21 participants using purposive sampling from AIDS Service Organizations, HIV care clinics, and other community-based and sexual health organizations across Canada. Digital flyers were initially distributed via email to the lead researchers' professional network, and then on social media platforms such as Twitter, Facebook, and LinkedIn. The flyers provided the lead researcher's email, who assessed participant eligibility. Inclusion criteria for this study required community members to (1) self-identify as Black, (2) be 18 years of age or older, (3) live in Canada, (4) speak and understand English comfortably, and (5) have access to an android phone or iPhone. HIV service providers were required to meet the above criteria and have worked in the HIV sector in a clinical or non-clinical capacity for 12 months out of the last 5 years.

3.3   Study Procedures

In total, there were 21 participants who were divided into Focus Group Discussions (FGDs). We concluded that this sample size was adequate for analysis based on data saturation and empirical evidence of sufficiency [21]. After participants were determined to be eligible for the study, they were invited to complete a pre-study questionnaire asking them to provide their demographic information and current knowledge of HIV and related prevention methods. Community members (CM) were asked to share their current knowledge of HIV transmission, prevention, and their knowledge on where to access HIV-related support services. HIV service providers (SP) were asked to share their current experiences providing HIV care to Black communities and their opinions on current gaps in HIV-related services. After completing the pre-study questionnaire, participants were asked for their availability to participate in a FGD with 4 or 5 other participants. FGDs were conducted virtually using Microsoft Teams and lasted an average of 45 min long. There were three FGDs completed with community members (N = 11). There were two FGDs completed with service providers (N = 10). FGDs were facilitated by the lead researcher, who was knowledgeable about HIV prevention and the objectives of the mobile app. A notetaker also supported the sessions. We employed two FGD guides; one for CM and one for HIV SP. The FGD's covered four main topics: (1) general health of Black communities, (2) HIV prevention information needs of Black communities, (3) culturally responsive information needs of Black communities, and (4) preferred features of an mHealth app for HIV prevention. Participants were given a $10.00 gift card as an honorarium for their time.

3.4   Qualitative Data Analysis: Coding and Theme Development

We followed Braun and Clarke's six-phase framework [22] for conducting thematic analysis. Inductive coding techniques were used to categorize the data and generate an understanding of participants' subjective experiences and motivation. This method was selected for its analytical flexibility and applicability across diverse ontological and epistemological viewpoints [23]. Initially, the researchers read and re-read the transcripts to familiarize themselves thoroughly with the data. To enhance the rigor and trustworthiness of the qualitative data analysis, inter-rater reliability was assessed. Two independent reviewers conducted thematic analysis separately on a subset of transcripts for CM ($n = 5$) and SP ($n = 5$). Cohen's kappa coefficient was calculated to measure the consistency between reviewers. A kappa score of 0.82 was obtained, indicating a high level of agreement between raters [24]. Discrepancies in coding were discussed until consensus was reached, and definitions of codes were refined accordingly. The iterative process ensured consistency in coding and theme development. A codebook was created for each participant group, and codes were applied to the dataset. These codes were analyzed to identify broader themes, which were refined through discussion until consensus was reached. Finally, the themes were used to create a narrative capturing Black communities' perspectives on using an mHealth app for HIV prevention.

4   Results

4.1   Participant Characteristics

A total of 11 community members and 10 HIV service providers participated in the FGDs (Table 1). Generally, our participants were diverse in terms of age, gender, ethnicity and level of education.

Table 1. Participant characteristics.

Characteristic	Community members ($N = 11$)	Service providers ($N = 10$)
Age (years)	18−25 (36%), 26−35 (36%), 36−45 (18%), 45−55 (9%)	26−35 (20%), 36−45 (50%), 45−55 (30%)
Gender	Cis-woman (73%), non-binary (9%), non-gender conforming (9%), prefer not to answer (9%)	Cis-woman (70%), cis-man (30%)
Ethnicity	African (73%), Caribbean (27%)	African (60%), Caribbean (40%)
Education level	Secondary school diploma (18%), College certificate or diploma (18%), university bachelor's degree (45%), Master's, doctorate or professional degree (18%)	Secondary school diploma (10%), College certificate or diploma (20%), university bachelor's degree (40%), Master's, doctorate or professional degree (30%)
Employment status	Working full-time (45%), working part-time (45%), on government assistance (9%)	Working full-time (80%), working part-time (20%)
Province	Ontario (64%), Alberta (9%), British Columbia (9%), and Nova Scotia (9%)	Ontario (100%)
Work experience (years)	N/A	1−3 (20%), 3−5 (10%), 5 + (70)
Work setting	N/A	AIDS service organization (80%), community health center (20%)

4.2 Perspectives and Experiences of Black Communities Regarding the Use of mHealth for HIV Prevention

Results were categorized into five overarching themes for both community members [CM] and service provider [SP] FGDs to guide the development of a culturally responsive mHealth HIV prevention app for Black communities. The first theme, *general health concerns*, encompassed population health and personal health concerns as expressed by participants. The second theme, *cultural responsiveness,* addressed stigma, cultural barriers to accessing HIV prevention information, and culturally specific information sharing. The third theme, *HIV prevention for Black communities*, highlighted existing stigma, HIV risk assessment, and PrEP knowledge and uptake. The fourth theme, *mHealth application preferences*, explored desired app features, persuasive strategies, and mHealth app concerns. Excerpts are presented with minor spelling and grammatical corrections. The final theme, *persuasive strategies and design preferences* highlighted the preferred features that would promote behavior change and encourage user engagement and retention in the app.

Theme 1: General Health Concerns. The top health concerns from community members included chronic conditions such as diabetes, and hypertension, as well as mental health, and access to affordable care. Community members expressed that general health priorities often take precedence over HIV prevention. One participant said, *"Healthy food is expensive, and without it, managing weight and other conditions becomes impossible"* [CM7]. Service providers noted that HIV often intersects with chronic health issues such as diabetes, hypertension, and mental health challenges. Therefore, addressing these broader concerns was seen as essential for increasing engagement with HIV prevention tools. For example, one SP said, *"People's first concern isn't always HIV—it's the chronic conditions they're already managing. So, we should link HIV prevention to overall wellness to make it more relevant"* [SP3].

Theme 2: Cultural Responsiveness. Participants consistently highlighted the stigma surrounding HIV in Black communities, rooted in cultural, religious, and societal beliefs. Community members expressed concerns about judgment and discrimination. One participant expressed, *"HIV is still seen as a death sentence in our communities; people avoid testing out of fear of being judged"* [CM3]. To parallel this thought, service providers emphasized the need for strategies to normalize HIV prevention and testing. *"We need to use positive narratives and testimonials from respected community figures to combat stigma"* [SP6]. Expanding on the concept of storytelling, one community member said, *"When I think about HIV and living with HIV, I think of [family member name]. And a lot of people see him and they don't know his story. So if you could identify other persons living with HIV to show people that its not a life sentence. I think even more important than just telling people, like if you take these medications you'll be okay, would be helpful getting those stories across to people to reduce the stigma"* [CM2].

Both groups identified language barriers, mistrust of healthcare systems, and culturally irrelevant materials as significant obstacles. CM stressed the importance of localized content, stating, *"Some older adults can't access information because it's only available in English"* [CM1]. One SP suggested storytelling as the preferred method of communication in many Black cultures, and that group-based education would improve education uptake. One SP said, *"People trust stories; they're easier to connect with than facts alone. That would work well to share information in culturally meaningful ways"* [SP9]. Another community member reflected, *"I do like the idea of, like, having, like, proper representation of, like, people that look like us reflected in a project like that"* [CM7].

Participants stressed the need for culturally relevant content, such as using visuals, narratives, and languages that resonate with diverse Black identities. *"I would definitely incorporate multiple languages, not just English and French. I've seen some service organizations develop things in different African languages and Patois and Creole, so that's something that is emerging that I'm seeing and I'm really excited about"* [CM10].

Theme 3: HIV Prevention for Black Communities. When discussing specific HIV prevention measures, specifically PrEP, limited knowledge of eligibility for and accessibility of the medication was noted by both community members and service providers. One SP mentioned, *"We need to explain who PrEP is for and how people can access it"* [SP3]. Another SP said, *"PrEP uptake remains low because people don't know enough about it. We need to explain eligibility and benefits clearly"* [SP8]. For community members who were aware of PrEP, they were not aware of where to access it and plainly said, *"I've heard of PrEP, but I don't know where to get it or if it's for me"* [CM10]. Once more, the stigma surrounding HIV was cited as a barrier preventing people from seeking appropriate resources. One CM said, *"People think taking PrEP means you're promiscuous, which stops them from even learning about it"* [CM2].

Theme 4: *mHealth Application Preferences.* Participants across focus groups articulated a clear need for an mHealth app that is accessible, user-friendly, and culturally relevant. For example, one CM said, *"If it's not easy to use, people won't bother"* [CM2]. Participants emphasized that an mHealth application for HIV prevention amongst Black communities should be compatible across Android and iPhone platforms and should cater to diverse needs, ensuring inclusivity across age groups, literacy levels, and cultural backgrounds. One SP highlighted the need to consider older adults in the design of the app, stating, *"Please make it user-friendly and simple for everyone to use, including the older generation"* [SP2]. Regarding being mindful of cultural ways of sharing information, a CM noted, *"Religion and spiritual beliefs have to be taken into account because I think that informs how we engage in sexual health topics in general and HIV prevention. With that in mind, we need to consider that folks will receive information in different ways or they won't even engage because of religious, cultural or spiritual practices"* [CM4].

Theme 5: Persuasive Strategies and Design Preferences. When discussing persuasive technologies to encourage app use, participants identified strategies to keep users engaged and encourage consistent app usage. These strategies include community engagement. One SP expressed, *"Creating safe online spaces for peer interaction can help build trust and reduce stigma"* [SP3]. Another noted the impact of one dimension of cultural responsiveness, which is the impact of seeing reflective images in the app. They explained how this would positively influence app usage, noting, *"Seeing oneself in the app, through relatable visuals and narratives, would foster trust and engagement"* [SP3]. SP provided rich insights into the clinical content and resource navigation tools to be included on the app. Regarding HIV information, they highlighted the need to provide comprehensive information about HIV transmission, prevention, and treatment, including FAQs and side effects of medications like PrEP, as essential. *"The app should provide clear, translated information to address misconceptions about PrEP"* [SP2]. One service provider highlighted an often-neglected area of HIV prevention, which is condom negotiation especially amongst cis-and trans-women said, *"for people who identify as women, and that includes trans folks, there should be a section on negotiating sex and negotiating condom use because there's a lot of power dynamics that happen there and women especially have challenges negotiating safe sex in those relationships"* [SP5]. A CM corroborated this by emphasizing the need to recall intersectionality and the fact that HIV affects different subcommunities in different ways, saying, *"Really taking into consideration from a cultural perspective, who is impacted by HIV, so whether its nationality, race, and other intersections of sexual orientation, gender, to make it more tailored"* [CM2].

Regarding resource navigation, SP highlighted the need for the app to offer a geolocation feature and provide a directory of Black-friendly health service organizations and testing locations. One participant emphasized that *"We need a service map where some-one can get access to Black-friendly health service organizations or community health centres. I think people are always looking for contact information or where places are located"* [SP3]. Another added, *"It would be good if it could show where to get PrEP and where you can go get tested or where you can go if you have received a positive response"* [SP10]. Participants identified additional strategies to keep users engaged and encourage consistent app usage. These strategies include community engagement, personalized health tracking and push notifications. One SP expressed, *"Creating safe online spaces for peer interaction can help build trust and reduce stigma"* [SP3]. Another service provider highlighted that tracking things like medication, could support adher-ence for those on medication said, *"Adherence is an issue. So you know, if you can have a tracker or something that reminds people to take their medication, I think that would also help"* [SP2]. Finally, SP emphasized the need for data privacy measures, highlight-ing concerns rooted in ethical HIV disclosure and the historical exploitation and lack of data sovereignty experienced by Black communities in health research. One SP said, *"Ensuring that guidelines for data collection and use are clearly outlined is essential"* [SP8], while another SP explained, *"It's critical to have clear privacy policies, especially when users may disclose sensitive health information on the platform"* [SP4].

5   Discussion

This study engaged Black community members and HIV service providers across Canada in the ideation of a mobile application designed to respond to the multi-level barriers to comprehensive HIV prevention. Participants were engaged to understand their prefer-ences for the content, functionality, format, and design of an mHealth app and to examine their willingness to access HIV education on a mobile application. They provided many suggestions including the functionality of the app, visual and health education content, layout and navigation, as well as privacy features.

5.1   Design Recommendations

Based on the collected data, we determined five features that incorporate persuasive design principles defined by Oinas-Kukkonen and Harjumaa [25] to ensure the app, named *MyHealthCore* (***Co**mmunity **Re**source*), aligns with the community's needs and expectations. Some initial sketches of the features for upcoming development are shown in Fig. 1. The five features are as follows:

1. **Home Screen:** The home screen (Fig. 1a) will be designed using **primary task support** to offer users a dashboard with immediate access to the app's primary features and real-time news on advancements in HIV prevention and care. Using **tunneling**, users will be guides to select a headline from the news carousel, users will be led to an external website to read the full article.
2. **MyHealthEducation:** This feature (Fig. 1b) is an educational hub within the app, offering a search-enabled interface for users to access a range of HIV-related topics. In this section, users are met with a menu of options including HIV 101, Testing,

Prevention, Treatment, and PrEP, each leading to a repository of detailed information. **Tailoring** provides users with the option to customize their education based on their interests. **Self-monitoring** of knowledge is done through the completion of quizzes that assess user's learning progress on HIV-related topics.

3. **MyHealthConnect:** This feature (Fig. 1c) encourages **social support** by offering a gateway for users to engage with their community and healthcare professionals. Users can navigate to the feature where they have the option to view Community Stories; a platform to share and learn from collective experiences.

4. **MyHealthLocator:** This feature (Fig. 1d) relies on **reduction** to simplify the process of navigation to essential HIV health services such as AIDS Service Organizations (ASOs), HIV testing centres, PrEP clinics, and community-based organizations. Relying on **tailoring**, the geolocation feature will allow users to filter services by province. Using their current location, they will access maps in the browser and have directions to each service.

5. **MyHealthTracker:** An integral feature (Fig. 1e) of the app, this will be designed to help users monitor various aspects of their health. Designed using the principle of **simulation**, this centralized tracker provides options to record and review tests, schedule and manage appointments, log symptoms as they occur, monitor medication schedules, and mental health progress. Additionally, **dialogue support** will be embedded in the form of reminders to send notifications for appointments and medication schedules to encourage adherence.

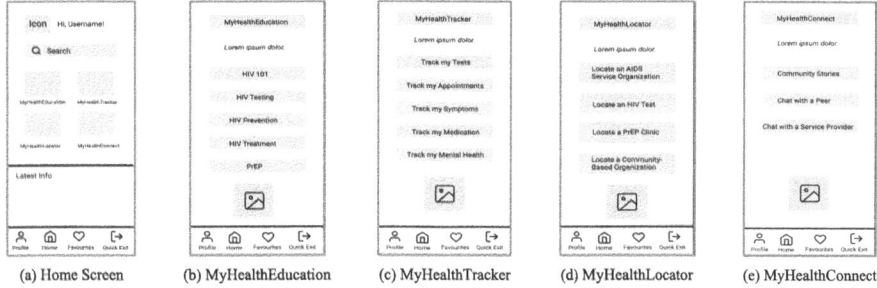

| (a) Home Screen | (b) MyHealthEducation | (c) MyHealthTracker | (d) MyHealthLocator | (e) MyHealthConnect |

Fig. 1. Initial sketches of features for upcoming development of the MyHealthCore app.

5.2 Implications for Development

The findings from our study underscore several key persuasive technology design and health information considerations. First, addressing stigma is paramount. Incorporating positive narratives and culturally resonant storytelling can help normalize HIV prevention and reduce fear of judgment. Beyond research showing feedback, appropriate reminders, and in-app support from peers are key elements for promoting retention [26], this study uncovered that features such as geolocation for nearby testing centers, interactive risk assessments, and push notifications for reminders (strategies that enable a system to remind users to perform the target behavior [27]) were identified as essential for facilitating access and sustained engagement. Second, participants emphasized the importance of inclusivity in imagery and language to reflect the diversity within Black communities [28, 29]. Multilingual options, visuals of individuals from different cultural backgrounds, and intergenerational content were highlighted as strategies to foster trust and relatability. Additionally, the app must ensure ease of use through simple navigation, intuitive design, and compatibility with varying levels of digital literacy.

5.3 Limitations

Despite its strong methodological basis, this study has limitations. One limitation is that the sample size, though diverse, may not fully capture the heterogeneity within Black communities across Canada. While the study explored user preferences, another limitation is that it did not evaluate the feasibility or effectiveness of the proposed app features and health content, which will require further testing in real-world contexts.

5.4 Directions for Future Work

The findings from this study provide a strong foundation for the next phases of mHealth app development. Future work will proceed through the following four stages:

1. **Integrating Theoretical Frameworks.** This step will involve incorporating established behavior change models, such as Fogg's Behavior Model [30], the Self-Determination Theory [31], or the Health Belief Model [32] to effectively frame participant's behavioral change and optimize engagement in the app.
2. **Wireframe Design and Evaluation.** The initial step involves completing the wireframe or low-fidelity sketches of the app's layout and features. These wireframes will then be evaluated through participatory design sessions with additional community members and service providers to ensure that the app aligns with user needs and cultural expectations.
3. **Prototype Design and Evaluation.** Building on the wireframes, an interactive prototype will be developed, incorporating the features and design elements identified in this study. Usability testing with Black users and service providers will be conducted to refine functionality, navigation, and aesthetics.
4. **App Development and Evaluation.** The final stage involves full app development, followed by pilot testing to assess its impact on key outcomes such as HIV knowledge, app usability, and perceived usefulness. A mixed-methods evaluation will explore user satisfaction, behavioral changes, and scalability to other underserved populations.

By advancing through these stages, the study aims to translate the insights gained into a functional, impactful mHealth solution that addresses the unique barriers faced by Black communities.

6   Conclusion

In conclusion, this study explored the perspectives of Black community members and HIV service providers to inform the design and development of a culturally responsive and clinically relevant HIV prevention mHealth app. To the best of our knowledge, this is one of the first studies in Canada to integrate cultural responsiveness, persuasive design, and technology to address gaps in the prevention arm of the HIV care cascade among Black populations. Our findings offer valuable insights to guide the next stages of this work, including the design and evaluation of low- and medium-fidelity prototypes, culminating in the development of the full application.

Acknowledgments. This research was undertaken, in part, thanks to funding from the Canada Research Chairs Program. We acknowledge the support of the Natural Sciences and Engineering Research Council of Canada (NSERC) through the Discovery Grant. The research is conducted as part of the Dalhousie University Persuasive Computing Lab.

References

1. Public Health Agency of Canada: https://www.canada.ca/en/public-health/services/pub lications/diseases-conditions/hiv-canada-surveillance-report-december-31-2022.html. Last accessed 25 Oct. 2024
2. Statistics Canada Information sheet: https://www.statcan.gc.ca/en/dai/smr08/2024/smr08_ 278/infosheet. Last accessed 25 Oct. 2024
3. Current Trends for HIV in Ontario: https://www.ohesi.ca/. Last accessed 25 Oct. 2024
4. Challacombe, L.: The epidemiology of HIV in Canada. Catie. pp. 1–5 (2013)
5. Etowa, J., et al.: Community perspectives on addressing and responding to HIV-testing, pre-exposure prophylaxis (PrEP) and post-exposure prophylaxis (PEP) among African, Caribbean and Black (ACB) people in Ontario, Canada. BMC Public Health. (2022)
6. Baidoobonso, S., et al.: HIV risk perception and distribution of HIV risk among African, Caribbean and other black people in a Canadian city: mixed methods results from the BLACCH study. BMC Public Health. (2013)
7. Logie, C.H., et al.: A structural equation model of HIV-related stigma, racial discrimination, housing insecurity and wellbeing among African and Caribbean Black women living with HIV in Ontario, Canada. PLoS One. (2016)
8. Mauka, W., et al.: Development of a mobile health application for HIV prevention among at-risk populations in urban settings in east africa: A participatory design approach. JMIR Form. Res. (2021)
9. Tesema, N., et al.: Mobile phone apps for HIV prevention among college-aged black women in atlanta: mixed methods study and user-centered prototype. JMIR Form. Res. (2023)
10. Mihan, R., Kerr, J., Maticka-Tyndale, E.: HIV-related stigma among African, Caribbean, and Black youth in Windsor, Ontario. AIDS Care - Psychol. Socio Med. Asp. AIDS/HIV. **28**, 758–763 (2016)
11. Logie, C.H., James, L.I., Tharao, W., Loutfy, M.R.: HIV, gender, race, sexual orientation, and sex work: A qualitative study of intersectional stigma experienced by HIV-positive women in Ontario, Canada. PLoS Med. (2011)
12. Jangu, N.W., Omorodion, F.I., Kerr, J.: The perception of religious leaders on HIV and their role in HIV prevention: a case study of African, Caribbean, and Black (ACB) communities in windsor. Ontario. J. Relig. Health. **62**, 1616–1635 (2023)
13. Xavier, J., et al.: Identifying the barriers and facilitators to culturally responsive HIV and PrEP screening for racial, ethnic, sexual, and gender minoritized patients: A scoping review protocol. PLoS One. (2023)
14. Winiarski., M.G., Beckett, E., Salcedo, J.: Outcomes of an inner-city HIV mental health programme integrated with primary care and emphasizing cultural responsiveness. AIDS Care Psychol. Socio Medical Asp. AIDS/HIV. **17**, 747–756 (2005)

15. Chandler, R., et al.: Digital health app to address disparate HIV outcomes among black women living in metro-atlanta: protocol for a multiphase, mixed methods pilot feasibility study. JMIR Res. Protoc. (2023)
16. Goldstein, M., et al.: Systematic review of mhealth interventions for adolescent and young adult HIV prevention and the adolescent HIV continuum of care in low to middle income countries. AIDS Behav. **27**, 94–115 (2023)
17. Danielson, C.K., et al.: Feasibility of delivering evidence-based HIV/STI prevention programming to a community sample of African American teen girls via the internet. AIDS Educ. Prev. **25**, 394–404 (2013)
18. James, D.C.S., Harville, C.: Smartphone usage, social media engagement, and Willingness to participate in mHealth weight management research among African American women. Heal. Educ. Behav. **45**, 315–322 (2018)
19. What is Community-Based Research?: https://paninbc.ca/research-and-evaluation/what-is-cbr/ Last accessed 25 Oct. 2024
20. Holkup, P.A., Tripp-Reimer, T., Salois, E.M., Weinert, C.: Community-based participatory research: an approach to intervention research with a native american community. Adv. Nurs. Sci. **27**, 162–175 (2004)
21. Braun, V., Clarke, V.: Using thematic analysis in psychology. Qual. Res. Psychol. **3**, 77–101 (2006)
22. Braun, V., Clarke, V.: Thematic analysis. In: APA handbook of research methods in psychology. Vol 2: Research designs: Quantitative, qualitative, neuropsychological, and biological, pp. 57–71. American Psychological Association, Washington (2012)
23. Thomas, D.R.: A General Inductive approach for analyzing qualitative evaluation data. Am. J. Eval. **27**, 237–246 (2006)
24. McHugh, M.L.: Interrater reliability: the kappa statistic. Biochem. Medica. **22**, 276–282 (2012)
25. Oinas-Kukkonen, H., Harjumaa, M.: Persuasive systems design: key issues, process model, and system features. Commun. Assoc. Inf. Syst. **24**, 485–500 (2009)
26. Amagai, S., et al.: Challenges in participant engagement and retention using mobile health apps: literature review. J. Med. Internet Res. (2022)
27. Alqahtani, F., Al Khalifah, G., Oyebode, O., Orji, R.: Apps for mental health: an evaluation of behavior change strategies and recommendations for future development. Front. Artif. Intell. (2019)
28. Naderbagi, A., et al.: Cultural and contextual adaptation of digital health interventions: narrative review. J. Med. Internet Res. (2024)
29. Vigil-Hayes, M., et al.: Integrating cultural relevance into a behavioral mHealth intervention for native american youth. Proc. ACM Hum. Comput. Interact. 5, (2021)
30. Fogg, B.: A behavior model for persuasive design. ACM Int. Conf. Proceeding Ser. (2009)
31. Ryan, R.M., Deci, E.L.: Self-determination theory and the facilitation of intrinsic motivation, social development, and well-being. Am. Psychol. **55**, 68–78 (2000)
32. Rosenstock, I.M.: The health belief model and preventive health behavior. Heal. Educ. Behav. **2**, 354–386 (1977)
33. Don't Die App. https://dontdieapp.notion.site
34. Oinas-Kukkonen, H., Harjumaa, M.: A systematic framework for designing and evaluating persuasive systems. In: Oinas-Kukkonen, H., Hasle, P., Harjumaa, M., Segerståhl, K., Øhrstrøm, P. (eds.) Persuasive Technology: Third International Conference on Persuasive Technology, PERSUASIVE 2008, Oulu, Finland, 4–6 June 2008, Proceedings, pp. 164–176. Springer, Cham (2008). https://doi.org/10.1007/978-3-540-68504-3_15
35. Oinas-Kukkonen, H., Harjumaa, M.: Persuasive systems design: key issues, process model, and system features. Commun. Assoc. Inf. Syst. **24**(1), Article 28, 485–500 (2009). https://doi.org/10.17705/1CAIS.02428

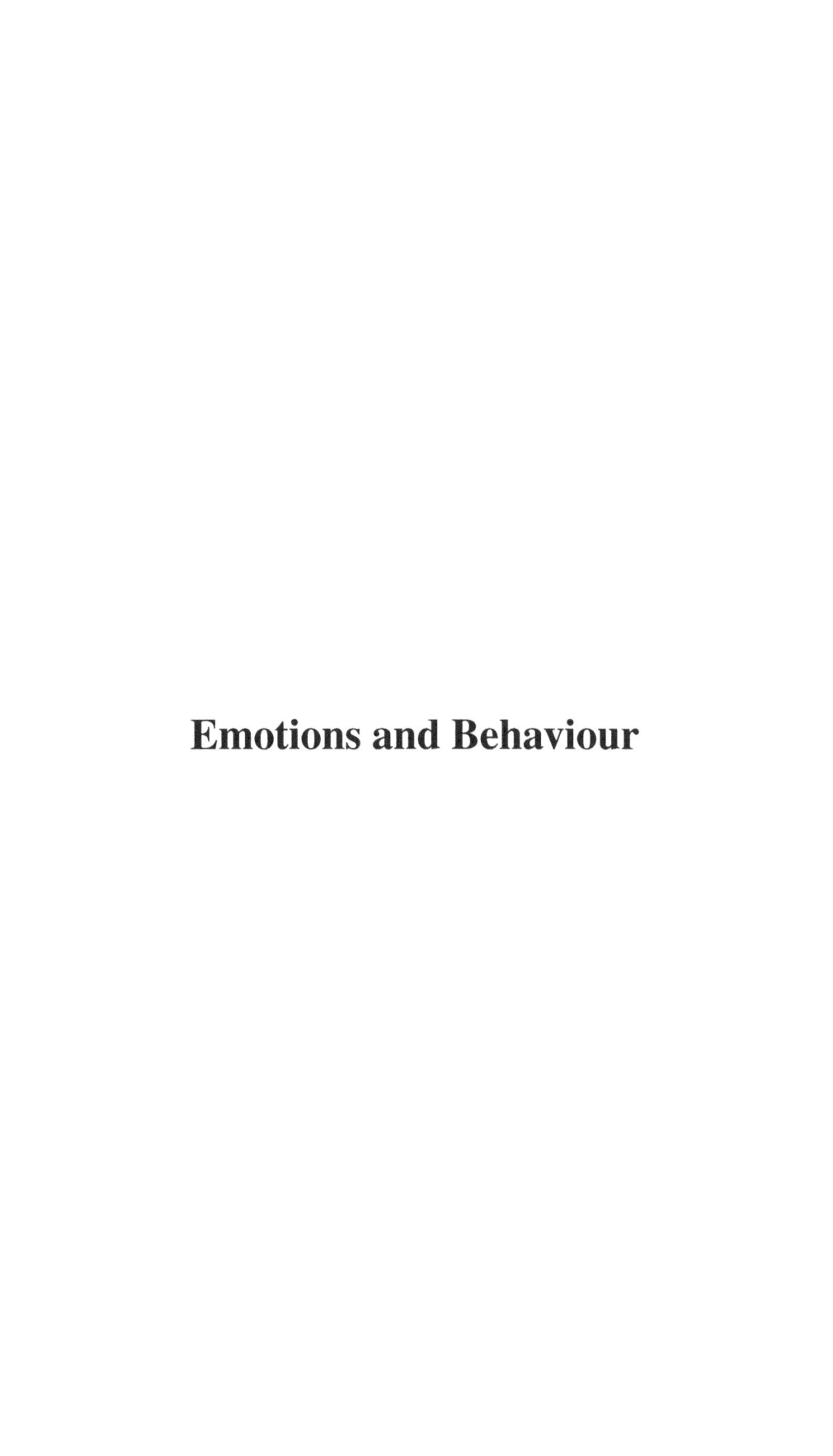

Emotions and Behaviour

Health Risk Management Using Persuasive Technology: A Scoping Review

Stanley Ebhohimhen Abhadiomhen[1,2(✉)] [iD],
Emmanuel Onyekachukwu Nzeakor[1], and Kiemute Oyibo[1] [iD]

[1] Department of Electrical Engineering and Computer Science, York University,
4700 Keele Street, Toronto, ON M3J 1P3, Canada
kiemute.oyibo@yorku.ca
[2] Department of Computer Science, University of Nigeria, Nsukka 400241, Nigeria
sabhadio@yorku.ca

Abstract. Persuasive technology (PT) uses techniques such as goal-setting and feedback to promote behavioral changes, and its effectiveness in mitigating various health conditions has been demonstrated in numerous studies. However, no systematic or scoping review has explored the application of PT in general health risk management. Existing reviews tend to focus on specific risk factors or health conditions, leaving a gap in exploring the broader application of PT in mitigating different health risks. This paper aims to expand the scope of existing reviews to include a wide range of health conditions managed through PT. A scoping review was performed following the approach outlined by Tranfield et al. and the PRISMA guidelines for reporting systematic/scoping reviews. The search was conducted across 5 databases. From an initial pool of 688 studies, 126 were removed due to duplication. Of the 21 studies included in the final analysis, 7 (33.33%) focused on general health risks. Physical activity was the most frequently targeted behavior in all but 5 studies (76.19%). Web-based platforms and mobile health applications were the most used digital technology (38.09% each), followed by wearable devices (19.05%). Feedback was the most employed PT technique (52.38%), with goal-setting (33.33%) and personalization (38.10%) also being frequently utilized. Despite the reported effectiveness of PT-based interventions, it remains unclear how to design the most effective tailored messages for diverse populations (especially underserved populations) without assuming population homogeneity (one-size-fits-all approach). Further research is required to address this gap and develop more tailored and personalized interventions.

Keywords: health risk management · persuasive technology · tailored interventions · behavioral changes

1 Introduction

According to the World Health Organization report [54], chronic diseases such as diabetes, hypertension, and obesity account for 70% of mortality worldwide,

K. T. Win et al. (Eds.): PERSUASIVE 2025, LNCS 15711, pp. 203–216, 2025.
https://doi.org/10.1007/978-3-031-94959-3_15

highlighting the need for robust health risk management (HRM) strategies to mitigate the prevalence of these conditions. HRM encompasses health risk assessment [41] to categorize individuals or populations into different health risk groups based on the likelihood of being affected by certain illnesses. Once health risks are assessed, interventions and strategies are implemented to manage the identified risks through targeted behavioral changes [19]. However, traditional health care models have several limitations [21]. These include structural inequities, such as geographical barriers (e.g. rural or remote locations with limited healthcare facilities) and socioeconomic barriers (e.g. low income or lack of health insurance), which can hinder access to healthcare resources for low-income populations. [1]. In addition, most traditional systems struggle during public health emergencies [23], as evidenced by the strain on many healthcare facilities during the COVID-19 pandemic [58].

Digital health (DH) focuses on addressing these limitations through the integration of technology into healthcare systems [34] to enhance engagement and efficiency in healthcare delivery. DH technologies include wearable devices, web-based applications, mobile health applications, health informatics, and telemedicine, all of which aim to improve healthcare outcomes [37]. At the core of DH initiatives is persuasive technology (PT) [42], which aims to change behaviors through persuasion and influence. In healthcare, PT seeks to foster healthy behaviors by delivering tailored and personalized interventions to promote HRM [6]. Target behaviors often include adopting healthier lifestyles, increasing physical activity, and improving diet using PT techniques such as goal-setting, gamification (through elements like points, badges, and leaderboards to boost engagement), real-time feedback on progress (such as steps walked, or weight lost), and timely reminders or nudges to help users stay on track [46]. Social tools are also commonly used to motivate users through social comparisons or peer pressure [33], for example, by showing how users' progress compared with their friends. As a result of the evidence-based effectiveness of PT techniques, many health risk-related studies [4,5,22,47] have largely incorporated them.

However, no systematic or scoping review has explored their application in general health risk management. Existing reviews in this area, such as those by Idrees et al. [29], Aldenaini et al. [3], Jaffar et al. [32], Grady et al. [25], and Sediva et al. [56], primarily focus on specific health conditions and do not consider the broader application of PT in general HRM. This gap in the literature forms the core rationale for the current review. Therefore, the main objective of this scoping review is to analyze and synthesize findings from published studies (across various chronic diseases) that used PT techniques for health risk management. Accordingly, this review was guided by the following research questions: (1) What health conditions are commonly managed with PT interventions? (2) What PT techniques are mostly used in HRM? (3) Which health behaviors are most frequently targeted by PT interventions in the context of HRM, and how effective are these techniques in fostering target behavior change? (4) What are the current research gaps in using PT for HRM, and which areas require further investigation?

2   Methodology

Tranfield et al.'s [57] three-step framework (planning, search and screening, and synthesizing and reporting) was followed to conduct the scoping review. The planning phase, which involved defining review objectives and developing the search protocol–including identifying relevant databases, formulating search strings, and establishing eligibility criteria for article retrieval, was conducted by the first author (FA) and the last author. Searching was performed by the FA across five databases: IEEE Xplore, Scopus, Web of Science, ACM Digital Library, and Medline. Screening, including title/abstract (TA) and full-text (FT) screening, was performed independently by the FA and the second author (SA), with 136 articles progressing to the FT screening after TA screening, and 21 articles being included in the final analysis. Data extraction was done collaboratively by the FA and the SA using Google spreadsheet, from where the data was processed, organized, and tabulated for further analysis. The reporting phase was carried out by the FA. Due to space limitations, some details were presented concisely, but the findings were presented relatively in accordance with the PRISMA 2020 checklist [48].

Eligibility Criteria: The eligibility criteria included studies written in English and published in peer-reviewed journals or conference proceedings. Eligible studies focused on health risk management and incorporated persuasive technology elements or behavior change support systems, such as employing digital tools (e.g., apps, wearables) aimed at influencing health behavior. Studies that reported the effectiveness of interventions (e.g., smoking cessation, weight reduction, increased physical activities) were included. Articles not written in English, non-peer-reviewed publications, studies not related to chronic disease based human health risk management, and those without persuasive elements were excluded. The search strategy incorporates the following string: ("health risk") AND ("management" OR "assessment*" OR "evaluation*" OR "monitoring" OR "tracking") AND ("persuasive" OR "behavio* change") AND ("technolog*" OR "system*" OR "app*"). These terms were carefully identified through a combination of relevant keywords related to health risk management, persuasive technology, and the associated digital platforms, based on existing literature and expert recommendations. The search was conducted without restrictions on publication date to ensure comprehensive coverage of relevant studies. However, the final search was completed in December 2024, which serves as the cutoff for included studies.

Data Synthesis Method: Data were synthesized qualitatively, focusing on key themes such as geographical characteristics, focused health conditions, targeted health behaviors, digital domains, and PT techniques. A narrative synthesis approach [9], incorporating both thematic and descriptive analysis, was used to analyze the findings. The results are presented using tables and charts, generated with MATLAB R2021a.

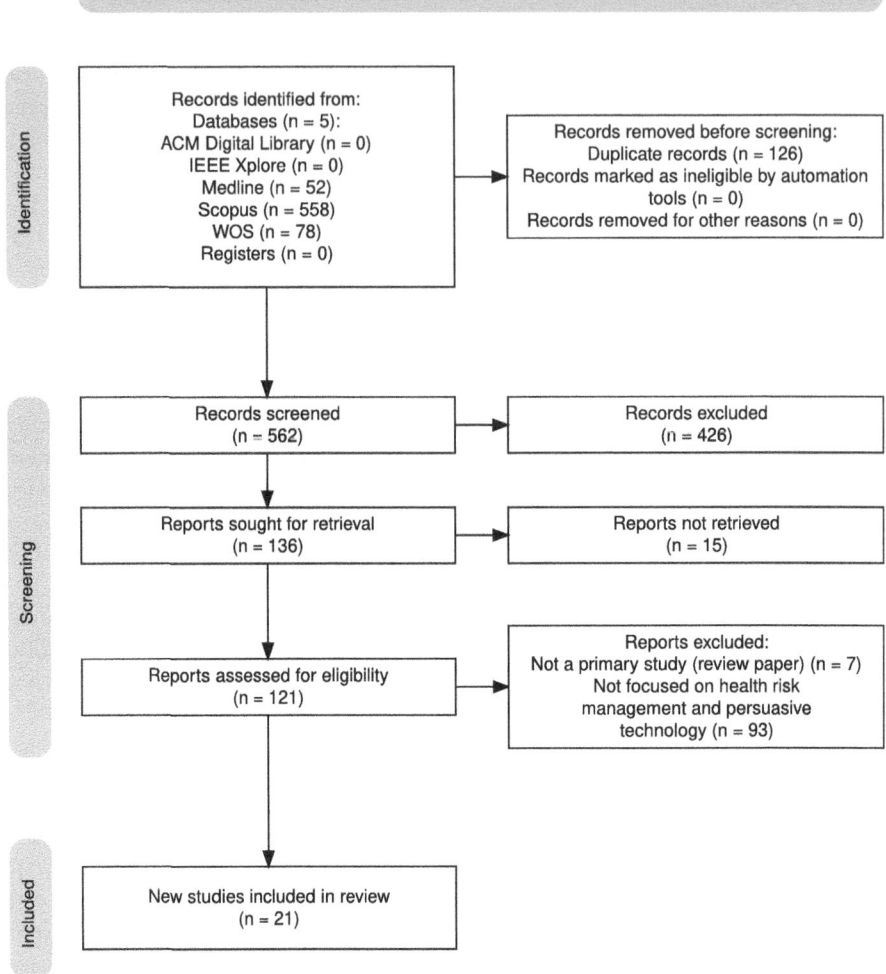

Fig. 1. PRISMA flowchart showing the screening and inclusion process of articles in the scoping review. WOS: Web of Science. This figure was generated using a tool by Haddaway et al. [27].

3 Result

In this section, we present the findings of the scoping review and analysis, supplemented by tables and charts that directly addressed the research questions.

3.1 Selection of Sources of Evidence

The screening and selection of articles for the scoping review followed the PRISMA flowchart, as shown in Fig. 1. Initially, 688 articles were retrieved from three databases. After removing 126 duplicates (18.31%), 562 unique articles remained for TA screening. Consequently, 426 articles (75.80% of the 562 screened articles) were excluded during the TA screening phase due to irrelevance to the topic. This left 136 articles for full-text screening. Of these, 115 articles (84.56% of the 136) were further excluded for not meeting the inclusion criteria, resulting in 21 articles being included in the scoping review and analysis.

Table 1. Characteristics of the included studies. HR: Health Risks, DP: Digital Platform, GHR: General Health Risks, CH: Cardiometabolic Health, CR: Cancer Risk, MD: Metabolic disorders, CD: Cardiovascular disease, LH: Lung health, MM: Mass media, WBA: Web-based application, MHA: Mobile health application, IVRT: Interactive voice response technology

Author	HR	Target Behavior	DP	PT Elements
Lupton et al. [40] (2014, Australia)	Obesity	Weight loss via healthier eating, physical activity	MM	Goal-setting, feedback, social support
Burrell et al. [11] (2023, USA)	Obesity	Weight loss via lifestyle habits	Email	Coaching, goal-setting, tracking
Cowdery et al. [16] (2007, USA)	GHR	Smoking, weight management, nutrition, physical activity, alcohol use	WBA	Motivation
Hui et al. [28] (2015, USA)	GHR	Stress management, weight management, physical activity	WBA	Health risk framing
Miller et al. [43] (2024, USA)	Obesity and CR	Weight loss via physical activity and nutrition	WBA	Goal-setting, feedback
Forte et al. [13] (2022, Netherlands)	CH	Improved diet and physical activity	MHA	Personalization, coaching, tracking
Gerber et al. [24] (2024, USA)	Diabetes	Tailored lifestyle and weight management	Wearable WBA	Affirmations, Trend alerts, Goal attainment
Powley et al. [52] (2023, UK)	Frailty	Physical activity, nutrition, weight management	MHA	Personalization, coaching, goal-setting, feedback
Kim et al. [36] (2019, South Korea)	MD	Low-sodium diet, moderate physical activity	MHA	Personalization, Self-monitoring, feedback, peer support

(continued)

Table 1. (*continued*)

Author	HR	Target Behavior	DP	PT Elements
Schulz et al. [55] (2014, Netherlands)	GHR	Increased physical activity, nutrition	WBA	Tailoring, feedback, motivation
Groarke et al. [26] (2019, UK)	Cancer	Increased physical activity	MHA Wearable	Personalization, Goal-setting, feedback
Kwon et al. [38] (2020, USA)	CD	Improved dietary quality	MHA	Personalization, Feedback, tips
Colkesen et al. [15] (2011, Netherlands)	CD	Physical activity, improved diet	WBA	Tailoring, feedback, self-reporting
Brekel-Dijkstra et al. [10] (2015, Netherlands)	CD	Increased physical activity, healthy diet	WBA	Personalization, Goal-setting
Gasca et al. [22] (2008, Mexico)	GHR	Physical activity, improved diet	MHA	Social support, goal-setting, feedback, gamification
Perez et al. [49] (2009, USA)	GHR	Improved diet (fruit, vegetables)	WBA	Personalization, tips, rewards
Crucian et al. [17] (2017, UK)	GHR	Increased physical activity	Wearable	Just-In-Time Adaptive Intervention
Alhasani et al. [4] (2023, Canada)	GHR	Stress management	MHA	Personalization, reminders, social role
Almutari et al. [5] (2024, Saudi Arabia)	CD	Increased physical activity	MHA	Reminders, tips, rewards
Kytö et al. [39] (2023, Finland)	Diabetes	Self-tracking of glucose and lifestyle factors	Wearable	Feedback, self-monitoring
Cohn et al. [14] (2018, USA)	LH	Smoking behavior	IVRT	Self-monitoring, awareness, feedback

3.2   Results of Synthesis

The results of the scoping review are presented through graphs and tables, structured into key themes: geographical characteristics, focused health risks, and PT methodologies: digital domains, PT techniques, and targeted health behaviors. Table 1 provides the broad characteristics of the included articles.

Geographical characteristics: Out of the 21 studies included in our analysis, 8 (38.10%) studies emanated from the USA [11,14,16,24,28,38,43,49], 1 (4.76%) study originated from Canada [4] and 1 (4.76%) study from Mexico [22], resulting in a total of 10 (47.62%) studies from North America. Europe contributed 8 (38.10%) studies, with 4 (19.05%) from the Netherlands [10,13,15,55], 3 (14.29%) from the UK [17,26,52], and 1 (4.76%) from Finland [39]. Oceania had 1 (4.76%) study from Australia [40]. Asia contributed 2 (9.52%) studies, including 1 (4.76%) from South Korea [36], and 1 (4.76%) from Saudi Arabia [5].

Health risks: As shown in Fig. 2, the addressed health risks are as follows: Obesity was reported in 3 studies (14.29%) [11,40,43], Cancer in 2 studies (9.52%) [26,43], Cardiovascular disease in 4 studies (19.05%) [5,10,15,38], Cardiometabolic health in 1 study (4.76%) [13], Diabetes in 2 studies (9.52%) [24,39], Frailty in 1 study (4.76%) [52], Lung health in 1 study (4.76%) [14], and Metabolic disorders in 1 study (4.76%) [36]. General Health Risks were the focus of 7 studies (33.33%) [4,16,17,22,28,49,55]. Regarding targeted health behaviors, physical activity was the most frequently targeted behavior, with all but 5 studies [4,14,38,39,49] considering increased physical activity for health risk management, particularly for weight management in individuals at risk of obesity. Weight management was specifically targeted in 7 studies (33.33%) [11,16,24,40,43,52]. Dietary behavior changes were targeted in 10 studies (47.62%) [13,15,16,22,36,38,43,49,52,55], and stress management in 2 studies (9.52%) [23,37]. Also, multiple behaviors were targeted together in several studies, with physical activity and dietary behavior changes being the most combined, appearing in 8 studies (38.10%) [10,15,16,22,36,40,43,52]. Other combinations included stress management with weight management (4.76%) [28].

Furthermore, the digital technologies used in the studies primarily fall into three categories: web-based, mobile-based, and wearable platforms. Web-based applications were used in 8 studies (38.09%) [10,15,16,24,28,43,49,55]. Mobile health applications were also featured in 8 studies (38.09%) [4,5,13,22,26,36, 38,52]. Wearable technologies were employed in 4 studies (19.05%) [17,24,26, 39], including fitness trackers like Fitbit and other health monitoring devices. Other digital PT interventions that do not fit neatly into the above categories include email [11], interactive voice response technology [14], and mass media approaches [40]. For the PT techniques employed in the studies, we extracted the unique elements as shown in Fig. 2. Goal-setting was reported in 7 studies (33.33%) [10,11,22,26,40,43,52]; Feedback appeared in 11 studies (52.38%) [14, 15,22,26,36,38–40,43,52,55]; Coaching was mentioned in 3 studies (14.29%) [11, 13,52]; Motivation was included in 2 studies (9.52%) [16,55]; Health risk framing appeared in 1 study (4.76%) [28]; Personalization was used in 8 studies (38.10%) [4,10,13,26,36,38,49,52]; Self-monitoring was noted in 3 studies (14.29%) [14, 36,39]; Tips was used in 3 studies (14.29%) [5,38,49]; Peer support was seen in 1 study (4.76%) [36]; Social support was included in 2 studies (9.52%) [22,40];

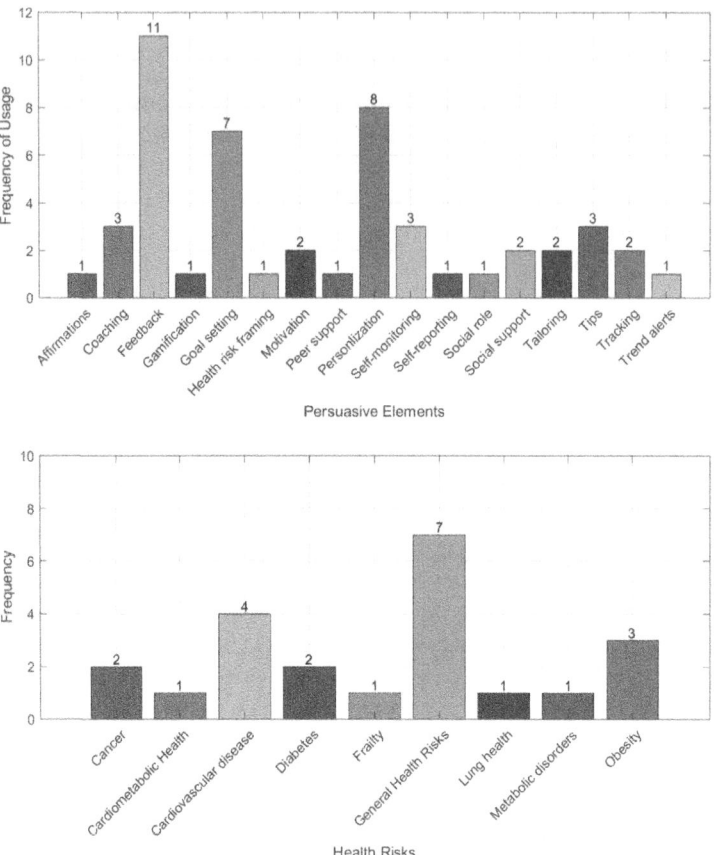

Fig. 2. The top figure illustrates the frequency of use for key persuasive technology elements, while the bottom figure depicts the health risks addressed in the included studies.

Tailoring was found in 2 studies (9.52%) [15, 55]; Tracking was mentioned in 2 studies (9.52%) [11, 13]; Trend alerts were employed in 1 study (4.76%) [24]; Self-reporting appeared in 1 study (4.76%) [15]; Social role was employed in 1 study (4.76%) [4]; Gamification was used in 1 study (4.76%) [22]. Of the 21 studies, 16 demonstrated positive behavioral changes, while 5 showed limited or mixed effectiveness [4, 11, 28, 40, 55].

4   Discussion

In the following section, we discuss the main findings of the scoping review, drawing on the presented results.

4.1   Interpretation of Findings

The geographical distribution of studies included in our analysis highlights significant disparities in research contributions across regions. North America accounted for the highest proportion of studies (47.62%), with the majority originating from the United States (38.10%). Europe followed closely, contributing 38.10% of the studies, with the Netherlands leading the region with four studies (19.05%). This dominance may be attributed to extensive healthcare funding and advanced research infrastructure in these countries [50]. As Polin et al. [51] noted, high-income countries such as the United States have prioritized public health research due to their commitment to improving population health through innovative health interventions. Additionally, the large-scale adoption of digital health technologies in these countries [44] has likely provided a fertile ground for digital health research. Nevertheless, a notable observation is the lack of contributions from underserved populations, including low- and middle-income regions such as Africa. This underrepresentation aligns with findings in literature [35], which emphasize persistent challenges such as limited funding, insufficient research infrastructure, and a lack of integration of digital health technologies into public health systems in these areas. For example, Africa, despite facing significant health challenges such as non-communicable and infectious diseases, remains underrepresented in global health studies [30]. This disparity further highlights the urgent need for increased investments in research capacity and digital health innovation, which could significantly enhance health outcomes in resource-limited settings.

Furthermore, our review reveals a diverse focus on various health risks, with some studies targeting diseases, such as obesity (14.29%), cardiovascular disease (19.05%), and cancer (9.52%). The relatively higher representation of obesity and cardiovascular disease aligns with their high global prevalence and established associations with non-communicable diseases, which are major public health concerns in high-income countries [31,45]. Cardiovascular disease, for example, is often prioritized in research due to its significant impact on healthcare systems and mortality rates globally [20]. On the other hand, the focus on general health risks in 33.33% of studies reflects a broader public health approach, aiming to address multiple risk factors that contribute to a variety of diseases Additionally, our review shows a strong focus on physical activity and dietary behavior changes as the most targeted behaviors in many studies (with physical activity in all but five studies and dietary behavior in 10 studies). This underscores the significant role sedentary lifestyles and poor diets play in the development of non-communicable diseases [7]. Correspondingly, Beltrán-Carrillo et al. [8], demonstrated that increasing physical activity and improving dietary habits are key interventions for managing these health risks. Moreover, the behavioral outcomes from the included studies provide reasonable evidence to support the effectiveness of physical activity [22] in mitigating several risk factors.

Additionally, several interventions led to better dietary habits [10,43] and enhanced self-management of health conditions [39]. However, some studies reported limited or mixed effectiveness. For instance, poor sleep quality negatively impacted behavior change [28], and certain strategies, like rewards, were not perceived as persuasive [4]. Moreover, no significant weight loss was observed in one intervention [11], highlighting variability in outcomes across studies. We also reported the commonly employed PT elements in the included studies, where feedback techniques emerged as the most frequently used (52.38%). This reason for this result is not farfetched due to the established effectiveness of feedback in promoting behavior change through continuous reinforcement [53]. Goal-setting and personalization (each used in 33.33% and 38.10% of studies, respectively) are also evidence-based strategies for enhancing engagement and maintaining long-term behavioral changes. The inclusion of techniques like coaching, self-monitoring, and social support have also been linked to improve health outcomes, especially when combined with physical activity and dietary changes [18].

4.2   Limitations of Existing Studies

Although existing PT-based HRM interventions have demonstrated effectiveness, several limitations persist. One primary challenge is how to design persuasive messages that can effectively address the diverse needs of various populations, particularly underserved groups. Many studies still adopt a one-size-fits-all approach, assuming population homogeneity, which may not account for the unique characteristics and needs of specific demographic groups. To enhance the impact of these interventions and better influence people's readiness and motivation to change health behavior, future research should focus on developing more personalized approaches that account for cultural, socioeconomic and behavioral differences. Such approaches should emphasize perceived benefits and reduce barriers to change (e.g. time and financial constraints) based on the Health Belief Model [59]. In addition, studies are needed that explore how personalized messaging can be optimized (e.g., through multitask learning [2] or graph learning techniques [12]) for different population segments, especially in low-resource settings where health disparities are more pronounced.

5   Conclusions

This paper presented a scoping review synthesizing studies based on persuasive technologies for health risk management. The primary aim was to understand the current state of PT applications in HRM. Our review revealed that improving diet and physical activity were the most frequently targeted behavioral changes across the included studies. This highlights their critical role in managing non-communicable diseases such as obesity, cardiovascular diseases, and diabetes. In particular, physical activity was a central focus, with many studies targeting its role in weight management. Similarly, dietary behavior changes were also a major focus, demonstrating the importance of addressing both physical activity and diet in managing health risks. In addition, our review identified that PT elements, such as goal-setting, feedback, and personalization, emerged as key strategies in enhancing the effectiveness of the behavioral interventions.

Goal-setting provided participants with specific targets to strive toward, while feedback helped reinforce positive behaviors and offered guidance for improvement. Personalization allowed for tailored interventions that addressed individual needs, preferences, and circumstances. These strategies, when integrated into PT applications, were found to significantly enhance health behavior change efforts.

Limitations of the Current Study: Despite the positive outcomes observed, our study has limitations. Even though we tried to cover all possible related terminologies, the search string used in our search may not have been exhaustive. Notably, no results were found in IEEE Xplore or the ACM Digital Library, perhaps due to their limited coverage of behavioral science and health technology-focused publications. Additionally, the review did not include a certainty assessment to access the certainty of evidence reported in the included studies. We plan to address this in the future expansion of the review. Furthermore, additional databases may be explored to expand the scope of our review and capture PT frameworks, enhancing the depth of the analysis.

Acknowledgments. This work was undertaken thanks in part to funding from the Connected Minds Program, supported by Canada First Research Excellence Fund, Grant No. CFREF-2022-00010.

References

1. Abhadiomhen, S.E., Nzeakor, E.O., Oyibo, K.: Health risk assessment using machine learning: systematic review. Electronics **13**(22), 4405 (2024)
2. Abhadiomhen, S.E., Nzeh, R.C., Ganaa, E.D., Nwagwu, H.C., Okereke, G.E., Routray, S.: Supervised shallow multi-task learning: analysis of methods. Neural Process. Lett. **54**(3), 2491–2508 (2022)
3. Aldenaini, N., Oyebode, O., Orji, R., Sampalli, S.: Mobile phone-based persuasive technology for physical activity and sedentary behavior: a systematic review. Front. Comput. Sci. **2**, 19 (2020)
4. Alhasani, M., Oyebode, O., Orji, R.: SereneMind: design and evaluation of a persuasive mobile app for managing stress among adults. In: 2023 IEEE 11th International Conference on Serious Games and Applications for Health (SeGAH), pp. 1–8. IEEE (2023)
5. Almutari, N.S., Alqahtani, F., Orji, R., Chan, G.: StepsBooster-S: a culturally tailored step-based persuasive application for promoting physical activity. Int. J. Hum.-Comput. Interact. 1–24 (2024)
6. Alslaity, A., Oyebode, O., Vassileva, J., Orji, R.: Personalized Persuasive Technologies in Health and Wellness: From Theory to Practice. Springer (2024)
7. Ameer Arsalan Hadi, P.: Nutritional status and sedentary lifestyle of individuals a review. Int. J. Mod. Agric. **10**(2) (2021)
8. Beltran-Carrillo, V.J., Megias, A., Gonzalez-Cutre, D., Jimenez-Loaisa, A.: Elements behind sedentary lifestyles and unhealthy eating habits in individuals with severe obesity. Int. J. Qual. Stud. Health Well-Being **17**(1) (2022)
9. Braun, V., Clarke, V.: Using thematic analysis in psychology. Qual. Res. Psychol. **3**(2), 77–101 (2006)

10. van den Brekel-Dijkstra, K., Rengers, A.H., Niessen, M.A., de Wit, N.J., Kraaijenhagen, R.A.: Personalized prevention approach with use of a web-based cardiovascular risk assessment with tailored lifestyle follow-up in primary care practice-a pilot study. Eur. J. Prev. Cardiol. **23**(5), 544–551 (2016)
11. Burrell, C.: A quasi-experimental study on adult weight loss using a multidimensional approach among a rural population. SAGE Open Med. **11**, 20503121231187744 (2023)
12. Cai, M., Shen, X., Abhadiomhen, S.E., Cai, Y., Tian, S.: Robust dimensionality reduction via low-rank laplacian graph learning. ACM Trans. Intell. Syst. Technol. **14**(3), 1–24 (2023)
13. Castela Forte, J., et al.: Changes in blood lipid levels after a digitally enabled cardiometabolic preventive health program: pre-post study in an adult dutch general population cohort. JMIR Cardio **6**(1), e34946 (2022)
14. Cohn, A.M., Elmasry, H., Ehlke, S.J.: Utilization, receptivity and reactivity to interactive voice response daily monitoring in risky drinking smokers who are motivated to quit. Tobacco Induced Dis. **16** (2018)
15. Colkesen, E.B., et al.: Initiation of health-behaviour change among employees participating in a web-based health risk assessment with tailored feedback. J. Occup. Med. Toxicol. **6**, 1–7 (2011)
16. Cowdery, J.E., Suggs, L.S., Parker, S.: Application of a web-based tailored health risk assessment in a work-site population. Health Promot. Pract. **8**(1), 88–95 (2007)
17. Cruciani, F., Nugent, C., Cleland, I., McCullagh, P.: Rich context information for just-in-time adaptive intervention promoting physical activity. In: 2017 39th Annual International Conference of the IEEE Engineering in Medicine and Biology Society (EMBC), pp. 849–852. IEEE (2017)
18. Eid, N.M.: Exploring the effectiveness of supporting dietary weight loss interventions with health coaching and telemonitoring: an integrative nutrition approach (2024). Preprints
19. Fu, Z., Burger, H., Arjadi, R., Bockting, C.L.: Effectiveness of digital psychological interventions for mental health problems in low-income and middle-income countries: a systematic review and meta-analysis. Lancet Psychiatry **7**(10), 851–864 (2020)
20. Gaidai, O., Cao, Y., Loginov, S.: Global cardiovascular diseases death rate prediction. Curr. Probl. Cardiol. **48**(5) (2023)
21. Garnelo, L., Parente, R., Puchiarelli, M., Correia, P.C., Torres, M.V., Herkrath, F.J.: Barriers to access and organization of primary health care services for rural riverside populations in the amazon. Int. J. Equity Health **19**, 1–14 (2020)
22. Gasca, E., Favela, J., Tentori, M.: Persuasive virtual communities to promote a healthy lifestyle among patients with chronic diseases. In: Briggs, R.O., Antunes, P., de Vreede, G.-J., Read, A.S. (eds.) CRIWG 2008. LNCS, vol. 5411, pp. 74–82. Springer, Heidelberg (2008). https://doi.org/10.1007/978-3-540-92831-7_7
23. George, C.E., Inbaraj, L.R., Rajukutty, S., De Witte, L.P.: Challenges, experience and coping of health professionals in delivering healthcare in an urban slum in India during the first 40 days of COVID-19 crisis: a mixed method study. BMJ Open **10**(11), e042171 (2020)
24. Gerber, S., et al.: Development and feasibility of an eHealth diabetes prevention program adapted for older adults-results from a randomized control pilot study. Nutrients **16**(7), 930 (2024)
25. Grady, A., et al.: The effectiveness of strategies to improve user engagement with digital health interventions targeting nutrition, physical activity, and overweight

and obesity: systematic review and meta-analysis. J. Med. Internet Res. **25**, e47987 (2023)

26. Groarke, J.M., et al.: Examining the impact of a personalized self-management lifestyle program using mobile technology on the health and well-being of cancer survivors: protocol and rationale for a randomized controlled trial (the moving on study). JMIR Res. Protocols **8**(8), e13214 (2019)

27. Haddaway, N.R., Page, M.J., Pritchard, C.C., McGuinness, L.A.: PRISMA 2020: an R package and shiny app for producing PRISMA 2020-compliant flow diagrams, with interactivity for optimised digital transparency and open synthesis. Campbell Syst. Rev. **18**(2), e1230 (2022)

28. Hui, S., Grandner, M.A.: Associations between poor sleep quality and stages of change of multiple health behaviors among participants of employee wellness program. Prevent. Med. Rep. **2**, 292–299 (2015)

29. Idrees, A.R., Kraft, R., Mutter, A., Baumeister, H., Reichert, M., Pryss, R.: Persuasive technologies design for mental and behavioral health platforms: A scoping literature review. PLOS Digit. Health **3**(5), e0000498 (2024)

30. Inam, M., et al.: Health data sciences and cardiovascular disease in Africa: needs and the way forward. Curr. Atheroscler. Rep. **26**(11), 659–671 (2024)

31. Islam, A.S., Sultana, H., Refat, M.N.H., Farhana, Z., Kamil, A.A., Rahman, M.M.: The global burden of overweight-obesity and its association with economic status, benefiting from steps survey of who member states: a meta-analysis. Prevent. Med. Rep. (2024)

32. Jaffar, A., Tan, C.E., Mohd-Sidik, S., Admodisastro, N., Goodyear-Smith, F.: Persuasive technology in an mhealth app designed for pelvic floor muscle training among women: systematic review. JMIR Mhealth Uhealth **10**(3), e28751 (2022)

33. Ji, K., Me, R.C., Kamarudin, K.M.: A review of persuasive technology and design to healthy lifestyle. Int. J. Art Design **7**(2), 101–113 (2023)

34. Jimenez, G., et al.: Digital health competencies for primary healthcare professionals: a scoping review. Int. J. Med. Inform. **143**, 104260 (2020)

35. Jones, N., Bailey, M., Lyytikainen, M.: Research capacity strengthening in Africa: trends, gaps and opportunities. Technical report, Overseas Development Institute (2007)

36. Kim, T.Y., et al.: Effects of a mobile healthcare service provided by public health centers on practicing of health behaviors and health risk factors. Nurs. Res. Pract. **13**(6), 509–520 (2019)

37. Knight, S.R., Ng, N., Tsanas, A., Mclean, K., Pagliari, C., Harrison, E.M.: Mobile devices and wearable technology for measuring patient outcomes after surgery: a systematic review. NPJ Digit. Med. **4**(1), 157 (2021)

38. Kwon, B.C., et al.: Improving heart disease risk through quality-focused diet logging: pre-post study of a diet quality tracking app. JMIR Mhealth Uhealth **8**(12), e21733 (2020)

39. Kytö, M., et al.: Supporting the management of gestational diabetes mellitus with comprehensive self-tracking: mixed methods study of wearable sensors. JMIR Diabetes **8** (2023)

40. Lupton, D.: "How do you measure up?" assumptions about "obesity" and health-related behaviors and beliefs in two Australian "obesity" prevention campaigns. Fat Stud. **3**(1), 32–44 (2014)

41. Mariappanadar, S.: Improving quality of work for positive health: interaction of sustainable development goal (SDG) 8 and SDG 3 from the sustainable HRM perspective. Sustainability **16**(13), 5356 (2024)

42. McGowan, A., Sittig, S., Bourrie, D., Benton, R., Iyengar, S.: The intersection of persuasive system design and personalization in mobile health: statistical evaluation. JMIR Mhealth Uhealth **10**(9), e40576 (2022)
43. Miller, M., Valenzuela, R., Salinas, J.J.: Change in nutrition behavior after participating in an obesity-related cancer education program in El Paso, Texas. Cancer Control **31**, 10732748241261568 (2024)
44. Mwanza, J., Telukdarie, A., Igusa, T.: Impact of industry 4.0 on healthcare systems of low-and middle-income countries: a systematic review. Health Technol. **13**(1), 35–52 (2023)
45. World Health Organization: Obese and overweight (2024)
46. Oyibo, K.: ComTech: towards a unified taxonomy of persuasive techniques for persuasive technology design. Comput. Hum. Behav. Rep. **14**, 100372 (2024)
47. Oyibo, K., Adaji, I., Vassileva, J.: Susceptibility to fitness app's persuasive features: differences between acting and non-acting users. In: Adjunct Publication of the 27th Conference on User Modeling, Adaptation and Personalization, pp. 135–143 (2019)
48. Page, M.J., et al.: The PRISMA 2020 statement: an updated guideline for reporting systematic reviews. BMJ **372** (2021)
49. Philyaw Perez, A., Phillips, M.M., Cornell, C.E., Mays, G., Adams, B.: Promoting dietary change among state health employees in Arkansas through a worksite wellness program: the healthy employee lifestyle program (HELP). Prevent. Chronic Dis. (2009)
50. Plancikova, D., Duric, P., O'May, F.: High-income countries remain overrepresented in highly ranked public health journals: a descriptive analysis of research settings and authorship affiliations. Crit. Public Health **31**(4), 487–493 (2021)
51. Polin, K., Hjortland, M., Maresso, A., van Ginneken, E., Busse, R., Quentin, W.: "Top-three" health reforms in 31 high-income countries in 2018 and 2019: an expert informed overview. Health Policy **125**(7), 815–832 (2021)
52. Powley, N., et al.: Digital health coaching to improve patient preparedness for elective lower limb arthroplasty: a quality improvement project. BMJ Open Qual. **12**(4), e002244 (2023)
53. Prue, D.M., Fairbank, J.A.: Performance feedback in organizational behavior management: a review. J. Organ. Behav. Manag. **3**(1), 1–16 (1981)
54. Schmidt, H., et al.: Chronic disease prevention and health promotion. In: Public Health Ethics: Cases Spanning the Globe, pp. 137–176 (2016)
55. Schulz, D.N., et al.: Effects of a web-based tailored multiple-lifestyle intervention for adults: a two-year randomized controlled trial comparing sequential and simultaneous delivery modes. J. Med. Internet Res. **16**(1), e26 (2014)
56. Sediva, H., Cartwright, T., Robertson, C., Deb, S.K.: Behavior change techniques in digital health interventions for midlife women: systematic review. JMIR Mhealth Uhealth **10**(11), e37234 (2022)
57. Tranfield, D., Denyer, D., Smart, P.: Towards a methodology for developing evidence-informed management knowledge by means of systematic review. Br. J. Manag. **14**(3), 207–222 (2003)
58. Walby, S.: The COVID pandemic and social theory: social democracy and public health in the crisis. Eur. J. Soc. Theory **24**(1), 22–43 (2021)
59. Ye, W., Li, Q., Yu, S.: Persuasive effects of message framing and narrative format on promoting COVID-19 vaccination: a study on Chinese college students. Int. J. Environ. Res. Public Health **18**(18), 9485 (2021)

Evaluation of an Emotion-Aware Persuasive Framework Based on Peripheral Interaction for Reducing Physical Strain in Office Environments

Franci Suni-Lopez[1]($\boxtimes$)(iD) and Nelly Condori-Fernandez[2]($\boxtimes$)(iD)

[1] Laboratorio de Inteligencia Artificial, Universidad de Lima, Lima, Peru
fsuni@ulima.edu.pe
[2] Centro Singular de Investigación en Tecnoloxías Intelixentes (CiTIUS),
Universidade de Santiago de Compostela, 15782 Santiago de Compostela, Spain
n.condori.fernandez@usc.es

Abstract. Repetitive Strain Injuries (RSIs) are a leading cause of workplace disability and absenteeism, particularly among office workers engaged in prolonged computer-based tasks. This study evaluates the effectiveness of EMotivA, a persuasive system designed to promote active breaks and mitigate the risk of RSIs. A quantitative pretest-postest design was conducted with 20 office workers over one workweek, during which EMotivA dispatched persuasive notifications every 40 min to encourage brief, light physical activities.

The system aimed to *increase the frequency and regularity of active breaks* and *reduce musculoskeletal discomfort*, measured using the Cornell Musculoskeletal Discomfort Questionnaire (CMDQ). Results showed a significant increase in active breaks and a marked improvement in time dedicated to physical activities. CMDQ scores revealed a significant reduction in musculoskeletal discomfort post-intervention ($t(19) = 3.152$, $p = 0.005$, $d = 0.705$). These findings demonstrate that EMotivA effectively fosters healthier work habits and reduces physical discomfort, emphasizing its potential as a tool for occupational health management.

Keywords: RSIs · Persuasive Systems · Workplace Well-being · Emotion-Aware Technology · Behavioral Change

1 Introduction

Sedentary behavior is prevalent in modern workplaces, especially among office workers who spend prolonged hours seated at desks [2]. This lifestyle is strongly associated with Repetitive Strain Injuries (RSIs), a leading cause of disability and absenteeism globally, negatively impacting productivity and employee well-being [13]. RSIs are linked to prolonged sitting and poor posture, common in office environments where workers remain in static positions for long periods without breaks. Inadequate ergonomic interventions exacerbate these risks, highlighting the need for effective solutions to mitigate such injuries [8].

A joint report by the World Health Organization (WHO) and the International Labour Organization highlights the global burden of RSIs on occupational health, affecting both high- and low-income countries[1]. Key ergonomic risk factors, such as static positions and repetitive movements, are identified as primary contributors to the prevalence of these disorders [13,33]. Addressing these factors through proactive strategies is critical for promoting healthier workplaces and improving employee well-being. Active breaks-brief periods of physical activity throughout the workday-counteract the negative impacts of prolonged sitting. Studies show that regular active breaks reduce musculoskeletal pain, alleviate stress, and improve mood, enhancing well-being and productivity [27]. However, consistent adoption remains a challenge due to factors such as lack of motivation, forgetfulness, and disruptions to workflow.

In response, persuasive technologies have emerged as promising tools to facilitate behavior change by subtly influencing individuals' actions and decisions [11,23]. These systems leverage psychological principles and contextual information to encourage healthy behaviors while minimizing intrusiveness. By integrating persuasive strategies into daily tools and environments, these technologies can create supportive systems that foster the development and maintenance of beneficial habits. However, their effectiveness depends on the ability to deliver timely and contextually appropriate interventions tailored to users' needs and preferences [3,15].

While existing systems primarily focus on tracking user behavior, they often lack the emotional and contextual adaptation necessary to enhance their effectiveness. Our contribution lies in the development of EMotivA (*Emotion Motivation Awareness*), an innovative emotion-aware persuasive framework designed to reduce physical strain and promote healthy behaviors in office settings through peripheral interaction. EMotivA unobtrusively monitors users' emotional and contextual states, enabling personalized, timely interventions to encourage active breaks. Its modular and adaptive architecture ensures seamless integration into various office environments, enhancing its applicability and effectiveness across different organizational contexts. This study provides empirical evidence on the effectiveness of emotion-aware persuasive systems in mitigating RSIs through minimally intrusive interventions. By demonstrating how such systems can be effectively integrated into office environments, this research contributes to advancing the field of persuasive technologies and offers new insights into promoting healthier workplace behaviors.

This paper is structured as follows: Sect. 2 discusses related works, focusing on persuasive applications aimed at promoting healthy behaviors in office environments. Section 3 provides a detailed overview of the EMotivA framework, emphasizing its emotion-aware and adaptive approach. The experimental design and methodology are outlined in Sect. 4. Sections 5 and 6 present the study's

---

[1] https://www.who.int/publications/i/item/9789240034945.

findings and analyze potential threats to validity, ensuring the robustness of the results. Finally, Sect. 7 summarizes the key contributions, addresses the study's limitations, and proposes directions for future research.

2   Related Works

Persuasive systems have garnered significant attention for their potential to enhance workplace health and well-being. Numerous studies demonstrate the efficacy of mobile applications and digital platforms in promoting behavior change. For instance, Singh et al. [29] reported that a web-based program significantly improved physical activity, mood, and energy levels among employees. Similarly, Kekkonen et al. [17] developed an application incorporating stress management and sedentary behavior reduction, yielding notable improvements in user adherence, although variations in acceptance were observed.

While these systems show promise, they predominantly rely on explicit task-based strategies, such as reminders and activity tracking, which can disrupt workflow and reduce long-term engagement. More nuanced approaches, such as those integrating peripheral interaction or emotional context, remain underexplored. For example, Ataguba and Orji [5] introduced a real-time posture detection system, achieving high accuracy in promoting ergonomic adjustments. However, its focus on physical posture neglects broader aspects of well-being, such as emotional state or personalized intervention timing. Similarly, Zhang and Jemmott [37] utilized mobile applications and wearable devices but emphasized static feedback mechanisms rather than adaptive, emotion-aware interventions.

Table 1 summarizes prior studies, highlighting their technologies, strategies, outcomes, and effectiveness. While systems like Zhang and Jemmott [37] and Geurts et al. [12] achieved full success by integrating comprehensive features such as tracking and personalization, most others reported partial success. These limitations often stem from short intervention durations, lack of emotional adaptation, or disruptions to workflow, making them less effective in achieving holistic and sustained improvements in workplace well-being. EMotivA addresses these gaps by integrating peripheral interaction, real-time emotional analysis, and adaptive feedback mechanisms to deliver minimally intrusive and contextually relevant interventions. Unlike previous systems with mixed effectiveness, EMotivA dynamically adapts to users' states, enhancing both engagement and outcomes. This approach not only promotes sustained behavioral change but also achieves a balance between productivity and well-being, setting a new standard in workplace health interventions.

3   Configuration of the EMotivA Framework

EMotivA is an innovative, emotion-aware persuasive framework designed to enhance workplace well-being by promoting healthy behaviors and reducing physical strain among office workers. As shown in Fig. 1, its five-layer architecture integrates peripheral interaction techniques, real-time emotional analysis,

Table 1. Summary of related works on persuasive systems for promoting health and well-being in workplace settings, categorized based on [3].

Authors	Technology	Persuasive strategies	Evaluation method	Duration	Participants	Effectiveness
Singh et al. (2024) [29]	Mobile-responsive web platform	Tracking, reduction, rewards, self-monitoring, social support, goal setting	Quantitative	6 weeks	11575 adults	Partially successful
Jung-Krenzer et al. (2024) [15]	IoT prototype	Tracking and monitoring	Mixed	45 to 90 min	5 adults	Partially successful
Ataguba and Orji (2024) [5]	None	Tracking, reduction, tunneling, self-monitoring, personalization, reminder, social comparison, rewards	Quantitative	None	269 unspecified	Partially successful
Kekkonen et al. (2023) [17]	Mobile app	Tracking, self-reflection, self-monitoring, personalization, social comparison, social support	Qualitative	56 days	1225 adults	Partially successful
Za et al. (2022) [36]	Mobile app	Tracking, reduction, self-monitoring, rewards, personalization	Qualitative	3 weeks to 6 months	20 adults	Fully successful
Zhang and Jemmott (2019) [37]	Mobile app, Fitbit tracker	Tracking, personalization, elf-monitoring, reminder, social support	Quantitative	3 months	91 young adults	Fully successful
Kasteren et al. (2019) [16]	Fitbit tracker, ambient temperature	Tracking, self-monitoring	Quantitative	2 months	15 adults	Partially successful
Oyibo et al. (2019) [26]	Mobile app	Tailoring, personalization, goal-setting, self-monitoring, rewards, social support	Mixed	1 month	120 adults	Partially successful
Wang and Reiterer (2019) [34]	Computer PC System	Tracking and monitoring, personalization, self-monitoring, reminder, surface credibility	Mixed	3 weeks	8 adults	Partially successful
Geurts et al. (2019) [12]	Mobile app	Tracking, tunneling, tailoring, personalization, goal-setting, self-monitoring, praise, expertise, social support	Mixed	10 weeks	13 elderly	Fully Successful

and adaptive feedback mechanisms to deliver minimally intrusive and contextually relevant interventions. By seamlessly embedding itself into employees' daily routines, EMotivA encourages active breaks and ergonomic adjustments while minimizing disruptions to workflow. This section describes the configuration of EMotivA's layers, focusing on how each component addresses the challenges of RSIs in office environments. By leveraging real-time emotional analysis, the framework tailors its interventions to the user's current emotional and physical condition, ensuring that messages are both relevant and engaging. The integration of peripheral interaction ensures that these interventions are delivered subtly, maintaining user productivity while fostering sustainable workplace habits.

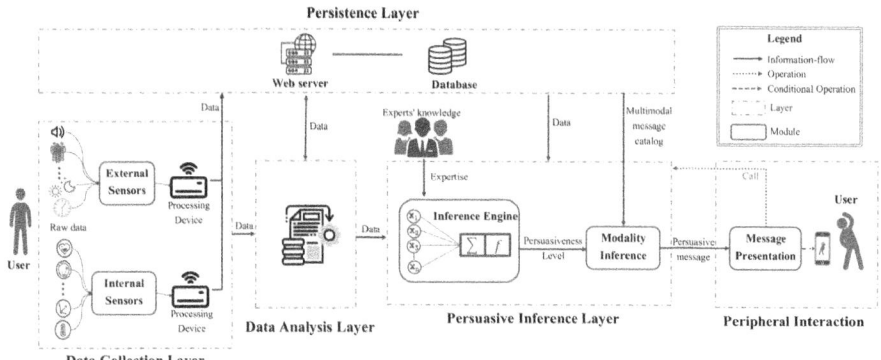

Fig. 1. Overview of EMotivA framework architecture.

3.1 Data Acquisition and Analysis

EMotivA gathers real-time physiological, behavioral, and contextual data while ensuring these inputs are transformed into actionable insights for decision-making. The system employs non-intrusive devices optimized for efficient data capture. The E4-Wristband, worn on the non-dominant hand, records key physiological metrics such as Electrodermal Activity (EDA) and accelerometer data, which indicate stress levels and physical movement [14, 38]. A smartphone application complements this by collecting contextual data such as ambient noise levels, screen activity, and battery status, while also serving as a hub for synchronizing information with the wristband. Additionally, a webcam captures facial expressions for emotion recognition and attention detection, employing privacy safeguards to store only numerical descriptors derived from the data [35]. All collected data is anonymized and securely transmitted to cloud storage for further processing.

The analysis phase transforms the gathered data into personalized, context-sensitive insights. Demographic characteristics (e.g., age, occupation) are combined with psychological traits assessed via the BFI-2-S personality test [21] to enable tailored persuasive strategies. Physiological stress is detected through EDA signals processed with noise filtering and symbolic aggregation to identify stress episodes [31], while facial emotions such as joy or sadness are classified using pre-trained neural network models like ResNet-34. Attention levels are evaluated through head pose and gaze direction, categorizing attention into low, medium, or high [30]. Accelerometer data is analyzed to differentiate between movement and inactivity using predefined thresholds [32], ensuring that interventions align with the user's current state.

To support these processes, the persistence layer provides secure and efficient storage and access to the data streams processed by EMotivA. For this case study, a robust technology stack was implemented to enable real-time data synchronization. React was used to develop a user-friendly frontend for managing facial emotion detection, while Django served as the backend for data processing and communication with the database. Both components were deployed on Microsoft Azure, ensuring scalability, security, and high availability. Data storage was managed with Google Cloud Firestore, a NoSQL database chosen for its ability to efficiently handle dynamic data and support real-time queries. This setup ensures seamless integration with mobile and web applications, providing the Persuasive Inference Layer with timely access to the data required for effective interventions.

3.2   Persuasive Inference Layer

The Persuasive Inference Layer is the core decision-making component of the EMotivA framework, responsible for generating and delivering personalized persuasive messages based on the user's current activity and state. This layer continuously monitors physical activity, and when insufficient movement is detected for a 40-minute period, it evaluates the user's interruptibility using a predictive model. If the user is deemed interruptible, the system determines the appropriate level of persuasiveness and selects the delivery modality-visual or auditory-to ensure the message is effective yet minimally disruptive [22].

The persuasive strategy is based on Cialdini's principles of persuasion [7], which are organized hierarchically to vary the strength of influence. For this study, three key principles were implemented: *Liking* (L1), leveraging affinity to motivate action; *Reciprocity* (L2), appealing to the natural inclination to return favors; and *Commitment and Consistency* (L3), which fosters behavior aligned with prior commitments [24,25]. The system maps these levels to specific modalities for delivering messages:

- In the visual modality, the smartphone screen color changes to reflect the persuasiveness level: yellow for L1 (Liking), orange for L2 (Reciprocity), and red for L3 (Commitment and Consistency). These colors are chosen to subtly draw attention without being intrusive, capitalizing on their psychological effects [10,19,20].
- In the auditory modality, the system uses the smartphone's text-to-speech functionality to deliver spoken reminders that encourage active breaks

in a non-intrusive manner. These messages were evaluated by eight persuasion experts according to three criteria-clarity, representativeness, and effectiveness-using Aiken's V [1, 28] with a minimum threshold of 0.7 for acceptance. Five messages surpassed this threshold and were adopted, while those scoring below it were adjusted or discarded.

If the user is classified as non-interruptible, the system reschedules the intervention, increasing the delay incrementally to 5, 10, 15, and 20 min. Beyond this, if the user remains unavailable, a mandatory intervention is triggered to prevent prolonged inactivity, adhering to a maximum inactivity limit of 60 min [9]. This escalation ensures that the system balances responsiveness with user context, minimizing unnecessary interruptions while prioritizing health-promoting actions.

After a message is delivered, the system monitors the user's response to determine if the recommended activity is performed within five minutes. If the user does not engage in the activity, the system dynamically adjusts the persuasiveness level or delivery modality and resends the message. Conversely, if the activity is completed or if physical activity is detected before the 40-minute threshold, the inactivity counter resets, and the system resumes monitoring. This adaptive feedback loop ensures that the system remains contextually relevant and effective in sustaining user engagement over time. This intervention strategy is depicted in Fig. 3 (See Appendix A).

4   Experimental Design of the Office Case Study

The experiment followed a quantitative pretest-posttest design with a single group of 20 office workers. Conducted over a standard workweek, the EMotivA system delivered persuasive notifications every 40 min, encouraging participants to take light walks lasting at least three minutes. These active breaks were designed to mitigate the risk of Repetitive Strain Injuries (RSIs), improve ergonomic practices, and promote healthier workplace habits.

The primary objective of this study was to evaluate the **effectiveness** of **EMotivA** in increasing the frequency and regularity of active breaks and reducing musculoskeletal discomfort among office workers. Effectiveness, as defined by the International Organization for Standardization (ISO 9241-11), refers to the extent to which a system achieves its intended goals under specified conditions. In this context, effectiveness is measured by the system's capacity to achieve its intended behavioral and ergonomic outcomes within the office environment. To assess effectiveness, the study posed the following research questions:

- **RQ1:** How effectively does the persuasive system increase the frequency and regularity of active breaks among office workers?
- **RQ2:** How effectively does the persuasive system reduce musculoskeletal discomfort reported by office workers after its implementation?

4.1   Variables and Hypotheses

This study was designed to evaluate the effectiveness of EMotivA in promoting healthier workplace behaviors and reducing physical discomfort. The **independent variable** was the system intervention, which involved personalized persuasive notifications delivered through visual or auditory modalities. These notifications were dynamically tailored to users' emotional and contextual states, leveraging Cialdini's principles of persuasion to maximize engagement and relevance.

The **dependent variables** were defined to comprehensively measure the system's effectiveness. First, the **frequency and duration of active breaks** were objectively logged by the system throughout the workweek, providing quantitative data on behavioral changes. Second, **musculoskeletal discomfort** was assessed using the CMDQ questionnaire, a validated instrument that captures self-reported discomfort across key body regions, such as the neck, back, and extremities. Together, these variables allow for an empirical evaluation of EMotivA's ability to address both behavioral and ergonomic challenges. The following **alternative hypotheses** were formulated to evaluate the system's effectiveness:

- H_1: EMotivA significantly increases the frequency and regularity of active breaks among office workers compared to baseline behaviors.
- H_2: EMotivA significantly reduces musculoskeletal discomfort among office workers compared to baseline levels.

4.2   Participants

The study included 20 office workers who spent a minimum of six hours daily performing computer-based tasks, ensuring the relevance of the collected data for a sedentary work environment. Participants were recruited voluntarily through internal announcements, with detailed explanations of the study's objectives and procedures provided beforehand. The group had a balanced gender composition (55% male and 45% female) and a mean age of 22.3 years, ranging from 19 to 31. The majority were from Systems Engineering (55%), followed by Civil Engineering (30%) and Communication Sciences (15%), reflecting a young, early-career cohort. Informed consent was obtained from all participants, ensuring their understanding of the study's purpose, procedures, and their right to withdraw at any time without consequences. As a gesture of appreciation, institutional merchandise was provided, encouraging participation while reinforcing ethical standards such as transparency and respect for participants' rights.

4.3   Instruments

To comprehensively assess the effectiveness of the persuasive system, the study employed a combination of technological tools and validated questionnaires specifically designed to measure the relevant variables. Two custom applications were developed: a mobile application that interacted with participants' smartphones to send and display persuasive messages while collecting contextual data, and a web application connected to participants' computer webcams, enabling real-time facial emotion recognition and attention evaluation (as detailed in Sect. 3). To evaluate changes in ergonomic variables, the study employed the CMDQ [4], a validated and psychometrically reliable instrument suitable for Peruvian populations. This questionnaire assesses musculoskeletal discomfort in various body regions, including the neck, shoulders, back, and extremities, recording the frequency, intensity, and severity of perceived discomfort during the workday to provide a detailed overview of the physical impact of work activities.

4.4   Procedure

The experiment was divided into four stages: recruitment, pretest, system intervention, and postest, ensuring comprehensive data collection and a rigorous evaluation of outcomes. **Recruitment:** Participants were recruited voluntarily through internal announcements and personalized invitations, with the study's purpose, procedures, and ethical considerations thoroughly explained. Informed consent was obtained before participation, and the study was approved by the *Research and Ethics Committee* of the Psychology Faculty at the University of Lima, Peru.

In the **pretest phase**, a 20-minute EDA baseline measurement was conducted using the E4-Wristband, followed by the completion of the CMDQ to assess discomfort levels. Demographic data and information about participants' existing active break habits were collected to establish physiological and subjective baselines critical for evaluating the intervention.

The intervention spanned one workweek, during which participants engaged in six-hour daily sessions (totaling 30 h). In this case study, EMotivA was designed to motivate office workers to take a three-minute light walk every 40 min of inactivity, mitigating the negative effects of a sedentary lifestyle as supported by previous research [6, 9, 18]. The system sent persuasive auditory or visual messages at these intervals to reduce physical fatigue and prevent RSIs, while being calibrated to ensure the prompts remained effective without disrupting workflow continuity.

In the **postest phase**, participants repeated the CMDQ to evaluate changes in musculoskeletal discomfort and answered specific questions assessing the system's effectiveness, satisfaction, and impact on well-being and habits. Brief interviews provided qualitative insights into participants' experiences, offering additional context to complement the quantitative data and identifying areas for potential improvement.

5   Results

The results of this study provide a comprehensive evaluation of EMotivA's effectiveness in promoting active breaks and reducing musculoskeletal discomfort among office workers. By integrating quantitative analyses and comparisons with previous systems, the findings highlight the framework's ability to drive meaningful behavioral and ergonomic improvements.

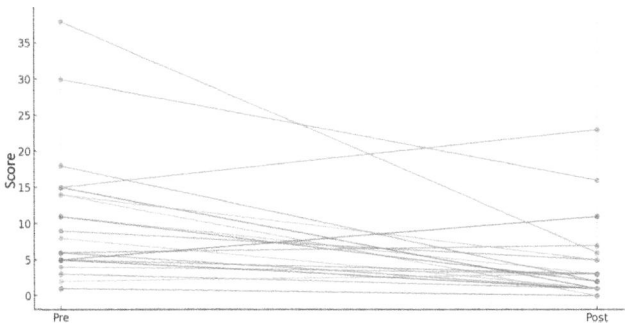

Fig. 2. Individual changes in CMDQ scores by participant.

5.1   RQ1: How Effectively does the Persuasive System Increase the Frequency and Regularity of Active Breaks Among Office Workers?

Before the intervention, active breaks were infrequent, with 40% of participants reporting taking breaks *"rarely"* and 30% *"sometimes"*. Additionally, 85% of participants spent less than 10 min daily on such activities. After the intervention, 95% of participants increased the frequency of their breaks, with 60% allocating 5–10 minutes and 30% dedicating 10–20 minutes daily. This improvement underscores EMotivA's ability to drive sustained behavioral change through contextually adaptive and minimally intrusive notifications. In contrast, prior studies such as Singh et al. [29] and Kekkonen et al. [17] sought to increase physical activity but achieved only partial success, largely due to their reliance on static feedback mechanisms and limited adaptability to user-specific contexts. Furthermore, post-intervention feedback revealed that 90% of participants experienced improvements in their overall well-being, with 25% reporting significant improvement and 65% noting some improvement. These results further validate EMotivA's effectiveness in meaningfully engaging users, fostering regular active breaks, and enhancing workplace well-being.

5.2   RQ2: How Effectively does the Persuasive System Reduce Musculoskeletal Discomfort Reported by Office Workers After Its Implementation?

The study revealed a significant reduction in musculoskeletal discomfort following the intervention. A Shapiro-Wilk test confirmed that the differences in

CMDQ scores followed a normal distribution ($p = 0.134$), validating the use of a paired tt-test for analysis. The tt-test results indicated a statistically significant improvement ($t(19) = 3.152$, $p = 0.005$), with an average reduction of 6.3 points in CMDQ scores and a moderate to large effect size (Cohen's $d = 0.705$). This effect size highlights a meaningful practical impact, reinforcing EMotivA's efficacy as an ergonomic intervention. Figure 2 illustrates the individual changes in CMDQ scores, showing consistent reductions across participants.

Notably, the percentage of participants engaging in physical activities, such as short walks during breaks, increased from 40% to 55%. This indicates that EMotivA not only encouraged more frequent breaks but also facilitated more effective activities to alleviate physical discomfort. Compared to previous systems, such as the posture detection approach by Ataguba and Orji [5], which achieved partial success by focusing solely on ergonomic adjustments, EMotivA offered a more holistic solution. By incorporating emotional context and adaptive feedback, EMotivA delivered timely and relevant prompts that significantly reduced discomfort. Additionally, while Zhang and Jemmott [37] reported fully successful outcomes, their reliance on static feedback mechanisms limited adaptability, a challenge EMotivA addressed through its dynamic and personalized interventions.

6   Threats to Validity

6.1   Internal Validity

A key potential threat to internal validity relates to the reliance on self-reported measures for tracking active breaks and musculoskeletal discomfort. Although the CMDQ is a validated instrument, self-reports may be influenced by recall bias or overestimation of behavioral change. Additionally, the Hawthorne effect-where participants modify their behavior due to the awareness of being observed-was a concern. However, this effect was mitigated by conducting the experiment in participants' usual office settings, without requiring them to alter their normal tasks or workflow; they were free to ignore or postpone the system's notifications, thus reducing the likelihood of artificially inflated engagement. Furthermore, the absence of a formal usability evaluation presents another limitation, although it was partially mitigated by sending notifications to the periphery of the participant's attention to minimize disruption to ongoing tasks.

6.2   External Validity

The relatively small, homogeneous sample of 20 young professionals (aged 19 to 31) constrains the generalizability of these findings to broader populations that may differ in age range, occupational roles, or technological familiarity. Additionally, the study did not include a control or comparison group, limiting the ability to benchmark EMotivA's effectiveness against other interventions or baseline conditions. The reliance on specific devices (E4-Wristband, smartphones, webcams) may also reduce applicability in workplaces with limited technological resources or different policies regarding personal devices. Nonetheless, the fact that the experiment was carried out in actual office environments, where participants followed their usual work routines, reinforces the practical relevance of the results and partially offsets these limitations.

6.3 Construct Validity

The operationalization of active breaks as three-minute walks every 40 min may not fully encapsulate the variety of physical activities that could mitigate the effects of sedentary behavior. Additionally, the study focused on short-term outcomes, such as musculoskeletal discomfort and active break frequency, without evaluating long-term adherence or broader health impacts. These factors limit the construct validity of the study in assessing the comprehensive benefits of EMotivA, particularly its sustained effectiveness over extended periods or in diverse workplace environments.

6.4 Ecological Validity

The study was conducted in participants' actual work environment, reinforcing its ecological validity. However, the structured approach to scheduling breaks may not fully reflect the diverse tasks and schedules found in various office settings. In this sense, the inclusion of an interruptibility prediction module allows the system to better adapt to each user's context, minimizing unwanted interruptions and supporting a more user-aware approach to active breaks.

7   Conclusions

This study highlights the effectiveness of the EMotivA system in promoting healthier workplace habits and reducing musculoskeletal discomfort among office workers. By leveraging emotion-aware and adaptive interventions, EMotivA successfully addressed the challenges of sedentary behavior through personalized and minimally intrusive notifications. The findings demonstrate a substantial increase in the frequency and regularity of active breaks among participants, with the majority dedicating significantly more time to physical activities compared to their baseline behaviors. These results underscore EMotivA's ability to embed sustainable behavioral changes seamlessly into daily workflows.

The reduction in musculoskeletal discomfort further validates the system's ergonomic impact. Participants reported notable improvements in physical well-being, particularly those with higher baseline discomfort. The rise in effective activities, such as light walking, highlights the importance of tailoring interventions to not only increase activity levels but also promote the quality of these behaviors. EMotivA's integration of emotional and contextual data ensured that interventions were timely and relevant, enhancing both engagement and effectiveness. Compared to existing systems, EMotivA represents a significant advancement in persuasive technologies by addressing key limitations such as static feedback, lack of emotional adaptability, and intrusive implementation. Its holistic approach demonstrates the potential for emotion-aware frameworks to set a new standard in workplace health interventions.

Future research should explore the long-term sustainability of these behavioral changes and validate the system's effectiveness in diverse workplace environments. Expanding the framework to include additional metrics, such as emotional well-being and job satisfaction, could provide a more comprehensive evaluation of its impact. Moreover, incorporating advanced AI techniques for enhanced personalization and experimenting with emerging technologies, such as augmented reality, could further optimize the system's adaptability and user experience.

Acknowledgements. N. Condori Fernández acknowledges the support of the XAI4SOC project (grant PID2021-123152OB-C21), funded by the Spanish Ministry of Science and Innovation, the State Research Agency (MCIN/AEI/ 10.13039/501100011033), and the European Social Fund (ESF) through the "Investing in your future" initiative. Additionally, F. Suni Lopez would like to acknowledge the support of the Laboratorio de Inteligencia Artificial at the Universidad de Lima for providing advanced technological resources that were instrumental in the successful execution of our experiments.

Appendix A   EMotivA Strategy

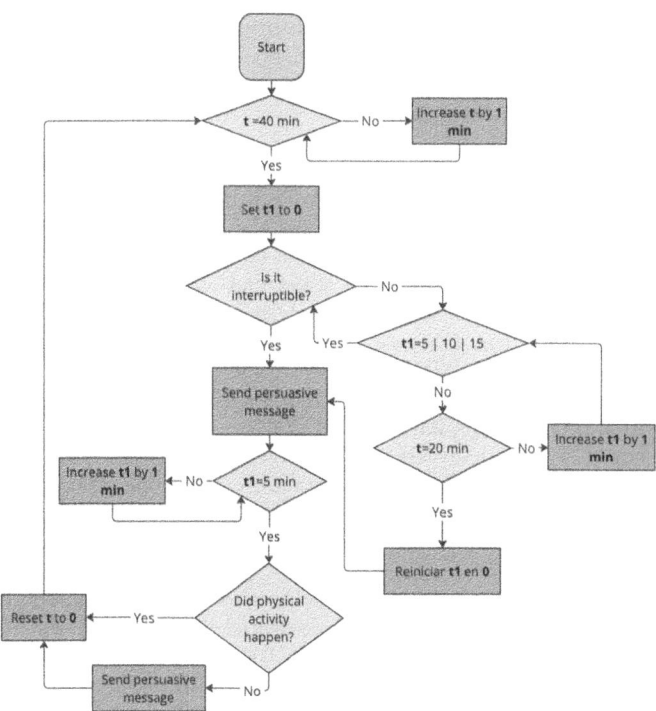

Fig. 3. Flowchart of the Persuasive Inference Layer's intervention strategy.

References

1. Aiken, L.R.: Content validity and reliability of single items or questionnaires. Educ. Psychol. Measur. **40**(4), 955–959 (1980)
2. Akksilp, K., et al.: The physical activity at work (paw) program in Thai office workers: mixed methods process evaluation study. JMIR Formative Res. **9**, e57604 (2025)
3. Aldenaini, N., Alqahtani, F., Orji, R., Sampalli, S.: Trends in persuasive technologies for physical activity and sedentary behavior: a systematic review. Front. Artif. Intell. **3** (2020)
4. Astete-Cornejo, J.M., Asencios-Hidalgo, J.R.: Validation of the Cornell musculoskeletal discomfort questionnaires in textile workers in Peru. Revista Brasileira de Medicina do Trabalho **21**(04), 01–07 (2023)
5. Ataguba, G., Orji, R.: Toward the design of persuasive systems for a healthy workplace: a real-time posture detection. Front. Big Data **7** (2024)
6. Buckley, J.P., et al.: The sedentary office: an expert statement on the growing case for change towards better health and productivity. Br. J. Sports Med. **49**, 1357–1362 (2015)
7. Cialdini, R.B.: Influence: The Psychology of Persuasion. HarperCollins (2007)
8. Demissie, B., Bayih, E.T., Demmelash, A.A.: A systematic review of work-related musculoskeletal disorders and risk factors among computer users. Heliyon **10**(3), e25075 (2024)
9. Dempsey, P.C., Sacre, J.W., Larsen, R.N., Straznicky, N.E., Sethi, P., Cohen, N.D., et al.: Interrupting prolonged sitting with brief bouts of light walking or simple resistance activities reduces resting blood pressure and plasma noradrenaline in type 2 diabetes. J. Hypertens. **34**(12), 2376–2382 (2016)
10. Elliot, A.J., Aarts, H.: Perception of the color red enhances the force and velocity of motor output. Emotion **11**(2), 445–449 (2011)
11. Fogg, B.: A behavior model for persuasive design. In: Proceedings of the 4th International Conference on Persuasive Technology. Persuasive 2009. ACM (2009)
12. Geurts, E., et al.: Walkwithme-personalized goal setting and coaching for walking in people with multiple sclerosis. UMAP 51–60 (2019)
13. Hulshof, C.T., et al.: The prevalence of occupational exposure to ergonomic risk factors: a systematic review and meta-analysis from the who/ilo joint estimates of the work-related burden of disease and injury. Environ. Int. **146**, 106157 (2021)
14. Islam, M.R., Kabir, M.M., Mridha, M.F., Alfarhood, S., Safran, M., Che, D.: Deep learning-based IoT system for remote monitoring and early detection of health issues in real-time. Sensors **23**(11), 5204 (2023)
15. Jung-Krenzer, T., Kirchner-Krath, J., Retz, C., Altmeyer, M.: Leaf your chair behind - calm persuasion for frequent sitting breaks among office-workers. In: Proceedings of Mensch und Computer 2024, MuC 2024, pp. 111–128. ACM (2024)
16. van Kasteren, Y., et al.: Thermal comfort and physical activity in an office setting. PervasiveHealth (2019)
17. Kekkonen, M., et al.: Examining the fidelity and dose of a mobile health app for micro-entrepreneurs' recovery from work-related stress. In: TKTP 2023: Annual Symposium for Computer Science 2023. CEUR Workshop Proceedings (2023)
18. McLean, L., Tingley, M., Scott, R.N., Rickards, J.: Computer terminal work and the benefit of microbreaks. Appl. Ergon. **32**(3), 225–237 (2001)
19. Mehta, R., Demmers, J., van Dolen, W.M., Weinburg, C.B.: When red means go: non-normative effects of red under sensation seeking. J. Consum. Psychol. **27**(1), 91–97 (2017)

20. Mehta, R., Zhu, R.J.: Blue or red? Exploring the effect of color on cognitive task performances. Science **323**(5918), 1226–1229 (2009)
21. Michie, S., van Stralen, M.M., West, R.: The behaviour change wheel: a new method for characterising and designing behaviour change interventions. Implementation Sci. **6**(1) (2011)
22. de Miguel, J., Gallardo, I., Horcajo, J., Becerra, A., Aguilar, P., Briñol, P.: El efecto del estrés sobre el procesamiento de mensajes persuasivos. Revista de Psicología Social **24**(3), 399–409 (2009)
23. Oinas-Kukkonen, H., Harjumaa, M.: Persuasive systems design: key issues, process model, and system features. In: Proceedings of the 4th International Conference on Persuasive Technology, pp. 1–8. ACM (2009)
24. Orji, R.: Persuasion and culture: Individualism-collectivism and susceptibility to influence strategies. In: Proceedings of the Eleventh International Conference on Persuasive Technology, pp. 30–41. Springer, Cham (2016)
25. Orji, R., Mandryk, R.L., Vassileva, J.: Gender, Age, and Responsiveness to Cialdini's Persuasion Strategies, pp. 147–159. Springer, Cham (2015)
26. Oyibo, K., et al.: Ben'fit: design, implementation and evaluation of a culture-tailored fitness app. PervasiveHealth (2019)
27. Park, S., et al.: Sedentary behaviors and physical activity of the working population measured by accelerometry: a systematic review and meta-analysis. BMC Public Health **24**(1) (2024)
28. Penfield, R.D., Giacobbi, P.R., Jr.: Applying a score confidence interval to Aiken's v index. Meas. Phys. Educ. Exerc. Sci. **18**(1), 21–31 (2014)
29. Singh, B., Ferguson, T., Deev, A., Deev, A., Maher, C.A.: Evaluation of the "15 minute challenge": a workplace health and wellbeing program. Healthcare **12**(13), 1255 (2024)
30. Singh, T., Mohadikar, M., Gite, S., Patil, S., Pradhan, B., Alamri, A.: Attention span prediction using head-pose estimation with deep neural networks. IEEE Access **9**, 142632–142643 (2021)
31. Suni Lopez, F., Condori-Fernandez, N., Catala, A.: Towards Real-Time Automatic Stress Detection for Office Workplaces, pp. 273–288. Springer, Cham (2019)
32. Suni-Lopez, F., Condori-Fernandez, N., Catala, A.: Understanding implicit user feedback from multisensorial and physiological data: a case study. In: Proceedings of the IEEE/ACM 42nd International Conference on Software Engineering Workshops, ICSE 2020, pp. 563–569. ACM (2020)
33. Wang, C., Lu, E.Y., Sun, W., Chang, J.R., Tsang, H.: Effectiveness of interventions on sedentary behaviors in office workers: a systematic review and meta-analysis. Public Health **230**, 45–51 (2024)
34. Wang, Y., Reiterer, H.: The point-of-choice prompt or the always-on progress bar?: a pilot study of reminders for prolonged sedentary behavior change (2019)
35. Wu, Y., Ji, Q.: Facial landmark detection: a literature survey (2018)
36. Za, S., Scornavacca, E., Pallud, J.: Enhancing workplace competence acquisition through a persuasive system. IseB **20**(4), 819–846 (2022)
37. Zhang, J., Jemmott, J.B., III.: Mobile app-based small-group physical activity intervention for young African American women: a pilot randomized controlled trial. Prev. Sci. **1**, 1–10 (2019)
38. Zhou, Y., Chen, P., Fan, Y., Wu, Y.: A multimodal feature fusion brain fatigue recognition system based on Bayes-gcForest. Sensors **24**(9), 2910 (2024)

On People's Susceptibility to Persuasive Techniques in Social Engineering: Is It About the Technique or Their Readiness to Be Persuaded?

Aya Muhanad[1]([⊠]) [iD], Ala Yankouskaya[2] [iD], Khaled M. Khan[1] [iD],
Mahmoud Barhamgi[1] [iD], and Raian Ali[3] [iD]

[1] College of Engineering, Qatar University, Doha, Qatar
{aya.muhanad,k.khan,mbarhamgi}@qu.edu.qa
[2] Department of Psychology, Bournemouth University, Poole, UK
ayankouskaya@bournemouth.ac.uk
[3] College of Science and Engineering, Hamad Bin Khalifa University, Doha, Qatar
raali2@hbku.edu.qa

Abstract. Social engineering (SE) typically involves persuasive elements that influence victims to take risky security actions. Among the recognised principles of persuasion are Cialdini's principles: social proof, likeability, authority, commitment and consistency, reciprocity, and scarcity. Research has shown differences in the prevalence of persuasive techniques in SE attempts, but whether these techniques differ in manipulative power in general, and specifically when security risks are present and known, remains unexplored. More broadly, does the technique matter as much as the readiness to be persuaded and take risks? Can individuals be grouped by their receptiveness to persuasion across all Cialdini principles in the context of SE attempts? To explore this topic, we presented participants with a social media scenario in which a member requests volunteers to install an app and provide feedback. We designed 12 scenarios, highlighting the presence or neutralisation of each principle. Our online study involved 329 participants from the Arab Gulf Cooperation Council (GCC) countries and 223 from the United Kingdom. Using K-Means clustering, we identified distinct cluster profiles in both samples. Clustering revealed that, across both regions, participants in each cluster exhibited consistent susceptibility levels to all principles. For example, in the Arab sample, we identified three clusters reflecting low, medium, and high susceptibility. This study concludes that vulnerability to persuasion in potential SE attacks appears consistent, regardless of the technique. This suggests that susceptibility to persuasion and readiness to take risks may have a more significant impact than the specific persuasion technique used.

Keywords: Social engineering · Trust · Cialdini's principles · Risk-taking · Persuasion · Clustering

K. T. Win et al. (Eds.): PERSUASIVE 2025, LNCS 15711, pp. 232–246, 2025.
https://doi.org/10.1007/978-3-031-94959-3_17

1 Introduction

Persuasion, a fundamental aspect of human interaction, is an active attempt to influence decision-making processes [1]. With the exponential growth of the internet and broadcasting channels, individuals are now exposed to persuasive messages more than ever before [2]. This increased exposure underscores the need for research to understand its effects on people. A significant body of literature explores the impact of persuasion, highlighting its role in shaping decision-making, e.g. [3, 4]. Understanding how persuasion influences individuals is paramount, as it serves diverse purposes, such as enhancing educational outcomes, where teachers use persuasive techniques to help students acquire new knowledge [5], and promoting positive behaviours, like encouraging hygiene practices among hospital visitors [6].

Persuasion is not merely a singular tactic; it encompasses a variety of strategies designed to influence others. One notable classification of these strategies is provided by Robert Cialdini, who identifies six principles that are frequently employed in marketing and other domains [7]: social proof, which highlights how the behaviours of others can influence us; likeability, which emphasises the stronger impact individuals we admire or personally favour have on us; authority, which highlights our tendency to trust experts more; commitment and consistency, which pertains the need to remain consistent with previous commitments; reciprocity, which denotes the feeling to repay kindness; and scarcity, which posits that items that are rare are considered more valuable.

While persuasion principles can yield beneficial outcomes, they can also be abused to encourage risky behaviours. Social engineering (SE) attacks exploit human vulnerabilities to acquire sensitive information or breach systems illicitly [8] and often incorporate the aforementioned persuasion principles to achieve their objectives. Since these attacks rely on human vulnerabilities, the human needs to be persuaded for these attacks to be successful. Various analyses of SE attacks reveal the high use of these principles; a study analysing 207 phishing emails indicated that most attacks use at least one of Cialdini's principles [9]. A similar study examining vishing attacks, another form of SE, has also demonstrated the prevalent use of persuasion principles [10]. Studies have been conducted to measure the impact of these principles [11, 12], but not many focus on their effectiveness in online scenarios that involve risk. One study investigates the exact influence of each Cialdini principle on victims of potential SE attempts, revealing that the principles remain effective even if the victim is aware of an online risk [13]. This emphasizes the urgent need to address vulnerabilities to the malicious application of persuasion principles.

Numerous studies explored the human factors contributing to susceptibility to persuasion, including personality traits [14–17], linking certain personalities with vulnerability to specific persuasion principles. However, prior research suggests that personality traits [18] and cognitive styles [19] do not comprehensively account for vulnerability to Cialdini's principles in SE attempts. One new approach to tackle this problem is to examine whether individuals are inherently susceptible to persuasion regardless of the technique used. This means that if an individual is highly influenced by one principle, it may also carry across to the other principles.

Drawing parallels to other domains, we can find that various treatments aimed at influencing people's behaviour may not all be effective for every individual. For instance, multisensory learning, an approach that engages multiple sensory inputs such as hearing, touch and sight, has improved learning [20] and created a more immersive educational experience [21]. However, research indicates that certain sensory approaches can be more effective for specific groups than other sensory approaches [22]. This suggests that while the different approaches designed to affect learning may all be useful, their effectiveness can vary among people. Similar findings have emerged in studies on motivational strategies, which aim to boost motivation to achieve behavioural change [23]. While motivational strategies are generally effective in helping individuals reach their goals, some research explains that certain strategies may resonate with specific groups. In contrast, others may not have the desired impact [24]. Connecting this to the effectiveness of persuasion principles raises the question: If one persuasion principle successfully influences an individual, will others have a similar effect?

With this study, we aim to determine whether people are generally susceptible to persuasion and exhibit certain low or high vulnerability level to various persuasion principles in a consistent style. Generally, studies measuring vulnerability under persuasion principles often rely on secondary data, such as phishing emails [25], which typically embody multiple principles simultaneously, limiting the ability to analyse each principle in isolation. Alternatively, other research uses distinct scenarios for each principle [26], which can introduce covariates that affect the measurement. Our analysis has addressed these limitations by designing scenarios around the same storyline for each persuasion principle. In this study, we address the following research question.

RQ: Does susceptibility to social engineering vary by the persuasion technique used, or is it consistent and driven by an individual's overall readiness to be persuaded and take risks?

2   Method

This section explains how we answered our research question by explaining how we designed the SE scenarios, then detailing the data collection process, and finally describing the statistical analyses used.

2.1   Scenario Design

In order to measure risk-taking due to the influence of Cialdini's principles in a potential SE attempt, we presented participants with the scenario that they are part of a social media group where one member, named Majid for Arab participants and Oliver for United Kingdom (UK) participants, asks for volunteers to try out his new app and provide feedback. These names were carefully chosen not to have religious connotations and for each cultural group to reduce religious and cultural biases. The app collects personal data such as age, dietary info, and location to provide customised recommendations such as offers at local shops and future health planning. The important part of this scenario is that this request could be malicious or legitimate; we ensured this by asking participants about their risk perception in installing the app and excluded those who did not perceive any risk with installing the app from Majid (Oliver for the UK). To measure the effect of each principle, we created scenarios representing the presence and absence of each of Cialdini's principles. Figure 1 shows an example of the scenarios of authority and social proof. The presence of authority was presented by Majid (Oliver for the UK), who has an extensive social media profile with certificates from well-known organisations and a work history at several companies. As for the absence, no such information on expertise was provided. For the social proof principle, its presence was shown by displaying that many users have installed and liked the app, while the absence has only five downloads and zero comments. A similar approach was taken for the remaining principles. The order of the 12 scenarios was randomised for each participant to reduce any learning effects.

Each scenario underwent a face validation, a process done to confirm whether each scenario presents one and only one of Cialdini's principles. We asked six individuals to familiarise themselves with these principles and match each principle with the scenarios. We also asked them to provide feedback on the illustrations. Based on the feedback, some adjustments have been made; for example, the social proof absence was initially zero downloads. Since this is quite an extreme form of the absence of social proof we converted it to five downloads instead.

The full details of the study and dataset are available on the Open Science Framework link provided in Supplementary Material section.

Fig. 1. The presence (left) and absence (right) of authority (top) and social proof (bottom)

2.2   Participants and Data Collection

We conducted the surveys with 329 participants (age range 18–60, M = 35.67, SD = 10.15, 144 females) from the Arab Gulf Cooperation Council (Arab GCC) countries, which include Bahrain, Kuwait, Oman, Saudi Arabia, the United Arab Emirates, and Qatar. Additionally, we gathered responses from 323 participants (age range 18–60, M = 38.48, SD = 12.51, 188 females) in the UK, specifically from England, Northern

Ireland, and Wales. Due to the limited number of survey respondents who identified as "other" or chose not to disclose their gender, we excluded these responses from the analysis. The full dataset can be retrieved from the OSF link provided earlier. We developed our surveys using Survey Monkey (surveymonkey.com) and distributed them with assistance from TGM Research (tgmresearch.com). An Arabic version of the survey was sent to participants from the GCC, while an English version was provided to participants in the UK. The Arabic survey was developed using the back-translation process [27], which involves translating the text from English to Arabic and then back to English again to compare it to the original version. All participants were required to be at least 18 years old, identify with the cultural norms of either the UK or Arab GCC, be familiar with social media, and be generally willing to assist strangers online. Exclusion criteria included failing attention checks during the survey, completing the survey in less than half the median time and not associating any risk in installing the app in the illustrated social media group scenario. Ethical approval was obtained from the Institutional Review Board of the last author's organisation, and participants provided informed consent before beginning the survey. They also had the option to withdraw at any point. Importantly, no personally identifiable information was collected, and the responses were only collected through our SurveyMonkey account and were stored in password-protected online folders.

To assess the effectiveness of each principle, participants were asked questions regarding their likelihood of installing the app and their level of trust in the software designer. After each scenario, we posed two questions. The first question was: "In a similar situation, how likely are you to install the app and give it a try?" Responses were recorded on a scale from one to six, where one represents "very unlikely" and six represents "very likely". This score is referred to as the *Install* variable. The second question pertained to *Trust*: "In a similar scenario, how much do you trust Oliver's transparency and intentions?" Participants rated their trust on a scale from one to six, where one represented "complete distrust", and six indicated "complete trust".

2.3 Data Analysis

Bootstrapped Descriptives. We started the data analysis with descriptive statistics to provide a general overview of participant levels of trust and the likelihood of app installation under the presence of the six persuasion principles. First, the levels for install (x) and trust (y) for each participant were paired as a single data point (x, y). A bootstrapped dataset was then created by resampling the data with replacements while maintaining the sample size equivalent to the number of participants. The mean of this bootstrapped dataset was then calculated and plotted as a single data point (x, y). This process was repeated 2000 times for the UK and Arab samples separately.

Exploratory Cluster Analysis. This analysis aimed to identify subgroups of participants exhibiting similar trust and risk-taking behaviour patterns. Calculating the difference between responses to the questions related to trust and the likelihood of app installation in scenarios with and without persuasion enabled us to assess the exact effect of each principle. However, for the clustering method, the variability within these calculated scores was too minimal. Since we aimed to observe general behaviour under the influence of all the six principles rather than precisely measuring the impact of the persuasion principle, we opted for using the responses to the two questions in scenarios where persuasion was present, as these variables had more significant variability.

The clustering variables included the level of trust participants had in the software designer (i.e. Oliver/Majid) and the likelihood of installing the app across all six principles, leading to 12 variables. These did not have to be standardised as the responses consisted of answers of the same interval. We employed the unsupervised machine learning technique k-means clustering using the standard R function in the *kmeans*() [stats package], which partitions objects into a specified number of k groups. The standard algorithm aims to reach an optimal solution for the sum of squared Euclidean distances between the objects and the corresponding centroid so that moving one object from one cluster to another will not reduce the within-cluster sum of squares [28]. To determine the number k, we used the *NbClust*() function in the NbClust R package, which provides 30 indices for finding the optimal number of clusters by varying combinations of k, distance measures and clustering methods [29]. Each final clustering model was validated using the silhouette coefficient (S_i). This coefficient measures an individual's similarity to others within the same cluster versus individuals in neighbouring clusters. The silhouette score ranges from 1 to -1, with values closer to 1 indicating well-defined clusters, while scores nearer to -1 suggest poor clustering.

3   Results

This section presents the results and clusters obtained in both the UK and Arab samples.

3.1   Overview of Trust and Install Scores Under the Presence of Persuasion Principles

The bootstrapped distributions for the Arab sample (Fig. 2) reveal variations in the level of trust participants placed in Majid when persuasion principles were present and the likelihood of installing the app. If the clouds overlap vertically, it indicates a similar level of risk-taking when persuasion is present. Horizontal overlap displays a level of trust. For instance, in the Arab sample, social proof and authority principles do not overlap regarding the likelihood of installing the app. Yet they show overlap regarding the level of trust. This means that when these two principles are present, similar levels of trust towards Majid are observed but with different levels of risk-taking (i.e., app installation). When examining the other principles in the graph, they demonstrate lower likelihoods of installing the app and trust levels in the lower left quadrant and exhibit slight overlap among their clouds. The bootstrapped distribution for the UK sample (Fig. 2) is slightly different from the Arab distribution. Generally, the trust and likelihood of app installation are lower than in the Arab sample. The highest point of the cloud centre reaches approximately (x ≈ 4.0, y ≈ 3.9) in the UK sample, in contrast with the Arab sample, where the centre of the social proof clouds is approximately situated (x ≈ 4.75, y ≈ 4.25). In the UK sample, the principles of reciprocity, social proof, and authority also show slightly more overlap than in the Arab sample, indicating that similar levels of risk-taking (installing the app) and trust are observed when these principles are present.

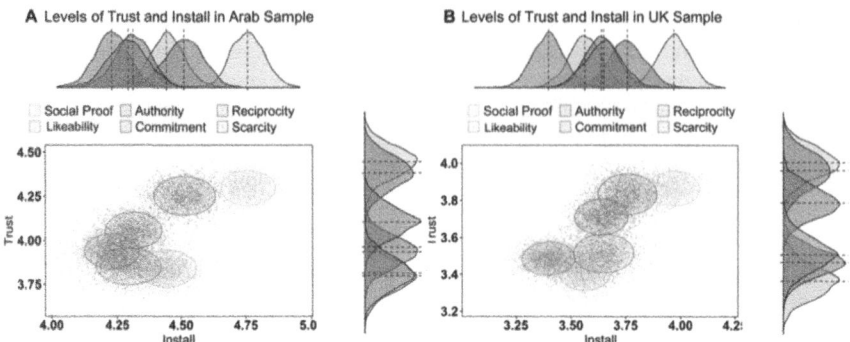

Fig. 2. Distributions of the levels of trust and installation under the presence of Cialdini's principles in Arab and UK samples. Note: The X-axis depicts the likelihood of app installation. The Y-axis depicts the level of trust. The higher the value in both axes, the stronger the influence.

3.2 Clusters

A k-means analysis was conducted to identify k groups based on 12 observations (Authority Install, Authority Trust, Commitment Install, Commitment Trust, Likeability Install, Likeability Trust, Reciprocity Install, Reciprocity Trust, Scarcity Install, Scarcity Trust, Social Proof Install and Social Proof Trust). This method enables us to cluster participants who exhibit similarities and have high intra-class similarity while effectively separating those who differ into distinct clusters and have low inter-class similarity. Following the majority rule, the analysis of 30 indices revealed that the optimal number of clusters for the UK sample is two (Cluster 1 size = 117, Cluster 2 size = 206), whereas, for the Arab sample, it is three (Cluster 1 size = 39, Cluster 2 size = 173, Cluster 3 size = 117) (see Fig. 3). The average silhouette width recorded was 0.38 for the UK sample and 0.25 for the Arab sample.

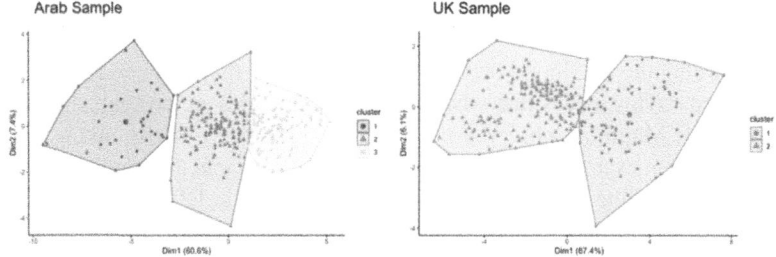

Fig. 3. Clustering solutions for the Arab and UK samples based on the likelihood of app installation and trust level. Plotted using the *factorextra* R package

We further analysed the levels of trust and the likelihood of app installation to create a profile for each cluster. For the Arab sample, we identified three clusters and calculated their means to gain insight into the characteristics of the individuals within each group. Additionally, we assessed the standard error to estimate the potential variation between the sample mean and the actual population value. The cluster means show a linear progression across the clusters: Cluster 1 exhibits the lowest mean scores for both trust and installation likelihood; Cluster 2 shows moderate levels for both. In contrast, Cluster 3 contains the highest scores across both trust and installation likelihood of all six persuasion principles (see Fig. 4). Cluster 1, which exhibits the lowest likelihood of app installation and trust levels, was the smallest, consisting of only 39 participants. This represents just 11.9% of the sample, indicating that only a small number of people in the sample show low vulnerability to Cialdini's principles. Clusters 2 and 3 represented 52.6% and 35.6% of the Arab sample.

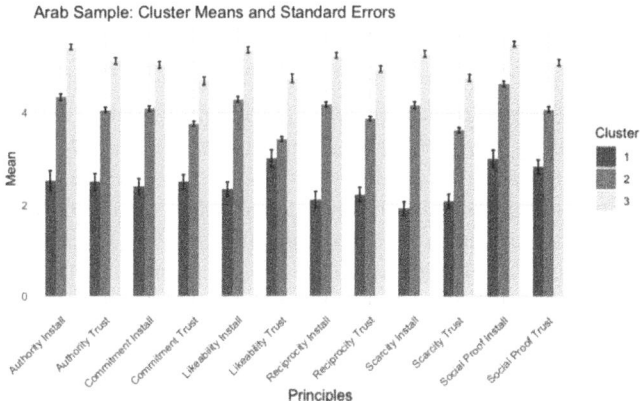

Fig. 4. Arab sample: cluster means and standard errors for trust and install levels

A similar analysis of the cluster means was conducted for the UK sample, for which we defined two clusters. The means of the clusters show a linear progression, with Cluster 1 exhibiting the lowest mean scores across all 12 variables. In contrast, Cluster 2 demonstrates elevated trust and installation likelihood levels for each of these six principles (see Fig. 5). Cluster 1, characterised by low vulnerability to persuasion, included 117 participants, accounting for 36% of the sample. While Cluster 2, representing individuals with high vulnerability, represented 64% of the UK sample.

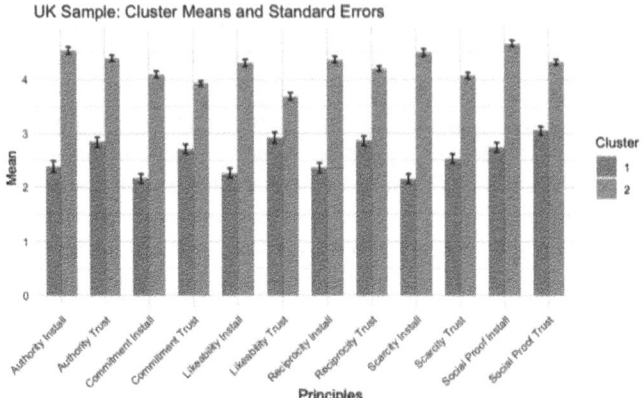

Fig. 5. UK sample: cluster means and standard errors for trust and install levels

4   Discussion

This paper seeks to determine whether behaviour in the context of an SE attempt that utilises persuasion aligns uniformly across Cialdini's principles. Prior research has primarily focused on correlating personality traits with specific persuasion strategies [14–17]; however, another study indicated that the influence of personality traits on risk-taking behaviour due to persuasion in an SE attempt is minimal [18]. Our clustering approach suggests that individuals highly vulnerable to one persuasion principle, in an SE context where risks are knowingly present, are likely vulnerable to others. This indicates that personalising each persuasion principle to individual characteristics may not be necessary to achieve influence. Instead, a generalised vulnerability to various techniques can be assumed once susceptibility to persuasion has been identified. Two clusters were identified in the UK sample, while three were identified in the Arab sample. We observed a consistent increase in vulnerability to all principles as we moved from one cluster to the next. The following subsections explore the similarities and differences between these increases. We first compare risk-taking tendencies under the influence of each principle across clusters in the UK sample, followed by the Arab sample (see 4.1), and then examine trust tendencies (see 4.2).

4.1   Comparing Risk-Taking Tendencies Under the Influence of Each Principle Across Clusters

In the UK sample, we identified two clusters, Cluster 1 with lower vulnerability to persuasion and Cluster 2 with higher; this is consistent for all six principles. On average, the high-vulnerability group is 89% more likely to install an app when these principles are present than the low-vulnerability group. The detailed increase in the likelihood of app installation in Cluster 2, relative to Cluster 1, shows increases of 70% for social proof, 90% for likeability, 90% for authority, 89% for commitment consistency, 85% for reciprocity, and 109% for scarcity. Interestingly, the influence of social proof on risk-taking least differentiates low from highly vulnerable individuals since it has the smallest increase. This could be explained by our herding nature, which suggests that humans tend to mimic the decisions of others far more often than making random decisions [30]. Our results indicate that the influence of social proof on risk-taking (i.e. installing the app) is most uniform between individuals with low and high vulnerability compared to other principles where the differences are more pronounced. Possibly because social proof is rooted in human origins. Another noteworthy observation involves scarcity, where the vulnerability increases by more than double. Low-vulnerable participants may have had a low desire for uniqueness [31] and high scepticism regarding the reasons behind scarcity-driven strategies, especially if they did not anticipate scarcity [32]. They may have easily noticed the persuasive tactic, as the scenario emphasises that only three vouchers remain out of 20 for the first app installers. In contrast, high-vulnerable participants seemed eager to seize the opportunity and were strongly influenced by scarcity; people often make such choices to avoid the regret of missing out on valuable chances [33]. The principles of likeability, authority, commitment consistency, and reciprocity demonstrate similar percentage increases from Cluster 1 to Cluster 2. This suggests that when a person is highly vulnerable to one of these principles, they are also likely to experience increased vulnerability to these principles.

In the Arab sample, three clusters were identified, focusing on the first two: Cluster 1 shows low vulnerability, and Cluster 2 exhibits medium vulnerability. On average, individuals with medium vulnerability were 84% more likely to install an app when these principles were present than those with low vulnerability. The detailed increases are as follows: 53% for social proof, 87% for likeability, 72% for authority, 71% for commitment consistency, 100% for reciprocity, and 121% for scarcity. While we iden-tified three clusters in the Arab sample and two in the UK sample, the first two clusters in the Arab sample show comparable results to those in the UK. Similar to the UK sample, the smallest difference in app installation likelihood between Cluster 1 and 2 was observed for social proof, with a 53% rise, suggesting that this principle is deeply rooted [30]. The most significant increase, at 121%, was for scarcity, suggesting similar characteristics to the UK sample, e.g. low desire for uniqueness among low-vulnerable individuals [31]. Unlike the UK sample, the vulnerability to reciprocity doubled in the medium-vulnerable group compared to the low-vulnerable group. This proposes that individuals with medium vulnerability are significantly influenced by reciprocity, con-sistent with prior findings that identify reciprocity as an influential persuasion principle among Arabs [34]. As for the remaining principles, the changes were similar, suggesting that vulnerability to one principle extends across the others, regardless of the technique used.

In the Arab sample, Cluster 2 represents medium vulnerability and makes up 53% of the Arab sample, while Cluster 3 represents 35% and exhibits the highest vulnerability. The differences in susceptibility to persuasion between medium and high-vulnerable individuals are notably smaller than between low and medium-vulnerable individuals. On average, there was a 25% increase in the likelihood of app installation from Cluster 2 to Cluster 3. The detailed increases are 20% for social proof, 24% for commitment consistency and 26% for each of the remaining four principles. Once again, social proof shows the smallest difference between the two groups, further supporting that it has the least impact on distinguishing individuals with different vulnerability levels. Interestingly, participants in Cluster 3 demonstrated a consistent 26% increase across the remaining principles, except for commitment, which had a 24% increase, a figure that is still very close. This indicates that vulnerability to these principles increased uniformly from Clusters 2 to 3. People are influenced to take risks because they rely on heuristics and biases [35]. High-vulnerable individuals may be more open to being influenced due to their reliance on these cognitive shortcuts, regardless of which principle is used.

4.2 Comparing Trust Tendencies Under the Influence of Each Principle Across Clusters

In the UK sample, the high-vulnerability group is on average 46% more trusting of an individual using persuasion, compared to the low-vulnerability group. High-vulnerable individuals showed a greater shift in their intention to install the app (average increase: 89%) but a smaller change in trust in the software designer's intentions (average increase: 46%) compared to low-vulnerable individuals. This indicates that individuals with high vulnerability differ from those with low vulnerability because their intentions are more easily influenced. In contrast, the influence on trust is less different. Trust is shaped by an individual's trust propensity, a generally stable trait [36]. The exact increases in trust levels from Cluster 1 to Cluster 2 were as follows: 42% for social proof, 26% for likeability, 55% for authority, 45% for commitment and consistency, 47% for reciprocity, and 61% for scarcity. Scarcity showed the largest increase among these principles. This indicates that individuals with high vulnerability exhibit a greater susceptibility to the influence of scarcity on their trust towards others, in contrast to those with low vulnerability.

In our scarcity scenario, the software engineer offers vouchers to the first 20 app installers and highlights that only three vouchers remain. This high increase in trust may come from the engineer's precise knowledge of the number of vouchers available, which may seem more credible than unrealistic scarcity appeals [37], like simply claiming the vouchers are in high demand. However, this does not fully explain why scarcity had a greater impact when differentiating the two groups than other principles, indicating a need for further investigation.

The second most significant difference in trust was observed from authority, suggesting that individuals with low and high vulnerability in the UK sample strongly differ in their trust towards experts. Since authority bias is related to trusting authoritative figures [38], lower susceptibility to this bias may play a role in distinguishing individuals with minimal vulnerability to persuasion from those who are more vulnerable. Interestingly, trust levels due to likeability least differentiated low from high-vulnerable individuals, with only a 26% increase. In contrast, social proof, commitment consistency and reciprocity showed noticeably higher and similar increases of 42%, 45% and 47%, respectively. This means that vulnerability increases similarly for these principles from Cluster 1 to Cluster 2, regardless of the principle used.

Comparing Cluster 1 (low-vulnerability) to Cluster 2 (medium-vulnerability) in the Arab sample, the detailed increases in trust levels are as follows: 47% for social proof, 13% for likeability, 64% for authority, 52% for commitment consistency, 77% for reciprocity, and 71% for scarcity. The smallest difference between the two groups was noted for likeability in the UK sample. Similarly, in the Arab sample, the smallest difference between low and medium-vulnerable individuals was linked to likeability. This suggests that likeability least differentiates the two groups regarding its effect on trust. We mentioned earlier that the effect of reciprocity on risk-taking strongly differentiated low from medium-vulnerable individuals in the Arab sample. A similar strong difference in trust levels between low and medium-vulnerable appeared again due to reciprocity, aligning with previous findings [34]. In the Arab sample, scarcity had the second-strongest effect on differentiating the groups in their trust levels followed by authority, a pattern similar to the UK sample. Thus, the effect of each principle on differentiating trust levels between Clusters 1 and 2 is nearly identical for the Arab and UK samples, with reciprocity being the notable exception. For all six principles, trust levels were more influenced in Cluster 2, suggesting that susceptibility to persuasion might have more to do with readiness to be influenced rather than which principle is used. Due to space constraints, we will not provide a detailed discussion comparing Cluster 2 to Cluster 3 in the Arab sample. However, the trends align with our findings, which indicate that increased vulnerability across the principles is consistent. For reference, the trust level increases are as follows: 41% for likeability, 28% for reciprocity, 33% for scarcity, and 24% for the remaining three principles.

4.3 Limitations

While our study identified interesting groups of individuals based on their vulnerability to persuasion, certain limitations exist. One key limitation is determining the optimal number of clusters. We addressed this by utilising 30 indices from the Nbclust R package, which aid in identifying the best value for k [29]. Additionally, we evaluated our clusters' meaningfulness by examining each cluster's behavioural characteristics. Although we employed robust methods for cluster estimation, the results require validation with an independent sample to confirm their generalisability. Other limitations include the lack of data to estimate the prevalence of the identified groups within each sample. Understanding the prevalence of each group would provide valuable insights for designing targeted strategies to reduce vulnerability to persuasion. Future research could tackle this limitation by conducting a study with a sample involving stratified quotas across various regions within the Arab and UK samples. Furthermore, distributing advertisements for the study may have introduced selection bias, as we targeted participants through TGM research. Additionally, the clusters exhibiting lower vulnerability do not represent resistance to persuasion. This paper does not address questions about resistance; instead, it concentrates on the consistency of behaviour.

5 Conclusion

This study shifts the focus from personality trait-specific vulnerabilities to general susceptibility profiles, paving the way for new approaches to mitigate the risks associated with persuasion-based manipulation. We assessed behaviour under the presence of persuasion principles during potential SE attempts. Utilising Likert scales, we measured risk-taking behaviour in SE attempts alongside trust levels in scenarios that utilise persuasion, which we used to cluster our participants, 329 from the Arab region and 323 from the UK. Our clustering analysis indicates that once vulnerability to one persuasion principle is detected, heightened vulnerability is also likely observed under the other principles. We found that risk-taking under the presence of social proof exhibited the least variation between low and highly vulnerable individuals in both samples, suggesting that this principle might be more deeply ingrained. Conversely, we found that vulnerability to scarcity most clearly distinguishes low-vulnerable from high-vulnerable individuals. This study highlights the importance of developing resistance strategies that address all persuasion tactics once vulnerability to one form of persuasion is found. Future research could explore how these susceptibility profiles evolve over time or in response to specific interventions, further enhancing our understanding of this dynamic. Moreover, comparable studies could be performed utilising alternative scenarios to ascertain whether the findings remain consistent.

Acknowledgements. This publication was supported by NPRP 14 Cluster grant # NPRP 14C-0916-210015 from the Qatar National Research Fund (a member of Qatar Foundation). The findings herein reflect the work and are solely the responsibility of the authors.

Author Contribution. RA, MB, and KMK designed the questionnaire and curated the data. All authors conceptualized the research presented in this paper. AY, RA, and AM designed the methodology for the statistical analysis. AM performed the analysis and wrote the initial draft. AY verified the analysis and extended it. AY, MB, KMK and RA reviewed and edited the paper.

Disclosure of Interests. The authors report there are no competing interests to declare.

Supplementary Material. The study design, dataset, and analysis files are available on the Open Science Framework (OSF) at the following link: https://osf.io/3tsez/.

References

1. Cacioppo, J.T., Cacioppo, S., Petty, R.E.: The neuroscience of persuasion: a review with an emphasis on issues and opportunities. Soc. Neurosci. **13**, 129–172 (2018). https://doi.org/10.1080/17470919.2016.1273851
2. Perloff, R.M., Perloff, R.M.: The Dynamics of persuasion: communication and attitudes in the 21st century. Routledge, New York (1993). https://doi.org/10.4324/9781410606884
3. Kaptein, M., Ruyter, B., Markopoulos, P., Aarts, E.: Adaptive persuasive systems: a study of tailored persuasive text messages to reduce snacking. ACM Trans. Interact. Intell. Syst. (TiiS) (2012). https://doi.org/10.1145/2209310.2209313
4. Spasova, L.: Degree of susceptibility to persuasion principles in advertising: measuring the persuasion principles as part of advertising influence. TJS. **20**, 227–237 (2022). https://doi.org/10.15547/tjs.2022.03.009
5. Hynd, C.: Persuasion and its role in meeting educational goals. Theor. Into Pract. **40**, 270 (2001).https://doi.org/10.1207/s15430421tip4004_9
6. Gaube, S., Fischer, P., Windl, V., Lermer, E.: The effect of persuasive messages on hospital visitors' hand hygiene behavior. Health Psychol. **39**, 471–481 (2020). https://doi.org/10.1037/hea0000854
7. Cialdini, R.B.: The science of persuasion. Sci. Am. **284**, 76–81 (2001)

8. Wang, Z., Sun, L., Zhu, H.: Defining social engineering in cybersecurity. IEEE Access. **8**, 85094–85115 (2020). https://doi.org/10.1109/ACCESS.2020.2992807

9. Akbar, N.: Analysing persuasion principles in phishing emails. https://essay.utwente.nl/66177/. Last accessed 17 Sep. 2024

10. Jones, K.S., Armstrong, M.E., Tornblad, M.K., Siami Namin, A.: How social engineers use persuasion principles during vishing attacks. Inf. Comput. Secur. **29**, 314–331 (2021). https://doi.org/10.1108/ICS-07-2020-0113

11. Tölken, L., Tolken, L.: The effects of Cialdini´s principles of persuasion and persuasive sources on purchase intention and persuasiveness on Facebook

12. Naruoei, B., Hakimpour, H., Mahmoodzadeh Vashshan, M., Mohammadi, M.: The effectiveness of Cialdini's principles on persuasion in digital marketing (A case study of Iran's furniture industry). Int. J. Nonlinear Anal. Appl. **15**, 135–148 (2024). https://doi.org/10.22075/ijnaa.2023.30051.4322

13. Mollazehi, A., Abuelezz, I., Barhamgi, M., Khan, K.M., Ali, R.: Do Cialdini's Persuasion principles still influence trust and risk-taking when social engineering is knowingly possible? In: Araújo, J., de la Vara, J.L., Santos, M.Y., Assar, S. (eds.) Research Challenges in Information Science: 18th International Conference, RCIS 2024, Guimarães, Portugal, May 14–17, 2024, Proceedings, Part I, pp. 273–288. Springer Nature Switzerland, Cham (2024). https://doi.org/10.1007/978-3-031-59465-6_17

14. Gkika, S., Skiada, M., Lekakos, G., Kourouthanassis, P.E.: Investigating the role of personality traits and influence strategies on the persuasive effect of personalized recommendations. Presented at the EMPIRE@RecSys (2016)

15. Liu, D., Campbell, W.K.: The Big Five personality traits, Big Two metatraits and social media: a meta-analysis. J. Res. Pers. **70**, 229–240 (2017). https://doi.org/10.1016/j.jrp.2017.08.004

16. Uebelacker, S., Quiel, S.: The social engineering personality framework. In: 2014 Workshop on Socio-Technical Aspects in Security and Trust. pp. 24–30 (2014). https://doi.org/10.1109/STAST.2014.12

17. Alkış, N., Taşkaya Temizel, T.: The impact of individual differences on influence strategies. Personality Individ. Differ. **87**, 147–152 (2015). https://doi.org/10.1016/j.paid.2015.07.037

18. Muhanad, A., Haris, R., Abouelezz, I., Barhamgi, M., Ali, R., Khan, K.M.: Do personality traits really impact susceptibility to persuasion in social engineering? A study among UK and Arab samples. https://www.researchsquare.com/article/rs-4902235/v1 (2024). https://doi.org/10.21203/rs.3.rs-4902235/v1

19. Abuelezz, I., et al.: Do cognition, affect, and intuition influence susceptibility to persuasion in social engineering among risk-aware targets?. https://papers.ssrn.com/abstract=4989373. (2024). https://doi.org/10.2139/ssrn.4989373

20. Neumann, M.: Neumann, M. M., Hyde, M., Neumann, D. L., Hood, M., Ford, R.: Multi-sensory methods for early literacy learning (pp. 197–216) (2011). In: G. Andrews and D. L. Neumann. (eds.). Beyond the Lab: Applications of Cognitive Research in Memory and Learning. Hauppauge, NY: Nova Science Publishers. Presented at the January 1 (2012)

21. Fan, Y., Chong, D.K., Li, Y.: Beyond play: a comparative study of multi-sensory and traditional toys in child education. Front. Educ. (2024). https://doi.org/10.3389/feduc.2024.1182660

22. Hoffer, S.M.: Adult learning styles: auditory, visual, and tactual-kinesthetic sensory modalities (1986). https://www.proquest.com/docview/303570390/abstract/DF5698CB407E49AEPQ/1

23. LCSW, M.S., Karen Dubin, M.D.: The role of motivation in behavioral change - SWEET INSTITUTE - continuing education for mental health professionals. https://sweetinstitute.com/the-role-of-motivation-in-behavioral-change/. Last accessed 25 Dec. 2024

24. Friederichs, S.A., Bolman, C., Oenema, A., Lechner, L.: Profiling physical activity motivation based on self-determination theory: a cluster analysis approach. BMC Psychol. **3**, 1 (2015). https://doi.org/10.1186/s40359-015-0059-2

25. Lawson, P., Pearson, C.J., Crowson, A., Mayhorn, C.B.: Email phishing and signal detection: how persuasion principles and personality influence response patterns and accuracy. Appl. Ergon. **86**, 103084 (2020). https://doi.org/10.1016/j.apergo.2020.103084

26. Parsons, K., Butavicius, M., Delfabbro, P., Lillie, M.: Predicting susceptibility to social influence in phishing emails. Int. J. Hum. Comput. Stud. **128**, 17–26 (2019). https://doi.org/10.1016/j.ijhcs.2019.02.007

27. Brislin, R.W.: Back-translation for cross-cultural research. J. Cross Cult. Psychol. **1**, 185–216 (1970). https://doi.org/10.1177/135910457000100301

28. Hartigan, J.A., Wong, M.A.: Algorithm AS 136: a K-means clustering algorithm. Appl. Statistics **28**(1), 100 (1979). https://doi.org/10.2307/2346830

29. Charrad, M., Ghazzali, N., Boiteau, V., Niknafs, A.: NbClust: an R package for determining the relevant number of clusters in a data set. J. Stat. Soft. (2014). https://doi.org/10.18637/jss.v061.i06

30. Baddeley, M.: Copycats and Contrarians: Why We Follow Others and When We Don't. Yale University Press (2019). https://doi.org/10.12987/9780300231823

31. Shi, X., Li, F., Chumnumpan, P.: The use of product scarcity in marketing. Eur. J. Mark. **54**, 380–418 (2020). https://doi.org/10.1108/EJM-04-2018-0285

32. Mukherjee, A., Lee, S.Y.: Scarcity appeals in advertising: the moderating role of expectation of scarcity. J. Advert. **45**, 256–268 (2016)

33. Gabler, C.B., Myles Landers, V., Reynolds, K.E.: Purchase decision regret: negative consequences of the steadily increasing discount strategy. J. Bus. Res. **76**, 201–208 (2017). https://doi.org/10.1016/j.jbusres.2017.01.002

34. Alnunu, M., Amin, A., Abu-Rayya, H.M.: The susceptibility to persuasion strategies among arab muslims: the role of culture and acculturation. Front. Psychol. **12**, 574115 (2021). https://doi.org/10.3389/fpsyg.2021.574115

35. Muhanad, A., Abuelezz, I., Khan, K., Ali, R.: On how Cialdini's Persuasion principles influence individuals in the context of social engineering: a qualitative study. In: Barhamgi, M., Wang, H., Wang, X. (eds.) Web Information Systems Engineering – WISE 2024: 25th International Conference, Doha, Qatar, December 2–5, 2024, Proceedings, Part III, pp. 373–388. Springer Nature Singapore, Singapore (2025). https://doi.org/10.1007/978-981-96-0570-5_27

36. Mayer, R.C., Davis, J.H., Schoorman, F.D.: An integrative model of organizational trust. Acad. Manag. Rev. **20**, 709–734 (1995). https://doi.org/10.2307/258792

37. Aguirre-Rodriguez, A.: The effect of consumer Persuasion knowledge on scarcity Appeal Persuasiveness. J. Advertising **42**(4), 371–379 (2013). https://doi.org/10.1080/00913367.2013.803186

38. Tredinnick, L., Laybats, C.: Evaluating digital sources: trust, truth and lies. Bus. Inf. Rev. **34**, 172–175 (2017). https://doi.org/10.1177/0266382117743370

Behavior Change Games

AMRageddon V1: The Design and Usability Evaluation of a Digital Escape Room Game for Antimicrobial Resistance Education Through Persuasive Technology

Avis Anya Nowbuth[1]([✉]) [iD], Vikram Singh Parmar[2] [iD], Andrea Porras Elizo[2,3] [iD], Aslak Irgens Steinsbekk[4] [iD], and Ashis Jalote Parmar[2] [iD]

[1] Department of Neuromedicine and Movement Sciences, Norwegian University of Science and Technology, Torgarden, Norway
`anya.a.nowbuth@ntnu.no`
[2] Department of Design, Norwegian University of Science and Technology, Torgarden, Norway
`{vikram.s.parmar,ashis.jalote.parmar}@ntnu.no`
[3] Design Thinkers and Makers S.L., Madrid, Spain
[4] Department of Public Health and Nursing, Norwegian University of Science and Technology, Torgarden, Norway
`aslak.steinsbekk@ntnu.no`

Abstract. Antimicrobial resistance (AMR) is projected to cause 8.22 million deaths annually by 2050, impacting 12 of the 17 Sustainable Development Goals (SDGs) and posing a major global health threat. Despite this, medical students often feel unprepared and lack confidence in prescribing antimicrobials, highlighting the need for improved education on AMR and stewardship. This paper presents the design and pilot testing of persuasive technology in AMRageddon v1, a gamified learning tool developed for final-year medical students to address these gaps. The tool integrates social cues from persuasive technology, employing physical (interactive graphics), psychological (problem-solving puzzles), language (positive reinforcement), social dynamics (achievement recognition), and social roles (role-play as doctors solving clinical cases) cues. Usability and user experience were assessed using the System Usability Scale (SUS), the shortened User Experience Questionnaire (UEQ-S), and focus group discussions (FGDs) structured by Bowen's feasibility framework. Twenty-three final-year Norwegian medical students participated, yielding a high usability score (SUS: 78.75) and exceptional hedonic qualities, placing AMRageddon v1 among the top 10% of benchmarked tools. Qualitative findings highlighted strong acceptability, demand, and adaptability, with students emphasizing the game's relevance to clinical practice and global health. The interactive, case-based content was particularly engaging, and the integration of social cues from persuasive technology enhanced its perceived effectiveness. These results suggest AMRageddon v1 is a promising tool for AMR education, promoting confidence and preparedness among final-year medical students.

Keywords: Persuasive Technology · Antimicrobial Resistance · Medical Education · Digital Escape Room

K. T. Win et al. (Eds.): PERSUASIVE 2025, LNCS 15711, pp. 249–263, 2025.
https://doi.org/10.1007/978-3-031-94959-3_18

1 Introduction

Antimicrobial resistance (AMR) is forecasted to contribute to 8.22 million deaths annually by 2050, currently affecting 12 of the 17 sustainable development goals (SDGs) thereby representing a leading global health threat and emphasizing the urgent need for innovative interventions [23, 24]. Studies have shown that students feel unprepared and have low confidence in prescribing antimicrobials, and the need for education on AMR and stewardship [3, 13]. As future prescribers, medical and veterinary students play a key role in combating AMR by applying evidence-based practices in antimicrobial stewardship. In the context of AMR, terminology and abbreviations are criticised for being abstract, difficult to pronounce, lacking in memorability; and fails to evoke a sense of urgency or risk perception and can hinder understanding and necessary behavioural changes to combat AMR [18–20].

Educational interventions have shown improvements of self-reported knowledge, confidence and attitudes related to health [33, 39]. Persuasive games are interactive systems that are designed to change behaviour and attitudes through persuasive strategies, and are effective in promoting behavioural change [26]. Persuasive technology applies principles of behavioural psychology to motivate players toward specific learning outcomes or behaviour changes [6]. BJ Fogg's work highlights the unique ability of interactive systems, like games, to act as persuasive tools by mimicking social behaviours, providing feedback, and eliciting emotional responses [14, 15]. These characteristics position digital games as an effective channel to foster active learning – where students engage directly with content [21, 34] – over passive learning, where information is passively received [34]. Active learning has been characterized with student engagement and participation, and considered to be a better learning experience, deeper learning and improved retention of information [34]. Current gamification tools that exist to address AMR are (a) tailored for one sector only (human healthcare), (b) focus on one educational topic (microbiology or pharmacology), and (c) are specific for consultant physicians or infectious disease doctors [27].

Digital escape rooms (DER) are new approaches to medical education, where immersive, game-based experiences improve the learning process, by promoting active engagement, critical thinking and teamwork among students. By integrating medical scenarios into puzzles, students can apply theoretical knowledge to practical situations, thereby improving retention and understanding of complex medical concepts [28, 32]. Studies have demonstrated that such interactive methods can boost student motivation, collaboration skills, and confidence in clinical settings [28, 32]. While further research is needed to establish the long-term knowledge and memorability effects, current evidence supports DER as an optimal supplement to traditional lectures [2, 32].

When designing an intervention, specifically a digital educational intervention, usability is a key component that needs to be evaluated to determine the adoption and feasibility of the intervention [31, 41]. Usability testing is essential in product development; however, it is often overlooked, especially in the field of AMR education [27]. Effective usability testing allows the development of products that are intuitive and accessible even for users with varying levels of technical expertise, even more so where complex terminology can impede understanding and appropriate actions, essential for promoting accurate interpretation and application of AMR-related information. The International

Organization for Standardization (ISO) 9241–210 standards defined usability important to bridge the gap between technical content and user comprehension [16].

To address these various challenges, we developed a game to make the learning experience captivating. We present key AMR principles in a simplified and relatable manner and help students to internalize the consequences of misuse and the importance of proactive behaviours. We use persuasive strategies like storytelling, captivating visuals, and interactive problem solving to convey abstract concepts into tangible learning outcomes. In this paper, we present the design, usability evaluation of a persuasive DER game (AMRageddon v1) to promote knowledge among students about AMR across the One Health sectors. This study aims at usability evaluation of AMRageddon v1, a persuasive DER focused on educating final year medical students at Norwegian University of Science and Technology (NTNU) about AMR. The design of AMRageddon v1 integrates social cues from persuasive technology. This paper makes the following contributions: we illustrate that AMRageddon v1 is perceived effective and applicable in an educational context and has a foundation for further reiterations. By applying BJ Fogg's behaviour model and Bowen's feasibility framework, we provide a thorough evaluation of the usability, persuasiveness, and practicality of AMRageddon v1. This offers valuable insights for designing educational games that meet user needs and curricular demands. The study validates the role of a persuasive DER in education for teaching AMR. It also lays the groundwork for future research on scalable, adaptable, and interdisciplinary applications of educational games.

2   Methods

2.1   Design Phase: *BJ Foggs Social Cues Embedded in User Centred Approach*

The design of AMRageddon v1 is grounded in BJ Foggs Social Cues [15]. BJ Foggs social cues were selected as it builds on the principle that humans tend to respond to computers, interfaces, and other non-human entities as if they were social beings [14, 15], therefore allowing us to create a system that feels intuitive, relatable, and compelling, motivating behaviour change in ways that feel natural and engaging to the user [14]. It features interactive elements such as drag-and-drop medical tools, dynamic question-answer interfaces, multimedia content (images, videos, sound clips), and simulated patient charts. The platform allows for both synchronous (team-based) and asynchronous (individual) gameplay. We employed a user-centred design approach for designing user interactions specifically focusing on creating engaging interfaces and experiences between the end-users and digital systems. This approach aims to improve user satisfaction, makes the interfaces intuitive and enjoyable and incorporates the emotional and functional needs of the users [17, 38]. AMRageddon v1 incorporates elements such as role-playing, virtual collaboration, and teamwork which fosters active participation and peer learning. It also evokes emotive responses by incorporating storytelling using the "theme of Armageddon," representing a world where antibiotics are ineffective rendering minor infections deadly. Our game includes rewards and achievements and level progression which immerses players in the critical importance of antimicrobial stewardship. We used metaphors which emphasize the prescriber's responsibility, that test and reinforce key concepts memorably. Consistency across all the levels, rooms and game elements aligned with the theme, reducing cognitive burden and confusion, allowing players to focus on challenges rather than navigation. AMRageddon v1 enhances learnability by minimizing cognitive load through interactive graphics, clear visual cues, and straightforward instructions in accessible language [38]. Feedback mechanisms, such as emotional reinforcement, success celebrations, and reciprocal game responses thereby keeping players motivated and invested and allowing for a balance between learning and entertainment. In developing the game, the design team utilized Figma for (an open-source software) for prototyping, ensuring a visually engaging and user-centered interface. The architecture includes a sitemap that maps user navigation across the game's core modules, each designed to teach specific aspects of AMR tailored for medical, veterinary, and dental students worldwide.

2.2 Design Content: *Game Design Embedded in Interaction Design*

AMRageddon v1 was structured around two levels: background and a medical scenario that require students to solve puzzles, diagnose conditions, and make treatment decisions within a set time limit. AMRageddon v1's design leverages narrative-driven gameplay to immerse students in a simulated clinical environment, promoting problem-solving, critical thinking, and teamwork. Each puzzle or challenge represents a step toward solving a question to "escape the room" while reinforcing core AMR concepts. Puzzle elements were incorporated to challenge players with tasks such as interpreting lab results, identifying medical errors, diagnosing conditions, selecting appropriate treatments, and managing critical care situations. AMRageddon v1 draws from BJ Fogg's persuasive cues to maximize student engagement and reinforce learning outcomes. The game incorporates these five cues – physical, psychological, language, social dynamics and social roles – in a structured approach to influence behavior change and knowledge retention (Fig. 1). Each cue served a distinct purpose to create an immersive and persuasive learning experience for students, specifically in improving knowledge, attitudes and practices related to AMR.

Physical Cues. These included elements that create a sense of presence through visual design and interaction [15]. AMRageddon v1 used an *attractive design theme* (Fig. 1a) related to the consequences of the overuse and misuse of antibiotics: the theme of "Armageddon". This makes the game engaging and reinforces the urgency of AMR. Additionally, the name of the game was created for the same purpose. This approach uses Fogg's principle of attractiveness, making the experience enjoyable and memorable while drawing attention through the thematic connection (e.g., using "AMRageddon" name and visually to highlight the gravity of AMR).

Psychological Cues. This assume emotions and preferences to create a human-like, emotionally responsive systems [15]. We used *emotional language*, where empathic responses are displayed when players face challenges or successfully complete a puzzle. This enhances the sense of connection, and makes the system feel more supportive. Additionally, the puzzles in this prototype are *interpretation-based puzzles* (Fig. 1b.), where students must rely on and apply deeper understanding, instead of simple recall. This creates a system that is more credible and engages with students. AMRageddon v1 has a version of personalized feedback, minimally, where responses based on individual performance are offered, thus fostering a sense of understanding, and increasing motivation by supporting personalized learning.

a. Physical cue: b. Psychological: c. Social roles cue: d. Social dynamics:
urgency theme   interpretation   role-play   achievements

Fig. 1. Example screens from Design of AMRageddon v1 used to teach final-year medical students about AMR

Language Cues. These were incorporated to make the game seem more social and human-like through the language used [15]. Features such as *praise for success*, used positive languages after puzzle completion, boosting self-esteem and motivating players to continue. Friendly and consistent *offers for support*, through the "/clue" system helped ensure that players felt supported during difficult challenges, increasing engagement. The concept of turn-taking through *interactive dialogue* (Fig. 1c.), simulated natural conversation, fostering a cooperative interaction that kept players deeply involved in the game. Lastly, *authority in language*, presented by virtual doctors, was used to enhance trust and credibility, encouraging players to take guidance more seriously.

Social Dynamic Cues. This mirrors real-world behaviors such as cooperation, reciprocity, and peer influence [15]. *Reciprocity* was created by offering help or clues in return for continued efforts, making players feel obligated to progress further. AMRageddon v1 encouraged *teamwork* and fostered a sense of belonging and cooperation, which is related to the real-world clinical teamwork skills needed in practice. AMRageddon v1 was designed to remind players of their past choices – the *commitment and consistency* aspect of social dynamics, and principle vital in clinical decision-making. Lastly, upon completing a puzzle or level, *praise and recognition* (Fig. 1d.) through badges and certificates reinforced the social rewards and motivating players to continue the game.

Social Role Cues. This involves embedding recognizable human roles to guide behavior [15]. The game was designed to allow students to act as doctors in solving clinical cases (*role playing*) (Fig. 1c.), which deepened engagement by making decisions feel more meaningful and closely aligned with their future professional roles. *Tangible rewards* like certificates of completion, and achievement badges (Fig. 1d.) acknowledged competence and progression, thereby reinforcing players' professional identity, and encouraging continued participation.

3   Study Design

In order to evaluate the perceived persuasiveness and usability of AMRageddon v1, we conducted a game lecture using AMRageddon v1, and collected data using a Focus Group Discussion (FGD), and the validated System Usability Scale (SUS), the shortened User Experience Questionnaire (UEQ-S), Perceived Persuasiveness Scale (PPS), and post intervention.

3.1   Participants and Recruitment

(N = 23) final-year medical students participated in AMRageddon v1 lecture during their One Health elective, after which they were invited to complete the SUS and UEQ surveys. Study details were presented at the lecture, followed by written information via web announcements and emails. Interested students completed the surveys and registered for a FGD held five days later. A total of 23 final-year medical students participated, representing the target group, of which five additional students contributing to FGDs for deeper qualitative insights. The FGDs provided nuanced perspectives, complementing SUS and UEQ findings for a comprehensive evaluation of the AMRageddon v1 prototype. Students received an information sheet detailing study objectives, methods, and confidentiality, with informed consent obtained prior to participation. Direct communication and email announcements facilitated recruitment.

3.2   Testing Procedure and Data Collection

The game-lecture comprised of a non-mandatory pre-allocated timeslot within their lecture's week. One researcher was present in the room, with an additional three external supervisors to observe and provide support if needed. The game-lecture consisted of four steps: (1) a cognitive pre-test; (2) explanation of the game concept, rules and process; (3) 45 min of playing the digital escape room, and (4) invitation to complete the opinion surveys and interviews. All data were collected though Nettskjema post-lecture by sending one survey to the students using announcement feature on their web-based notice board and additional individual emails. User satisfaction and experience was evaluated using SUS and UEQ, namely attractiveness, clarity and stimulation.

3.3   Data Analysis

SUS, UEQ-S and PPS. Students completed a SUS survey post-intervention to evaluate usability, with scores ranging from 0 to 100 (scores above 68 indicating above-average usability [22, 40]. A sample size of 12–14 participants is typically recommended [40].

Additionally, the perceived persuasiveness scale (4-items) by Drozd et al. measured relevance, credibility, habitual change and influence of the game [12]. The UEQ-S assessed user experience across attractiveness, perspicuity, efficiency, and dependability using an eight-item on a seven-point scale [35–37]. We chose the UEQ-S for its ability to efficiently capture essential user experience dimensions without overwhelming participants, ensuring higher response rates. Its concise format encouraged higher response rates, with a recommended sample size of 16–20 participants [35, 36]. Scores were analyzed using the UEQ-S Data Analysis Tool, evaluating internal reliability and benchmarking results. Quantitative data from SUS and UEQ-S were analyzed descriptively, with mean scores, standard deviations, and SUS adjective-grade scales used for interpretation.

FGD. A semi-structured FGD, based on Bowen's framework [8], explored final-year medical students experiences and suggestions for AMRageddon v1. Students registered via a survey link, and sessions lasted 60 min, including consent and an overview. Discussions were audio-recorded, led by the primary researcher, observed by a supervisor, and supported by a note-taking assistant. Qualitative data were transcribed verbatim and analyzed using framework analysis to identify recurring themes. The FGD results are presented and structured according to areas of focus described by Bowen et al. [12].

4 Results

4.1 Participant Demographics

(N = 26) final-year medical students attended the game-lecture, with 18 completing the UEQ and SUS surveys. Five students, all female, aged 24–29, attended the FGD. Among survey respondents (n = 18), 83.3% (n = 15) were female, and all had attended the game-lecture. Regarding gaming habits, 61.1% (n = 11) reported playing digital games recreationally, mostly a few times a year (45.5%, n = 5), with fewer playing occasionally (27.3%, n = 3) or daily (9.1%, n = 1). Action/adventure and puzzle/logic games were the most popular genres (50% each), while educational/serious games and simulation/strategy were least favored (12.5%).

4.2 Quantitative Usability Assessment

SUS scores provided an overview of AMRageddon v1's usability, with an average score of 78.61, classified as "good" on the Bangor (2009) and grade "C" on Brooke (2013) scales [7, 9]. This score surpasses the benchmark of 68, indicating above-average usability [11]. Final-year medical students rated the system above average for positive aspects: learnability (3.33/5), confidence (3.06/5), ease of use (3.17/5), and moderately low for function integration (2.89/5), while moderate-low scores for the negative aspects: complexity (3.17/5), support needs (3.17/5), inconsistency (3.33/5), and cumbersomeness (3.35/5) suggest minimal usability issues (Fig. 2b). A lower score for game re-playability (M = 2.61) highlights areas for improvement. Overall, the system was intuitive and met user needs, but improvements could focus on integration and reducing perceived complexity. Persuasiveness was analyzed using a one-sample t-test on the perceived persuasiveness scale. The mean score (M = 3.72, SD = 0.46) was significantly above the neutral rating of 3 t (17) = 6.64, p < 0.001), indicating high persuasiveness (Fig. 2c). The UEQ-S analysis revealed pragmatic and hedonic quality scores. Pragmatic quality, reflecting usability (e.g., supportiveness, clarity), scored 1.50 (SD = 0.26, 95% CI = [1.39–1.62]), while hedonic quality, indicating excitement and innovation, scored higher at 2.33 (SD = 0.45, 95% CI = [2.13–2.54]) (Fig. 2d-2). The overall score was 1.92 (95% CI = [1.78–2.05]), favoring hedonic aspects (Fig. 2e). Compared to benchmarks from 468 studies [36, 37], AMRageddon v1 ranked above average for pragmatic quality and within the top 10% for hedonic quality and overall user experience. These results confirm the system's strong usability, engaging design, and innovative appeal.

4.3   Experience with Testing AMRageddon V1

Acceptability. Final-year medical students experience with the prototype was positive, finding it enjoyable and engaging compared to traditional lectures. One student shared, *"I was looking forward to doing something interactive."* Another stressed its appeal: *"I'm very tired of their regular lectures, so I think it's nice to have some variation."*

Demand. There was clear demand for gamified educational methods to increase engagement and attendance. One student observed, *"more people would come to the lectures if they were more like this, because fewer and fewer come during the semester."*

Practicality. Final-year medical students valued the game's active learning approach. *"With playing the game, you have to answer the questions to complete the game, and then you are more responsible for actually obtaining the knowledge,"* noted one. Another said, *"It made learning about AMR more interesting and fun."* Its relevance to clinical decision-making was also praised: *"It's nice to learn how to choose the right antibiotic in the right scenario because we don't focus that much on that in lectures."*

Integration. Students expressed enthusiasm for expanding the game to broader topics and education levels. Its relevance to global health issues and the One Health framework was noted: *"The part about humans, animals, and the use of antibiotics for veterinarians and in cattle industries was something we haven't thought that much about."*

Impact. Students stressed the importance of responsible prescribing. *"We're going to be medical doctors for decades, and we will probably come to a point where what we have learned in medical school doesn't work anymore."* The game's introduction of the One Health perspective was considered enlightening: *"That was a very good part because that's things we haven't been thinking that much about."* (Table 1)

5   Discussion

This study evaluated the persuasiveness, usability, and feasibility of AMRageddon v1, a gamified tool designed to teach final-year medical students about AMR, including its background and clinical application. The results demonstrate that AMRageddon v1 is user-friendly and engaging, with a "good" SUS score (78.75) and "excellent" hedonic quality ratings, confirming its effective design and appeal. These findings suggest that, with refinement, the game could be a valuable addition to the medical curriculum, enhancing student engagement and AMR knowledge.

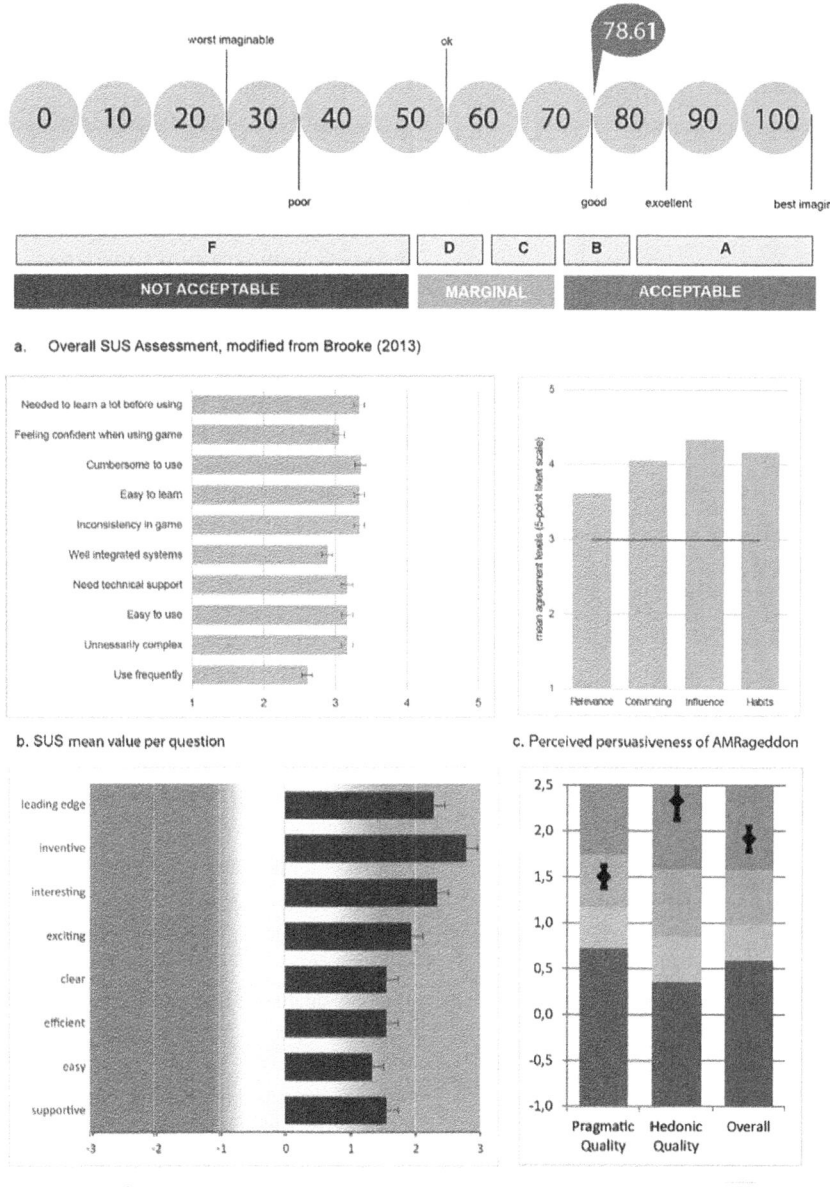

Fig. 2. AMRageddon v1 field testing results from SUS, PP scale and UEQ

5.1 Persuasiveness of AMRageddon V1

The visual appeal and ease of navigation in AMRageddon v1 were highly rated, with "excellent" hedonic quality scores on the UEQ-S, supporting research that visually engaging interfaces boost user engagement [36]. The intellectually stimulating clinical

Table 1. Claimed effect of the DER and evidence in our results

Claimed Effect	Evidence in Results
Above-average usability	SUS score: 78.61 ("good" usability, above benchmark of 68)
Excellent hedonic quality and engaging user experience	In the top 10% of benchmarked tools, highlighting its engaging and innovative design
	Pragmatic quality (UEQS): 1.50/3 (above average for usability)
	Hedonic quality (UEQS): 2.33/3 (top 10% for excitement/innovation)
Effective use of persuasive technology	Mean persuasiveness score (M = 3.72) above neutral t (17) = 6.64, p < 0.001
	FGDs highlighted roleplaying, badges, and teamwork as key motivators
Intuitive design with moderate usability challenges	Positive usability scores: Learnability (3.33/5), confidence (3.06/5), ease of use (3.17/5)
	Negative usability scores: Complexity (3.17/5), support needs (3.17/5), inconsistency (3.33/5), cumbersomeness (3.35/5)
	Function integration scored moderately low (2.89/5)
Improved clinical relevance and decision-making	Students praised real world scenarios (e.g., "*learn how to choose the right antibiotic in the right scenario*")
	One Health was noted as enlightening in FGDs
Active learning and critical thinking	Students reported active responsibility (e.g., "*you have to answer questions to complete the game*")
Motivation through gamification	Hedonic quality (UEQS) ranked "excellent," driven by rewards, storytelling, and immersive design
	Students described the game as "fun," "interactive," and preferable to lectures
Behavior changes potential (responsible prescribing)	FGDs emphasized long-term consequences (e.g., "*what we learned won't work anymore*")
	Feedback on prescribing decisions and global health implications resonated with students
Demand for gamified education	Students stated, "*more people would come to lectures if they were like this.*"

(continued)

Table 1. (*continued*)

Claimed Effect	Evidence in Results
Re-playability and scalability	Re-playability scored lower (M = 2.61), indicating room for improvement
	Students suggested expanding content (e.g., viral/fungal resistance, organ specific diseases)
	Results validated feasibility for curricular integration

case scenario promoted active learning, aligning with Fogg's (2009) persuasive technology concept that engagement and motivation drive user behavior [14]. Similar strategies in SmileApp [30] and Drop Dash [6] have effectively improved motivation and positive habits. The game's progressive difficulty balanced challenge and skill, fostering user flow, consistent with findings by Agyei et al. on incremental challenges sustaining motivation [4]. Social dynamic cues, such as peer collaboration and role-play, created accountability and professional competence, echoing Fogg's (2003) framework [15]. These methods align with Andreasen et al.'s work on VR-based collaborative learning enhancing engagement [5] and Ndulue and Orji's findings on group-based interactions improving persuasive games' impact [25]. Role-playing simulated professional scenarios, fostering behavioral alignment with professional norms [5]. AMRageddon v1 had high ratings for influence prescribing behaviors (4.0) and "make [me] consider my prescribing habits" (4.17) on the perceived persuasiveness scale indicating students found the content trustworthy and applicable [12, 41]. These results validate AMRageddon v1 as a potential effective, persuasive educational tool.

5.2 Behavior Change Potential

AMRageddon v1 demonstrated its ability to promote behavior change by encouraging critical thinking about prescribing practices and the global implications of AMR. Final-year medical students valued its interactive learning approach, with one stating, "*It reinforced the importance of thinking about resistance when prescribing.*" This aligns with de Freitas and Liarokapis (2011), who found that game-based learning enhances knowledge through realistic scenarios that foster critical thinking [10, 11]. Another student emphasized long-term consequences of antibiotic misuse "*We will probably come to a point where what we have learned in medical school doesn't work anymore.*" The game's real-world scenarios and decision-making elements align with Oinas-Kukkonen and Harjumaa's Persuasive Systems Design model, using immediate feedback to reinforce responsible prescribing behaviors and heighten awareness of AMR as a global health issue [29]. These elements reflect Fogg's persuasive design framework, which emphasizes motivation through positive reinforcement and interactivity [14].

5.3 Implications for Design

The findings from our study offer insights for designing persuasive educational tools in healthcare contexts. This study provides valuable insights for designing persuasive educational tools in healthcare, specifically for final-year medical students. Prioritizing usability is essential to create a seamless and engaging learning experience. User-centered design principles, such as immediate, actionable feedback and intuitive navigation, are critical to maintaining user engagement and enhancing effectiveness [4, 14, 15]. The integration of gamified elements-such as rewards, challenges, and real-world scenarios-proved particularly effective in motivating users and fostering knowledge retention. These features not only enhance the learning process but also align with the principles of persuasive technology, which emphasize interactivity, personalization, and accessibility [15, 20, 21]. For example, real-world scenarios that reflect clinical challenges promote active learning and critical thinking, equipping learners with practical skills for real-life applications.

5.4 Limitations, Strengths and Future Work

Our study highlights the importance of integrating persuasive systems to enhance the usability and engagement of gamified learning tools. Since students experienced technical issues that hindered their gameplay and their overall learning experience, resolving these technical problems is vital before implementing the game in a wider educational setting. The small screen limited group interaction, hindering the potential benefits of collaborative learning. A key limitation of this study is the potential for self-selection bias, as participation was voluntary. This may have led to an overrepresentation of individuals with a particular interest in gamified learning, limiting the generalizability of the findings. Future recommendation for AMRageddon v1 is to develop a version of the game that can be played on larger screens or individual laptops to facilitate better communication and when students select the "multiplayer" version. Students expressed a desire for more information on viral and fungal resistance, and in alignment with the literature, the design team can consider broadening the game to include a wider range of AMR topics thereby ensuring comprehensive coverage. Studies have shown that aligning game content with learners' professional needs increases perceived value and participation rates [9, 40]. Future iterations to maximize the impact of AMRageddon include optimizing the interface for group collaboration and resolving technical glitches to improve the user experience and make the game more accessible. Additionally, the absence of a control group in the initial evaluation restricts our ability to fully validate the observed effects. To address this, we conducted a follow-up pilot study incorporating a control group in both medical and veterinary settings. We also plan to expand the content to include additional AMR-related medical topics, such as how AMR affects organ-specific diseases, as suggested by the final-year medical students.

6 Conclusion

AMRageddon v1 prototype employs persuasive technology principles and demonstrates the successful application of these principles in its design to engage users, improve knowledge, and encourage behavior change related to AMR. By integrating interactivity, real-world scenarios, and the One Health perspective, AMRageddon v1 created an impactful learning experience that final-year medical students found both enjoyable and educational. This approach effectively showcases how persuasive technology can provide valuable insights into user experiences, usability, and overall satisfaction further highlighting the importance in design when developing educational or dissemination tools. While technical issues limited its full potential, the game's strengths highlight its promise as a scalable and adaptable tool for medical education, offering an idea that can be applied to similar interventions.

References

1. Abt, C.C.: Serious Games. University Press of America (1987)
2. Acebo-Seguín, C., et al.: The effectiveness of the Escape Room as an educational methodology in the Infarction Code. Enfermeria Clinica (2024). https://doi.org/10.1016/j.enfcli.2024.02.003
3. Adekanye, U.O., et al.: Knowledge, attitudes and practices of veterinarians towards antimicrobial resistance and stewardship in Nigeria. Antibiotics 9(8), 453 (2020)
4. Agyei, E.E.Y.F., et al.: Evaluating the persuasive potential from software design specifications. In: Baghaei, N., et al. (eds.) Persuasive Technology: 19th International Conference, PERSUASIVE 2024, Wollongong, NSW, Australia, April 10–12, 2024, Proceedings, pp. 15–25. Springer Nature Switzerland, Cham (2024). https://doi.org/10.1007/978-3-031-58226-4_2
5. Andreasen, E.M., et al.: Usability Evaluation of the Preoperative ISBAR (Identification, Situation, Background, Assessment, and Recommendation) Desktop Virtual Reality Application: Qualitative Observational Study. JMIR Hum. Factors 9(4), e40400 (2022). https://doi.org/10.2196/40400
6. Anukem, S., et al.: DROP DASH: A Persuasive Mobile Game to Promote Healthy Hydration Choices Using Machine Learning. In: Baghaei, N., et al. (eds.) Persuasive Technology: 19th International Conference, PERSUASIVE 2024, Wollongong, NSW, Australia, April 10–12, 2024, Proceedings, pp. 54–64. Springer Nature Switzerland, Cham (2024). https://doi.org/10.1007/978-3-031-58226-4_5
7. Bangor, A., et al.: Determining what individual SUS scores mean: adding an adjective rating scale. J. Usability Stud. 4(3), 114–123 (2009)
8. Bowen, D.J., et al.: How we design feasibility studies. Am. J. Prev. Med. 36(5), 452–457 (2009). https://doi.org/10.1016/j.amepre.2009.02.002
9. Brooke, J.: SUS: a retrospective. J. Usability Stud. 8, 29–40 (2013)
10. de Freitas, S., Liarokapis, F.: Serious games: a new paradigm for education? In: Ma, M., et al. (eds.) Serious Games and Edutainment Applications, pp. 9–23. Springer London, London (2011). https://doi.org/10.1007/978-1-4471-2161-9_2
11. De Freitas, S.I.: Using games and simulations for supporting learning. Learn. Media Technol. 31(4), 343–358 (2006). https://doi.org/10.1080/17439880601021967
12. Drozd, F., et al.: Exploring perceived persuasiveness of a behavior change support system: a structural model. In: Bang, M., Ragnemalm, E.L. (eds.) Persuasive Technology. Design for Health and Safety, pp. 157–168. Springer Berlin Heidelberg, Berlin, Heidelberg (2012). https://doi.org/10.1007/978-3-642-31037-9_14

13. Dyar, O.J., et al.: European medical students: a first multicentre study of knowledge, attitudes and perceptions of antibiotic prescribing and antibiotic resistance. J. Antimicrob. Chemother. **69**(3), 842–846 (2014). https://doi.org/10.1093/jac/dkt440

14. Fogg, B.: A behavior model for persuasive design. In: Proceedings of the 4th International Conference on Persuasive Technology, pp. 1–7 Association for Computing Machinery, New York, NY, USA (2009). https://doi.org/10.1145/1541948.1541999

15. Fogg, B.J.: Chapter 5 – Computers as persuasive social actors. In: Fogg, B.J. (ed.) Persuasive Technology, pp. 89–120. Morgan Kaufmann, San Francisco (2003). https://doi.org/10.1016/B978-155860643-2/50007-X

16. ISO, I.: 9241-210: 2019 Ergonomics of human-system interaction. Part 210: Human-centred design for interactive systems (2019)

17. Jalote-Parmar, A., et al.: Development of an innovative user centered design driven mHealth app for female athletes- "The Coral App." In: IEEE International Conference on Systems, Man, and Cybernetics (SMC). IEEE International Conference on Systems, Man, and Cybernetics (SMC), Sarawak, Malaysia (2024)

18. Karvanen, M., Cars, O.: The language of antimicrobial and antibiotic resistance is blocking global collective action. Infect. Dis. **56**(6), 487–495 (2024). https://doi.org/10.1080/23744235.2024.2332455

19. Krockow, E.M., et al.: Existing terminology related to antimicrobial resistance fails to evoke risk perceptions and be remembered. Commun. Med. **3**(1), 1–11 (2023). https://doi.org/10.1038/s43856-023-00379-6

20. Krockow, E.M.: Nomen est omen: why we need to rename 'antimicrobial resistance.' JAC-Antimicrob. Resist. **2**(3), dlaa067 (2020). https://doi.org/10.1093/jacamr/dlaa067

21. Kruschke, J.K.: Bayesian approaches to associative learning: from passive to active learning. Learn. Behav. **36**(3), 210–226 (2008). https://doi.org/10.3758/LB.36.3.210

22. Lewis, J.R.: The system usability scale: past, present, and future. Int. J. Hum.-Comput. Interact. **34**(7), 577–590 (2018). https://doi.org/10.1080/10447318.2018.1455307

23. Mantegazza, L., et al.: Circular Health: exploiting the SDG roadmap to fight AMR. Front. Cell. Infect. Microbiol. (2023). https://doi.org/10.3389/fcimb.2023.1185673

24. Naghavi, M., et al.: Global burden of bacterial antimicrobial resistance 1990–2021: a systematic analysis with forecasts to 2050. The Lancet (2024). https://doi.org/10.1016/S0140-6736(24)01867-1

25. Ndulue, C., Orji, R.: Exploring the influence of game framing and gamer types on the effectiveness of persuasive games. In: Baghaei, N., Ali, R., Win, K., Oyibo, K. (eds.) Persuasive Technology: 19th International Conference, PERSUASIVE 2024, Wollongong, NSW, Australia, April 10–12, 2024, Proceedings, pp. 207–221. Springer Nature Switzerland, Cham (2024). https://doi.org/10.1007/978-3-031-58226-4_16

26. Ndulue, C., Orji, R.: Games for change—a comparative systematic review of persuasive strategies in games for behavior change. IEEE Trans. Games. **15**(2), 121–133 (2023). https://doi.org/10.1109/TG.2022.3159090

27. Nowbuth, A.A., et al.: Gamification as an educational tool to address antimicrobial resistance: a systematic review. JAC-Antimicrob. Resist. (2023). https://doi.org/10.1093/jacamr/dlad130

28. Nowbuth, A.A., Parmar, V.S.: Escaping the ordinary: a review of escape rooms in medical and veterinary education. BMC Med. Educ. **24**(1), 1506 (2024). https://doi.org/10.1186/s12909-024-06512-w

29. Oinas-Kukkonen, H., Harjumaa, M.: Persuasive systems design: key issues, process model, and system features. Commun. Assoc. Inform. Syst. (2009). https://doi.org/10.17705/1CAIS.02428

30. Orji, J., et al.: SmileApp: the design and evaluation of an mhealth app for stress reduction through artificial intelligence and persuasive technology. In: Baghaei, N., Ali, R., Win, K.,

Oyibo, K. (eds.) Persuasive Technology: 19th International Conference, PERSUASIVE 2024, Wollongong, NSW, Australia, April 10–12, 2024, Proceedings, pp. 237–251. Springer Nature Switzerland, Cham (2024). https://doi.org/10.1007/978-3-031-58226-4_18

31. Park, G.E., et al.: Mobile application for digital health coaching in the self-management of older adults with multiple chronic conditions: a development and usability study. Healthc Inform Res. **30**(4), 344–354 (2024). https://doi.org/10.4258/hir.2024.30.4.344

32. Park, G.L., et al.: Fostering competencies: a scoping review of escape rooms in medical education. Med. Sci. Educ. (2025). https://doi.org/10.1007/s40670-024-02270-y

33. Parmar, V., Keyson, D., deBont, C.: Persuasive technology for shaping social beliefs of rural women in India: an approach based on the theory of planned behaviour. In: Oinas-Kukkonen, H., et al. (eds.) Persuasive Technology, pp. 104–115. Springer Berlin Heidelberg, Berlin, Heidelberg (2008). https://doi.org/10.1007/978-3-540-68504-3_10

34. Qablan, A.: Active learning: strategies for engaging students and enhancing learning. In: Abdallah, A.K., et al. (eds.) Cutting-Edge Innovations in Teaching, Leadership, Technology, and Assessment:, pp. 31–41. IGI Global (2024). https://doi.org/10.4018/979-8-3693-0880-6.ch003

35. Schrepp, M., et al.: A comparison of SUS, UMUX-LITE, and UEQ-S. J. User Experience **18**, 2 (2023)

36. Schrepp, M., et al.: Applying the user experience questionnaire (UEQ) in different evaluation scenarios. In: Marcus, A. (ed.) Design, User Experience, and Usability. Theories, Methods, and Tools for Designing the User Experience: Third International Conference, DUXU 2014, Held as Part of HCI International 2014, Heraklion, Crete, Greece, June 22-27, 2014, Proceedings, Part I, pp. 383–392. Springer International Publishing, Cham (2014). https://doi.org/10.1007/978-3-319-07668-3_37

37. Schrepp, M., et al.: Design and evaluation of a short version of the user experience questionnaire (UEQ-S). Int. J. Interact. Multimed. Artific. Intell. **4**(6), 103 (2017). https://doi.org/10.9781/ijimai.2017.09.001

38. Siyu, F., et al.: The application of interaction design to human emotion and pleasure based on interactive concepts. In: Affective and Pleasurable Design. AHFE Open Acces (2024). https://doi.org/10.54941/ahfe1004685

39. Tirupakuzhi Vijayaraghavan, B.K., et al.: Improving antimicrobial resistance awareness among medical students in india: the sensitization of medical students on antimicrobial resistance (SOS-AMR) study. J. Med. Educ. Curricular Dev. (2024). https://doi.org/10.1177/23821205241239842

40. Tullis, T., Stetson, J.: A Comparison of Questionnaires for Assessing Website Usability (2006)

41. Vlachogianni, P., Tselios, N.: Perceived usability evaluation of educational technology using the System Usability Scale (SUS): a systematic review. J. Res. Technol. Educ. **54**(3), 392–409 (2022). https://doi.org/10.1080/15391523.2020.1867938

PetBuddy: An Examination of Augmented Reality Mobile Health Game for Promoting Physical Activity

Priyal Srivastava⬤, Gerry Chan$^{(\boxtimes)}$⬤, Oladapo Oyebode⬤, and Rita Orji⬤

Faculty of Computer Science, Dalhousie University, Halifax, NS, Canada
gerry.chan@dal.ca

Abstract. Mobile games have the potential to increase physical activity (PA). However, not all games can capture and sustain interest in PA, as it is challenging to maintain user engagement once the initial novelty diminishes. This research explores how augmented reality (AR) and idle game design, combined with persuasive strategies, can reduce sedentary behavior. We designed, developed and evaluated *PetBuddy*, a mobile health game aimed at promoting PA. Sixty-five young adults (between 18–35 years old) played the game for 10 days and completed a questionnaire about their experience. This is followed by an interview of 17 participants. Results revealed significant increases in PA with users meeting the World Health Organization's recommended activity levels and adopting healthier behavioral changes. Participants reported that the persuasive strategies implemented as game features (particularly competition) and the game experience motivated them to participate in PA. The findings from this research provide a deeper understanding of how mobile games can be designed to encourage PA.

Keywords: Augmented Reality · Exercise Games · Fitness Games · Gamification · Mobile Health (mHealth) · Persuasive Technology · Physical Activity

1 Introduction

Physical inactivity is one of the leading causes of global mortality, contributing to chronic conditions such as heart disease, diabetes, and cancer [1]. Furthermore, a significant portion of the global population fails to meet recommended physical activity (PA) guidelines [2], leading to various health risks. Research shows that participation in regular PA is essential for reducing these risks and promoting longevity [3]. However, many individuals find traditional forms of exercise unappealing, which limits their motivation to engage in PA. Some common complaints associated with PA include factors such as lack of social support, perceived feelings of exhaustion, and inconvenience of environmental conditions [4].

Playing active video games, such as Ring Fit Adventure (Nintendo Co, Ltd.), or mobile augmented reality (AR) games such as Pokémon Go [5], have been shown to increase PA short-term and, in contrast to most existing interventions and mobile health (mHealth) apps, can potentially reach inactive populations [6]. Moreover, digital devices such as smartwatches and fitness trackers encourage PA by monitoring activity levels and promoting good health habits [7, 8]. Due to the rising popularity of fitness trackers, step-based games (e.g., Pikmin Bloom [9]) are also gaining much traction because of their convenience and ability to encourage PA [10–12]. Games that encourage PA are commonly referred to as "exergames" [13]. Research shows that exergames can make exercise more enjoyable, especially for those who are reluctant to engage in traditional forms of exercise [14, 15]. Yet, not all exergames can capture and sustain interest in PA, as it is challenging to maintain user engagement once the initial novelty diminishes [11, 16]. Therefore, designing games that are both fun and motivating is crucial for sustaining participation in PA.

Current reviews on gamification apps used in mHealth to increase PA levels emphasizes the necessity of optimizing the implementation of specific game mechanics and relevant theoretical frameworks [17]. As such, this research explores the potential of a mobile intervention that incorporates game experiences and gamification elements, specifically targeting walking. We present the design, development, and evaluation of "PetBuddy" – a mobile exergame that incorporates Augmented Reality (AR), emotional influence, and idle game (designs that support long absences from the game [18]) to promote PA. AR technology can enhance the gaming experience by integrating virtual elements into the real world, making the experience of PA more interactive and engaging. Additionally, emotional engagement is incorporated to further motivate users and sustain their interest and idle game design is incorporated to prevent over exhaustion. Additionally, the Persuasive Systems Design (PSD) model, a conceptual framework for developing and evaluating persuasive behavior change technologies [19], is applied to further motivate positive changes in PA. The PSD model suggests that persuasive design features, such as personalization, feedback, reminders, and rewards, can positively influence user behavior by encouraging desired actions.

This study seeks to answer the research question: *"How effective are the persuasive strategies implemented PetBuddy for promoting PA?"* To answer the question, we designed, developed and evaluated an AR-driven mobile health game to promote PA through walking. Employing a mixed-methods approach, we conducted an in-the-wild evaluation with 65 participants that played the game for 10 days and completed a questionnaire about their experience. Quantitative results showed that the game is persuasive and a combination of AR features along with competitive elements are effective at increasing PA levels. Qualitative results showed that daily reminders and engagement with the app reinforced participation in PA, suggesting a positive behavior change.

We contribute to ongoing efforts in designing virtual pets and artificial companionship for healthcare [20, 21], as well as developing games that encourage PA [22, 23]. Our work offers three main contributions to the field of persuasive technology and mobile game design. First, we show that the *PetBuddy* app can increase moderate to vigorous PA, particularly for those who do not meet the World Health Organization (WHO)'s recommended level of 600 metabolic equivalent of task (MET) – a way to measure the intensity of physical activity by estimating how much oxygen the body uses [24]. Second, a user study shows that the combination of idle game design, AR and persuasive strategies is effective at convincing users to engage in PA. Third, the research offers a new approach to the design of mobile health games and exercises games in general. Based on our findings we offer valuable insights into future research and practical applications in developing mobile games that encourage PA, particularly those that apply AR and a mobile, step-based design.

2 Background and Related Work

2.1 Augmented Reality and Physical Activity

Recent years have witnessed the emergence of AR, technology that combines virtual reality with reality [25], where virtual 3D objects are seamlessly integrated into real-time 3D environments [26]. Presently, AR finds applications primarily in health-related fields, such as managing gait issues in older adults or within medical and surgical practices [27]. This technology holds promise for promoting and engaging healthy adults in PA through gamification [28]. AR applications give users the opportunity to see the real world with added digital elements, making it more exciting and interactive [27].

In one study, Farič et al. [29] investigated people's motivation and experience using a narrative-based AR exergame app called Zombies, Run! (ZR) for PA. The app immerses users in a post-apocalyptic world where running helps them collect supplies and build a base. Key findings include that ZR's gamification and storyline effectively motivated longer and more consistent exercise sessions. The study highlights that AR apps with engaging narratives can enhance PA by changing perceptions and fostering long-term healthy habits. In a different study, Odenigbo et al. [30] created an app called "The Journey" that uses AR to encourage PA in young adults by letting them explore touristic sites and earn virtual assets. Users can explore virtually or in person, track their steps, and unlock rewards by meeting goals. With daily targets based on activity levels and the implementation of a leaderboard to encourage competition, the app effectively motivates increased PA both indoors and outdoors.

In general, AR technology is increasingly employed in health-related fields to encourage PA through immersive and enjoyable experiences. Despite global declines in PA influenced by digital technology, integrating AR into exergaming and health interventions shows promise in promoting PA.

2.2 Idle Game Design

Idle games, or incremental games, are a genre where gameplay runs mostly autonomously with minimal player input [31]. These games typically involve accumulating points through both idle and active actions, with upgrades enhancing point gains [32]. This genre, which began in the early 2000s, has gained popularity due to its accessibility and appeal to multitasking and efficient time use [33].

A study conducted by Alharthi et al. [34] analyzed 66 idle games and 10 non-idle games to examine their mechanics, rewards, and interactivity. The research emphasizes how idle games enable progress with minimal engagement, challenging traditional gameplay norms. It also explores cognitive offloading and ludic efficiency in game design. In another study, Villareale et al. [18] investigated the potential of idle games for promoting PA and behavioral change. By surveying 11 popular idle games, they identified gameplay loops and design patterns that could enhance social exergames. Key design considerations include timed actions and player-driven auto-play, which could improve engagement and motivation.

Overall, idle games have become significant in gaming, offering opportunities for promoting consistent engagement and behavioral change through their unique gameplay structure.

2.3 Applying Persuasive Strategies in Games

Persuasive strategies are methods used in designing persuasive technologies (PTs) to encourage positive behaviors and attitudes [35]. Socially oriented strategies like competition, comparison, and cooperation are widely employed in persuasive and gamified systems due to their effectiveness in leveraging social dynamics to drive behavior change. For example, Orji [36] studied these socially-oriented strategies to assess their effectiveness in promoting health behaviors, and reported that socially-oriented strategies are perceived as persuasive with the social comparison strategy being the most persuasive. It was also reported that one strength of competition is that it makes one committed and gives a sense of accomplishment.

In a different study, Ndulue and Orji [39] conducted a systematic review of persuasive games and reported that the reward strategy was the most common, especially in promoting PA, with self-monitoring and rehearsal also prevalent. In one more study, Chan et al. [37] examined how different player traits are associated with interest in social features of an exercise game for improving player experience through better player matching using common and complementary characteristics. The researchers reported that persuasive strategies such as competition and rewards (earning points) are particularly appealing for those who score high on achiever and player-oriented traits, while strategies such as cooperation and authority are preferable for those who score high on philanthropist and socializer-oriented traits. Their study, however, remained at a conceptual level, utilizing storyboards as the research method.

Overall, persuasive strategies are crucial for designing effective games that motivate PA. The use of diverse strategies, including competition and rewards, demonstrate the effectiveness of these approaches in encouraging positive behavior change, particularly in promoting PA.

3 PetBuddy App Design and Development

3.1 System Design

We developed a mobile app to promote PA and integrate AR features, focusing on both frontend and backend technologies. For frontend development, we used Flutter [38], an open-source user interface (UI) toolkit by Google, chosen for its cross-platform capabilities and ability to create smooth, engaging user interfaces for Android devices. The app accurately tracks step counts using the pedometer Flutter package which connects with the device's sensors. For AR experiences, we implemented the ARCore Flutter package enabling interactive 3D models that respond to real-world surroundings. The backend was developed with REST APIs in Java, with MySQL as the database management system, hosted on an AWS EC2 instance for scalability. This setup efficiently stores and retrieves data such as user profiles and step counts. Overall, the app was carefully designed to provide a robust, engaging experience that encourages PA, specifically tailored for Android users.

3.2   User Interface Design and Persuasive Strategies as Game Features

The development of PetBuddy employed a user-centered design approach [39], by first sketching initial wireframes (Fig. 1) to refining our ideas and creating a medium-fidelity interactive prototype to identify potential issues and gather feedback, before moving forward onto the development of a fully functional app (Fig. 2). During the initial wireframe and prototyping stages, users were asked to interact with the prototype and provide insights on usability, ease of navigation, and engagement. We also observed user behaviors and took note of any challenges they faced while using the prototype, such as difficulty understanding certain features or confusion around the icons and AR experience. The feedback we received for improving the app included simplifying the user interface and enhancing the visual elements. Participants also suggested adding visual cues and feedback mechanisms, such as progress indicators, and refining the overall interaction flow. All these recommendations were considered and incorporated into the final development of the fully functional app.

The design was focused on offering an engaging exergame experience that promotes PA through walking. The design process centered around three core objectives: enhancing user motivation, leveraging immersive game experiences with AR, and integrating emotional engagement with idle game mechanics to prevent over exhaustion. Inspired by the 'Tamagotchi effect' (an emotional attachment to machines, robots or even software [40]), and drawing on Intrinsic Motivation Theory, which suggests that people are more likely to sustain behaviors they find inherently enjoyable [41], and the PSD model [19], we aimed to make walking both fun and rewarding. *PetBuddy* taps into eliciting feelings of intrinsic motivation [42] by transforming a routine activity into a rewarding experience, promoting PA adherence. A dog was specifically chosen as the virtual pet because it aligns with the physical activity theme, as research shows that dog owners tend to be more physically active than non-dog owners [43]. Among other motivational theories and models (e.g., ARCS model [44]), the PSD model was selected for this research because it provides a structured framework for incorporating persuasive design features to encourage specific user behaviors—in this case, increasing PA through a mobile game.

Upon authentication, users are taken to the home screen, featuring a dog avatar that shows either sadness or happiness. The dog starts off sad, indicating hunger, and users can make it happy by walking and collecting food items. Once the dog is fed, it becomes happy. The happy/sad dog face aligns with the principle of **normative influence** (provide means for gathering together people who have the same goal and make them feel norms [19]) by visually reinforcing social norms. When users see a happy dog face after meeting their step goals, it provides social validation and positive reinforcement. In contrast, a sad dog face signals a lack of progress or failure to meet the step goal, motivating users to improve their actions to avoid this negative feedback. The happy stage which starts

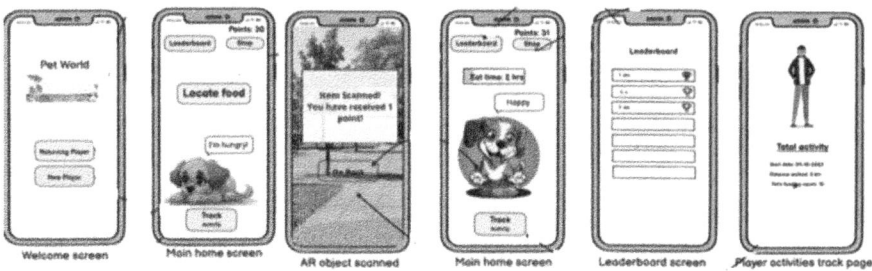

Fig. 1. Wireframes at the initial stages of creating PetBuddy.

when the dog is fed lasts for 2.5 h allows users to take breaks. This idle game mechanic promotes healthy usage habits, encouraging long-term engagement without fostering addiction. To make the dog happy, users must walk 500 steps. This is tracked (Fig. 2a) by the pedometer feature of the mobile phone allowing the user to **monitor** (allow people to track their own behaviors, providing information on both past and current states [45]) their progress and make necessary adjustments to achieve their goals. After collecting the food item, users are **rewarded** (offer virtual rewards to users for performing the target behavior [45]) in the form of points (Fig. 2b) and encouraged to walk more. As shown in Fig. 2c, the app limits food box collection to three times before disabling the "start walking" button. This is done to prevent overexertion and the negative effects of excessive walking [46], using an idle game mechanic [18].

Once users achieve the 500-step goal, they can collect a food box through an AR experience (Fig. 2d), visible in their real-world environment using the AR Flutter plugin. Successfully collecting and feeding the food box to the dog earns users 50 points, which can be spent on in-app accessories like a bowl, toy, clothes, or a house in the Shop (Fig. 2e) to **customize** (allows users to adapt a system's contents and functionalities to their needs and choices [45]) the dog avatar. The leaderboard screen (Fig. 2f) displays the top 10 performers to inspire and motivate others, fostering a sense of **social comparison** (provide means for comparing performance with performance of other users [19]) and **competition** (provide a means for competing with others [19]) and encouraging continued participation and fitness commitment. It is important to note that competition only appeals to competitive individuals. Research shows that while collaborative users may perform better in a competitive environment, they generally dislike it, and although may continue playing to finish the game, are unlikely to engage with such games again [47].

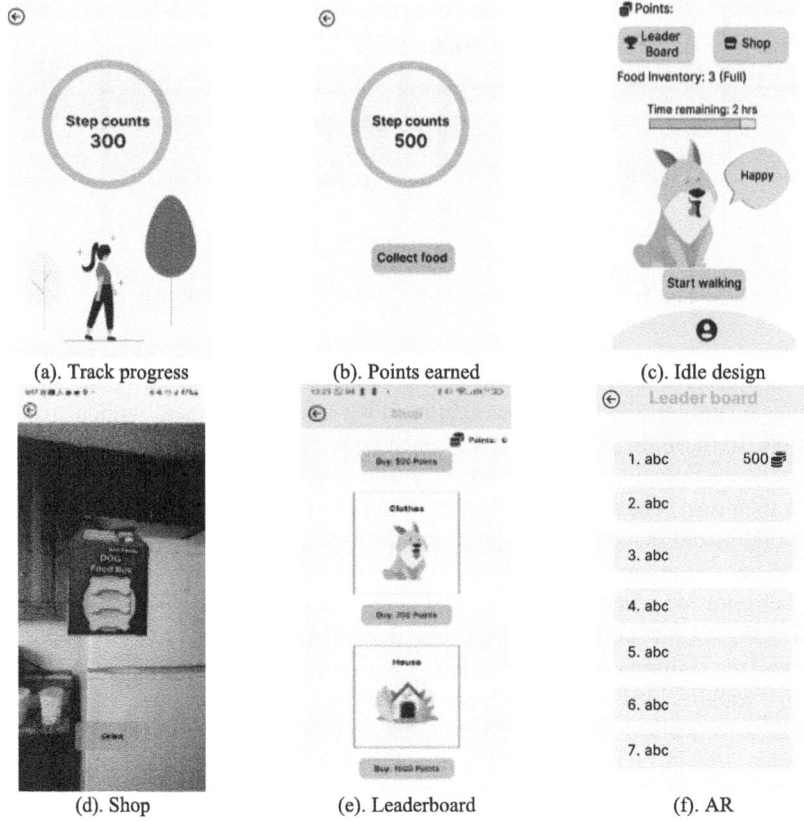

(a). Track progress   (b). Points earned   (c). Idle design

(d). Shop   (e). Leaderboard   (f). AR

Fig. 2. PetBuddy UI and implementation of persuasive strategies and AR experience.

4 User Study Design

To evaluate the effectiveness of *PetBuddy*, for promoting PA, we used a mixed-methods user study approach. Both quantitative and qualitative data were collected for analysis. The evaluation consisted of four steps: (1) complete a pre-study questionnaire, (2) use of the app for 10 days, (3) complete a post-study questionnaire, and (4) participate in an optional semi-structured interview.

4.1 Recruitment and Procedures

After obtaining approval from the university Research Ethics Board, participants were recruited by advertising on social media channels such as LinkedIn. Participants were required to be 18 years or older, be proficient in English, and own an Android smartphone with web access. Participants who met the inclusion criteria were invited to proceed with the four-step procedure as follows:

- **Step 1**: After reading the consent form and understanding the nature of their partici-pation, participants completed a demographics questionnaire about their age, gender, and level of education, as well as the global physical activity questionnaire (GPAQ) [48] developed by the WHO to estimate an individual's level of PA in 3 domains (work, transport and leisure time) and has been shown to be a valid measure of moderate-to-vigorous PA [49].

- **Step 2**: After completing Step 1, participants were provided with a link to download *PetBuddy* and were asked to use it for 10 days. To ensure that all participants had the AR feature working and were able to use it, participants were asked to complete a short test by interacting with the feature and confirming its functionality before starting the study.
- **Step 3**: After 10 days, participants completed a post-study questionnaire. In addition to the GPAQ, the questionnaire also consisted of statements that evaluated usability and perceived persuasiveness of the app. In particular, usability was evaluated using the System Usability Scale (SUS) developed by Lewis and Sauro [50]. The SUS consists of 10 items and has been used to evaluate a wide range of products and applications, including mHealth apps [51, 52]. Perceived persuasiveness was measured using a scale (4-items) developed by Drozd et al. [53]. This scale has been validated and employed in many studies including Orji et al. [54]. Participants indicated their level of agreement on a 7-point Likert scale (1 = strongly disagree to 7 = strongly agree).
- **Step 4**: An optional interview was made available to those participants who were interested in providing more about their experiences with the *PetBuddy* app. Interviews were conducted online and took approximately 30 min.

4.2 Data Analysis

A total of 65 participants were included in the quantitative analysis, providing a comprehensive dataset. Out of the 65 participants, 17 participants volunteered to participate in the optional interview. Results were analyzed using both quantitative and qualitative data analysis techniques. Numerical data collected in the questionnaire were analyzed using descriptive statistics and frequency histograms to first explore the data. Next, paired samples t-tests were used to analyze the GPAQ scores (both before and after the study), and one-sample t-tests were used to determine whether the subjective ratings on usability and perceived persuasiveness are above the neutral point, and significant. Verbal data collected from the optional, semi-structured interviews were analyzed using a thematic analysis.

5 Results

5.1 Participant Demographics

The demographics of our study population ($N = 65$) are shown in Table 2. In general, most participants fall in the age bracket of 26 to 35 years old (46%), most of the participants were female (57%) while for academic qualification, and the majority held a bachelor's degree (49%).

Table 2. Participants' demographic information ($N = 65$).

Characteristics	Frequency (%)
Age (years old)	18–25 (45%), 26–35 (46%), 36–45 (3%), over 46 (6%)
Gender identity	Male (43%), female (57%)
Education level	High school degree (9%), college diploma (9%), bachelor's degree (49%), master's degree (31%), doctoral degree (2%)

5.2 Quantitative Results

Prior to analyzing GPAQ scores, in accordance with GPAQ guidelines [55], participants' responses were converted into actual MET values per week. The WHO recommends a minimum of 150 min of moderate to vigorous activity per week, which is approximately 600METs. Results (Fig. 3) of a paired-samples t-test showed a significant difference between the baseline/before ($M = 528.62$, $SD = 238.70$) which did not meet the WHO's recommended level of 600MET, and after ($M = 692.92$, $SD = 210.01$) the intervention period of 10-days exceeded the threshold of 13%, $t(64) = -5.93$, $p < .001$, $d = 0.74$. This suggests a medium to large effect, indicating a substantial practical significance of the intervention with respect to promoting PA.

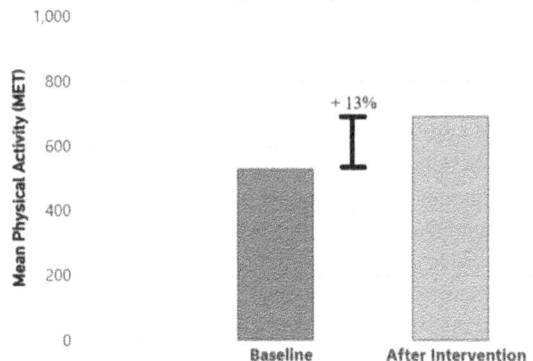

Fig. 3. Increase in PA between the baseline and after the intervention period.

Next, SUS scores were analyzed to provide an overview of the usability of *PetBuddy*. The SUS revealed an average score of 75.12 ($SD = 15.06$), suggesting that the overall usability of the app is "above average" [56]. Furthermore, results of a one-sample t-test comparing mean usability scores against a neutral point of 3 indicated that users' SUS ratings are statistically significant, $t(64) = 38.52$, $p < 0.001$.

Finally, we analyzed the persuasiveness scores collected about the game experience (AR, emotion, and idle game), and the persuasive strategies (competition, reward, self-monitoring and customization) implemented as game features. For the game experience, results (Fig. 4) showed that the AR experience had a mean score of 5.82 ($SD = 1.07$), with a significant t-test result, $t(64) = 13.75, p < .001$, and a large effect size ($d = 1.71$), suggesting it is highly persuasive. The emotion game experience, featuring happy/sad dog face (Fig. 2b), scored 5.46 ($SD = 1.12$), with $t(64) = 10.50, p < .001$, and a large effect size ($d = 1.12$), suggesting a strong emotional influence. The idle game experience had a mean score of 4.92 ($SD = 1.34$), with $t(64) = 5.67, p < .001$, and a moderate effect size ($d = 1.34$), suggesting it is persuasive, but not as persuasive compared to the experience of AR and emotional influence. As for the persuasive strategies, results (Fig. 5) showed that self-monitoring (track progress) had a significant t-test result, $t(64) = 11.80, p < .001$, ($M = 5.57, SD = 1.07$), indicating it was highly persuasive. Customization (the shop) was also significantly persuasive, $t(64) = 7.56, p < .001$, ($M = 5.21, SD = 1.30$) and though less so than the self-monitoring strategy. Reward (points) was also highly persuasive $t(64) = 12.73, p < .001$, ($M = 5.76, SD = 1.11$). Competition (leaderboard) had the highest persuasiveness score ($M = 6.21, SD = 1.01$), with $t(64) = 17.63, p < .001$, making it the most persuasive strategy.

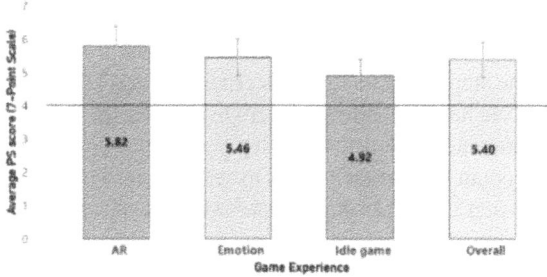

Fig. 4. Perceived persuasiveness of the game experience. The black line indicates the neutral rating of 4.

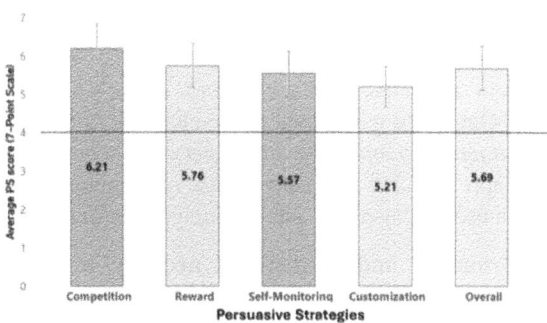

Fig. 5. Perceived persuasiveness of strategies. The black line indicates the neutral rating of 4.

5.3 Qualitative Results

To further explore users' experience of the app, we conducted interviews with 17 participants who expressed interest at the end of the study by providing their email addresses.

Participants were invited to share their thoughts about their experience using *PetBuddy*. The questions focused on what they liked, disliked, and areas they felt could be improved. We analyzed the feedback to identify recurring themes and reached data saturation [57], meaning no new insights emerged. Interview recordings were transcribed and a thematic analysis method developed by Braun and Clarke [58] was used to uncover patterns and themes in the data. The themes were coded by reviewing the interview data, identifying recurring patterns, and categorizing them into meaningful themes. Each theme was then labeled and organized to reflect the key findings of the analysis. Our analysis revealed five themes as discussed in the subsequent sections. The excerpts are presented with minor spelling and grammatical corrections.

Theme 1: Goal setting and step tracking aids progress monitoring thereby facilitating behavior change. The users appreciated the app's ability to set goals and track their progress, which helped them stay accountable and work towards increasing their PA levels. Observing their achievements and improvements over time reinforced positive behavior change. This was evident when one participant said *"the app helped me measure my daily steps, which I didn't do before"* [P07], while a different participant commented *"I've increased my daily step count since using the app and it has kept me motivated"* [P32]. Furthermore, the step count feature was crucial for tracking participants' PA and influencing their exercise habits. It allowed users to monitor their daily progress, which helped them remain motivated and meet their step goals. Furthermore, participants noted that seeing their step count encouraged them to walk more. For example, one participant said *"seeing my step count throughout the day helped me stay on track"* [P01], while a different participant said *"setting a specific step goal gave me something to aim for"* [P30]. Overall, this suggests that the step tracking feature increased participants' awareness of their activity levels and provided a tangible measure of their progress.

Theme 2: Social aspects and competition increase motivation to engage in PA. The social features, such as seeing others' progress on the leaderboard and engaging in friendly competition, were strong motivators for many users. For example, one participant said *"the competition created by the leaderboard motivated me to walk more"* [P16], while another participant said *"competing with friends added a fun, competitive element to my routine"* [P22]. One more participant pinpointed that *"the leaderboard was the most appealing part. It made me open the app to get more scores"* [P02]. Collectively, this suggests that the app was able to create a sense of community and social support which helped maintain user engagement and encouraged continued PA.

Theme 3: Habit formation and consistency are key to sustaining behavior change. Several users mentioned that the app helped them form new habits and become more consistent with their PA routines. For example, one participant said *"I've become more consistent with my daily walks. The app motivates me to meet my step goals every day"* [P30]. Another participant said *"yes, it made me more consistent with my exercise routine"* [P07]. One more participant said *"I've added a 15–20-min walk to my schedule, improving my overall physical activity"* [P02]. Altogether, these results demonstrate that daily reminders and engagement with the app reinforced these positive habits, leading to sustained behavior change.

Theme 4: The app helped overcome barriers to PA and provided support. Some users noted that the app helped them overcome barriers to PA, such as lack of motivation or accountability. For example, a participant said that *"the app helped me regain confidence and become more active"* [P16], while a different participant mentioned *"the app made me more conscious of my physical activity. I now set daily walking goals, which is something I never did before"* [P22]. One more participant explained that *"the app pushes me to exercise even when I was feeling lazy"* [P17]. In general, this suggests that the app provided the necessary support and encouragement to help users stay on track and make positive changes in their lives.

Theme 5: Gamification elements (persuasive strategies) enhance motivation and engagement. The app's gamification features (persuasive strategies), such as the leaderboard, rewards, and AR interactions, were frequently mentioned as motivating and engaging. For example, one participant said *"the leaderboard and reward system encouraged me to walk more"* [P02], while another participant thought that *"the AR made walking more enjoyable"* [P32]. One more participant said *"the leaderboard was my favorite feature and kept me motivated to walk more"* [P01]. These comments suggest that gamification elements tapped into users' competitive nature and made the experience more enjoyable, increasing the likelihood of continued use and behavior change.

6 Discussion

The purpose of this research was to evaluate the effectiveness of the *PetBuddy* app for promoting PA and to gather insights for enhancing its impact across diverse user demographics. Using a mixed-methods approach, we found that *PetBuddy* shows potential to increase PA in the short term, particularly among those initially less active. In general, our results showed that *PetBuddy* is usable, and the game features (persuasive strategies), as well as the game experience, are effective at influencing users to reconsider their PA habits. Based on our results, we offer the following four recommendations that will aid mHealth game application developers and researchers who are designing technologies that promote PA.

Design Recommendation 1: Include goal setting and progress tracking features to support users in the behavior change efforts. Beyond research showing that the use of wearable activity trackers during exercise and gradual feature updates can keep users interest in PA high [59], our results suggest that setting goals and realizing achievements and improvements over time can reinforce positive behavior change, and in turn, motivate PA. Thus, designers should include goal setting and progress tracking features to support users in their behavior change efforts. For example, the system can help the user set manageable goals (both long-term and short-term) so that users can gradually see the progress they have made. This should be particularly beneficial for beginners who are at the start of an exercise program, enabling them to incorporate PA into their daily routines and continue to thrive.

Design Recommendation 2: Incorporate social features and elements of competition to increase user motivation. Research shows that playing in teams or meeting at (virtual) meeting points is an important motivator for PA [60]. Our results demonstrate the importance of social support for maintaining user engagement. As such, we invite designers to consider including social features and elements of competition to boost user motivation and create a supportive community. Balance competition with cooperation and ensure a positive social experience for all users. For example, a system can offer two different modes of play (1) head-to-head (competition), and (2) same team (cooperation) to satisfy different user preferences.

Design Recommendation 3: Focus on features that promote habit formation and consistence to encourage PA over the long-term. Habit formation can be challenge, and Fogg [61] suggest breaking down large habits into small, manageable steps. We observed that the use of the app helped users form new habits and become more consistent with their PA routines. As such, designers should focus on features that promote habit formation and consistency, such as daily reminders and streaks. For example, the system can award bonus points after two consecutive days or weeks of meeting a step target.

Design Recommendation 4: Consider the common barriers to PA and incorporate features that help users overcome them. Research suggests that lack of social support, perceived feelings of exhaustion, and inconvenience of environmental conditions are common complaints associated with PA [4]. Our results showed that *PetBuddy* was able to help users tackle their lack of motivation to engage in PA. Thus, designers should consider the common barriers to PA and incorporate features that help users overcome them. The system can ask the user to complete a profile which includes the barriers that they have, and the content and design can be personalized based on the user's responses. For example, if a user prefers to exercise with friends, then the system can suggest an exercise buddy – a virtual avatar or real person.

6.1   Limitations and Directions for Future Work

While we reported on some interesting results, there are limitations. First, the research was restricted to Android smartphones, limiting the generalizability of the findings to other platforms like iOS. Future studies should include multiple smartphone platforms to enhance applicability. Second, compatibility issues with AR Core exclude some mobile models from participating fully. Thus, exploring alternative AR development tools for broader device compatibility is necessary. Third, the 10-day study period may not capture long-term effects, so incorporating control groups and adopting longer study designs will be crucial for assessing long-term effectiveness of *PetBuddy*.

7   Conclusion

In closing, this study explored how the *PetBuddy* app can enhance PA through persuasive strategies. The app, featuring AR, was designed to create an engaging experience to make increasing PA enjoyable. This research contributes to advancing knowledge in the domain of persuasive technology and designing mobile games for encouraging healthy behavior changes. It highlights that engaging games are crucial for maintaining interest, and by incorporating AR, emotional influences, and persuasive strategies, *PetBuddy* offers a novel approach to promote PA. The findings emphasize the importance of user engagement and motivation, showing that incorporating rewards, self-monitoring, customization, and competition can enhance PA adherence. This research highlights AR's potential in health promotion by making PA fun and interactive, suggesting avenues for future research.

Acknowledgements. This research was undertaken, in part, thanks to funding from the Canada Research Chairs Program. We acknowledge the support of the Natural Sciences and Engineering Research Council of Canada (NSERC) through the Discovery Grant. The research is conducted as part of the Dalhousie University Persuasive Computing Lab.

References

1. Katzmarzyk, P.T., Friedenreich, C., Shiroma, E.J., Lee, I.M.: Physical inactivity and non-communicable disease burden in low-income, middle-income and high-income countries. Br. J. Sports Med. **56**, 101–106 (2022)
2. Guthold, R., Stevens, G.A., Riley, L.M., Bull, F.C.: Global trends in insufficient physical activity among adolescents: A pooled analysis of 298 population-based surveys with 1.6 million participants. Yearb. Paediatr. Endocrinol. (2020)
3. Lee, I.M., Paffenbarger, R.S., Hennekens, C.H.: Physical activity, physical fitness and longevity. Aging Clin. Exp. Res. **9**, 2–11 (1997). https://doi.org/10.1007/bf03340123
4. Myers, R.S., Roth, D.L.: Perceived benefits of and barriers to exercise and stage of exercise adoption in young adults. Heal. Psychol. **16**, 277–283 (1997)
5. Barkley, J.E., Lepp, A., Glickman, E.L.: "Pokémon go!" may promote walking, discourage sedentary behavior in college students. Games Health J. **6**, 165–170 (2017)
6. Althoff, T., White, R.W., Horvitz, E.: Influence of pokémon go on physical activity: Study and implications. J. Med. Internet Res. **18**(12), e315 (2016). https://doi.org/10.2196/jmir.6759
7. Lynch, C., Bird, S., Lythgo, N., Selva-Raj, I.: Changing the physical activity behavior of adults with fitness trackers: a systematic review and meta-analysis. Am. J. Heal. Promot. **34**, 418–430 (2020)
8. Zhao, Z., Arya, A., Orji, R., Chan, G.: Effects of a personalized fitness recommender system using gamification and continuous player modeling: System design and long-term validation study. JMIR Serious Games. **8** (2020)
9. Pikman Bloom. https://pikminbloom.com/
10. Neupane, A., Hansen, D., Sharma, A., Fails, J.A., Neupane, B., Beutler, J.: A review of gamified fitness tracker apps and future directions. In: CHI Play 2020 – Proceedings of the Annual Symposium Computational Interaction Play, pp. 522–533 (2020)
11. Caro, K., Feng, Y., Day, T., Freed, E., Fox, B., Zhu, J.: Understanding the Effect of Existing Positive Relationships on a Social Motion-based Game for Health, pp. 77–87 (2018)
12. Chan, G., Alslaity, A., Reen, J.K., Anukem, S., Orji, R.: Gardenquest: using hexad player types to design a step-based multiplayer persuasive game for motivating physical activity. In: Meschtscherjakov, A., Midden, C., Ham, J. (eds.) Persuasive Technology: 18th International Conference, PERSUASIVE 2023, Eindhoven, The Netherlands, April 19–21, 2023, Proceedings, pp. 337–356. Springer Nature Switzerland, Cham (2023). https://doi.org/10.1007/978-3-031-30933-5_22
13. Oh, Y., Yang, S.P.: Defining Exergames & Exergaming. Meaningful Play (2010)

14. Moholdt, T., Weie, S., Chorianopoulos, K., Inge Wang, A., Hagen, K.: Exergaming can be an innovative way of enjoyable high-intensity interval training. BMJ Open Sport Exerc, Med. 3(1), e000258 (2017)
15. Glen, K., Eston, R., Loetscher, T., Parfitt, G.: Exergaming: Feels good despite working harder. PLoS One. 12 (2017)
16. Garde, A., et al.: A multi-week assessment of a mobile exergame intervention in an elementary school. Games Health J. 7, 43–50 (2018)
17. Xu, L., et al.: The Effects of mHealth-Based Gamification Interventions on Participation in Physical Activity: Systematic Review. JMIR mHealth uHealth. 10, (2022)
18. Villareale, J., Gray, R.C., Furqan, A., Fox, T., Zhu, J.: Enhancing social exergames through idle game design. In: ACM International Conference Proceeding Ser. (2019)
19. Oinas-Kukkonen, H., Harjumaa, M.: Persuasive systems design: key issues, process model, and system features. Commun. Assoc. Inf. Syst. 24, 485–500 (2009)
20. Alex, M., Lottridge, D., Wünsche, B.C.: Artificial companions in stroke rehabilitation: Likeability, familiarity and expectations. In: Proceedings of the Annual Hawaii International Conference System Science 2020-Janua, 3789–3798 (2020)
21. Cho, M.G.: A Study on Augmented Reality-based Virtual Pets for the Elderly Living Alone. Int. Conf. ICT Converg. 2021-Octob, pp. 1280–1283 (2021)
22. Chan, G., Arya, A., Orji, R., Zhao, Z., Stojmenovic, M., Whitehead, A.: Player matching for social exergame retention. In: Extended Abstracts of the 2020 Annual Symposium on Computer-Human Interaction in Play, pp. 198–203. ACM, New York, NY, USA (2020)
23. Altmeyer, M., Lessel, P., Jantwal, S., Muller, L., Daiber, F., Krüger, A.: Potential and effects of personalizing gameful fitness applications using behavior change intentions and Hexad user types. User Model. User-adapt. Interact. (2021)
24. Kinetics, H., Roderbirken, K., Republic, F.: Metabolic equivalents (METS) in exercise testing, exercise prescription, and evaluation of functional capacity. Clin. Cardiol. 13, 555–565 (1990)
25. Chen, Y., Wang, Q., Chen, H., Song, X., Tang, H., Tian, M.: An overview of augmented reality technology. J. Phys.: Conf. Ser. 1237(2), 022082 (2019)
26. Philippe, A.G., Goncalves, A., Korchi, K., Deshayes, M.: Exergaming in augmented reality is tailor-made for aerobic training and enjoyment among healthy young adults. Front. Public Heal. 12 (2024)
27. Azuma, R.T.: A survey of augmented reality. Presence: teleoperators and virtual environments. Presence Teleoperators Virtual Environ. 42, 1451–1462 (1997)
28. Geelan, B., et al.: Augmented exergaming : increasing exercise duration in novices. In: OzCHI Australian Conference on Computational Interactiuon, pp. 1–9 (2016)
29. Farič, N., Potts, H.W.W., Rowe, S., Beaty, T., Hon, A., Fisher, A.: Running app "zombies, run!" users' engagement with physical activity: a qualitative study. Games Health J. 10, 420–429 (2021)
30. Odenigbo, I.P., Reen, J.K., Eneze, C., Friday, A., Orji, R.: The journey: an AR gamified mobile application for promoting physical activity in young adults. In: UMAP2022 - Adjunct Proceedings of the 30th ACM Conference on User Modeling, Adaptation and Personalization, pp. 342–353. ACM, New York, NY, USA (2022)
31. Purkiss, B., Khaliq, I.: A study of interaction in idle games & perceptions on the definition of a game. In: 2015 IEEE Games Entertain. Media Conf. GEM 2015 (2016)
32. Cutting, J., Gundry, D., Cairns, P.: Busy doing nothing? What do players do in idle games? Int. J. Hum. Comput. Stud. 122, 133–144 (2019). https://doi.org/10.1016/j.ijhcs.2018.09.006
33. Stebbins, S.: The rise in popularity of idle games and their impact on modern time management (2020)
34. Alharthi, S.A., Alsaedi, O., Toups Dugas, P.O., Tanenbaum, T.J., Hammer, J.: Playing to wait: a taxonomy of idle games. In: Conference on Human Factors Computing Systsem – Proceedings (2018)

35. Alslaity, A., Chan, G., Orji, R.: A panoramic view of personalization based on individual differences in persuasive and behavior change interventions. Front. Artif. Intell. **6** (2023)
36. Orji, R.: Why are persuasive strategies effective? Exploring the strengths and weaknesses of socially-oriented persuasive strategies. In: de Vries, P., Oinas-Kukkonen, H., Siemons, L., Beerlage-de Jong, N., van Gemert-Pijnen, L. (eds.) Persuasive Technology: Development and Implementation of Personalized Technologies to Change Attitudes and Behaviors: 12th International Conference, PERSUASIVE 2017, Amsterdam, The Netherlands, April 4–6, 2017, Proceedings, pp. 253–266. Springer International Publishing, Cham (2017). https://doi.org/10.1007/978-3-319-55134-0_20
37. Chan, G., Arya, A., Orji, R., Zhao, Z., Whitehead, A.: Increasing motivation in social exercise games: personalising gamification elements to player type. Behav. Inform. Technol. **43**(11), 2608–2638 (2023)
38. google_ml_kit I Flutter Package
39. Vredenburg, K., Mao, J.-Y., Smith, P.W., Carey, T.: A survey of user-centered design practice, pp. 471–478 (2002)
40. Taylor, N.: Introduction. In: Taylor, N. (ed.) Cinematic Perspectives on Digital Culture, pp. 1– 9. Palgrave Macmillan UK, London (2012). https://doi.org/10.1057/9781137284624_1
41. Miller, K.A., Deci, E.L., Ryan, R.M.: Intrinsic motivation and self-determination in human behavior. Contemp. Sociol. **17**, 253 (1988)
42. Ryan, R.M., Mims, V., Koestner, R.: Relation of reward contingency and interpersonal context to intrinsic motivation: a review and test using cognitive evaluation theory. J. Pers. Soc. Psychol. **45**, 736–750 (1983)
43. Westgarth, C., Christley, R.M., Jewell, C., German, A.J., Boddy, L.M., Christian, H.E.: Dog owners are more likely to meet physical activity guidelines than people without a dog: an investigation of the association between dog ownership and physical activity levels in a UK community. Sci. Rep. **9** (2019)
44. Keller, J.M.: Development and use of the ARCS model of instructional design. J. Instr. Dev. **10**, 2–10 (1987)
45. Orji, R., Tondello, G.F., Nacke, L.E.: Personalizing persuasive strategies in gameful systems to gamification user types. In: Conference on Human Factors in Computing Systems – Proceedings (2018)
46. Bumgardner, W.: Are There Negative Effects of Walking Too Much? (2024)
47. Song, H., Kim, J., Tenzek, K.E., Lee, K.M.: The effects of competition and competitiveness upon intrinsic motivation in exergames. Comput. Human Behav. **29**, 1702–1708 (2013)
48. Armstrong, T., Bull, F.: Development of the world health organization global physical activity questionnaire (GPAQ). J. Public Health (Bangkok) **14**, 66–70 (2006)
49. Cleland, C.L., Hunter, R.F., Kee, F., Cupples, M.E., Sallis, J.F., Tully, M.A.: Validity of the Global Physical Activity Questionnaire (GPAQ) in assessing levels and change in moderate-vigorous physical activity and sedentary behaviour. BMC Public Health. **14** (2014)
50. Lewis, J.R., Sauro, J.: The factor structure of the system usability scale. Lect. Notes Comput. Sci. (including Subser. Lect. Notes Artif. Intell. Lect. Notes Bioinformatics). 5619 LNCS, pp. 94–103 (2009)
51. Isaković, M., Sedlar, U., Volk, M., Bešter, J.: Usability pitfalls of diabetes mHealth apps for the elderly. J. Diab. Res. **2016**, 1–9 (2016). https://doi.org/10.1155/2016/1604609
52. Santoso, I.S., Ferdinansyah, A., Sensuse, D.I., Suryono, R.R., Kautsarina, Hidayanto, A.N.: Effectiveness of gamification in mhealth apps designed for mental illness. In: Proceeding – 2021 2nd International Conference on ICT Rural Dev. IC-ICTRuDev (2021)
53. Drozd, F., Lehto, T., Oinas-Kukkonen, H.: Exploring perceived persuasiveness of a behavior change support system: a structural model. In: Bang, Magnus, Ragnemalm, Eva L. (eds.) PERSUASIVE 2012. LNCS, vol. 7284, pp. 157–168. Springer, Heidelberg (2012). https://doi.org/10.1007/978-3-642-31037-9_14

54. Orji, R., Vassileva, J., Mandryk, R.L.: Modeling the efficacy of persuasive strategies for different gamer types in serious games for health. User Model. User-Adapted Interact. **24**(5), 453–498 (2014). https://doi.org/10.1007/s11257-014-9149-8

55. Global Physical Activity Questionnaire Analysis Guide GPAQ Analysis Guide Global Physical Activity Questionnaire (GPAQ) Analysis Guide (2002)

56. Bangor, A., Kortum, P., Miller, J.: Determining what individual SUS scores mean: adding an adjective rating scale. J. usability Stud. **4**, 114–123 (2009)

57. Hennink, M., Kaiser, B.N.: Sample sizes for saturation in qualitative research: a systematic review of empirical tests. Soc. Sci. Med. **292**, 114523 (2022)

58. Braun, V., Clarke, V.: Using thematic analysis in psychology. Qual. Res. Psychol. **3**, 77–101 (2006)

59. Zhao, Z., Arya, A., Whitehead, A., Chan, G., Etemad, S.A.: Keeping Users Engaged through Feature Updates. Presented at the (2017)

60. Schwarz, A., et al.: Mobile exergaming in adolescents' everyday life—contextual design of where, when, with whom, and how: The smartlife case. Int. J. Environ. Res. Public Health. **15** (2018)

61. Fogg, B.J., Euchner, J.: Designing for behavior change—new models and moral issues: an interview with B.J. Fogg. Research-Technology Management **62**(5), 14–19 (2019). https://doi.org/10.1080/08956308.2019.1638490

The Motivational Appeal of Persuasive Strategies in a Healthy Eating Behaviour Change Game

Chinenye Ndulue[1]([⊠]) [iD], Oladapo Oyebode[2] [iD], and Rita Orji[2] [iD]

[1] MacEwan University, Edmonton, Canada
nduluec@macewan.ca
[2] Dalhousie University, Halifax, Canada
{oladapo.oyebode,rita.orji}@dal.ca

Abstract. Persuasive game designers employ persuasive strategies to improve the effectiveness of behaviour change games. Since persuasive strategies are intended to motivate the players toward the desired behaviours, the motivational appeal of these persuasive strategies can play an important role in the effectiveness of these behaviour change games. Therefore, it is important to understand the effectiveness of persuasive strategies and their motivational appeal. To advance research in this direction, this paper explores the relationship between the effectiveness of four popular persuasive strategies (reward, competition, praise, suggestion) and their motivational appeal in a persuasive game for healthy eating. In a study of 124 participants, our results showed that all the persuasive strategies were perceived to be effective in promoting behaviour change. We also discovered that the reward, competition and suggestion strategies showed a completely consistent relationship with all the motivational appeal dimensions. We also observed the strongest motivational appeal dimension for rewards was attention, competition and praise predominantly impacted satisfaction, while relevance stood out as the most significant motivational appeal dimension for suggestions. We conclude by offering some insights on how to implement persuasive strategies that amplify the four motivational appeal dimensions, in order to design games with better persuasive appeal.

Keywords: persuasive games · persuasive strategies · behaviour change · reward · competition · suggestion · praise · serious games · healthy eating

1 Introduction

Behaviour change games or persuasive games have garnered significant attention as potent instruments for driving behaviour change and shaping attitudes across diverse aspects of life. These games, falling under the umbrella of serious games and games for change, uniquely combine entertaining gameplay with a behaviour change agenda. By leveraging the inherent allure of games, persuasive games subtly guide players toward desired behaviours and attitudes [5]. The true potential of persuasive games lies in

K. T. Win et al. (Eds.): PERSUASIVE 2025, LNCS 15711, pp. 281–295, 2025.
https://doi.org/10.1007/978-3-031-94959-3_20

their capacity to captivate and motivate players while effectively conveying persuasive messages that promote desired positive behaviours [17]. Research has proven the effectiveness of persuasive games across various domains including Disease Prevention [6, 23], Healthy Nutrition [18, 21, 28] and Physical Activity [8, 10, 13].

However, the effectiveness of these games could be impacted by a variety of factors. For example, research has shown that the effectiveness of persuasive games can be impacted by factors such as age groups [36, 45], gender groups [36, 46], gamer types [32], gamification user type [31], personality types [3, 33].

Another factor that can affect the effectiveness of persuasive games is the motivational appeal of the persuasive strategies implemented in them [35]. The ARCS motivational appeal model [19] is based on a combination of four motivational dimensions namely attention (A), relevance (R), confidence (C), and satisfaction (S). These dimensions represent specific aspects of motivation that can determine how appealing persuasive game features can be. Therefore, since the motivational appeal of system features can affect users' perception towards the system, it is important to investigate the relationship between the perceived effectiveness of persuasive games and their motivational appeal. These results will enable designers and researchers to design their persuasive games to harness the full potential of these strategies when developing games for behaviour change.

Specifically, in this paper, we explore the following research questions:

R1: What is the perceived effectiveness of behaviour change games for healthy eating?
R1: What is the relationship between the motivational appeal of persuasive strategies and their effectiveness in a behaviour change game for healthy eating?

To answer these research questions, we designed a Pac-Man-styled persuasive game for healthy eating. Then, we carried out a study of 124 participants to investigate the motivational appeal and the effectiveness of different persuasive strategies, using the ARCS motivational appeal questionnaire and the persuasiveness questionnaire. Our results revealed that all the persuasive strategies were significantly effective in the game for healthy eating. We also discovered that the reward, competition and suggestion strategies showed a completely consistent relationship with all the motivational appeal dimensions, while the praise strategy showed no relationship with the attention dimension. We also observed the strongest motivational appeal dimension for rewards is attention, while competition and praise predominantly impacted satisfaction. In contrast, relevance stood out as the most significant motivational appeal dimension for suggestions. We conclude by offering some insights on how to implement persuasive strategies that amplify the four motivational appeal dimensions, in order to design games with better persuasive appeal.

2 Literature Review

In this section, we offer essential background for the research presented in this paper. We provide a brief overview of established persuasive system design frameworks, explore the implementation of persuasive strategies in various applications and explore motivational appeal research.

2.1 Persuasive Strategies

Unlike traditional games, PGs are designed to promote behaviour change and reinforce desired behaviours. They achieve this desired behaviour change through the intentional implementation of persuasive strategies. Therefore, persuasive strategies are techniques employed in persuasive games to motivate behaviour change.

In the domain of persuasive systems design, several frameworks and models outline specific persuasive strategies. Notable examples include the Persuasive Systems Design (PSD) model proposed by Oinas-Kukkonen et al. [25], the Fogg Behavioral Model [15], and Cialdini's principles of persuasion [43]. These frameworks provide valuable insights into the techniques used to create effective persuasive systems. For this research, we selected four persuasive strategies from the PSD model which are rewards, competition, praise and suggestions. These strategies are among the most frequently used strategies in persuasive game design [27, 31]. Table 1 shows the definitions of these strategies.

Table 1. Persuasive strategies and their descriptions

Strategies	Description
Rewards	Offering positive incentives or reinforcements to players, such as points, badges, or virtual loot boxes, to motivate and encourage desired behaviours or actions
Competition	Encouraging players to compete with others, thereby motivating them to achieve desired goals or outcomes using techniques such as social challenges, ranking charts and leaderboards
Praise	Utilizing positive feedback or compliments to reinforce desired behaviours or achievements
Suggestions	Offering recommendations to players and suggesting specific actions or behaviours to motivate them to adopt desired habits or decisions

2.2 Persuasive Strategies

Recent research highlights a growing trend in the development and application of persuasive games across various domains. One illustrative example is the 'Playful Bottle' [11] game, designed to promote healthy nutrition habits, specifically targeting office workers to ensure adequate daily water consumption. The game incorporates a range of persuasive strategies, including Self-Monitoring, Simulation, Reward, Reminders, Liking, Competition, Comparison, and Recognition. Through the integration of a smart mug with sensors connected to a mobile phone, the game tracks users' water consumption habits. As players increase their water intake, their virtual tree blossoms, but neglecting water consumption results in withering – simulation. Points are awarded to players based on their water intake, forming a reward system.

Similarly, 'SmokeScreen' [37] targets high school students, motivating them to steer clear of behaviours that could lead to tobacco abuse. Employing Simulation, Rehearsal,

Reward, and Similarity strategies, the game lets players select and navigate virtual characters representing students within a virtual school. Decision-making in response to scenarios that may lead to tobacco usage is a key aspect, with players rewarded for healthy choices and penalized with a loss of health points for poor decisions. The game concludes after a series of decisions, allowing players to observe the overall impact on their avatar's health – a simulation strategy.

Additional examples of persuasive games include 'LunchTime' [29], designed to motivate healthy eating through Reward, Competition, and Comparison strategies, and 'Nourish Your Tree' [34], a game promoting physical activity through various persuasive strategies like Self-monitoring, Simulation, Praise, Suggestion, Reminders, Rewards, Competition, and Recognition.

2.3 Motivational Appeal Constructs

There has been a lot of research that tries to understand human motivation. They have resulted in motivational theories, such as Self-determination theory [39] and Expectancy–Value theory [47] and the ARCS model of motivation [19]. The ARCS model of motivation is based on research in the psychology of human motivation to identify four key dimensions that drive and sustain motivation: Attention, Relevance, Confidence, and Satisfaction [19].

In this research, we opted for the ARCS model because it is a widely applied and established motivational model [143], with components derived from a comprehensive synthesis of research on human motivation [1]. Additionally, the ARCS model serves as a robust macro-theory that integrates various notable motivational theories, including the Self-Efficacy theory, Expectancy-Value theory, Reinforcement theory, Social learning theory, and Cognitive Evaluation theory [19, 41].

Moreover, since the ARCS motivation model has demonstrated associations with behaviour and behaviour change [16], human-computer interaction and persuasive technology researchers have utilized the ARCS model to guide the design and evaluation of behaviour change interventions. For instance, it has been widely employed to assess the motivational appeal of persuasive systems across diverse domains such as health interventions[2, 42], and persuasive games [12, 48]. Abdessettar applied the ARCS motivation model in creating a persuasive smart mobile school for children [1], and Zulkifli et al. used the ARCS questionnaire to evaluate the motivational appeal of an interactive persuasive system [157]. Various persuasive system designers have also incorporated elements of the ARCS motivation model into their intervention designs. For example, Stockdale et al. integrated the Confidence construct of the ARCS model in a persuasive intervention to promote breastfeeding among first-time mothers, aiming to boost their confidence in their breastfeeding ability [42]. Similarly, Yusoff et al. [49] adapted the Attention construct to enhance the motivational appeal of persuasive elements within their persuasive game. Table 2 provides a summary of the ARCS model of motivation dimensions, adapted from Orji et al. [26] and Oladapo et al. [35].

3   Method

In this section, we describe our methodology: the measurement instrument used in our study, provide an overview of participants' demographics, and details of our data analysis methods.

3.1   Game Design

As indicated earlier, we adapted the popular Pac-man game for healthy eating. The maze is populated with both healthy food items like fruits and vegetables and unhealthy food items like candies and junk food. Both types of food items are constantly moving around the maze. The player's objective is twofold: Pac-Man needs to consume all the healthy food items while simultaneously avoiding the unhealthy foods, all within a specified time limit. Players gain points for every healthy food item consumed, however, if Pac-Man encounters an unhealthy food item, points are deducted. The healthier items contribute positively to the player's score, while encounters with unhealthy items result in a penalty. This version of Pac-Man creates a dynamic and challenging gameplay experience where players must make quick decisions to balance collecting points through healthy food consumption and avoiding penalties by steering clear of unhealthy foods. The design encourages players to prioritize healthy choices while penalizing interactions with unhealthy items, promoting a balanced and health-conscious gameplay approach (see Fig. 1).

3.2   Measurement Instrument

While designing the game, we intentionally implemented four persuasive strategies from the PSD model. They are Reward, Competition, Suggestion, and Praise strategies.

Table 3 shows the implementations of these strategies while Fig. 2 shows screenshots of some of the strategies.

Following the game design phase, the game underwent evaluation by two game design experts to identify and address potential design issues. To collect feedback from participants on the effectiveness of these strategies, we developed a survey that asked users to rate their perceived effectiveness of the strategies.

Following the game design phase, the game underwent evaluation by two game design experts to identify and address potential design issues. To collect feedback from participants on the effectiveness of these strategies, we developed a survey that asked users to rate their perceived effectiveness of the strategies.

To minimize potential bias caused by question order, we generated four survey versions, each featuring the same questions but arranged in a randomized sequence. The survey collected the perceived effectiveness of the overall game and the four persuasive strategies implemented in the game. To do this, we used a scale adapted from Thomas et al. [44] and Drodz et al. [14]. The scale is a well-established measure used to evaluate the perceived persuasiveness of system features, and it has been utilized in various Human-Computer Interaction (HCI) and related research studies [7, 14, 27, 30]. The scale consisted of the following questions:

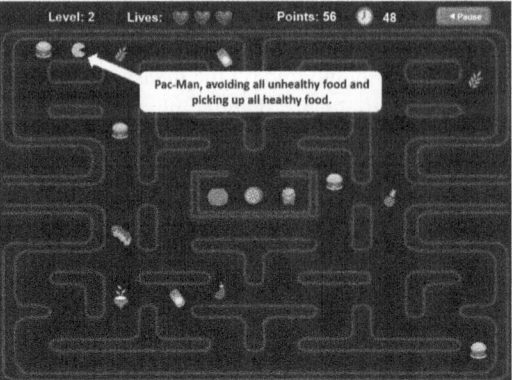

Fig. 1. Screenshot of the gameplay.

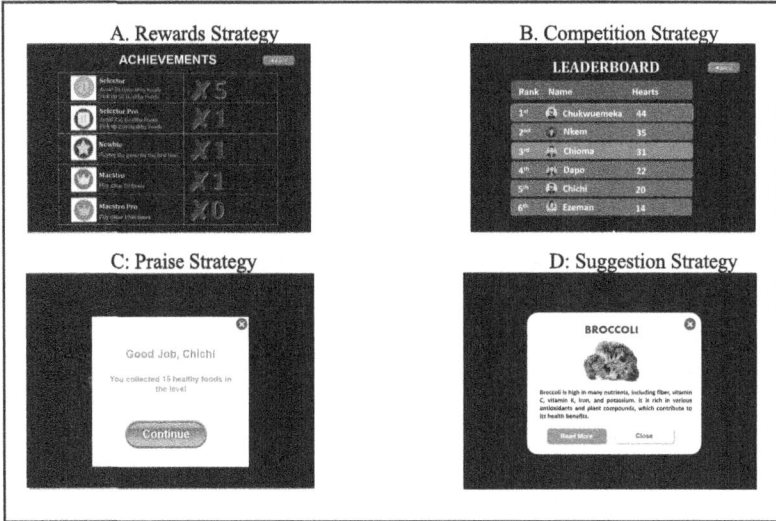

Fig. 2. Screenshots of the persuasive strategies implemented

   i. "This feature/game would influence me to eat healthily."
  ii. "This feature/game would convince me to eat healthily."
 iii. "This feature/game would be personally relevant to me."
  iv. "This feature/game would make me reconsider my eating habits."
   v. "The feature/game would make or motivate me to use the app."

We measured these questions on a 7-point Likert scale ranging from "1 = Strongly disagree" to "7 = Strongly agree" for each strategy and the overall game. Furthermore, we collected the motivational appeal of participants using the ARCS model of motivation questionnaire, consisting of 12 items measured on a 5-point Likert scale (ranging from "1 – Strongly Disagree" and "5 – Strongly Agree"). We adapted this questionnaire from Orji et al. [26].

Table 2. The constructs or dimensions of the ARCS Model of Motivation

Construct	Definition
Attention	For a system to motivate users, it must arouse and sustain their attention
Relevance	To motivate users, a system must reflect users' interests and goals. A system that is perceived as helpful and useful in terms of helping users accomplish their goals is more likely to motivate users. To be relevant, a system must be goal-oriented, motive-matching, and make use of familiar concepts
Confidence	People do not like taking on a task with little or no probability of success. Although success is never guaranteed, and people like to be challenged, a challenge that is beyond a user's capability could demotivate them. Users' confidence levels are often correlated with their motivation and the amount of effort put forth towards achieving an objective
Satisfaction	To motivate users and sustain their motivation, they must derive some satisfaction and reward for their effort

Table 3. Persuasive strategies and their implementations

Strategy	Implementation
Reward	Badges and points for completing in-game achievements. For example, players obtained the selector badge by collecting 50 healthy foods and avoiding 50 unhealthy foods (Fig. 2A)
Competition	A leaderboard of points earned in-game. Players are ranked according to the points accumulated while playing the game (Fig. 2B)
Suggestion	Random pop-up tips about healthy eating or unhealthy eating practices. For example, players received tips that both encouraged healthy eating and discouraged indulging in unhealthy options, striking a balance between positive and negative reinforcement (Fig. 2D)
Praise	Image and textual positive feedback for completing in-game achievements (Fig. 2C)

3.3 Demographic Information

We initially recruited 409 participants, all of whom installed the game on their personal computers. The participants were instructed to dedicate a minimum of 15 min per day over three consecutive days to engage with the game. Upon completing the gameplay period, they were required to fill out a survey, capturing their perceptions regarding the game's effectiveness and the implementation of the four strategies within the game. Following the exclusion of participants who did not complete the survey, a total of 124 participants were included in the subsequent analysis. The demographic distribution of participants is illustrated in Table 4.

Table 4. Demographic distribution for the study.

Total	124
Gender	Females = 31, Males = 93
Age	18–25 = 29, 26–35 = 64, 36–45 = 31
Education	Bachelors = 78, Masters = 19, High School = 7, Diploma = 7

3.4 Data Analysis

To analyze the data we collected, we employed established analytical tools, techniques, and procedures to derive meaningful insights that answered our research questions. The following summary outlines the key steps undertaken in the data analysis process:

i. We used Cronbach's alpha to check the reliability of the responses collected with the scale. The reliability analysis showed that all the scales were internally consistent, with a combined Cronbach's alpha value of 0.72 which is an acceptable level of reliability [9].

ii. Using Statistical Package for the Social Sciences (SPSS), we conducted a One-Sample t-test on the overall rating of the game and each persuasive strategy implemented. This was done to verify the perceived effectiveness of the overall game and each persuasive strategy implemented.

iii. Using SmartPLS 4 [38], we applied Partial Least Squares Structural Equation Modeling (PLS-SEM) to develop models illustrating the relationships between the persuasiveness of strategies and the four ARCS motivational constructs. PLS-SEM is a widely utilized method for estimating path models that unveil intricate interconnections between observed and latent variables [40]. The choice of PLS-SEM over other approaches, such as covariant-based methods, stems from its suitability for handling complex predictive models [20], and it has demonstrated success in estimating relationships between variables in the context of Human-Computer Interaction (HCI) research [3, 22, 35]. Models were developed for each motivational appeal construct, addressing one strategy at a time. Figure 3 illustrates the PLS-SEM structural model, displaying the relationships between the ARCS motivational constructs and each strategy.

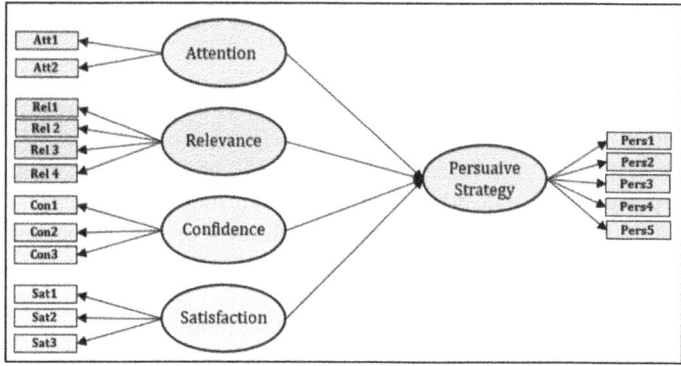

Fig. 3. PLS-SEM structural model showing the relationship between the ARCS motivational constructs and each persuasive strategy.

4   Results

In this section, we present the results of our study, arranged according to our research questions.

4.1   The Effectiveness of the Four Persuasive Strategies

To answer Research Question 1 (R1) – *What is the perceived effectiveness of behaviour change games for healthy eating?* – we conducted one-sample t-tests on the mean scores of user ratings for the overall game and the four persuasive strategies, referencing the neutral rating of 4 on a 7-point persuasiveness scale. Our findings indicated that the overall game was perceived as significantly effective in its persuasive impact – $(t(123) = 36.88, p < .001)$. Furthermore, all the persuasive strategies deployed within the game were perceived as significantly effective, as illustrated in Table 5.

Table 5. T-Test of the mean values user rating of the game and the persuasive strategies implemented. (All means were significant at $p < .0001$, test value $= 4$).

Strategies	df = 123				
	p	M	SD	t	p
Overall	.001	5.79	0.540	36.89	.001
Reward	.001	6.04	0.852	26.59	.001
Competition	.001	6.08	0.856	27.04	.001
Praise	.001	5.48	0.915	17.96	.001
Suggestion	.001	5.57	0.841	20.71	.001

4.2   The Relationship Between the Effectiveness of the Persuasive Strategies and Their Motivational Appeal

To address Research Question 2 (R2) – *What is the relationship between the motivational appeal of persuasive strategies and their effectiveness in a behaviour change game for healthy eating?* – we developed a structural model showing the relationship between the persuasiveness of the strategies and their motivational appeal. We aimed to understand the relationships between the effectiveness of the four persuasive strategies *(reward, competition, praise, suggestion)* and the four dimensions of motivational appeal: *attention, relevance, confidence,* and *satisfaction.* Table 6 shows the path coefficients of these relationships, with the bolded values indicating stronger relationships and the '-' denoting no relationship.

Our results showed that all persuasive strategies exhibited significant relationships with relevance, confidence, and satisfaction. Although reward, competition, and suggestion showed significant relationships with attention, praise did not.

Analyzing the overall strength of relationships across motivational dimensions, attention displayed a stronger relationship with only the reward strategy ($\beta = 0.345$, p < 0.001). This implies that the reward strategy particularly stood out in terms of its impact on capturing individuals' attention.

Concerning confidence, no distinct patterns of stronger relationships were identified across the four strategies. However, relevance exhibited stronger relationships with both the praise ($\beta = 0.275$, p < 0.001) and suggestion ($\beta = 0.321$, p < 0.001) strategies. This suggests that the participants perceived a higher relevance of persuasive strategies centred around praise and suggestion.

Satisfaction, on the other hand, demonstrated the highest number of stronger relationships with competition ($\beta = 0.291$, p < 0.001), praise ($\beta = 0.451$, p < 0.001), and suggestion ($\beta = 0.261$, p < 0.001). This indicates that these three strategies were particularly effective in eliciting higher levels of satisfaction among individuals.

Table 6. Standard path coefficients and significance of relationships in the game. Bolded coefficients have significance levels of p < .001, while unbolded coefficients have significance levels of p < .05. "–" represents non-significant coefficients.

Strategy	ATT	REL	CON	SAT
Reward	**0.345**	0.287	0.239	0.163
Competition	0.272	0.233	0.179	**0.291**
Praise	-	**0.275**	0.130	**0.451**
Suggestion	0.193	**0.321**	0.200	**0.261**

ATT = Attention, REL = Relevance, CON = Confidence, SAT = Satisfaction

5 Discussion

In this section, we will discuss the results concerning the motivational appeal of persuasive strategies implemented in persuasive games. Through this discussion, we aim to provide a comprehensive understanding of the impact of persuasive strategies on player motivation.

5.1 Confidence

Our findings revealed that confidence emerged as a significant factor for all the persuasive strategies. This emphasizes its central role in shaping player motivation and highlights its universal importance in driving engagement and fostering positive behaviour change. Confidence, closely tied to the concept of self-efficacy, reflects an individual's belief in their ability to successfully execute specific tasks or behaviours [4]. Its significance across different strategies suggests its widespread influence on player motivation. Players are more likely to be motivated when they feel confident in their capacity to meet the challenges presented in the game and achieve positive outcomes. For persuasive game designers, recognizing the universal significance of confidence opens avenues for intentional design choices. Strategies that actively boost players' confidence, such as providing positive feedback, acknowledging achievements, and offering personalized support, can contribute to a more motivating and engaging gaming experience. Furthermore, designing game scenarios that gradually build and reinforce players' confidence levels can further improve behaviour change games.

5.2 Attention and Reward Strategy

Attention showed the strongest significance with the reward strategy. This is understandable since rewards in games act as potent stimuli to capture players' attention, drawing them into the gameplay experience and encouraging further interaction.

Another reason for this significance could be due to the principle of immediate gratification [24]. Players are more likely to pay attention to elements within the game that offer immediate rewards or feedback. By providing instant gratification for desired actions or accomplishments, rewards maintain players' attention and motivate continued engagement with the persuasive content embedded in the game.

Furthermore, the interaction between attention and rewards creates a dynamic feedback loop within persuasive games. As players pay attention to rewarded elements within the game, they are motivated to continue engaging with the gameplay experience. In turn, the reinforcement provided by rewards sustains players' attention and encourages them to explore further, deepening their immersion in the persuasive content.

Therefore it is important to design rewards with well-timed and engaging visual cues to capture and maintain attention. These rewards can also be tied to gameful challenges and decision-making scenarios to actively involve players, fostering a sense of agency and investment, thereby increasing attention.

5.3 Satisfaction

Interestingly, our findings revealed that satisfaction was a significant factor for all the persuasive strategies. However, satisfaction also had the highest number of stronger significance to the persuasive strategies. It was strongly related to competition, praise and suggestion. The prominence of satisfaction suggests that players are not solely motivated by the immediate impact of persuasive elements but are deeply influenced by their overall sense of gratification and enjoyment derived from the game. Understanding the significance of satisfaction becomes pivotal in tailoring behaviour change interventions that extend beyond the immediate persuasive cues, considering the holistic gaming experience. Given its notable impact, game designers are encouraged to strategically incorporate elements that contribute to player satisfaction. Persuasive strategies such as leaderboards, praise, and gameful suggestions, which have demonstrated stronger significance, can be further refined and optimized to enhance the overall satisfaction of players. For example, badges and leaderboards can be designed not just as markers of achievement but as elements that contribute to a sense of accomplishment and progress. Positive reinforcement through praise and well-timed suggestions can be woven seamlessly into the gameplay, creating moments that elevate player satisfaction.

5.4 Relevance and Suggestion Strategy

Relevance, as a key motivational dimension, demonstrated significant relationships with all the persuasive strategies, showing the strongest relationship with the suggestion strategy. This finding suggests that the suggestion strategy can play an important role in aligning the persuasive message in behaviour change games with the relevance of the content. It also implies that the suggestion strategy is an important tool for making the game content personally meaningful and pertinent to the player, enhancing its overall relevance. Understanding the dynamics of relevance allows for the strategic tailoring of persuasive interventions to maximize their impact. Designers can leverage the suggestion strategy to enhance the perceived relevance of the content and increase its motivational appeal. In practical terms, these findings offer valuable insights for persuasive game designers aiming to optimize the motivational appeal of behaviour change interventions. By strategically incorporating suggestion elements, designers can create interventions that resonate with players on both cognitive and emotional levels. This may involve implementing well-timed and contextually relevant suggestions that align with the behaviour goals of the game, ensuring that they contribute meaningfully to the overall motivational experience.

6 Conclusion

In conclusion, this study aimed to explore the relationship between the effectiveness of persuasive strategies and their motivational appeal in a behaviour change. The results collectively contribute to the growing body of knowledge on the design and optimization of behaviour change games. Designers and researchers alike can draw upon these findings to tailor interventions that not only capture attention and relevance but also foster confidence and satisfaction, ultimately driving sustained motivation for positive behaviour change.

While these recommendations in our work offer valuable guidance for designing behaviour change games, it is crucial to acknowledge the study's limitations. Future research could explore additional contextual factors, participant demographics, and game design elements to further refine our understanding of the intricate relationships between persuasive strategies and motivation. Additionally, ongoing research should investigate the long-term effects of persuasive strategies on sustained behaviour change and also explore the impact of game framing on the motivational appeal and effectiveness of these games.

References

1. Abdessettar, S., et al.: Persuasive technologies for efficient adaptable self-education kids smart mobile school project. In: The Eighth International Conference on Mobile, Hybrid, and On-line Learning
2. Al-Tawfiq, J.A., Pittet, D.: Improving hand hygiene compliance in healthcare settings using behavior change theories: reflections. Teach. Learn. Med. **25**(4), 374–382 (2013). https://doi.org/10.1080/10401334.2013.827575
3. Anagnostopoulou, E., et al.: Exploring the links between persuasion, personality and mobility types in personalized mobility application. In: Vries, P.W., Oinas-Kukkonen, H., Siemons, L., Jong, N.B., Gemert-Pijnen, L. (eds.) PERSUASIVE 2017. LNCS, vol. 10171, pp. 107–118. Springer, Cham (2017). https://doi.org/10.1007/978-3-319-55134-0_9
4. Bandura, A.: Self-efficacy: toward a unifying theory of behavioral change. Adv. Behav. Res. Therapy **1**(4), 139–161 (1978). https://doi.org/10.1016/0146-6402(78)90002-4
5. Baranowski, T., et al.: Playing for real. Am. J. Prevent. Med **34**(1), 74-82.e10 (2008). https://doi.org/10.1016/j.amepre.2007.09.027.
6. Brown, S.J., et al.: Educational video game for juvenile diabetes: results of a controlled trial. Med. Inform. **22**(1), 77–89 (1997). https://doi.org/10.3109/14639239709089835
7. Busch, M., et al.: More than sex: the role of femininity and masculinity in the design of personalized persuasive games. In: Meschtscherjakov, A., De Ruyter, B., Fuchsberger, V., Murer, M., Tscheligi, M. (eds.) Persuasive Technology, pp. 219–229. Springer International Publishing, Cham (2016). https://doi.org/10.1007/978-3-319-31510-2_19
8. Chen, Y.X., et al.: Opportunities for persuasive technology to motivate heavy computer users for stretching exercise. In: Lecture Notes in Computer Science (including subseries Lecture Notes in Artificial Intelligence and Lecture Notes in Bioinformatics) (2014)
9. Chin, W.W.: The partial least squares approach for structural equation modeling. Modern Methods Bus. Res. 295–336 (1998)
10. Chittaro, L., Sioni, R.: Turning the classic snake mobile game into a location-based exergame that encourages walking. In: Lecture Notes in Computer Science (including subseries Lecture Notes in Artificial Intelligence and Lecture Notes in Bioinformatics) (2012)
11. Chiu, M.-C., et al.: Playful bottle: a mobile social persuasion system to motivate healthy water intake. In: Proceedings of the 11th International Conference on Ubiquitous Computing, pp. 185–194, New York, NY, USA (2009)
12. Derbali, L., Frasson, C.: Players' motivation and EEG waves patterns in a serious game environment. In: Lecture Notes in Computer Science (including subseries Lecture Notes in Artificial Intelligence and Lecture Notes in Bioinformatics). 6095 LNCS, PART 2, pp. 297–299 (2010). https://doi.org/10.1007/978-3-642-13437-1_50/COVER
13. Dickinson, A., et al.: Ukko: Enriching persuasive location based games with environmental sensor data. In: CHI PLAY '15 Proceedings of the 2015 Annual Symposium on Computer-Human Interaction in Play (2015)

14. Drozd, F., et al.: Exploring perceived persuasiveness of a behavior change support system: a structural model. In: Bang, M., Ragnemalm, E.L. (eds.) Persuasive Technology. Design for Health and Safety, pp. 157–168. Springer Berlin Heidelberg, Berlin, Heidelberg (2012). https://doi.org/10.1007/978-3-642-31037-9_14

15. Fogg, B.: A behavior model for persuasive design (2009)

16. Gopalan, V., et al.: A review of the motivation theories in learning 020043 (2017)

17. Hamari, J., et al.: Does gamification work? – a literature review of empirical studies on gamification. In: Proceedings of the Annual Hawaii International Conference on System Sciences (2014)

18. Kadomura, A., et al.: Sensing fork and persuasive game for improving eating behavior (2013)

19. Keller, J.M.: Development and use of the ARCS model of instructional design. J. Instruct. Dev. **10**(3), 2–10 (1987). https://doi.org/10.1007/BF02905780/METRICS

20. Kupek, E.: Beyond logistic regression: Structural equations modelling for binary variables and its application to investigating unobserved confounders. BMC Med. Res. Methodol. (2006). https://doi.org/10.1186/1471-2288-6-13

21. Lin, T., et al.: A persuasive game to encourage healthy dietary behaviors of kindergarten children. In: Adjunct Proceedings of the 8th International Conference on Ubiquitous Computing (2006)

22. Ndulue, C., et al.: Personality-targeted persuasive gamified systems: exploring the impact of application domain on the effectiveness of behaviour change strategies. User Model User-Adap. Inter. **32**(1–2), 165–214 (2022)

23. Ndulue, C., Orji, R.: STD PONG : An african-centric persuasive game for risky behaviour change. In: Adj. Proceedings of Persuasive Technology Conference (2018)

24. O'Donoghue, T., Rabin, M.: The economics of immediate gratification. J. Behav. Dec. Mak. **13**(2), 233–250 (2000). https://doi.org/10.1002/(SICI)1099-0771(200004/06)13:2%3c233::AID-BDM325%3e3.0.CO;2-U

25. Oinas-Kukkonen, H., Harjumaa, M.: Persuasive systems design: key issues, process model, and system features. Commun. Assoc. Inform. Syst. **24**(1), 485–500 (2009)

26. Orji, R., et al.: Deconstructing persuasiveness of strategies in behaviour change systems using the ARCS model of motivation. Behav. Technol. **38**(4), 319–335 (2019). https://doi.org/10.1080/0144929X.2018.1520302

27. Orji, R., et al.: Improving the efficacy of games for change using personalization models. ACM Trans. Comput.-Hum. Interact. **24**(5), 1–22 (2017). https://doi.org/10.1145/3119929

28. Orji, R., et al.: LunchTime: a slow-casual game for long-term dietary behavior change. Pers. Ubiquit. Comput. **17**(6), 1211–1221 (2013). https://doi.org/10.1007/s00779-012-0590-6

29. Orji, R., et al.: LunchTime: a slow-casual game for long-term dietary behavior change. Pers. Ubiquit. Comput. **17**(6), 1211–1221 (2013). https://doi.org/10.1007/s00779-012-0590-6

30. Orji, R., Vassileva, J., Mandryk, R.L.: Modeling the efficacy of persuasive strategies for different gamer types in serious games for health. User Model. User-Adap. Inter. **24**(5), 453–498 (2014). https://doi.org/10.1007/s11257-014-9149-8

31. Orji, R., et al.: Personalizing persuasive strategies in gameful systems to gamification user types. In: Conference on Human Factors in Computing Systems - Proceedings (2018)

32. Orji, R., et al.: Tailoring persuasive health games to gamer type. In: Proceedings of the SIGCHI Conference on Human Factors in Computing Systems - CHI'13, New York, New York, USA, p. 2467 (2013)

33. Orji, R., et al.: Towards personality-driven persuasive health games and gamified systems. In: Conference on Human Factors in Computing Systems – Proceedings (2017)

34. Oyebode, O., et al.: Nourish your tree! developing a persuasive exergame for promoting physical activity among adults. In: 2020 IEEE 8th International Conference on Serious Games and Applications for Health, SeGAH 2020 (2020)

35. Oyebode, O., et al.: Tailoring persuasive and behaviour change systems based on stages of change and motivation. In: Conference on Human Factors in Computing Systems – Proceedings (2021). https://doi.org/10.1145/3411764.3445619
36. Oyibo, K., et al.: Investigation of the persuasiveness of social influence in persuasive technology and the effect of age and gender. In: CEUR Workshop Proceedings (2017)
37. Pentz, M.A., et al.: A videogame intervention for tobacco product use prevention in adolescents. Addict. Behav. **91**, 188–192 (2019). https://doi.org/10.1016/j.addbeh.2018.11.016
38. Product | SmartPLS
39. Ryan, R.M., Deci, E.: Self-determination theory and the facilitation of intrinsic motivation, social development, and well-being. Am. Psychol. **55**(1), 68–78 (2000). https://doi.org/10.1037/0003-066X.55.1.68
40. Sarstedt, M., Cheah, J.-H.: Partial least squares structural equation modeling using SmartPLS: a software review. J. Market. Anal. **7**(3), 196–202 (2019). https://doi.org/10.1057/s41270-019-00058-3
41. Small, R.V.: Motivation in Instructional Design. ERIC Digest. ERIC Publications; ERIC Digests in Full Text. ERIC Clearinghouse on Information and Technology, 4-194 Center for Science and Technology, Syracuse, NY 13244-4100 (free while supplies lasts) (1997)
42. Stockdale, J., et al.: Applying the ARCS design model to breastfeeding advice by midwives in order to motivate mothers to personalise their experience. Evid. Based Midwifery (2014)
43. The Science of Persuasion – Scientific American: 2004. https://www.scientificamerican.com/article/the-science-of-persuasion/. Accessed 11 March 2019
44. Thomas, R.J., et al.: Can i influence you? Development of a scale to measure perceived persuasiveness and two studies showing the use of the scale. Front. Artif. Intell. (2019). https://doi.org/10.3389/frai.2019.00024
45. van Velsen, L., et al.: Tailoring persuasive electronic health strategies for older adults on the basis of personal motivation: Web-based survey study. J. Med. Internet Res. **21**(9), e11759 (2019). https://doi.org/10.2196/11759
46. de Vries, R.A.J., et al.: A word of advice: how to tailor motivational text messages based on behavior change theory to personality and gender. Pers. Ubiquit. Comput. **21**(4), 675–687 (2017). https://doi.org/10.1007/s00779-017-1025-1
47. Wigfield, A., Eccles, J.S.: Expectancy – value theory of achievement motivation. Contemp. Educ. Psychol. **25**(2000), 68–81 (2000). https://doi.org/10.1006/ceps.1999.1015
48. Ying, M.-H., Yang, K.-T.: A game-based learning system using the ARCS model and fuzzy logic (2013). https://doi.org/10.4304/jsw.8.9.2155-2162.
49. Yusoff, Z., Kamsin, A.: Game rhetoric: interaction design model of persuasive learning for serious games. In: Zaphiris, P., Ioannou, A. (eds.) LCT 2015. LNCS, vol. 9192, pp. 644–654. Springer, Cham (2015). https://doi.org/10.1007/978-3-319-20609-7_60

Personality and Individual Differences

(Un)sustainable Personalities: The Role of Personality When Persuading to Adopt Sustainable Behaviours

Elena Minucci$^{(\boxtimes)}$ ⓘ, Martin Lages ⓘ, and Simone Stumpf ⓘ

University of Glasgow, Glasgow, UK
elena.minucci@glasgow.ac.uk

Abstract. Achieving a sustainable future requires behaviour change on a large scale. One possible approach is to improve persuasive technology by mirroring each users' personality, but research on this is very limited. In this work, we explore whether the Big Five personality traits underpin differences in persuasive text for sustainability, both in terms of content and linguistics. We also investigate whether personality scores can be reliably predicted from persuasive text, using machine learning (ML) techniques. Our results show that personality traits appear to influence some aspects of the content, but not linguistics; however, predicting personality is more successful through linguistics than content. We provide a follow-on analysis of which features are most informative to predict personality scores. Based on these results, we provide recommendations for automatic personality recognition and synthesis in persuasive technologies.

Keywords: Persuasive Technology · Personality Traits · Personality Recognition · Personality Synthesis · Machine Learning · LIWC · Linguistics

1 Introduction

Building a sustainable future for all requires an interplay of updates in infrastructure and large-scale individual behaviour change, as indicated by the United Nations [45]. One major obstacle to large-scale behaviour change technologies is that individuals differ widely; as such, individual user characteristics need to be taken into account to ensure effective, personalised interactions [3, 8]. One of the most reliable predictors of behaviour change is personality [13, 41]. Personality is defined as a set of individual characteristics which underpin behaviour, and which are thought to be relatively stable across one's lifespan [18, 40]. Many persuasive technologies across various domains, such as health [35, 38], counselling [23] and product recommendations [22], already take personality into account, either by measuring the user's personality using questionnaires [35, 38] or, more rarely, by manipulating the "personality" of the technology itself, such as building "extroverted" [22] or "dominant" technologies [34]. However, current personality-adaptive technologies generally fail to capture the complexity of human personality, often focusing on only a single personality trait [1, 6, 17, 33] or focusing on general-purpose text rather than persuasive text. To inform personality-aware persuasive

© The Author(s), under exclusive license to Springer Nature Switzerland AG 2025
K. T. Win et al. (Eds.): PERSUASIVE 2025, LNCS 15711, pp. 299–314, 2025.
https://doi.org/10.1007/978-3-031-94959-3_21

technologies, there is a need to explore how personality affects persuasive communication, both in terms of content (*what* is said) and linguistics (*how* it is said). Our research questions are as follows:

RQ1: Do personality traits predict differences in persuasive writing, either for linguistic or content features?
RQ2: Is it possible to predict personality traits from persuasive writing? Which features matter?

One major limitation to advance research in this area is the lack of suitable datasets linking persuasive texts to personality traits. To investigate these research questions, we collected written samples from people attempting to persuade others to take up sustainable behaviours. We used multivariate regression to find personality markers in the content and linguistics features of their writing. Then, we explored personality prediction from persuasive writing using machine learning (ML) and explainable artificial intelligence (XAI) approaches. Our contributions are as follows:

- We provide a publicly available dataset linking personality traits to persuasive text, using sustainable behaviour as domain to further research in this area.
- We provide evidence of personality markers in persuasive text that can be used to inform personality recognition and synthesis in persuasive technologies.

2 Related Work

Human personality is a complex construct; current personality research favours models which assess personality on a spectrum, such as the Big Five [18] and HEXACO [5], over models which use categorical personality types, such as MBTI [27]. The most widely used personality model is the Big Five model, which assesses personality along five independent traits: Extraversion, Agreeableness, Conscientiousness, Neuroticism and Openness to experience [18]. Differences along these personality traits have been observed to influence both how humans produce [4, 24] and respond [2, 29] to language. This has been replicated across various general-purpose texts [4, 24], such as stream of consciousness essays [21, 29], self-narratives [21], and blog posts [42]. However, for persuasive texts, the role of personality traits is underexplored.

In general, individuals show a preference for technologies that mirror their personality traits [21, 22], which is defined as similarity-attraction paradigm. To achieve similarity, we need persuasive technologies that are both aware of the user's personality, *and* able to embody a personality that resonates with the personality of the user. These two challenges are referred to as *personality recognition* and *personality synthesis*, respectively. Personality recognition is concerned with predicting a human's true personality from interaction with a system, while personality synthesis is concerned with giving a realistic personality to conversational systems [40]. Personality recognition in persuasive technologies is often not automated; most technologies will ask the user to self-report their personality [31, 35, 38]. There is a substantial body of research on automatic personality recognition in general-purpose text [11, 30], but not in persuasive text. Personality synthesis is understudied in persuasive systems. The few systems that have attempted it only considered one personality trait at a time and used extreme categories, such as comparing the persuasiveness of a highly extrovert versus a highly introvert system [22, 34]. It has been previously acknowledged [15] that using extreme categories is problematic, as it is not a true reflection of human personality, which involves nuanced interplay across the five traits. There is a lack of research on how people with different personality traits communicate persuasively, which can then form a basis for personality synthesis and recognition. This research is hampered by the absence of a dataset linking personality traits and persuasive texts. Similar datasets typically pair personality scores with language use in generic, non-persuasive text [4, 26], while others [37] use estimations of personality traits with no access to ground truth. The current study aims to fill this gap.

3   Methods

3.1 Dataset Construction

Participants. The participant data used for this study, as well as all measures and prompts used are publicly available [28]. We recruited a sample of 137 native English speakers over 18 years of age through the Prolific participant pool [43]. This sample size was determined through an a-priori power analysis for multiple regression using G*Power [14], for alpha $= 0.05$, to detect a small-to-medium effect size ($f^2 = 0.09$), with 80% power. Participants were paid an average of £8.45/hour for their time. This study was approved by the Ethics Committee at University of Glasgow.

Materials. Personality was assessed through the Big Five Inventory (BFI) [18], which is a 44-item questionnaire scored on a 1–5 Likert scale. The BFI has excellent reliability and validity across cultures [16, 20] and is quick to administer, while accounting for more variance across individuals than shorter scales like Ten Items Personality Inventory [19]. Participants responded to five writing prompts. In each prompt, a fictitious character (e.g., "your neighbour Susan", "your friend Greg") shared their plans to commit to a sustainable behaviour and asked the participant's opinion on it. Each prompt mentioned a different sustainable behaviour, such as recycling, reducing driving, reducing meat consumption. These prompts were first piloted with 10 participants (not included in the final sample); we found that participants found it easier to type their responses across multiple textboxes rather than one single textbox, so our questionnaire accommodated this. An example prompt is displayed in Fig. 1.

3.2 Study Analyses

First, we excluded participants who wrote less than 100 words. This resulted in a final sample for analysis of 128 participants (66 females and 62 males), with a mean age of 36.44 (SD = 12.14, Min 19, Max 68). The minimum detectable effect size remained small-to-medium following exclusions ($f^2 = 0.10$). We concatenated all text written by each participant, which resulted in one writing sample per participant.

To investigate RQ1, we extracted linguistic features of the writing samples using Linguistic Inquiry and Word Count (LIWC) [9] software, which is the most widely used

Fig. 1. Example prompt from the Qualtrics questionnaire.

large lexicon for textual analysis. We selected five key linguistic features (see Table 1 for details) which have been linked to persuasiveness [37] in previous research: Word Count, Analytical Language, Certitude, Self-references and Lexical Diversity. While Lexical Diversity is not part of the original LIWC-22 dictionary, previous research [37] has suggested this addition. We ran a 5x5 multivariate regression model on R exploring whether personality traits scores predicted our chosen linguistic features. Next, we extracted content features through a thematic analysis [10]. In line with best practices for qualitative coding, we adopted an iterative process, where codes were merged or split to avoid repetitions, and sub-themes were added following discussion amongst the team of researchers. Eleven content features emerged from our thematic analysis, clustered along three broader themes: *reasons* to carry out a sustainable behaviour; *advice* on how to successfully carry out sustainable behaviours; and *evaluations* of sustainable behaviours, such as praise or criticism. These features are displayed in Table 2. To explore whether personality predicted differences in content features, we ran a 5×11 multivariate regression model on R.

To investigate RQ2, we compared the performance of three widely used ML approaches, which have previously been used with datasets of similar size: XGBoost (XGB) [12], Random Forest (RF) [32] and Support Vector Machine (SVM) [36]. We predicted personality scores as continuous variables, using three sets of predictors: all LIWC-22 features, our content features, and using a vectorised text approach. We employed a TF-IDF vectoriser for the latter task, as this has previously outperformed other vectorisers in personality recognition tasks [11]. We used 5-fold cross-validation for each of the models, splitting the dataset into 5 parts and using 4 for training and 1 for testing at each iteration. This ensures that all datapoints are used for both training and testing exactly once. We evaluated model performance using Mean Absolute Error (MAE). This metric was chosen because it is in the same scale as the outcome variable, and it is relatively resistant to outliers compared to similar metrics such as Root Mean Squared Error (RMSE). Altogether, this resulted in 45 ML models: 5 personality traits × 3 sets of predictors (linguistic features, content features, vectorised text features) × 3 types of models (RF, SVM, XGB). To check for differences in performance across these models, we ran a 5 × 3 × 3 ANOVA in R. We investigated the best performing models using beeswarm plots from SHAP [44], which is a XAI method used to interpret results of machine learning models. It assigns each feature a score that indicates how much that feature shifted the prediction higher or lower in each instance. SHAP beeswarm plots have been used for feature analysis in other domains [25], and the method is suitable for a study of this size as it requires a minimum of 100 samples [44].

4   Results

4.1   Data Description

Linguistic Features. Descriptives for the 5 key linguistic features are reported in Table 1. We observed large variances in word count, analytical language score and self-references in text, while lexical diversity scores were relatively similar across participants.

Table 1. Definition, means and SDs of selected linguistic features used to answer RQ1.

Linguistic features descriptives		
Feature	Definition	Mean (SD)
Word Count (WC)	Total word count	324.70 (184.08)
Analytical Language	Metric of logical, formal thinking	33.81 (18.86)
Certitude	Words relating to certitude (really, actually, of course, real) as a % of word count	0.74 (0.67)
Self-References	Use of "I" + "we" pronouns as a % of word count	3.04 (2.19)
Lexical Diversity	Unique words/total words	0.58 (0.06)

Content Features. Means and SDs for all content features are reported in Table 2. These are expressed as counts: for example, each participant mentioned environmental reasons 2.80 times on average. In general, we found that people provided a mix of reasons, advice and evaluations, but stated reasons more often than the other two features.

Personality Traits. Mean personality scores and standard deviations are reported in Table 3. When benchmarked against a large dataset of 1 M + entries [46], we found our dataset's personality spread was found to be comparable to the general population.

Table 2. Examples, definitions, means and sds for content features.

Content features descriptives				
Theme	Feature	Definition	Example	Mean (SD)
Reasons	Environmental Reasons	Used when a participant mentions environmental reasons to carry out the target behaviour	"You should be buying second hand clothes because it reduces your carbon footprint"	2.80 (2.40)
	Financial Reasons	Used when a participant mentions financial reasons to carry out the target behaviour	"Think at how much money you can save"	1.80 (1.23)
	Health Reasons	Used when a participant mentions health reasons to carry out the target behaviour	"a bonus of eating less meat is the health benefits you will most likely reap"	0.90 (0.96)
	Easy to Do	Used every time a participant mentions that the target behaviour is easy to carry out	"Super easy way to help reduce pollution"	0.54 (0.67)
Advice	Offers to Help	Used when the participant suggests to seek help from others, or directly offers to help	"I recycle a lot. Let me help you"	1.17 (1.68)
	Alternatives	Used when a participant suggests an alternative sustainable behaviour that is not in the prompt	"You could start with electricity consumption. I shut off a lot of my household electronics."	0.43 (0.88)
	Start Small	Used when a participant suggests a starting step that is easier to achieve than the target behaviour	"Start small – try to walk or cycle to work one day a week and then try to build it up."	0.80 (0.99)

(continued)

Table 2. (*continued*)

Content features descriptives

Theme	Feature	Definition	Example	Mean (SD)
Evaluations	Praise	Used when a participant uses words of praise or encouragement	"I'm so proud of you for thinking of this"	1.62 (1.73)
	Criticism	Used when a participant criticises the target behaviour	"Eating less meat doesn't necessarily reduce your carbon footprint, some fruit and veg may need to travel just as far"	0.17 (0.43)
	Scoping Questions	Used when a participant asks a question about circumstances that affect the target behaviour	"Is there much public transportation infrastructure near you?"	0.54 (0.99)
	Barriers	Used when a participant mentions obstacles to the target behaviour	"It's tough because fast fashion is convenient"	1.10 (1.29)

Table 3. Characteristics, means and SDs of Big Five personality traits in our dataset.

Personality trait descriptives

Trait	Characteristics	Mean (SD)
Extraversion	Low: reserved, thoughtful High: sociable, fun-loving	3.04 (0.85)
Agreeableness	Low: suspicious, uncooperative High: trusting, helpful	3.85 (0.58)
Conscientiousness	Low: impulsive, disorganized High: disciplined, careful	3.73 (0.72)
Openness	Low: prefers routine, practical High: imaginative, spontaneous	3.74 (0.66)
Neuroticism	Low: calm, confident High: anxious, pessimistic	2.83 (0.87)

4.2 RQ1. Do Personality Traits Predict Differences in Persuasive Writing?

Linguistic Features. We ran a multivariate multiple regression, setting the five personality traits as independent variables and our five linguistic features (word count, analytical language, certitude, self-references and lexical diversity) as dependent variables. The model was not significant (Pillai's V $= 0.23$, F(25, 610) $= 1.19, p = 0.237$), suggesting that personality traits did not predict differences in these linguistic features.

Content Features. We ran a multivariate regression, setting the 5 personality traits as independent variables and our 11 content features from Table 2 as dependent variables. The multivariate model was significant (Pillai's V $= 0.65$, F(55, 580) $= 1.58, p = 0.006$), suggesting that personality traits significantly predicted the content of persuasive text. Specifically, higher openness predicted more frequent mentions of health reasons, while higher extraversion and lower conscientiousness both predicted more frequent mentions of barriers to adopt a sustainable behaviour. The univariate models for health reasons and barriers are reported in Tables 4 and 5. No other models were significant. Gender differences were controlled for in both analyses for RQ1 and none were found.

Table 4. Impact of personality traits on mention of health reasons.

Impact of Personality traits on mention of health reasons Adj. $R^2 = 0.099$ $p = \mathbf{0.003**}$				
Predictor	B	Std. Error	β	p
Constant	1.142	1.003	1.142	0.257
Extraversion	0.022	0.109	0.008	0.838
Agreeableness	−0.272	0.172	−0.133	0.116
Conscientiousness	−0.150	0.143	−0.112	0.295
Openness	0.512	0.135	0.257	**<.001***** Adj.$R^2 = 0.098$
Neuroticism	−0.205	0.119	−0.472	0.086

Table 5. Impact of personality traits on mention of barriers.

Impact of Personality traits on mention of barriers Adj. $R^2 = 0.05$ $p = \mathbf{0.043*}$				
Predictor	B	Std. Error	β	p
Constant	1.946	1.385	1.946	0.162
Extraversion	0.300	0.151	0.256	**0.049*** Adj.$R^2 = 0.022$
Agreeableness	0.035	0.237	0.012	0.883
Conscientiousness	−0.580	0.197	−0.473	**0.004**** Adj.$R^2 = 0.043$
Openness	0.133	0.187	0.088	0.478
Neuroticism	−0.062	0.164	−0.080	0.705

4.3   RQ2. Is It Possible to Predict Personality Traits from Persuasive Writing? Which Features Matter?

We ran a total of 45 ML analyses, each predicting one of 5 personality trait scores from one of 3 sets of predictors (linguistic features, content features, vectorised text), using one of 3 types of models (RF, SVM, XGB). Figure 2 shows the MAE of each model.

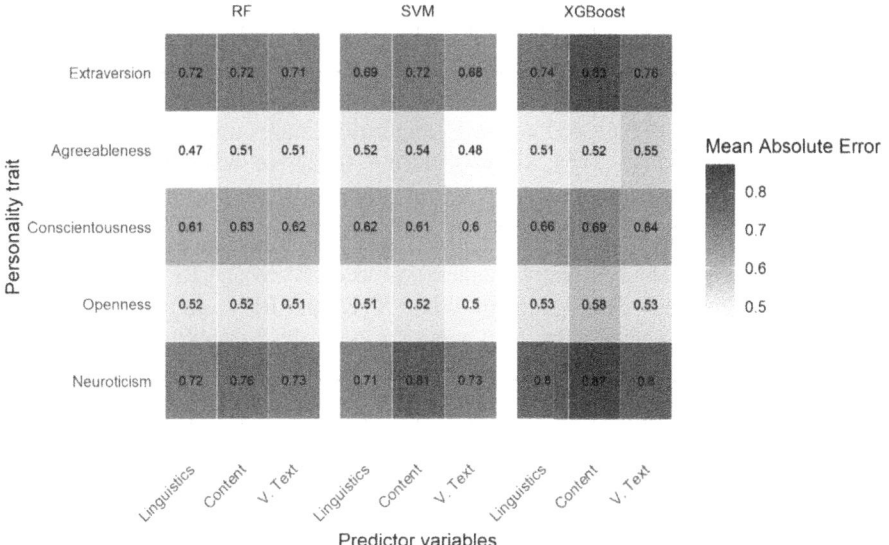

Fig. 2. Faceted heatmap of Mean Absolute Error by personality trait (Y axis), predictor (X axis) and ML model used (facets). Lighter colour indicates better performance.

Each personality trait was assessed from 1 to 5 points (range = 4). The mean error in prediction was 0.62, corresponding to an error margin of ±15.5% from the actual value. Error margins ranged from a minimum of 11.75% to a maximum of 21.75%. To identify differences in performance across traits, models and predictors, we ran a traits(5) × models(3) × predictors(3) ANOVA, which is reported in Table 6. We found significant main effects for all three independent variables, although effect sizes were small throughout. There were no significant interaction effects.

Table 6. Differences in MAE across traits, models and predictors..

Differences in MAE across traits, models and predictors						
	DF (nun, den)	Sum Sq	Mean Sq	F	η^2	p
Trait	4, 5715	59.9	14.97	71.22	0.047	**< 0.001***
Model	2, 5715	2.1	1.03	4.91	0.001	**0.007**
Predictor	2, 5715	1.6	0.79	3.78	0.001	**0.023***

There was a highly significant main effect for Personality Trait. Post-hoc Bonferroni comparisons showed that agreeableness (M = 0.51, SD = 0.36) and openness (M = 0.52, SD = 0.42) had significantly lower error rates than all other traits. These were also the traits with lower standard deviation. Conscientiousness (M = 0.63, SD = 0.44) was the next best trait, with significantly higher accuracy than extraversion (M = 0.73, SD = 0.52) and neuroticism (M = 0.76, SD = 0.54), both $p < .001$. There was also a significant main effect for the ML model used. Bonferroni comparisons showed that both SVM (M = 0.61, SD = 0.46) and RF (M = 0.62, SD = 0.46) performed significantly better than XGBoost (M = 0.65, SD = 0.49), $p = 0.016$ and $p = 0.037$, respectively. Lastly, there was a significant main effect for Predictors used. Post-hoc Bonferroni comparisons indicated that linguistic features were the best predictor (M = 0.61, SD = 0.44), followed by vectorised text (M = 0.62, SD = 0.46). Linguistic features were significantly more accurate than content (M = 0.65, SD = 0.50), $p = 0.024$ but there was no significant difference for vectorised text.

Feature Analysis Using SHAP Values. We focus our investigation on the best performing traits (Agreeableness and Openness), models (SVM and RF) and predictors (linguistic features and vectorised text). While SVM and RF reach similar accuracy when predicting personality traits, they appear to do so by considering different features. When predicting agreeableness from linguistic features, SVM produces directional results, meaning that feature value appears to skew impact positively or negatively. The most impactful linguistic features for predicting Agreeableness are reported in Fig. 3. SVM predicts higher agreeableness when the writing is longer, more analytical and shows higher social status (Clout). RF shows a range of emotion-related linguistic features such as Affect, Emotion, Positive Emotion, as well as cognition-related features such as Cognition, Cognitive Processes, Insight, Cause, Certitude. When predicting agreeableness from vectorised text, SVM considers more connecting words such as verbs, pronouns and adjectives ('my', 'your', 'good'). RF shows some words related to the task, such as 'bottle', 'area', 'recommend', as well as many evaluative words, such as 'feel', 'think', 'good', 'much', 'different', 'best'. Across both SVM and RF, the verb 'think' has a very high impact.

The most impactful linguistic features for Openness are reported in Fig. 4. SVM predicts increased Openness when text is more analytic, more authentic and shows lower social status. Word count has the highest impact but does not show a consistently positive or negative direction. RF seems to draw from broad semantic fields, such as Culture, Perception, Lifestyle. In vectorised text, SVM relies largely on function words. RF shows more words relating to sustainability, such as 'car', 'recycling', 'planet'.

5   Discussion

5.1   Limitations

The current study presents some limitations. Our writing prompts were designed to explore how people support others in meeting their goals, which is the main role of persuasive technology; we did not explore other facets of persuasion such as arguing

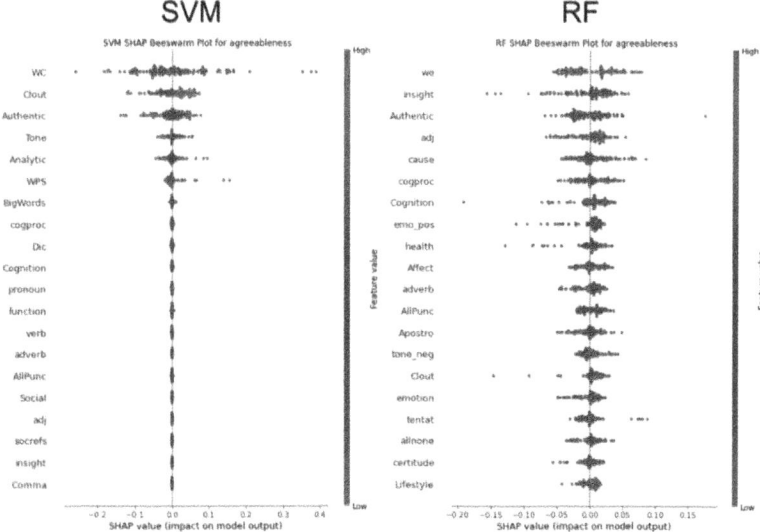

Fig. 3. SHAP Beeswarm plots showing most impactful linguistic features for predicting Agreeableness, using SVM (left) and RF (right). Each row represents one feature and each dot represents one instance of that feature. Feature values are on a red-to-blue gradient scale, with red indicating higher feature value.

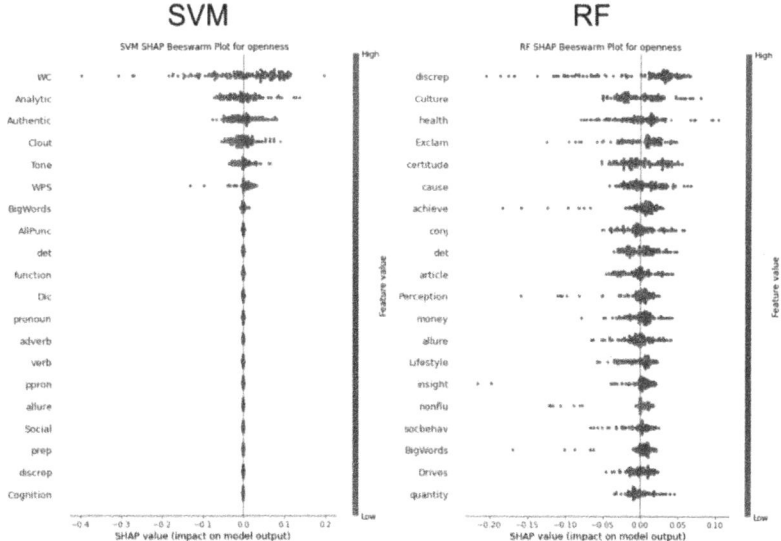

Fig. 4. SHAP Beeswarm plots showing most impactful linguistic features for predicting Openness, using SVM (left) and RF (right). See Fig. 3 caption for plot structure.

"for" or "against" sustainable behaviour. We also did not explore conversational persuasion, as no interaction with other people was required for this study. The data we collected is specific to sustainable behaviours and to native English speakers and it cannot be generalised to other domains or linguistic backgrounds. Lastly, the present study employs a relatively small sample size. This is common in human subject studies and the approaches we adopted for machine learning and explainable AI have previously been used on similar sample sizes. However, it is advisable to replicate these analyses on bigger samples to increase generalisability.

5.2   Implications for the Design of Persuasive Technologies

Personality Recognition: Different Personalities, Different Ways of Saying Things? Our results suggest that automatic personality recognition from persuasive texts may be a viable avenue, with an accuracy comparable to that of general-purpose text [11]. We found that Agreeableness and Openness can be predicted more accurately than the other three traits. The same trend has been previously observed in personality recognition using binary classification (high vs low scores on each trait) [39]. We also found that RF and SVM are well suited models for personality recognition. As RF and SVM leverage features differently, choosing one or the other may depend on the use case. RF is more resistant to differences in variable scaling and is less computationally expensive than SVM, which might make it more suitable for use cases that require timely interactions, such as chatbots. Our results show that SVM, in contrast, reaches similar accuracy to RF by utilizing less features, therefore it may be a better choice if only a small number of key features are available. Linguistic features were the best predictor of personality and we suggest that future persuasive technologies employ them in their personality recognition models.

Personality Synthesis: When is it Worth it? In order to inform personality synthesis, we explored whether personality influences how people communicate persuasively. One surprising finding was that personality did not predict linguistic features in our sample, even though we had selected linguistic features based on previous research linking them to persuasion in online text [37]. This finding contrasts with the majority of research using general-purpose text [15, 29]. One possible explanation is that these features are important for persuasive texts in general, independently of personality traits. As we found linguistic features to be a good predictor of personality, it is likely that the relationship between personality and persuasive text is more complex than previously thought, leveraging interactions across multiple linguistic features. In contrast, we found that personality predicts content of persuasive text. These personality markers in content could be used for personality synthesis; for example, a more "open" persuasive agent may mention health benefits more often.

Future Work. Our results point to personality differences in persuasive writing. Future research should explore whether these differences in writing result in increased persuasion. Since real-life persuasion is built on interaction, future work should investigate how the persuader's personality interacts with the listener's. Future research may also build on our findings by considering other user characteristics beyond personality, such as gender, age or cognitive style. Indeed, behaviour change is always a result of the interaction between individual differences and context [7], as different people experience different real-life behavioural cues and barriers. Future research should explore how people with different characteristics achieve behaviour change in different circumstances, and in other domains beyond sustainability.

6   Conclusion

This study contributed the first dataset linking personality traits with persuasive writing. We found that personality can predict selected content features of persuasive text, but not its linguistic features, and that personality recognition from persuasive text is a viable avenue, reaching similar accuracy to general-purpose text. Agreeableness and Openness can be predicted more accurately than all other traits. RF and SVM reach good accuracy in personality recognition and may have different ideal use cases. The present dataset, together with the results of our analyses provide the first steps towards personality recognition and synthesis in persuasive technology for sustainability.

Acknowledgments. This work was supported by the UKRI Centre for Doctoral Training in Socially Intelligent Artificial Agents, Grant Number EP/S02266X/1.

Disclosure of Interests.   The authors have no competing interests to declare that are relevant to the content of this article.

References

1. Ait Baha, T., et al.: The power of personalization: a systematic review of personality-adaptive chatbots. SN Comput. Sci. **4**(5), 661 (2023). https://doi.org/10.1007/s42979-023-02092-6
2. Alqahtani, F., et al.: Personality-based approach for tailoring persuasive mental health applications. User Model. User-Adap. Inter. **32**(3), 253–295 (2022). https://doi.org/10.1007/s11257-021-09289-5
3. Alslaity, A., et al.: A panoramic view of personalization based on individual differences in persuasive and behavior change interventions. Front. Artific. Intell. **6** (2023)
4. Argamon, S., et al.: Lexical predictors of personality types. In: Proceedings of the 2005 Joint Annual Meeting of the Interface and the Classification Society of North America, pp. 1–16 (2005)
5. Ashton, M.C., Lee, K.: The HEXACO model of personality structure and the importance of the h factor. Soc. Pers. Psychol. Compass **2**(5), 1952–1962 (2008). https://doi.org/10.1111/j.1751-9004.2008.00134.x
6. Balloccu, S., et al.: Unaddressed challenges in persuasive dieting chatbots. In: Adjunct Proceedings of the 29th ACM Conference on User Modeling, Adaptation and Personalization, pp. 392–395 ACM, Utrecht Netherlands (2021). https://doi.org/10.1145/3450614.3463602
7. Barsalou, L.W.: Situated simulation in the human conceptual system. Lang. Cognit. Process. **18**(5–6), 513–562 (2003). https://doi.org/10.1080/01690960344000026
8. Berkovsky, S., et al.: Adaptivity and personalization in persuasive technologies. In: 11th International Conference on Persuasive Technology, PERSUASIVE 2016, pp. 13–25. CEUR Workshop Proceedings (2016)
9. Boyd, R., et al.: The Development and Psychometric Properties of LIWC-22 (2022). https://doi.org/10.13140/RG.2.2.23890.43205

10. Braun, V., Clarke, V.: Thematic analysis. In: Maggino, F. (ed.) Encyclopedia of Quality of Life and Well-Being Research, pp. 1–7. Springer International Publishing, Cham (2020). https://doi.org/10.1007/978-3-319-69909-7_3470-2

11. Celli, F., et al.: The workshop on computational personality recognition 2014. In: Proceedings of the 22nd ACM international conference on Multimedia. pp. 1245–1246. ACM, Orlando Florida USA (2014). https://doi.org/10.1145/2647868.2647870

12. Chen, T., Guestrin, C.: XGBoost: a scalable tree boosting system. In: Proceedings of the 22nd ACM SIGKDD International Conference on Knowledge Discovery and Data Mining, pp. 785–794 ACM, San Francisco California USA (2016). https://doi.org/10.1145/2939672.2939785

13. Ciocarlan, A., et al.: Actual persuasiveness: impact of personality, age and gender on message type susceptibility. In: Oinas-Kukkonen, H., et al. (eds.) Persuasive Technology: Development of Persuasive and Behavior Change Support Systems: 14th International Conference, PERSUASIVE 2019, Limassol, Cyprus, April 9–11, 2019, Proceedings, pp. 283–294. Springer International Publishing, Cham (2019). https://doi.org/10.1007/978-3-030-17287-9_23

14. Faul, F., et al.: G*Power 3: a flexible statistical power analysis program for the social, behavioral, and biomedical sciences. Behav. Res. Methods **39**(2), 175–191 (2007). https://doi.org/10.3758/BF03193146

15. Feizi-Derakhshi, A.-R., et al.: Text-based automatic personality prediction: a bibliographic review. J. Comput. Soc. Sci. **5**(2), 1555–1593 (2022). https://doi.org/10.1007/s42001-022-00178-4

16. Fossati, A., et al.: The big five inventory (BFI). Eur. J. Psychol. Assess. **27**(1), 50–58 (2011). https://doi.org/10.1027/1015-5759/a000043

17. Galitsky, B.: Adjusting chatbot conversation to user personality and mood. In: Galitsky, B. (ed.) Artificial Intelligence for Customer Relationship Management: Solving Customer Problems, pp. 93–127. Springer International Publishing, Cham (2021). https://doi.org/10.1007/978-3-030-61641-0_3

18. Goldberg, L.R.: The development of markers for the Big-Five factor structure. Psychol. Assess. **4**(1), 26–42 (1992). https://doi.org/10.1037/1040-3590.4.1.26

19. Gosling, S.D., et al.: A very brief measure of the Big-Five personality domains. J. Res. Pers. **37**(6), 504–528 (2003). https://doi.org/10.1016/S0092-6566(03)00046-1

20. Hee, O.: Validity and reliability of the big five personality traits scale in Malaysia. Int. J. Innov. Appl. Stud. **5**(4), 309 (2014)

21. Hirsh, J.B., Peterson, J.B.: Personality and language use in self-narratives. J. Res. Pers. **43**(3), 524–527 (2009). https://doi.org/10.1016/j.jrp.2009.01.006

22. Jin, E., Eastin, M.S.: Birds of a feather flock together: matched personality effects of product recommendation chatbots and users. J. Res. Interact. Mark. **17**(3), 416–433 (2022). https://doi.org/10.1108/JRIM-03-2022-0089

23. Kolenik, T., et al.: PerMEASS – personal mental health virtual assistant with novel ambient intelligence integration. In: AAI4H@ ECAI, pp. 8–12 (2020)

24. Lee, C.H., et al.: The relations between personality and language use. J. Gen. Psychol. **134**(4), 405–413 (2007). https://doi.org/10.3200/GENP.134.4.405-414

25. Li, R., et al.: Use of machine learning models to predict in-hospital mortality in patients with acute coronary syndrome. Clin. Cardiol. **46**(2), 184–194 (2023). https://doi.org/10.1002/clc.23957

26. Mairesse, F., et al.: Using linguistic cues for the automatic recognition of personality in conversation and text. J. Artific. Intell. Res. **30**, 457–500 (2007). https://doi.org/10.1613/jair.2349

27. Mccaulley, M.H.: The myers-briggs type indicator: a measure for individuals and groups. Meas. Eval. Couns. Dev. **22**(4), 181–195 (1990). https://doi.org/10.1080/07481756.1990.12022929

28. Minucci, E.: ElenaMinucci/Pers-Pers-Dataset. https://github.com/ElenaMinucci/Pers-Pers-Dataset (2024)
29. Pennebaker, J.W., Lee, C.H.: The power of words in social, clinical, and personality psychology. Korean J. Thinking Problem Solv. **12**(2), 35–43 (2002)
30. Picca, D., Pitteloud, J.: Personality recognition in digital humanities: a review of computational approaches in the humanities. Digit. Sch. Humanit. **38**(4), 1646–1658 (2023). https://doi.org/10.1093/llc/fqad047
31. Prost, S., et al.: Contextualise! personalise! persuade! a mobile hci framework for behaviour change support systems. In: Proceedings of the 15th International Conference on Human-Computer Interaction with Mobile Devices and Services. pp. 510–515. Association for Computing Machinery, New York, NY (2013). https://doi.org/10.1145/2493190.2494434
32. Rigatti, S.J.: Random forest. J. Insur. Med. **47**(1), 31–39 (2017). https://doi.org/10.17849/insm-47-01-31-39.1.
33. Ruane, E., et al.: User perception of text-based chatbot personality. In: Følstad, A., et al. (eds.) Chatbot Research and Design: 4th International Workshop, CONVERSATIONS 2020, Virtual Event, November 23–24, 2020, Revised Selected Papers, pp. 32–47. Springer International Publishing, Cham (2021). https://doi.org/10.1007/978-3-030-68288-0_3
34. Ruijten, P.A.M.: The similarity-attraction paradigm in persuasive technology: effects of system and user personality on evaluations and persuasiveness of an interactive system. Behav. Inform. Technol. **40**(8), 734–746 (2021). https://doi.org/10.1080/0144929X.2020.1723701
35. Smith, K.A., et al.: Personalizing reminders to personality for melanoma self-checking. In: Proceedings of the 2016 Conference on User Modeling Adaptation and Personalization. pp. 85–93 Association for Computing Machinery, New York, NY, USA (2016). https://doi.org/10.1145/2930238.2930254
36. Suthaharan, S.: Support vector machine. In: Suthaharan, S. (ed.) Machine Learning Models and Algorithms for Big Data Classification: Thinking with Examples for Effective Learning, pp. 207–235. Springer US, Boston, MA (2016). https://doi.org/10.1007/978-1-4899-7641-3_9
37. Ta, V.P., et al.: An inclusive, real-world investigation of persuasion in language and verbal behavior. J. Comput. Soc. Sci. **5**, 883–903 (2022). https://doi.org/10.1007/s42001-021-00153-5
38. Trujillo, A., Buzzi, M.C.: Towards a fuzzy rule-based systems approach for adaptive interventions in menopause self-care. In: Adjunct Publication of the 26th Conference on User Modeling, Adaptation and Personalization, pp. 53–56 Association for Computing Machinery, New York, NY, USA (2018). https://doi.org/10.1145/3213586.3226193
39. Verhoeven, B., et al.: Evaluating content-independent features for personality recognition. In: Proceedings of the 2014 ACM Multi Media on Workshop on Computational Personality Recognition, pp. 7–10. ACM, Orlando Florida USA (2014). https://doi.org/10.1145/2659522.2659527
40. Vinciarelli, A., Mohammadi, G.: A survey of personality computing. IEEE Trans. Affective Comput. **5**(3), 273–291 (2014). https://doi.org/10.1109/TAFFC.2014.2330816
41. Xu, W., et al.: The utility of personality types for personalizing persuasion. In: Baghaei, N., Vassileva, J., Ali, R., Oyibo, K. (eds.) Persuasive Technology. PERSUASIVE 2022. Lecture Notes in Computer Science, 13213. Springer, Cham. (2022). https://doi.org/10.1007/978-3-030-98438-0_19
42. Yarkoni, T.: Personality in 100,000 Words: a large-scale analysis of personality and word use among bloggers. J. Res. Pers. **44**(3), 363–373 (2010). https://doi.org/10.1016/j.jrp.2010.04.001
43. About Prolific. https://www.prolific.com/about. Last accessed 25 Oct 2024

44. An introduction to explainable AI with Shapley values — SHAP latest documentation, https://shap.readthedocs.io/en/latest/example_notebooks/overviews/An%20introduction%20to%20explainable%20AI%20with%20Shapley%20values.html. Last accessed 21 Oct 2024

45. AR6 Synthesis Report: Climate Change 2023 — IPCC. https://www.ipcc.ch/report/sixth-assessment-report-cycle/. Last accessed 17 Oct 2024

46. Take a personality test – Open Source Psychometrics Project. https://openpsychometrics.org/. Last accessed 24 Feb 2025

Non-binary People are Harder to Persuade: Evidence and Insights

Victor Sonego[2]([✉]), Annye Braca[1] [iD], and Pierpaolo Dondio[1]([✉]) [iD]

[1] School of Computer Science, Technological University Dublin, Dublin, Ireland
{d18127085,pierpaolo.dondio}@tudublin.ie
[2] Faculty of Health and Medical Sciences, University of Copenhagen,
Copenhagen, Denmark
victor.sonego@sund.ku.dk

Abstract. We investigated the relationship between the effect of persuasion techniques on the individual and their gender, conceptualized as a three-value variable where participants could identify as male, female, or non-binary. While previous research has primarily examined the role of binary genders in persuasion, this study is the first to compare susceptibility to persuasion across binary and non-binary individuals. A total of 1,995 participants evaluated the persuasive impact of 30 statements representing 10 persuasion techniques (e.g., framing, social proof, flattery) across three contexts. Additionally, participants' personality traits and dysfunctional attitudes were assessed using the TIPI and DAS scales. Our findings revealed that non-binary participants were significantly less susceptible to persuasion, consistently assigning lower scores than both male and female participants across all techniques and contexts. The difference between non-binary individuals and binary genders was an order of magnitude greater than that between male and female participants, even after controlling for age, education, TIPI personality traits, and DAS dysfunctional attitudes. Mediation analysis indicated that 34.1% of the effect of gender on persuasion was explained by personality traits and dysfunctional attitudes, with Conscientiousness, Love, and Entitlement emerging as significant mediators. However, a substantial portion of the gender effect remained unexplained by these factors. To address this residual difference in persuasion scores, we propose two potential explanations: a stronger propensity among non-binary individuals to challenge and defy societal norms, and the influence of counterpublics and echo chambers in amplifying resistance to mainstream narratives and persuasive messaging.

Keywords: Persuasion · Gender studies · Personality traits ·
Non-Binary · LGBT

1 Introduction

Persuasion, a cornerstone of social influence, operates across diverse domains, from advertising to political discourse, leveraging our cognitive, emotional, and

K. T. Win et al. (Eds.): PERSUASIVE 2025, LNCS 15711, pp. 315–329, 2025.
https://doi.org/10.1007/978-3-031-94959-3_22

social tendencies. While research has explored how gender and personality influence susceptibility to persuasion [1,13], a critical gap remains in understanding how non-binary individuals respond to persuasive tactics. This study examines the relationship between persuasion and a three-value gender construct, where participants could self-identify as male, female, or non-binary, and it investigates the relationship between these three gender categories and the self-perceived effect of different persuasion techniques across various domains. Despite the increasing visibility of non-binary individuals, research on persuasion remains focused on binary gender categories, overlooking the unique experiences of those who identify outside this framework. This oversight is significant given the distinct challenges non-binary individuals face in affirming their identity within a binary-oriented society [10,31,33]. A more comprehensive understanding of the relationship between gender and persuasion offers a more inclusive understanding of psychological and social influence, and it can enhance the effectiveness of communication strategies. We expect that non-binary people may exhibit a lower susceptibility to persuasion, hypothesizing that the interplay of established minority social dynamics, and the process of deliberate self-reflection and critical examination of foundational social norms (i.e., the gender binary), may result in an increased tolerance to persuasion tactics.

The current study thus addresses the following research questions:

Q1. *Do non-binary individuals exhibit significantly different susceptibility to persuasion compared to binary individuals?*
    If such a difference is present, we also question:
Q2. *Do personality traits act as mediating factors?*
Q3. *What other factors might explain the difference in susceptibility to persuasion between binary and non-binary individuals?*

To answer our research questions, we exploit previous survey data published by Braca and Dondio in [5], where 1,995 participants rated the persuasive effect of 30 statements designed using 10 different persuasion techniques across three domains. This research represents a significant contribution to the understanding of the interplay between gender and persuasion, marking the first investigation into whether non-binary individuals differ in susceptibility to persuasion and it examines the role of personality traits as potential mediators. By addressing these questions, the study challenges binary-centric frameworks in persuasion research, integrates non-binary perspectives, and provides a more inclusive understanding of how gender identity intersects with social and cognitive processes. It also sheds light into how non-binary individuals navigate external influences and assert autonomy in a predominantly binary society.

2   Methodology

2.1   Data Collection

This study is based on an open-access dataset collected by two of the authors of this paper and published in [5], which is designed to simulate the peripheral route of persuasion. This dataset contains 1,995 valid participant submissions and includes information on demographics, personality traits, dysfunctional attitudes, and responses to persuasive statements. Braca and Dondio [5] recruited participants through the Prolific Academic platform (prolific.com), compensating them at an hourly rate of £9. Prolific is an online platform that connects researchers with diverse, high-quality participants for academic and market research studies. Data was collected using Qualtrics software (qualtrics.com).

Of 1,995 participants, 5.41% identified as non-binary. This reflects population estimates in English-speaking countries; A 2022 study found that 5% of the U.S. population identifies as non-binary, with a higher incidence among individuals aged 18–29 [7]. This is reflected in our dataset, where 42% of the respondents is under 26, and 37% is aged between 26 and 35. To address these factors, in our analysis we controlled for age and education.

The dataset provides insights into demographics, personality traits, dysfunctional attitudes, and agreement with persuasive techniques. Demographic variables include age, gender, and education level. Personality traits were measured with the Ten Item Personality Inventory (TIPI), which is a brief assessment tool designed to measure the Big Five personality traits: Extraversion, Agreeableness, Conscientiousness, Emotional Stability, and Openness to Experience. The Dysfunctional Attitude Scale (DAS) was used to assess attitudes related to Approval, Love, Achievement, Perfectionism, Entitlement, Omnipotence and Autonomy. The DAS is designed to evaluate dysfunctional beliefs and cognitive vulnerability, providing insights into an individual's psychological strengths based on their belief system. Finally, participants' agreement with statements using persuasive techniques was evaluated using a Net Promoter Score (NPS) ranging from 1 to 10, focusing on promoting paid news subscriptions, blood donations, and exercise. NPS is a metric used to gauge user and customer experience by measuring agreement with persuasive statements. In the context of the study, participants rated their agreement with persuasive statements on a scale from 1 (not convincing) to 10 (very convincing). This approach mirrors the NPS methodology commonly used in user and customer experience programmes.

Persuasive techniques were embedded within statements promoting positive outcomes across three distinct contexts: (1) subscribing to online news platforms adhering to professional standards and ethics, (2) donating blood, and (3) engaging in physical exercise. Each context was represented by statements sharing similar core content, but varying in the specific persuasive technique employed. For instance, to encourage exercise (Context 3), the social proof technique was employed in the statement, "Most people recognize the numerous benefits of being active-consider getting up and going for a healthy walk". Similarly, the flattery technique was used within the same context, as demonstrated by the statement, "Smart, successful people like you recognize that small wins matter. Standing up and walking around during the workday can lift your mood and improve your focus and attention".

2.2   The TIPI and DAS Scales

The TIPI instrument employs 10 brief statements, each designed to capture one of five traits: Openness to Experience, Conscientiousness, Extraversion, Agreeableness, and Neuroticism. To ensure balanced measurements, half of the items are worded to reflect the opposite of the intended trait (i.e. reverse-scored items). For these reverse-scored items, higher scores (e.g. "Agree strongly" on a 7-point Likert scale) actually indicate lower levels of the trait, while lower scores signify higher levels. This scoring method helps to control for response bias and ensures accurate assessment of each personality dimension [16].

The DAS assessment [9] involves participants evaluating 35 statements using a Likert scale ranging from 1 to 5. The resulting DAS value system comprises seven dimensions: Approval, Love, Achievement, Perfectionism, Entitlement, Omnipotence, and Autonomy.

Burns [9] described these dimensions as reflections of an individual's philosophy, making DAS a valuable tool to capture personal belief systems. Similarly, Braca and Dondio [2–4,6] argued that users resonate more with online statements employing persuasive techniques aligned with their linguistic style preferences. These preferences, which include specific language patterns, trigger cognitive biases central to persuasion. While DAS and cognitive biases approach the interpretation of information differently, both explore how individuals process and evaluate information [24,36].

DAS measures rigid, often negative underlying beliefs–like perfectionism, which sets unreasonable standards for oneself or others, or entitlement, which reflects expectations of effortless positive outcomes and the belief that bad events should not occur to good people [8,26]. In contrast, cognitive biases focus on unconscious mental shortcuts that lead to systematic errors in thinking. For example, confirmation bias drives individuals to seek information supporting their beliefs while dismissing contradictory evidence. Similarly, negativity bias prioritizes negative information over positive, often reinforcing dysfunctional attitudes [29].

Both DAS and cognitive biases offer insights into how individuals process information and form judgments, even though they approach this from slightly different angles. DAS beliefs create a lens through which we filter information, influencing our interpretations and judgments. Cognitive biases affect how we efficiently, but sometimes inaccurately, process information, which also impacts our judgment.

2.3   Data Analysis

Data analysis was carried out using R version 4.4 [30]. Since the persuasion scores assigned to each technique were not normally distributed, we employed non-parametric tests. A Kruskal-Wallis test was used to examine the differences in persuasion scores between genders, followed by a Wilcoxon signed-rank test to compare two groups. Mediator models were computed using the `lavaan` package [32]. Hierarchical models were computed using the `lmer` package. Robust regressions were computed using the `robustlmm` and `MASS` packages. When we performed multiple statistical tests, we used Bonferroni correction [38] to take a conservative stance and reduce false positive (Type I errors).

3   Results

Valid data was collected for 1,995 participants. The full survey dataset including descriptive statistics was published by Braca and Dondio in [5]. This study focuses on data and analyses relevant to our research questions. Table 1 presents descriptive statistics for the categorical variables used in this study: Education, Age Group, and Gender, with non-binary individuals comprising 5.41% (108 participants) of our dataset.

Table 1. Categorical variables considered in the study (N = 1,995).

Variable	Classes Distribution
Gender	Male: 941 (47.17%); Female: 946 (47.42%); Non-Binary: 108 (5.41%)
Age Group	Under 26: 841 (42.2%); 26–35: 749 (37.5%); 36–45: 249 (12.5%); 46–55: 97 (4.9%); 56–65: 37 (1.9%); Over 65: 22 (1.1%)
Education	Junior Cert: 29 (1.5%); High School: 390 (19.5%); College but No Degree: 437 (21.9%); Associate degree: 100 (5%); Bachelor: 778 (39%); Master: 223 (11.2%); PhD: 38 (1.9%)

Each participant scored a total of 30 statements, 10 for each of the three following persuasive contexts: (1) *subscribe to a News provider*, (2) *donate blood* and (3) *exercise* more, with each of the ten statements employing a different persuasion technique. Table 2 shows the mean and standard deviation of the scores, aggregated by techniques and domains. Notably, *blood donation* was the domain with the highest persuasion scores, significantly higher than the other two domains. Among the persuasion techniques, *Framing* was the most effective, and *Social Proof* the least effective.

3.1   Do Non-binary Individuals Exhibit Different Susceptibility to persuasion Compared to Binary Individuals?

We examined whether there was a significant difference in persuasion scores based on users' self-identified gender. To begin, we computed the mean scores by gender for each technique and domain. Figure 1 shows non-binary participants consistently assigned lower persuasion scores across all techniques and domains. A Kruskal-Wallis test confirmed the significant differences in persuasion scores across genders identified by the descriptive analysis across all techniques and domains. Table 3 presents χ^2 statistics for a Kruskal-Wallis test comparing the mean scores between the three gender groups, repeated for each domain and

Table 2. Mean persuasion scores by technique and domain.

Persuasion Technique	D1: News Subscription		D2: Blood Donation		D3: Exercise		All Domains	
	Mean	SD	Mean	SD	Mean	SD	Mean	**SD**
T1: Framing	5.58	2.54	8.66	1.86	7.73	2.27	7.32	2.22
T2: Social Proof	3.84	2.38	7.16	2.39	6.43	2.58	5.81	2.45
T3: Flattery	5.08	2.57	7.19	2.77	6.77	2.75	6.35	2.70
T4: Rhetorical Q.	4.81	2.72	6.50	2.64	6.56	2.72	5.96	2.69
T5: Antanagoge	5.23	2.67	7.07	2.49	6.75	2.54	6.35	2.57
T6: Logic	4.61	2.61	6.72	2.65	6.74	2.46	6.02	2.57
T7: Authority	5.23	2.67	7.07	2.49	6.75	2.54	6.35	2.57
T8: Pathos	5.40	2.51	7.59	2.20	6.80	2.50	6.60	2.40
T9: Priming	4.81	2.78	7.16	2.59	6.11	2.95	6.03	2.77
T10: Anaphora	5.23	2.64	7.55	2.32	7.29	2.30	6.69	2.42
ALL Techniques	5.01	2.61	7.29	2.41	6.86	2.52	6.38	2.51

persuasion technique. Bonferroni correction was used to adjust the p-values. The table also includes the mean and standard deviation for the three gender groups and the combined *Binary* group. The last column displays the 99% confidence interval for a Wilcoxon signed-rank test comparing differences between the mean scores assigned by non-binary participants and binary participants. There was a significant difference across the three gender groups for all the techniques and domains, and the scores assigned by non-binary people were consistently and significantly lower across all domains and techniques.

We performed the same analysis for each of the 30 statements. The Kruskal-Wallis test was significant at the 99% confidence level for 26 out of 30 mean scores, with non-significant cases limited to the blood donation domain using the techniques of *Social Proof, Antanagoge, Anaphora*, and *Logic*. Notably, the non-binary group had the lowest mean score in all 30 statements. Therefore, our analysis provides evidence that non-binary individuals were consistently harder to persuade.

Consistent with previous studies [1,28], we also found significant differences between the mean scores of male and female participants in 12 out of 30 statements. Regarding aggregated scores, there was no significant differences across the 3 domains between male and female, while 4 out of 10 techniques proved significant (*Logic, Framing, Priming* and *Pathos*). However, the gap between non-binary participants and the two binary groups was much larger and frequent than the one between male and female participants. The average persuasion score assigned by non-binary participants was 5.42 (SD = 1.31) against 6.35 (SD = 1.10) for male and 6.45 (SD = 1.08) for female participants.

To confirm the difference between non-binary and binary participants, we controlled for covariates - the five TIPI personality traits, the seven DAS attitudes, participants' age group, and their level of education. As we did for the Kruskal-Wallis test, we trained a model for each of the three domains and the

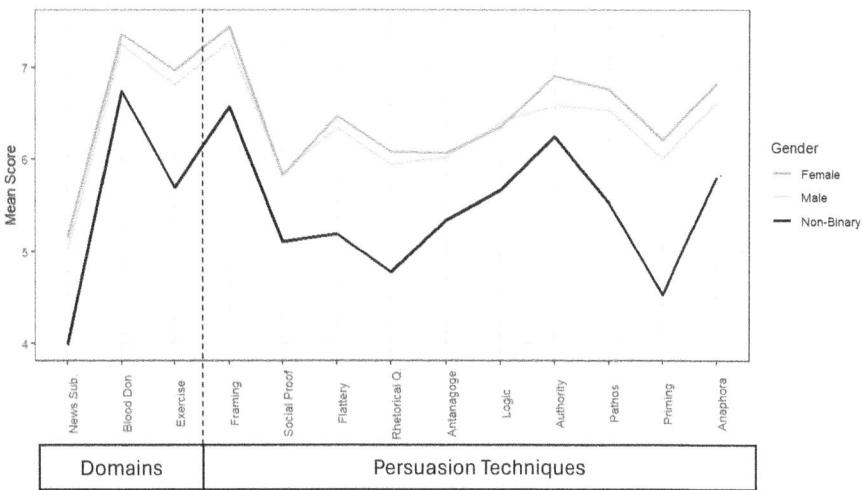

Fig. 1. Mean persuasion scores for each domain and persuasion technique. The mean scores assigned by non-binary participants are significantly lower than those assigned by binary participants. On the right, the Euclidean distance between the three gender groups computed using the mean persuasion sores for the ten techniques.

Table 3. For each domain and technique, χ^2 represents the chi-square statistic from a Kruskal-Wallis test comparing the mean scores across the three gender groups. The columns "Male", "Female", "Non-Binary", and "Binary" display the mean and standard deviation for each group, where "Binary" refers to the combined group of Male and Female participants. The last column presents the 99% confidence interval from a Wilcoxon signed-rank test, assessing whether the mean scores of Non-Binary participants were significantly lower than those of Binary participants. Bonferroni correction was used to adjust the significance levels.

Domain/Technique	K-W χ^2	Non-Binary	Female	Male	Binary (M + F)	Wilcox 99% CI (NB <B)
News Sub	40.05***	3.98 (1.85)	5.15 (1.85)	4.98 (1.85)	5.06 (1.85)	[0.7–1.7]
Blood Donation	14.11***	6.74 (1.71)	7.37 (1.71)	7.28 (1.67)	7.33 (1.69)	[0.1–1.1]
Exercise	44.89***	5.7 (1.86)	6.99 (1.85)	6.85 (1.77)	6.92 (1.81)	[0.8–1.8]
Framing	34.80***	6.57 (1.63)	7.46 (1.57)	7.28 (1.53)	7.37 (1.55)	[0.33–1.33]
Social Proof	15.38***	5.11 (1.91)	5.84 (1.86)	5.87 (1.81)	5.85 (1.84)	[0.33–1.33]
Flattery	30.17***	5.19 (2.36)	6.48 (2.18)	6.35 (2.13)	6.41 (2.15)	[0.67–2]
Rhetorical Q.	35.08***	4.77 (2.12)	6.09 (2.21)	5.95 (2.11)	6.02 (2.16)	[0.67–2]
Antanagoge	15.77***	5.34 (1.9)	6.09 (2.0)	6.04 (1.81)	6.06 (1.9)	[0.33–1.33]
Logic	14.44***	5.66 (1.85)	6.36 (2.14)	6.42 (1.88)	6.39 (2.01)	[0.33–1.33]
Authority	27.22***	6.24 (1.86)	6.91 (1.8)	6.58 (1.71)	6.75 (1.75)	[0.1–1.1]
Pathos	47.29***	5.53 (1.79)	6.77 (1.84)	6.54 (1.75)	6.66 (1.79)	[0.67–1.67]
Priming	55.03***	4.53 (2.14)	6.21 (2.2)	6.02 (2.11)	6.11 (2.15)	[1–2.33]
Anaphora	33.62***	5.81 (1.79)	6.84 (1.91)	6.64 (1.73)	6.74 (1.82)	[0.67–1.33]

ten persuasion techniques, matching the cases shown in Table 3. Since our data exhibited heteroskedasticity of residuals, we employed Humber regression [20], a robust regression model that assigns lower importance to outliers. Additionally, we used *Heteroskedasticity-Corrected Standard Errors* [37] to estimate p-values and confidence intervals. For each technique or domain we thus fitted the following regression model:

$$Y = \beta_g \cdot g + \beta_a \cdot a + \beta_e \cdot e + \beta_{1..5} \cdot \mathbf{X_{TIPI}} + \beta_{6..12} \cdot \mathbf{X_{DAS}} \tag{1}$$

The variable g represented gender, modelled as a binary variable with 0 encoding both male and female participants and 1 non-binary participants. The variables a and e represented the age group and the level of education of participants. The variables $\mathbf{X_{TIPI}}$ and $\mathbf{X_{DAS}}$ are two vectors, of size 5 and 7 respectively, representing the TIPI personality traits and the DAS attitudes of each participant. The regression models showed that the variable gender significantly predicted persuasion scores in all the domains and techniques but one. The most significant effect was found for *Priming* ($beta_g = -1.27$) and *Flattery* ($beta_g = -1.04$), while no significant effect was found for *Logic* ($beta_g = -0.28$, p=0.12). We also trained the same model for each of the 30 statements. The results were similar to those of the Kruskal-Wallis test, with gender being significant in 25 statements at the 99% confidence level. As with the Kruskal-Wallis test, the non-significant statements were all in the Blood Donation domain and corresponding to the following techniques: *Social Proof, Antanagoge, Anaphora, Logic*, and *Authority*. Overall, regression analysis confirmed that non-binary participants were less susceptible to persuasion even in fully controlled models.

3.2   Do Personality Traits Act as Mediating Factors?

To explain the effect of gender on persuasion scores, we tested whether personality traits and dysfunctional attitudes mediated the gender effect.

Following [15], mediation requires that the potential moderator M be predicted by the independent variable (here, *gender*). We therefore tested which of our 12 potential mediators (the TIPI and DAS variables) could be predicted by gender in a regression model controlling for age and education. Six traits were significantly predicted by gender: *Conscientiousness, Neuroticism, Love, Perfectionism, Entitlement*, and *Achievement* (Table 4). The traits Openness and Extraversion had p-values near the 0.05 significance threshold; however, we preferred to take a conservative approach and chose not to interpret them as significant.

After selecting the candidates for mediation according to the results of the regression model, we tested the model shown in Fig. 2 using the R package `lavaan`. The model tested the parallel mediation effect of the six selected personality traits and attitudes on the relationship between gender and persuasion scores. Three of the six mediators were significant: Conscientiousness, Love, and Entitlement. The mediated effect accounted for 34.1% of the total effect, indicating partial mediation. Therefore the TIPI and DAS variables explained a sub-

Table 4. For each TIPI and DAS variable Y_i, the table shows the coefficient β_g and its p-value of the model $Y_i = \beta_g \cdot g + \beta_a \cdot a + \beta_e \cdot e$, where g = gender (1 = non-binary), e = the level of education, a = age group.

TIPI			DAS		
Y_i	β_g	p-value	Y_i	β_g	p-value
Openness	0.28	0.051	Approval	−0.32	0.40
Conscientiousness	**−5.83**	**<0.001 ***	**Love**	**−1.7**	**<0.001 ***
Extraversion	-0.32	0.052	**Achievement**	**1.17**	**0.014 ***
Agreeableness	0.19	0.12	**Perfectionism**	**1.96**	**<0.001 ***
Neuroticism	**0.86**	**<0.001 ***	**Entitlement**	**1.73**	**<0.001 ***
			Omnipotence	−0.20	0.56
			Autonomy	−0.51	0.19

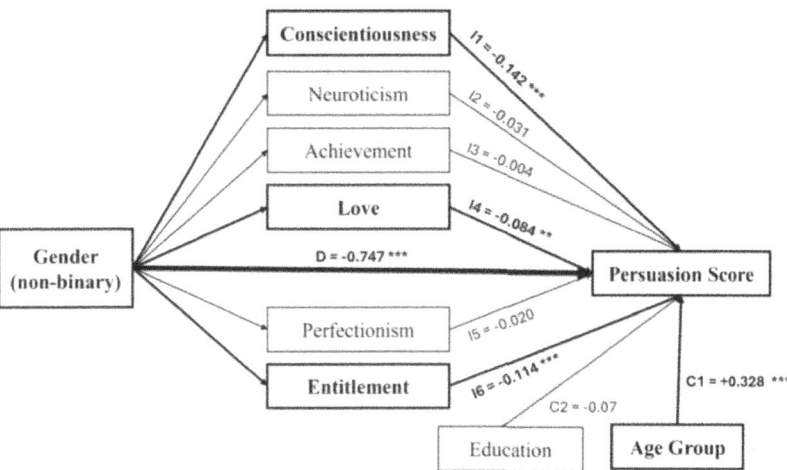

Fig. 2. Parallel mediation model. Love, Entitlement and Conscientiousness were significant partial mediators. The control covariate Age was also significant. The effect of Gender on the Persuasion scores was partially mediated: the direct effect was D = −0.747, while the total mediated effect was −0.387, for a total effect of −1.134; 34.1% of the effect was mediated.

stantial portion of the gender effect on persuasion, but the majority remained unexplained.

We repeated the analysis for each domain and technique separately, obtaining very similar results (Table 5). The moderators Conscientiousness and Entitlement were consistently significant, Love was significant in all cases except for the technique Priming, and Neuroticism showed weaker significance for Social Proof, Rhetorical Question, and Priming. The personality traits mediated an average of 38.5% (SD = 8.2%) of the total effect of gender on persuasion scores across the 10 techniques considered.

Table 5. Parallel mediation models for each domain and persuasion technique. The table shows the total and direct effect of gender on persuasion scores, the portion of effect modulated by the six mediators, and the p-value associated with each of them.

	Total	Direct	% Mediated	Cons.	Neur.	Achi.	Love	Perf.	Entitlement
D1	−1.109	−0.712	0.358	<0.001 ***	0.013	0.49	0.006 **	0.96	<0.001 ***
D2	−0.527	−0.279	0.471	<0.001 ***	0.18	0.29	0.024 *	0.27	<0.001 ***
D3	−1.134	−0.747	0.341	<0.001 ***	0.16	0.534	0.005 **	0.22	<0.001 ***
t1	−0.763	−0.562	0.263	0.001 ***	0.095	0.204	0.056	0.28	0.001 ***
t2	−0.687	−0.38	0.447	0.007 **	0.021 *	0.61	0.007 **	0.59	<0.001 ***
t3	−1.21	−0.739	0.389	<0.001 ***	0.087	0.86	0.005 **	0.67	<0.001 ***
t4	−1.188	−0.705	0.407	<0.001 ***	0.008 **	0.52	0.005 **	0.61	<0.001 ***
t5	−0.678	−0.369	0.456	0.005 **	0.081	0.445	0.009 **	0.256	<0.001 ***
t6	−0.686	−0.316	0.539	<0.001 ***	0.054	0.8	0.013 *	0.64	<0.001 ***
t7	−0.502	−0.288	0.426	<0.001 ***	0.73	0.48	0.048 *	0.326	0.001 ***
t8	−1.093	−0.78	0.286	<0.001 ***	0.251	0.323	0.009 **	0.363	0.001 ***
t9	−1.542	−1.07	0.306	<0.001 ***	0.043 *	0.727	0.005 **	0.385	<0.001 ***
t10	−0.882	−0.587	0.334	<0.001 ***	0.289	0.636	0.01 *	0.58	0.002 **

4   Discussion

Our first research question aimed to verify whether persuasion techniques had differing effects across the three gender types. Our analysis confirmed significant differences, with non-binary participants proving consistently harder to persuade. Across all domains and techniques, non-binary participants assigned significantly lower scores than males and females. While some significant differences were found between male and female groups, the gap between binary and non-binary participants was much larger and more frequent. In terms of persuasion scores, non-binary participants formed an isolated group almost equidistant from male and female participants, who were much closer to each other. These differences persisted after controlling for age, education, personality traits (TIPI), and dysfunctional attitudes (DAS).

To explain these differences, we tested whether personality traits and dysfunctional attitudes mediated the effect of gender on persuasion scores.

Traits and attitudes explained 34.1% of the total effect of gender on persuasion scores. Conscientiousness and the attitudes of Love and Entitlement were consistently significant across the 10 techniques analyzed, while Neuroticism had a weaker significant effect in only 3 techniques.

The finding that personality traits play a significant yet partial role in persuasion aligns with [25], who found that individual traits influence susceptibility to political messaging. Similarly, our research identified Conscientiousness as a key trait, while Neuroticism demonstrated a more selective impact, influencing only a subset of the persuasion techniques.

We hypothesize that the influence of Conscientiousness, Entitlement and Love may be related to the development of a greater level of individualism among non-binary individuals compared to binary gender-conforming people. This individualism may also partly explain their greater resistance to persuasion, as it correlates with an increased ability to withstand social pressures [21, 31, 35]. However, further research is needed to examine this potential link between non-binary identities and individualism, its origins, and its implications - such as whether it is a consequence of the marginalizing experiences of non-binary people in society.

Nonetheless, the mediation analysis, although significant, showed how the majority of the effect was not explained by personality traits nor attitudes, opening the discussion to other explanations. Despite the highly limited literature on non-binary individuals, we propose the following two explanations.

Hypothesis 1: The Questioning Mind Identity, Deconstruction, and Defiance. We hypothesize that non-binary individuals' resistance to persuasive techniques is rooted in their distinct experiences of deconstructing, challenging and defying societal norms, particularly the pervasive binary gender system. The process of establishing and defending a non-binary identity likely has consequences extending beyond the binary gender paradigm, also cultivating critical engagement with foundational societal assumptions and fostering a general skepticism toward normative pressures and persuasive influences [31, 33]. This heightened resistance to persuasive language may arise from the following interconnected factors:

1. *The I with themself: Identity formation and critical self-reflection.* Non-binary individuals realise at their gender identity through a process of deconstruction of traditional, binary gender norms. This deconstruction requires a continuous act of resistance against entrenched societal norms and paradigms [31]. This experience of challenging and ultimately rejecting one of society's most foundational constructs - the gender binary - encourages an active predisposition to question the intent, credibility, and assumptions underlying broader societal systems that perpetuate conformity and normative pressures, including persuasive messages. Indeed, persuasion techniques often rely on appealing to conformity or social proof, which might be less effective for individuals already accustomed to questioning and defying social expectations.

2. *The I and the social environment: Minority stress, hostile environment, and community*: The social environment - including both hostile and affirming influences - might play a key role in shaping non-binary individuals' resistance to persuasion. According to the Gender Minority Stress model [17, 18], an extension on the Minority Stress model [22], gender-diverse individuals face both distal stressors (external discrimination and marginalization) and proximal stressors (internalized stigma, concealment of identity, negative expectation of future events). These stressors lead to the development of protective coping mechanisms; one such mechanism is the seeking and establishment of a community of like-minded people. This dynamic is tied with Hypothesis 2, presented below, which explores the role of counterpublics and social echo

chambers in shaping the different response of non-binary people to the investigated persuasion techniques. Additionally, stressors may foster psychological adaptations such as increased skepticism towards authority, heightened self-awareness, and resilience against external pressures - all of which might contribute to a reduced susceptibility to persuasive techniques. The relationship between neuroticism and minority stress deserves further exploration. Higher levels of neuroticism, which are linked to minority stress [23], were found to be significantly more prevalent among non-binary participants compared to male and female participants.

3. *The I and authority: Lower baseline trust towards authority and institution*: Non-binary individuals often experience systemic exclusion and lack of recognition from the public and institutions, which may reduce their baseline trust in authority. Even in progressive societies, everyday challenges persist, such as binary gender requirements on documents, limited access to gender-neutral facilities, which also increase the risk facing discrimination and violence [10,27]. These experiences likely contribute to a perception of institutions as untrustworthy, promoting a reduced baseline trust in authority, which may be interpreted as a protective mechanism to distal stressors. This lower baseline trust translates into an increased resistance to institutional narratives and mainstream perspectives, including resilience against societal pressures and persuasive efforts that align with conventional norms.

Hypothesis 2: Counterpublics and Social Echo-Chambers. Another plausible explanation lies in the role of queer counter-spaces and social echo chambers in shaping communication dynamics, especially evidenced today through social media. Counterpublics are social groups that exist in isolation or partial isolation from dominant society, and which develop conscientious internal networks and cultural frameworks that oppose and resist dominant narratives and power structures [14]. At the same time, social echo chambers may contribute to non-binary individuals' resistance to persuasive messaging. This is a fundamentally social phenomenon, particularly evident today through social media platforms, where algorithms often create highly insular networks [11,34] where individuals primarily interact with like-minded peers and encounter content reinforcing their existing worldview, regardless of the specific platform. [12]. Queer counter-spaces [19], combined with echo chamber effects, may foster critical thinking and skepticism toward mainstream narratives, including persuasive techniques. This is plausible, as non-binary individuals often challenge societal norms and may be more attuned to recognizing manipulative tactics because they have experienced questioning and resisting societal expectations, requiring them to question constantly and challenge norms related to gender and identity.

Non-binary individuals might thus benefit from insular online communities in multiple ways, which directly or indirectly promote shared resistance to persuasive messaging.

5   Conclusions and Future Works

In this paper we investigated the relationship between persuasion and a more comprehensive three-value gender construct, (male, female, and non-binary).

Our findings revealed significant differences across the three gender groups. Non-binary participants were notably less susceptible to persuasion, consistently scoring lower than both male and female participants across all techniques and contexts. Although differences between male and female participants were observed, the gap between non-binary individuals and the two binary genders was much larger and more frequent. A mediation analysis showed that 35% to 45% of the gender effect could be attributed to personality traits and dysfunctional attitudes, with significant mediators including lower Conscientiousness and attitudes of Love (lower) and Entitlement (higher) among non-binary participants. However, a substantial portion of the gender effect remained unexplained by these factors. To account for this residual difference in persuasion scores, we propose two explanations: a greater inclination among non-binary individuals to challenge and defy societal norms, and the effect of counter-spaces and echo chambers in amplifying resistance to mainstream narratives and persuasive messaging.

These findings underscore the need for targeted research into the social dynamics and psychological traits of non-binary individuals. It also calls for a more detailed understanding of the role of queer counter-spaces and social media in the creation of the hypothesized echo chamber effect. By addressing these gaps, future research can provide a more nuanced understanding of the unique psychological profiles and social contexts of non-binary individuals.

Acknowledgments. This research is supported by the Science Foundation Ireland ADAPT Centre (www.adaptcentre.ie) (Grant 13/RC/2106_P2) at Technological University Dublin (www.tudublin.ie).

Disclosure of Interests. The authors have no competing interests to declare that are relevant to the content of this article.

References

1. Abdullahi, A.M., Oyibo, K., Orji, R., Kawu, A.A.: The influence of age, gender, and cognitive ability on the susceptibility to persuasive strategies. Information **10**(11), 352 (2019)
2. Braca, A.: Understanding consumer response to marketing communications: personality traits, demographics, and dysfunctional attitudes survey dataset (2023)
3. Braca, A., Dondio, P.: Developing persuasive systems for marketing: the interplay of persuasion techniques, customer traits and persuasive message design. Ital. J. Mark. **2023**(3), 369–412 (2023)
4. Braca, A., Dondio, P.: Persuasive communication systems: a machine learning approach to predict the effect of linguistic styles and persuasion techniques. J. Syst. Inf. Technol. (2023)

5. Braca, A., Dondio, P.: Survey data on dysfunctional attitudes, personality traits, and agreement with persuasive techniques. Data Brief 109473 (2023)
6. Braca, A., Spillane, B., Wade, V., Dondio, P.: Pilot data collection survey and analytical techniques for persuasion engineering systems. In: DiGo - Dialog for Good - Workshop on Speech and Language Technology Serving Society, Stockholm, Sweden (2019)
7. Brown, A.: About 5% of young adults in the U.S. say their gender is different from their sex assigned at birth. Pew Research Center (2022). Accessed 19 Sept 2024
8. Brown, G.P., Beck, A.T.: Dysfunctional attitudes, perfectionism, and models of vulnerability to depression. American Psychological Association (2002). ISBN 1557988420
9. David, D.: Burns. Feeling good. Signet Book (1981)
10. METRO Youth Chances: Youth chances summary of first findings: the experiences of LGBTQ young people in England. METRO, London (2014)
11. Cinelli, M., De Francisci, G., Morales, A.G., Quattrociocchi, W., Starnini, M.: The echo chamber effect on social media. Proc. Natl. Acad. Sci. **118**(9), e2023301118 (2021)
12. Cinelli, M., et al.: The COVID-19 social media infodemic. Sci. Rep. **10**(1), 1–10 (2020)
13. Ciocarlan, A., Masthoff, J., Oren, N.: Actual persuasiveness: impact of personality, age and gender on message type susceptibility. In: Oinas-Kukkonen, H., Win, K.T., Karapanos, E., Karppinen, P., Kyza, E. (eds.) PERSUASIVE 2019. LNCS, vol. 11433, pp. 283–294. Springer, Cham (2019). https://doi.org/10.1007/978-3-030-17287-9_23
14. Fattal, A.: Counterpublic. In: The International Encyclopedia of Anthropology, pp. 1–2 (2018)
15. Frazier, P.A., Tix, A.P., Barron, K.E.: Testing moderator and mediator effects in counseling psychology research. J. Couns. Psychol. **51**(1), 115 (2004)
16. Gosling, S.D., Rentfrow, P.J., Swann, W.B.: A very brief measure of the big-five personality domains. J. Res. Pers. **37**(6), 504–528 (2003)
17. Hendricks, M.L., Testa, R.J.: A conceptual framework for clinical work with transgender and gender nonconforming clients: an adaptation of the minority stress model. Prof. Psychol. Res. Pract. **43**(5), 460 (2012)
18. Hunter, J., Butler, C., Cooper, K.: Gender minority stress in trans and gender diverse adolescents and young people. Clin. Child Psychol. Psychiatry **26**(4), 1182–1195 (2021)
19. Kjaran, J.I.: Queer counterpublic spatialities. In: Critical Concepts in Queer Studies and Education: An International Guide for the Twenty-First Century, pp. 249–257 (2016)
20. Koller, M.: robustlmm: an R package for robust estimation of linear mixed-effects models. J. Stat. Softw. **75**(6), 1–24 (2016)
21. Markus, H.R.: Cultural variation in the self-concept. In: The Self: Interdisplinary Approaches. Springer (1991)
22. Meyer, I.H.: Prejudice, social stress, and mental health in lesbian, gay, and bisexual populations: conceptual issues and research evidence. Psychol. Bull. **129**(5), 674 (2003)
23. Bailey, J.M.: The minority stress model deserves reconsideration, not just extension. Arch. Sex. Behav. **49**(7), 2265–2268 (2020)
24. Monroe, S.M., Slavich, G.M., Torres, L.D., Gotlib, I.H.: Severe life events predict specific patterns of change in cognitive biases in major depression. Psychol. Med. **37**(6), 863–871 (2007)

25. Nai, A., Schemeil, Y., Valli, C.: A persuadable type? Personality traits, dissonant information, and political persuasion. Int. J. Commun. **17**, 22 (2023)
26. Nelson, L.D., Stern, S.L., Cicchetti, D.V.: The dysfunctional attitude scale: how well can it measure depressive thinking? J. Psychopathol. Behav. Assess. **14**(3), 217–223 (1992)
27. UN OHCHR. Discrimination and violence against individuals based on their sexual orientation and gender identity. Report of the United Nations High Commissioner for Human Rights, Geneva (2015)
28. Orji, R., Mandryk, R.L., Vassileva, J.: Gender, age, and responsiveness to Cialdini's persuasion strategies. In: MacTavish, T., Basapur, S. (eds.) PERSUASIVE 2015. LNCS, vol. 9072, pp. 147–159. Springer, Cham (2015). https://doi.org/10.1007/978-3-319-20306-5_14
29. Pratto, F., John, O.P.: Automatic vigilance: the attention-grabbing power of negative social information. J. Pers. Soc. Psychol. **61**(3), 380–391 (1991)
30. R Core Team. R: a language and environment for statistical computing. R Foundation for Statistical Computing, Vienna, Austria (2023)
31. Rankin, S., Beemyn, G.: Beyond a binary: the lives of gender-nonconforming youth. About Campus **17**(4), 2–10 (2012)
32. Rosseel, Y.: lavaan: an R package for structural equation modeling. J. Stat. Softw. **48**(2), 1–36 (2012)
33. Sue, D.W.: Microaggressions in everyday life: race, gender, and sexual orientation (2010)
34. Terren, L., Borge-Bravo, R.: Echo chambers on social media: a systematic review of the literature. Rev. Commun. Res. **9** (2021)
35. Triandis, H.C.: Individualism-collectivism and personality. J. Pers. **69**(6), 907–924 (2001)
36. Vanderhasselt, M.-A., De Raedt, R.: How ruminative thinking styles lead to dysfunctional cognitions: evidence from a mediation model. J. Behav. Ther. Exp. Psychiatry **43**(3), 910–914 (2012)
37. Venables, W.N., Ripley, B.D.: Modern Applied Statistics with S, 4th edn. Springer, New York (2002). ISBN 0-387-95457-0
38. Weisstein, E.W.: Bonferroni correction (2004). https://mathworldwolfram.com/

Gamified vs. Non-Gamified Language Learning: The Role of Working Memory and Gaming Disorder

Areej Babiker[1]([⊠]), Sameha Alshakhsi[1], Rabab Ali Abumalloh[2], Ala Yankouskaya[3], Dena Al-Thani[1], Magnus Liebherr[4], and Raian Ali[1]([⊠])

[1] College of Science and Engineering, Hamad Bin Khalifa University, Doha, Qatar
{arbabiker,salshakhsi,dalthani,raali2}@hbku.edu.qa
[2] College of Engineering, Qatar University Doha, Doha, Qatar
rabab.abumalloh@qu.edu.qa
[3] Department of Psychology, Bournemouth University, Poole, UK
ayankouskaya@bournemouth.ac.uk
[4] Department of Mechatronics, University Duisburg-Essen, Duisburg, Germany
magnus.liebherr@uni-due.de

Abstract. Learning is an essential human need, contributing to personal and intellectual growth influenced by various factors, including motivation. Gamification, the incorporation of game elements into non-game contexts, has been widely explored as a method to enhance learning and increase engagement and motivation to learning. While extensive research has examined the effectiveness of gamified learning on student performance, limited attention has been given to the role of working memory capacity and individuals gaming disorder tendency. Gamification could hypothetically consume memory or trigger a desire for gaming, potentially impacting learning. This paper is based on an experiment with 45 participants (53.33% female) aged between 18 and 27 years ($M = 21.51$, $SD = 2.63$) They learned Spanish through both gamified and non-gamified e-learning materials. We assessed learning outcomes based on immediate performance after the sessions and memory retention after two days. The experiment lasted 50 to 75 min. Our results showed no significant differences in post-session performance or memory retention between participants regardless of their gaming disorder tendency. Furthermore, working memory capacity did not correlate with the learning outcome. Despite males scoring higher than females in gaming disorder tendency, no significant differences were found in learning performance between genders. These findings suggest that gamification may not necessarily improve learning performance, although many participants expressed, through their qualitative feedback and actual interaction, more engagement in the gamified session as compared to the non-gamified session.

Keywords: Gamified learning · Cognition · Working memory · Memory retention · Gaming disorder · Language learning

K. T. Win et al. (Eds.): PERSUASIVE 2025, LNCS 15711, pp. 330–340, 2025.
https://doi.org/10.1007/978-3-031-94959-3_23

1 Introduction

The learning process may sometimes slow down, requiring motivation to sustain progress. Research has paid significant attention to motivation in learning, establishing theories to explain and predict learning behaviors [1]. This is particularly evident in language learning, where mastering a new language can be challenging and anxiety-inducing. Learning and remembering vocabulary and verb conjugation are tedious tasks influenced by factors such as working memory [2]. Working memory temporarily holds and manipulates information required for complex tasks [3] and has a limited capacity, which varies by age [4]. This variability could influence how learners process language tasks and interact with instructional designs. We hypothesize that gamification does not necessarily enhance learning, as it introduces additional information, which may consume additional working memory.

Another factor that could influence learning is gaming disorder, characterized by compulsive gaming behaviors that impact daily life and social functioning [5]. Studies suggest that greater engagement during learning is associated with lower levels of gaming disorder and that gaming disorder negatively correlates with academic performance [6]. We hypothesize that gaming elements in learning materials may influence gaming tendency, potentially compromising their benefits in enhancing engagement. Additionally, we are uncertain whether individuals with a high tendency for gaming will find gamification engaging. Gamification may also induce stress through social comparison, especially when leaderboards are used, negatively affecting experience [7]. Other influencing factors include Gender [8] and age [9].

The performance of language learners is measured using several types of tests. For example, Teng [10] assessed performance using working memory tasks: (1) an operation span test to assess complex working memory, and (2) a nonword repetition test to evaluate phonological short-term memory. Vocabulary retention has been measured using immediate post-tests (retention) and delayed tests (recall) [11]. Numerous methods such as incorporating interactive technologies, personalized learning and gamification, have been explored to enhance learner performance [12]. While there is growing advocacy for gamification, its effects in specific contexts remain unclear, particularly in relation to individual factors such as working memory [13].

Gamification has been recognized as a tool for improving learning outcomes and engagement, with platforms like Kahoot playing a key role [14]. It integrates game mechanics such as points, storytelling, and competition to enhance motivation and learning [15, 16]. Gamification strategies are linked to behavioral, motivational, and attitudinal constructs that enhance learning outcomes[17]. In language learning, gamification has gained popularity since 2015 and shown promising benefits despite some challenges [18]. Research suggests gamification enables students to engage through a "learn-by-failure" approach, reducing embarrassment in traditional settings [19]. However, the study did not find a significant impact on students' recall of factual knowledge.

Studies on gamification's effectiveness in learning show mixed results. Some research found benefits, such as increased knowledge retention in radiology education [20] and improved digital literacy performance [21]. However, other studies found no significant impact on learning performance in programming [22]. Shen et al. [23] suggested that gender differences might explain inconsistencies, as males tend to engage more in competitive, gamified environments. However, findings vary, with some studies showing higher female engagement in science education [24] and others reporting no gender influence on motivation [25]. Similarly, while gamified working memory tasks have shown improved performance in some studies [26], others found no effect on effort or task performance [27].

As learner characteristics were frequently overlooked in existing research [28], examines gamification's impact using a within-subject design, where participants engage in both gamified and non-gamified learning environments to account for cognitive and gaming disorder differences. In this study, learning performance refers to both the improvement in language vocabulary and sentence formation (referred to as learning gain) and the ability to retain information over time (referred to as retention). Based on the above discussion, this research aims to address the following research questions:

RQ1: Is there a difference in participants' learning performance between gamified and non-gamified modalities?
RQ2: Does working memory capacity correlate with learning performance considering both gamified and non-gamified learning modalities?
RQ3: Does learning performance differ between these modalities based on the personal factors of gender, working memory capacity, and gaming disorder tendency?

2   Methods

2.1   Participants

A total of 45 healthy participants (53.33% Female), aged between 18 and 27 (M = 21.51, SD = 2.63) were recruited from Qatar. Eligible participants were proficient in English language, over 18 years old, and had played games at least once in the past 12 months. The study received ethics approval from the Institutional Review Board (IRB) of the first author's university (ID: IRB-2025-37). Participants were compensated for their participation with coupons redeemable for snacks and coffee.

2.2   Learning Tasks

The learning tasks were chosen to be Spanish language, as Spanish is uncommon in the education system and is relatively engaging to learn in Qatar. The tasks were divided into two sessions, gamified and non-gamified and were designed as an interactive website. The gamified session incorporated drag-and-drop interactive questions, a point-based narrative revealing a blurred image, a leaderboard to enhance motivation, immediate feedback on answers, achievement badges such as "Sentence Master", scores/ points and a digital certificate to share with family and friends. The non-gamified session contained comparable learning content without gamified elements. The recorded videos of the portal we designed and learning tasks are available on the Open Science Framework (OSF), accessible via the link provided in Supplementary Material section.

The materials were reviewed by the Spanish language coordinator from an accredited language institute to ensure they are comparable in difficulty, with no overlap between the sessions to avoid interference in learning. Each learning session is designed to last between 12 to 15 min, depending on the participants' engagement with the material. The number of new words is comparable between the sessions and is considered basic, making the materials suitable for beginners. The sessions focus on equally interesting and practical topics, restaurant and travel, as these are commonly perceived as motivations for learning a new language. The order of the sessions is randomized to minimize any potential bias associated with task order.

2.3 Measures

A screening questionnaire was administered using the SurveyMonkey platform (survey-monkey.com) to identify eligible participants. The questionnaire included questions to assess demographics, interest in gamified learning, and interest in learning the Spanish language (participants who indicated no interest in either were excluded), as well as Spanish language proficiency (only participants with no prior knowledge or knowledge of fewer than 10 words were included).

Working Memory. Working memory was assessed using Digit Span Task (DST) implemented using PsyToolkit web-based platform [29]. DST requires participants to recall sequences of digits presented at increasing lengths to evaluate working memory capacity. This widely used task has been shown to measure not only short-term memory but also aspects of long-term associative learning.

Gaming Disorder Test (GDT). GDT was used to measure the level of gaming disorder among participants [30]. The scale assesses gaming behavior over the past 12 months, based on the World Health Organization (WHO) framework [31]. The GDT consists of four items rated on a 5-point Likert scale, ranging from 1 ("never") to 5 ("very often"). Hence, the theoretical range is between 4 and 20. The total score represents the level of GD, with higher scores indicating a higher level of gaming disorder symptoms. The scale reliability score in the current sample is $\alpha = 0.765$, indicating good reliability.

Pre-test and Post-test Performance. Participants completed pre-tests and post-tests to assess their Spanish language learning gain. The tests were designed using vocabulary and sentence construction introduced in both the gamified and non-gamified modalities. Pre-test scores provided a baseline for each participant, while post-test scores measured learning outcomes. The theoretical score range is between 0 and 11.

To evaluate learning improvement, a new variable, referred to as post-session, was calculated for each modality (gamified and non-gamified). Post-session denotes learning outcome and improvement [32] as shown in Eq. (1)

$$Post\text{-}session = (post\text{-}test - pre\text{-}test)/(total\ possible - pre\text{-}test) \tag{1}$$

Memory Retention. The follow-up assessment was conducted two days after the experiment. The assessment included two tests—one for the material of the gamified session and another for the material of the non-gamified session—featuring questions based on the words learned during the earlier sessions. These questions were different from the performance tests described earlier. The theoretical score range is between 0 and 10. We employed validated questionnaires to assess user experience, flow, emotions, success, effort and frustration. Furthermore, eye-tracking and heart rate data were collected as part of the study design; however, these measures were not analyzed in the current paper and will be addressed in future research.

2.4 Procedures

Selected participants received an experiment briefing, signed consent forms, and completed the DST and pre-questionnaires to evaluate their working memory and pre-existing knowledge of the Spanish language (specifically the knowledge on the materials presented in both gamified and non-gamified sessions). Subsequently, participants were seated in a luminance-controlled room about 67 cm from the eye-tracking system.

The experiment began with a 10-min trial to familiarize participants with the learning materials, followed by a 15-min gamified learning session. Afterward, participants completed questionnaires and a post-session test, followed by a 5-min stretching break. The second session, consisting of non-gamified learning, followed the same procedure. Finally, participants provided feedback on both sessions.

A follow-up assessment was conducted online two days after the experiment to evaluate overall memory retention of the learning materials from both sessions. A two-day interval for word retrieval is common in the literature [33].

2.5 Data Analysis

The data were analyzed using JASP software version 0.19.3.0. Descriptive statistics were computed for all variables, and normality was assessed using skewness and kurtosis thresholds, with acceptable thresholds set between -2 and 2 [34]. Pearson correlations were used to examine the relationships between the variables of interest. Point-biserial correlation was applied to analyze the association between gender and the variables of interest. Participants were grouped by GDT into low GD (scores below the sample mean) and moderate GD (scores equal to or greater than the sample mean) to analyze differences in performance and memory retention according to GD risk.

Levene's test for homogeneity of variances was performed prior to conducting the mixed ANOVA, and no violations were observed. Box plots showed outliers in non-gamified memory retention scores and non-gamified post-session variables. Considering the outliers as genuine data points, the analysis was conducted both with and without their inclusion, and no significant differences were observed in the results. Two separate mixed ANOVA, with working memory as a covariate were employed: one to assess differences in post session scores and another to assess differences in memory retention between gamified and non-gamified sessions. Additionally, Bayesian analysis was conducted using Bayes Factors to quantify the strength of evidence for the observed relationships.

3 Results

3.1 Participants Demographic and Descriptive Statistics

Table 1 presents the descriptive statistics for demographics and key study variables including gaming disorder test.

Table 1. Participants Demographic and Descriptive statistics ($N = 45$)

	Mean	SD	Skewness	Kurtosis	Min	Max
Age	21.51	2.63	0.33	−0.93	18	27
GDT Total	9.49	3.22	-0.04	−0.49	4	16
NG memory retention	6.62	2.20	−1.15	1.33	0	10
G memory retention	6.60	1.89	−0.53	−0.24	2	10
Working memory	6.20	1.22	0.39	−0.04	4	9
NG post-session	8.69	2.12	−1.09	0.92	3	11
G post-session	8.38	1.59	−0.70	0.52	4	11

NG: Non-Gamified, G: Gamified.

3.2 Correlation Analysis

Figure 1 presents Pearson's correlation analysis. Significant associations were observed between key variables. Gamified memory retention was significantly correlated with gamified post-session, and a similar association was observed in the non-gamified session. Interestingly, GDT was negatively associated with gender indicating that males had significantly higher total scores on the gaming disorder scale compared to females.

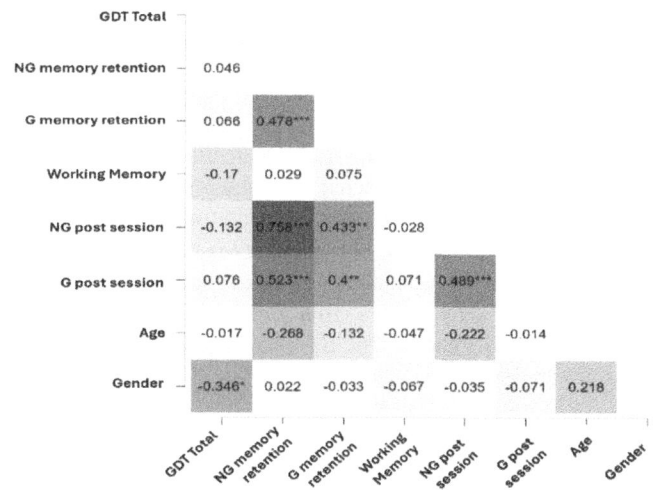

Fig. 1. Heatmap for the correlation analysis between the study variables. * $p < .05$, ** $p < .01$, *** $p < .001$. Note: Gender correlations are point-biserial (Male = 0, Female = 1)

3.3 Comparison of Post-Session in Gamified and Non-Gamified Modalities

To assess differences in post-session performance between the gamified and non-gamified sessions, a mixed ANOVA was conducted. As shown in Table 2, the main effect of post-session was not statistically significant. The interaction between post-session and working memory, and between post-session and GDT groups were not significant as well. To enhance the robustness of our findings, Bayesian mixed ANOVA was employed. The Bayesian analysis provided further evidence supporting the null hypothesis, as the Bayes factors (BF_{01}) for all models indicated moderate to strong support for the null hypothesis. The results of the Bayesian analyses are available on the OSF link provided in the Supplementary Material. The between-subjects analysis revealed no significant effects for GDT groups (low GD vs moderate GD) or working memory.

Table 2. Mixed ANOVA Results for Post-session performance

	F (1, 42)	p	BF_{01}
Within-Subjects Effects			
Post-sessions	0.82	.370	4.35
Post-sessions * GDT Groups	2.15	.150	10.58
Post-sessions * Working memory	0.74	.395	13.18
Between-Subjects Effects			
GDT Groups	0.50	.483	2.42
Working memory	0.00	.994	2.98

3.4 Comparison of Memory Retention in Gamified and Non-Gamified Modalities

To assess differences in memory retention between the gamified and non-gamified modalities, a mixed ANOVA was conducted. As shown in Table 3, the main effect of memory retention was not statistically significant. Additionally, the interaction between memory retention and GDT groups, and between memory retention and working memory were also not significant. The Bayesian analysis provided further evidence supporting the null hypothesis, as the Bayes factors (BF_{01}) for all models indicated moderate to strong support for the null hypothesis. The Bayesian analyses are available on the OSF link provided in the Supplementary Material.

4 Discussion

This study examined the role of gamification in language learning, particularly in relation to memory retention and participant's learning gain. Expanding on previous research, we considered participants' working memory capacity and gaming disorder levels, providing a new perspective on how prior gaming habits might influence learning performance.

Our findings revealed no significant difference between gamified and non-gamified modalities, regardless of working memory capacity and gaming disorder level. Bayesian analysis supported the null hypotheses for the main effects, indicating that the absence of significant differences is not due to sampling variability. This is in line with some previous

Table 3. Mixed ANOVA Results for Memory Retention

	F (1, 42)	p	BF_{01}
Within-Subjects Effects			
Memory Retention	0.19	.669	4.68
Memory Retention * GDT Groups	0.95	.335	12.89
Memory Retention * Working memory	0.17	.681	13.01
Between-Subjects Effects			
GDT Groups	0.09	.770	2.92
Working memory	0.18	.672	2.81

research that found no significant difference in learning performance between gamified and non-gamified conditions, including ultrasound training [35] and visual search tasks [36]. Similarly, gamification enhanced affect and task experience but not performance in a within-subject design [27]. However, our findings contrast with research suggesting gamification improves test scores[37] highlighting its complex impact on motivation and performance.

We also examined gaming disorder's (GD) effect on performance. Prior studies suggest engagement predicts lower GD, while GD negatively affects academic performance, including GPA[38]. Our findings showed no significant effect of GD scores (low vs. moderate) on learning gain or working memory, nor any correlation between GD and learning performance. This could be due to the relatively low to moderate GD scores of the participants, which may not have been sufficient to reflect severe levels of GD. However, the correlation results indicate that the prevalence of GD is higher in males than in females, consistent with previous research [39]. Moreover, our results align with studies reporting no effect of age or gender on learning performance but differ in showing no effect of gamification [40].

Gamification research presents mixed findings. Some studies report positive effects on student learning outcomes [41], yet others show increased motivation without performance gains [36]. Similarly, gamified and non-gamified applications showed no significant differences in usability or intrinsic motivation, possibly due to how participants perceived game elements like scoreboards [42]. While gamification can foster enthusiasm, provide feedback, fulfill recognition needs, and promote goal setting, it may also cause anxiety and stress, potentially compromising benefits if appropriate precautions and management strategies are not implemented [43]. These findings highlight the need for careful implementation of gamification elements to enhance learning while considering potential drawbacks and individual preferences.

This study has some limitations. The short duration of the learning materials may not have allowed enough time to capture long-term effects of gamification. Furthermore, the use of a single learning task may not reflect broader cognitive and behavioral changes. To mitigate these limitations and reduce variability in subject selection, we pre-selected participants who had a minimum knowledge of Spanish language and a minimum interest in gamified learning. This helped ensure that the participants were engaged with the material, although future studies could benefit from using diverse tasks and longer interventions to assess the long-term effects of gamification.

5   Conclusion

Gamification's impact on learning remains inconclusive due to individual differences and complex interactions. Our results indicate that while gamification enhances engagement, it does not significantly improve learning outcomes or memory retention. This aligns with previous research indicating that gamified and non-gamified cognitive training modalities show no significant differences in outcomes, despite increased engagement with the gamified version [44]. Future research may examine individual traits, prior gaming experience, and higher gaming disorder levels to understand gamification's effects better. Longitudinal studies could also assess its long-term impact and explore personalized gamification strategies to optimize learning benefits.

Acknowledgments. This publication was supported by NPRP 14 Cluster grant number NPRP 14C-0916–210015 from the Qatar National Research Fund (a member of Qatar Foundation). The findings herein reflect the work and are solely the responsibility of the authors.

Supplementary Material. The datasets associated with this study, along with a video recording of the e-learning platform we designed and the analysis files, are available on the Open Science Framework (OSF) at the following link: https://osf.io/ekw72.

References

1. Urhahne, D., Wijnia, L.: Theories of motivation in education: an integrative framework. Educ. Psychol. Rev. **35**(2), 1–35 (2023)
2. Palladino, P., Cornoldi, C.: Working memory performance of Italian students with foreign language learning difficulties. Learn. Individ. Differ. **14**, 137–151 (2004)
3. Willis, S., Goldbart, J., Stansfield, J.: The strengths and weaknesses in verbal short-term memory and visual working memory in children with hearing impairment and additional language learning difficulties. Int. J. Pediatr. Otorhinolaryngol. **78**, 1107–1114 (2014)
4. Cowan, N.: The magical number 4 in short-term memory: a reconsideration of mental storage capacity. Behav. Brain Sci. **24**, 87–114 (2001)
5. Wang, Q., Ren, H., Long, J., Liu, Y., Liu, T.: Research progress and debates on gaming disorder. Gen Psychiatr **32**, 100071 (2019)
6. Barata, G., Gama, S., Jorge, J., Gonçalves, D.: Identifying student types in a gamified learning experience. Int. J. Game-Based Learn. **4**, 19–36 (2014)
7. Shahri, A., Hosseini, M., Phalp, K., Taylor, J., Ali, R.: Towards a code of ethics for gamification at enterprise. Lect. Notes Bus. Inform. Process. **197**, 235–245 (2014)
8. Rafek, M.B., Ramli, N.H.L.B., Iksan, H.B., Harith, N.M., Abas, A.I.B.C.: Gender and language: communication apprehension in second language learning. Procedia Soc. Behav. Sci. **123**, 90–96 (2014)
9. Han, Z., Baohan, A.: Age and attainment in foreign language learning: the critical period account stands. Brain Lang. **246**, 105343 (2023)

10. Teng, M.F.: Effectiveness of captioned videos for incidental vocabulary learning and retention: the role of working memory. Comput. Assist. Lang Learn. 1–29 (2023)

11. Gorjian, B., Moosavinia, S.R., Ebrahimi Kavari, K., Asgari, P., Hydarei, A.: The impact of asynchronous computer-assisted language learning approaches on English as a foreign language high and low achievers' vocabulary retention and recall. Comput. Assist. Lang. Learn. **24**(5), 383–391 (2011). https://doi.org/10.1080/09588221.2011.552186

12. Yakubov, A., Nazarov, Y., Rodionov, A.A.: Advancing e-learning and m-learning environments incorporating ai and gamification to boost learner motivation. In: Proceedings – 2024 4th International Conference on Technology Enhanced Learning in Higher Education, TELE 2024, pp. 29–31 (2024)

13. Denden, M., et al.: The role of learners' characteristics in educational gamification systems: a systematic meta-review of the literature. Interact. Learn. Environ. **32**, 790–812 (2024)

14. Tsay, C.H.H., Kofinas, A., Luo, J.: Enhancing student learning experience with technology-mediated gamification: an empirical study. Comput. Educ. **121**, 1–17 (2018)

15. Almufareh, M.: The impact of gamification and individual differences on second language learning among first-year female university students in Saudi Arabia. Simul. Gaming **52**, 715–734 (2021)

16. Kapp, K.M.: The Gamification of Learning and Instruction: Game-Based Methods and Strategies for Training and Education. (Pfeiffer, 2012)

17. Landers, R.N., Armstrong, M.B., Collmus, A.B.: How to use game elements to enhance learning: applications of the theory of gamified learning. Serious Games Edutainm. Appl. **II**, 457–483 (2017)

18. Dehganzadeh, H., Dehganzadeh, H.: Investigating effects of digital gamification-based language learning: a systematic review. J. English Lang. Teach. Learn. **12**, 53–93 (2020)

19. Huang, W. H.-Y., Soman, D.: Gamification of Education. Research Report Series: Behavioural Economics in Action. Behavioural Economics in Action vol. 29 https://www.scirp.org/reference/referencespapers?referenceid=2512805 (2013)

20. Mobley, A., Chandora, A., Woodard, S.: The impact of gamification and potential of kaizen in radiology education. Clin. Imaging **103**, 109990 (2023)

21. Alnuaim, A.: The impact and acceptance of gamification by learners in a digital literacy course at the undergraduate level: randomized controlled trial. JMIR Serious Games **12**, e52017–e52017 (2024). https://doi.org/10.2196/52017

22. Ortiz Rojas, M.E., Chiluiza, K., Valcke, M.: Gamification in computer programming: effects on learning, engagement, self-efficacy and intrinsic motivation. In: 11th European Conference on Game-Based Learning (ECGBL), pp. 507–514. Acad Conferences LTD (2017)

23. Shen, W.-C., Liu, D., Santhanam, R., Evans, D.: Gamified Technology-Mediated Learning: The Role of Individual Differences. PACIS 2016 Proceedings (2016)

24. Klisch, Y., Miller, L.M., Wang, S., Epstein, J.: The impact of a science education game on students' learning and perception of inhalants as body pollutants. J. Sci. Educ. Technol. **21**, 295–303 (2012)

25. Almusharraf, N., Aljasser, M., Dalbani, H., Alsheikh, D.: Gender differences in utilizing a game-based approach within the EFL online classrooms. Heliyon **9**, e13136 (2023)

26. Ninaus, M., et al. Game elements improve performance in a working memory training task. Int. J. Serious Games **2** (2015)

27. Scharinger, C., Prislan, L., Bernecker, K., Ninaus, M.: Gamification of an n-back working memory task – Is it worth the effort? An EEG and eye-tracking study. Biol. Psychol. **179**, 108545 (2023)

28. Shortt, M., Tilak, S., Kuznetcova, I., Martens, B., Akinkuolie, B.: Gamification in mobile-assisted language learning: a systematic review of Duolingo literature from public release of 2012 to early 2020. Comput. Assist. Lang. Learn. **36**, 517–554 (2023)

29. Digit span task. https://www.psytoolkit.org/experiment-library/digitspan.html
30. Pontes, H.M., et al.: Measurement and conceptualization of gaming disorder according to the world health organization framework: the development of the gaming disorder test. Int. J. Ment. Health Addict. **19**, 508–528 (2021)
31. World Health Organization: ICD-11 Beta Draft: 6C51 Gaming Disorder (2020)
32. Hake, R.R.: Interactive-engagement versus traditional methods: a six-thousand-student survey of mechanics test data for introductory physics courses. Am. J. Phys. **66**, 64–74 (1998)
33. Barcroft, J.: Effects of opportunities for word retrieval during second language vocabulary learning. Lang. Learn. **57**, 35–56 (2007)
34. George, D., Mallery, M.: SPSS for Windows Step by Step: A Simple Guide and Reference, 17.0 Update. Pearson, Boston (2010)
35. Larsen, J.D., et al.: Education in focused lung ultrasound using gamified immersive virtual reality: a randomized controlled study. Ultrasound Med. Biol. **49**, 841–852 (2023)
36. Sliwinska, K.M.: Exploring the Gamification Paradox: Why Does Improved Engagement Not Lead to Improved Performance? Master's Theses (2019)
37. Huang, B., et al.: Investigating the effects of gamification-enhanced flipped learning on undergraduate students' behavioral and cognitive engagement. Interact. Learn. Environ. **27**, 1106–1126 (2019)
38. Samaha, M., Hawi, N.: Internet gaming disorder and its relationships with student engagement and academic performance. Int. J. Cyber Behav Psychol. Learn. **10**, 14–33 (2020)
39. Hawi, N., Samaha, M.: Relationships of gaming disorder, ADHD, and academic performance in university students: a mediation analysis. PLoS ONE **19**, e0300680 (2024)
40. Putz, L.M., Hofbauer, F., Treiblmaier, H.: Can gamification help to improve education? Findings from a longitudinal study. Comput. Human Behav. **110**, 106392 (2020)
41. Huang, R., et al.: The impact of gamification in educational settings on student learning outcomes: a meta-analysis. Educ. Tech. Res. Dev. **68**, 1875–1901 (2020)
42. Forde, S.F., Opwis, K., Mekler, E.D.: Informational, but not intrinsically motivating gamification? Preliminary findings. In: CHI PLAY 2016 – Proceedings of the Annual Symposium on Computer-Human Interaction in Play Companion, pp. 157–163 (2016)
43. Algashami, A., Vuillier, L., Alrobai, A., Phalp, K., Ali, R.: Gamification risks to enterprise teamwork: taxonomy, management strategies and modalities of application. Systems **7**, 9 (2019)
44. Mohammed, S., et al.: The benefits and challenges of implementing motivational features to boost cognitive training outcome. J. Cogn. Enhanc. **1**, 491 (2017)

Author Index

A

Abhadiomhen, Stanley Ebhohimhen   203
Abumalloh, Rabab Ali   330
Adaji, Ifeoma   74
Alhasani, Mona   147
Ali, Raian   232, 330
Alshakhsi, Sameha   330
Al-Thani, Dena   330

B

Babiker, Areej   330
Barhamgi, Mahmoud   232
Beheshti, Amin   3
Benlamine, Mohamed   89
Berjawi, Omran   117
Berkovsky, Shlomo   3
Braca, Annye   315

C

Chan, Gerry   131, 188, 264
Chittaro, Luca   61
Chumkasian, Waraporn   176
Condori-Fernandez, Nelly   217
Corrò, Christian   61

D

Dondio, Pierpaolo   315
Dosso, Cheyenne   89

E

Elizo, Andrea Porras   249

F

Fenza, Giuseppe   117
Fischer, Kerstin   32

G

Guan, Vivienne   18

H

Heintz, Christophe   89

J

Jensen, Lars C.   32
Jha, Smriti   131

K

Khan, Khaled M.   232
Khatoun, Rida   117
Klein, Michel   46

L

Lages, Martin   299
Langedijk, Rosalyn   32
Lee, Joohyun   18
Lewis, Frank   105
Liebherr, Magnus   330

M

Minucci, Elena   299
Morisseau, Tiffany   89
Muhanad, Aya   232
Musumbulwa, Kaminda Natasha   188

N

Ndulue, Chinenye   281
Nowbuth, Avis Anya   249
Nzeakor, Emmanuel Onyekachukwu   203

O

Oinas-Kukkonen, Harri   165
Orji, Rita   131, 147, 188, 264, 281
Oyebode, Oladapo   147, 188, 264, 281
Oyibo, Kiemute   203

P

Parmar, Ashis Jalote   249
Parmar, Vikram Singh   249
Petsoglou, Constantinos   176

K. T. Win et al. (Eds.): PERSUASIVE 2025, LNCS 15711, pp. 341–342, 2025.
https://doi.org/10.1007/978-3-031-94959-3

R
Rahman, Parinda   74

S
Saito, Junya   3
Sonego, Victor   315
Srivastava, Priyal   264
Steinsbekk, Aslak Irgens   249
Stumpf, Simone   299
Suni-Lopez, Franci   217

T
Taj, Fawad   46
Takeuchi, Shun   3
Taskan, Hasan Selkan   165

V
van Halteren, Aart   46
Vassileva, Julita   105
Vayre, Jean-Sébastien   89
Vitale, Jonathan   3
Vlahu-Gjorgievska, Elena   176

W
Win, Khin Than   18, 176

X
Xin, Kexuan   3

Y
Yamao, Sosuke   3
Yankouskaya, Ala   232, 330

The manufacturer's authorised representative in the EU is Springer
Nature Customer Service Centre GmbH, Europaplatz 3, 69115 Heidelberg,
Germany. If you have any concerns regarding our products, please
contact ProductSafety@springernature.com

Printed and bound by CPI Group (UK) Ltd, Croydon, CR0 4YY

28/04/2026

02098521-0006